Confessions of a Coding Monkey:

Learning the Subtle Art of Programming

Second Edition

MICHAEL A. WIRTH

The belief is still widespread in the computing community that C and its derivatives are programming languages—languages intended for people to write programs in. This is a regrettable misunderstanding.

—Bertrand Meyer

Kendall Hunt
publishing company

Kendall Hunt
publishing company

www.kendallhunt.com
Send all inquires to:
4050 Westmark Drive
Dubuque, IA 52004-1840

Copyright © 2007, 2010 by Michael A. Wirth

ISBN: 978-0-7575-8080-2

Printed in the United States of America
10 9 8 7 6 5 4 3 2

Dedication

For Kathleen and Mara

Contents

Confessions of a Coding Monkey

Programming is usually taught by examples.

—Niklaus Wirth

Learning to program has one fatal flaw. It can be seriously boring. Sometimes it feels as though we have become mere *coding monkeys*, an endearing term used to describe programmers required to produce large amounts of code. In reality, programming is a skill that once learned, can be used to create innovative solutions to problems. Programming does not merely imply learning the syntax of a programming language and spending all your time coding. Many books spend a lot of time—whole chapters, in fact—describing programming constructs in detail. Many of these provide a good technical description of the constructs and syntax of the language but often fail to show how they can be used effectively. We choose to take a more simplistic approach that shows the syntax, followed by examples used to explain the concepts. At the end of the day, though, we can show you pages upon pages of examples, but programming is an art which must be practiced in order to develop a true understanding. The adage "practice makes perfect" holds true.

C is not an easy language with which to come to terms. Indeed, it was never designed as a teaching language. It has its idiosyncrasies and "features," which make you wonder what its designers Kernighan and Ritchie were thinking. Yet C has endured, and long after other languages have been laid to rest, C will still be around. There are many textbooks on C; indeed the bookshelf in my office is lined with them. Sometimes I wonder how so many books can all be so similar. This is not meant to be a traditional book on C, although we will go through the process of learning the traditional constructs associated with the language. This is more of a tutorial guide to the art of programming, for which we will use C as the instructional language. It could just as well be Java, Pascal, or MAT-LAB. The basic constructs of programming do not change. This is by no means an ordinary book on C programming. I always said I wouldn't write just another textbook on C. Everything should be reasonably easy to understand. This book is for the novice programmer, which is the place we all start. The only true experts on C are Kernighan, Ritchie, and those fortunate enough to have used C for the past 30 years. This book is meant to introduce the elements of programming *using* C as an illustrative language. It is by no means a definitive guide on C.

What sets this apart from other texts? Well, a good portion of time is spent looking at topics like programming style and debugging from the point of view of a CS1 student. The examples given tend to be nontraditional. The programs are usually all dissected, in that we look at each element of the program and sometimes explore alternatives. The case studies throughout the text are drawn from potential real-world applications.

A Note on Examples

The code examples given throughout the book have been compiled using Pelles C or Gnu Common C (gcc). They are not designed to be the most optimized solutions on the planet, nor are the programs cryptic. I don't use a lot of shortcuts in C. I find them terribly difficult for the novice to understand. Part of what I didn't want this book to become is a text on C programming syntax. Syntax is used throughout the book, but remember that it is there to illustrate a concept. An ideal book introducing programming would endeavor to discuss the ideas behind a concept such as loops and illustrate them. I hope that is achieved here. A mix of discussion of structures and concepts is used in programming with illustrations provided in C.

Nor did I want this to become a book interspersed with 1,001 irrelevant examples. What you will find are examples packed with algorithms from various fields of application. The idea is modeled somewhat on the early books of Niklaus Wirth, such as *Pascal: User Manual and Report,* which is coauthored with Kathleen Jensen and provides a nice balance between syntax and examples, all in 167 pages. If you want more on the syntax of C, I have included some excellent reference books. I don't hope to cover every syntactic structure in this book, for to do so would turn it into a reference manual. I have included sections on debugging strategies and even flowcharting. The former is rarely taught in an introductory course, and the latter is rarely practiced anymore—at least not in the style of programming. Surprisingly it rears its head in object-oriented programming, so why not start programmers off on the right footing?

This book is all about examples. Small snippets of code are used to illustrate programming constructs, larger programs to integrate ideas and show how a program is constructed. All of the examples are focused on a central notion of real-world applications. We talk about creating a simple encryption algorithm, which although insecure by today's standards, illustrates how programming can be used to advocate security. The chapters discussing concepts are offset by what we term *case studies,* which are chapters devoted to solving specific problems. The programs will become longer and a little more complex as the book progresses, but as your skills improve, a program that today looks daunting may look simpler.

Who Is This Book For?

This book is intended for the novice programmer, the person who never thought he or she would end up in a programming class. The thought of learning programming, let alone C may seem somewhat daunting, but this book provides a grounding in the art of programming in such a manner that you will be able to solve real-world problems by writing programs.

Commonly Asked Questions and Replies

I know C already.

Mention that the introductory language is C, and more often than not, what you'll hear is "Why not Java?" or "I already learned C in high school." Really? There are many levels of programmers. Some are novices, some are intermediate programmers, and a few are experts. Some programmers are proficient in a number of different languages, while others are masters of just one or two. In truth, the only true experts are those who design a language or spend 20 years programming in it on a daily basis. The rest of us may be proficient in a language, but may not be aware of all its intricacies. We use it to solve problems.

C is, like, soooo old.

Yes, C is old, if you count being over thirty as old. But it works. Let's face it, with introductory programming, you are learning more than just a particular language syntax. You are learning about how to design an algorithm and what structures to use. At the end of the day the particular programming language used is unimportant. It is just a way of illustrating the concepts. Yet most introductory courses do devolve into courses on language structures and syntax.

Why can't we learn a visual language, and when will we build GUIs?

Why, oh, why? Start with something simple. Rome wasn't built in a day, you know, and it lasted for more than a millennium! The same cannot be said about a lot of the software designed today. Besides, many programs that function inside systems like robots don't even have GUIs (graphical user interfaces).

Why don't we learn Java, or C#?

Why not teach Java or C#? Yes it would be tempting to teach one of these languages, but the crux is that Java is not a core language in industry and C# is, to quote Bjarne Stroustrup, "just another proprietary language." There are always new languages and most of them seem to be descendants of C in one form or another. This is not a book about languages per se, although you will learn to code in C. Our goal is to help you master the structures and nuances associated with programming.

Case Studies

The case studies are tutorials devoted to designing and implementing real-world algorithms. Each of the case studies builds on the material learned so far.

Case Study	Topics
1. Home Energy Footprint	program structure, equation, data types
2. Dam Forces	I/O, equations, data types, defensive
3. Estimating Dinosaur Speed and Gait	variables, equations, if-else
4. Humidex	I/O, statements, equations, variables
5. Power of a Wind Turbine	I/O, data types, equations, input validation
6. Radiometric Dating	functions, switch, if, while
7. Ariane 5	debugging
8. Heron's Formula	formula, equations, algorithm design
9. Leap Years	if-else, expressions
10. Population Ecology	I/O, equations
11. Fibonacci	algorithms, recursion, functions, arrays
12. Sieve of Eratosthenes	functions, loops, arrays
13. Roman Numerals	switch, loops, strings, arrays, functions
14. Caesar Cipher	functions, strings
15. Compound Interest	I/O, equations, loops
16. Identifying the Age of a Tree	searching, 2D strings, arrays
17. A Global Positioning System	functions, parameter passing
18. Parking Cars	recursion, random numbers
19. Image Processing	file I/O, 2D arrays, functions
20. Counting Words	characters, while, if-else
21. Great Circle Distance	equations, math functions
22. Bubble Sort	arrays, functions, nested loops
23. The Calendar Problem	arrays, algorithm refinement
24. Talking to Mars	equations, program structure
25. Matching DNA	functions, strings
26. Calculating π	loops, decisions, functions
27. Random Password Generator	random numbers, strings
28. Round-off Errors	mathematical errors
29. ISBN Validation	strings, usability, I/O, functions
30. Timber Reforestation	decisions, loops, testing

Note that not every case study is presented in the same way. Sometimes we derive the program piece-by-piece and then show the whole program, while other times we show the whole program and then dissect the program.

Tales of Software

More than 50 percent of human programming will vanish
as computers take over.

—R. W. Kristinat, Hughes Aircraft Co.

Introduction

Humans use computers because they solve problems quickly and efficiently. In 650 BC, the Babylonians predicted weather from cloud patterns. Nowadays weather forecasting is achieved using numerical weather prediction models, which are computer simulations of the atmosphere. These models use observations of the Earth's surface of atmospheric pressure, temperature, wind speed, wind direction, humidity, and precipitation as a starting point from which to simulate the forthcoming state of the atmosphere. To do all this, you need extensive, complicated programs and even larger supercomputers to run the models. Examples of these supercomputers include a new system being installed at the Finnish Meteorological Institute for weather forecasting. The system is a Cray XT5m, with a theoretical peak performance of 34,000 billion floating-point calculations per second (34.6 teraflops). Wow, can any human match this? Probably not in speed or complexity, but maybe in intuition. Yet despite this, we still can't reliably predict weather. The caveat with computers is that there is no maybe. When you ask a question in a program, there are two responses: true or false. Partially that's because almost every computer built since the 1950s uses the binary number system of ones and zeros. Why binary? One aspect could be the simplicity and lower cost, in the same way that a light switch is simpler and less expensive than a dimmer.

Computers vs. Brains

How do computers stack up against the human brain? The brain is probably the most complex object known in human civilization. Nobody *really* knows how much capacity it has or how to unlock its computation power. Can computers mimic the function of the brain? In February 1996, Grand Chess Master Gary Kasparov went head-to-head with supercomputer Deep Blue in a tournament-style chess match. Deep Blue was a 32-node

IBM RS/6000 SP high-performance computer. Each node contained eight dedicated VLSI chess processors, for a total of 256 processors working in tandem. It had the capability of calculating 100 million possible chess moves per second. Deep Blue's programming code was written in C. Kasparov, capable of computing 3 moves per second, won the match 4–2. A year later a deeper Blue capable of 200 million chesses moves per second beat Kasparov 3.5–2.5.

How can a human, whose computability speed is so much slower, win? The answer lies in how calculations are performed. Computers can transfer data approximately 1 million times faster than the neurotransmitters in our brains. But where Deep Blue derived its playing strength from the brute force of its computing power, the human brain is highly adaptable, processing information from many sources simultaneously. It's not too hard to teach a computer to play chess: 32 pieces, each of which has a specific pattern of movement, a set of rules, some strategies, and the ability to simulate different scenarios—fast. But computers aren't intuitive—not yet anyway. Computers are good at some tasks, while humans are better at others.

Consider the task of robot vision. The retina has approximately 100 million neurons and processes about 10 one-million pixel images per second. It takes a robotic vision system about 100 computer instructions to derive a single edge from comparable (low-resolution) images. One hundred million instructions are needed to do a million detections, and it takes 1,000 million instructions per second (MIPS) to repeat them 10 times per second to match the retina.[1] The 1,500 cubic centimeter human brain is about 100,000 times as large as the retina, suggesting that matching overall human behavior will take about 100 million MIPS of computer power. The human visual system coupled with the brain is capable of tracking objects and extracting and analyzing information. The brain is therefore capable of processing visual information expediently. Computers can process images quickly, but usually this is restricted to specific tasks, such as automated mail sorting.

Computers are really good at calculating things that take brute force. In the second season Star Trek episode "Wolf in the Fold" (1967), Captain Kirk and Mr. Spock force an evil entity out of the starship Enterprise's computer by commanding the computer to "compute to the last digit the value of π," thus sending the computer into an infinite loop. There is, of course, no last digit of π. In August 2009, Daisuke Takahashi at the University of Tsukuba in Japan calculated π to 2.6 trillion digits in 29 hours on a supercomputer, a feat surpassed in December 2009 by Fabrice Bellard, a French computer scientist who added 100 billion digits on a PC (Intel Core i7) over 131 days. Compare this to Ludolph van Ceulen (1540–1610), a German mathematician who spent most of his life calculating π. He managed 35 digits:

$$3.14159265358979323846264338327950288$$

[1]Moravec, H., "When will computer hardware match the human brain?" *Journal of Evolution and Technology*, 1998, Vol. 1.

Software and Programming

Software is an entity that controls many of the devices we use every day, from the cars we drive to the processing of the cheese we eat. According to Heinz Zemanek, an Austrian computer pioneer, "software started with the translation of algebraic formulas into machine code."[2] This process of creating software is often termed *programming*, and the translation involves the use of a *programming language*. It wasn't until the late 1950s that the term software was first coined in a computing context by John W. Tukey:[3] "the *software* comprising the carefully planned interpretive routines, compilers, and other aspects of automotive programming." We generally perceive software as being composed of two elements: *instructions* and *data*. The instructions direct the processing of the data, and the data is interpreted and changed by the instructions. A good example is Google Maps, which uses data, in the form of satellite maps and databases of places, to drive its search capabilities. Searching is provided by way of algorithms to find the particular place being queried and pinpoint it visually on the map. Searching the restaurant "au Pied de Cochon, Montreal" in Google Maps will result in an address and satellite map showing the position of the restaurant.

What Programming Can Do

What is the future of computing? Indeed, what is the present? In the past 50 years, computer-based systems have become everyday entities in many aspects of life. Let's take a bit of time (no pun intended) and explore some of the applications of programs.

By the mid 1950s improvements in technology, such as the design of new motors and alloys, were pushing the envelope on what people felt the future held. In the 1950s computers were still largely relegated to research tasks. There are literally millions of applications for programs, from the mundane task of calculating interest in mortgage accounts to assisting in robotic surgery and recreating past civilizations. Indeed we could devote a whole book to looking at how computing influences our lives. By the 1960s computers were starting to take off. The Honeywell Kitchen Computer or H316 pedestal model of 1969 was a short-lived product made by Honeywell and offered by Neiman Marcus. It sold for $10,600, had a CPU speed of 2.5MHz, weighed approximately 150 pounds, and was used for storing recipes. It had a built-in cutting board and came with a few recipes. There is no evidence that any Honeywell Kitchen Computers were ever sold.

Now let's review some contemporary applications for programming.

---

[2]F.L. Bauer, "A Computer Pioneer's Talk: Pioneering Work in Software During the 50s in Central Europe, *History of Computing: Software Issues*, Springer Verlag (2002) 11–22.

[3]J. W. Tukey, "The Teaching of Concrete Mathematics," *The American Mathematical Monthly*, 65, no. 1 (1958): 1–9.

Robotic Milking

Consider the simple task of milking cows. Milking machines have been around for years, but it wasn't until recently that computers made their debut in this realm of agriculture. These robotic milking systems are cow-focused. The cows find their own way, in their own time, to the automated milking stalls, where a microchip implanted in the cow's collar is scanned by a computer system. The microchip holds information on the cow's milking history and health. The robotic milking machine, guided by lasers and ultrasound, then locates the cow's udder and prepares it by washing, sterilizing, and massaging the teats before collecting the milk. The milk is constantly cooled as it is piped to the storage system. The milk volume and color is also recorded, and if there is a problem, such as discoloration from blood in the milk, it will automatically be discarded.

Biometric Recognition at the Airport

With security at airports constantly increasing, there is a need to develop new means of identifying individuals. Old-style "rubber stamp" passports may be on their way out. Soon you may have a new passport that uses biometrics to authenticate your identity. *Biometrics* is the study of automated methods for uniquely recognizing humans based upon one or more intrinsic physical or behavioral traits, such as fingerprints or eye retinas. The passport's critical information is stored on a tiny Radio Frequency Identification (RFID) chip, much like information stored on smart cards. Such information may include retinal scans or fingerprints. Let's consider fingerprints. A fingerprint is an imprint made by the pattern of ridges (lines across fingerprints) and valleys (spaces between ridges) on the pad of a human finger. Fingerprint recognition is one of the oldest methods of biometric identification, going back to 6000 BC. Juan Vucetich was a Croatian-born Argentine anthropologist and police official who pioneered the use of fingerprinting in 1892. Fingerprint matching uses image processing and techniques in artificial intelligence to compare several features of a print pattern. First a fingerprint sensor is used to capture a live scan of a fingerprint, essentially a digital image of the fingerprint pattern. There are many types of sensors, including those that use visible light (optical), high-frequency sound waves (ultrasonic), or capacitance. Matching algorithms are then used to compare previously stored templates of fingerprints against candidate fingerprints for authentication purposes. Some of these algorithms are pattern-based, others are minutia-based. In pattern-based algorithms the candidate fingerprint is graphically compared with the template to determine the degree to which they match. Minutia-based algorithms compare several *minutia* features extracted from the original image stored in a template with those extracted from a candidate fingerprint.

Travel

Traveling somewhere, maybe from Toronto to Paris? Likely you will encounter electronics and the programs that run them everywhere—from the moment you check in and your baggage receives its *bag tag* to help airlines route your baggage to its final destination. Most bag tags incorporate a 10-digit numeric code in machine-readable barcode form that identifies a bag in an airport's Baggage Handling System (BHS). From the check-in counter, bags move into the BHS where they may be checked using a system that incorporates computed tomography to produce a 3-D or 2-D image of an entire bag, which is then analyzed. Machines such as the Boeing CTX9000 can analyze a bag every 6 seconds. No biometric passports yet? Well you probably have a machine-readable passport, which is checked using *optical character recognition* (OCR) as part of a system using a vast database of information. Going through security may require passing through a 3-D whole-body scanner, such as a millimeter wave scanner. Such scanners penetrate clothing and packaging to reveal and help pinpoint hidden weapons, explosives, drugs, and other contraband. When you finally get ready to board, you'll most likely be flying on an aircraft incorporating some form of *fly-by-wire* (FBW) technology with digital flight control systems. The Airbus A320 pioneered the use of digital FBW in 1988. In FBW a command applied using the Airbus sidestick "demands" a change in the flight path trajectory. The Airbus control computers then calculate and execute the deflection of the control surfaces required to achieve the change in flight path. Airbus is also pioneering an onboard computer system that will automatically maneuver an aircraft to avoid mid-air collisions.

Once you land in Paris at Charles de Gaulle airport, you may leave the airport on a fast train, such as the TGV (*train à grande vitesse*, French for "high-speed train"), which travels at speeds up to 320km/hr. For managing traffic speed and capacity on its TGV lines, the French National Railroad (SNCF) uses an automatic train control system named TVM430. This system displays instructions for train engineers and checks that these instructions are properly executed. Of course while in Paris you might travel on the Meteor, a fully automatic train that runs on 7km of track in the Paris metro (Line 14).

Reconstruction of the "Map" of Rome

The *Forma Urbis Romae*, or Severan Marble Plan, is a massive marble map of ancient Rome, created under the emperor Septimius Severus between 203 and 211. It originally measured 18 m wide by 13 m high and was carved into 150 marble slabs mounted on an interior wall of the Temple of Peace. Created at a scale of approximately 1 to 240, the map was detailed enough to show the floor plans of nearly every temple, bath, and insula in the central Roman city. The Plan was gradually destroyed during the Middle Ages, with the marble stones being used as building materials or for making lime. About 10 percent of the original surface area of the plan has since been recovered, in the form of more than 1,000 marble fragments. Piecing together the 1,186 surviving fragments of the plan is an activity that has engrossed scholars for centuries. Renaissance scholars managed to match and identify around 250 pieces, usually by recognizing famous landmarks such as the Colosseum and the Circus Maximus. Recently, however, a project at Stanford University[4] is digitizing the fragments and using algorithms in an attempt to reassemble more of the map.

Visual Analysis of Paintings

Paintings are nearly always assessed by human experts. Spotting a forged painting can take an expert potentially hours of analysis. However, a recent project named AUTHENTIC aims to develop a collection of software to help experts assess the authenticity of paintings.[5] Using image processing and machine learning, the visual structure of a painting can be quantified. The program works by analyzing characteristics such as complementary colors and texture as it relates to brushstrokes. The latter uses image processing to enhance brushstroke contours and then quantify the shape of the brushstroke.

Automated Mail Sorting

Most people have their mail delivered by hand. However what sort of process is involved in getting a piece of mail from location to location? Canada post processes approximately 30 million pieces of mail a day, delivering mail to 14 million addresses in Canada. Many mail systems use automated processing systems, and what lies at the heart of each of these systems? You guessed it: software running on computers to control machines of various types. The Siemens processing system can process 60,000 letters per hour, at a blazing 4 meters per second. Each system scanner reads and captures the address and image of 17 envelopes per second. The machines then sort the letters. All humans do is feed the machines with more letters and deliver the sorted mail. The software predominantly involved with the process is known as optical character recognition (OCR). In order to route the mail, the system must locate, read, and identify the postal code or country if the mail is to be sent overseas. The software has to deal with incorrectly addressed and illegible addresses as well as those written using character sets other than English. Once deciphered, the address is registered and printed on each letter as a barcode. Siemens postal recognition technology, ARTRead, also allows different types of mail such as parcels to be processed. The system captures the front of the envelope as an image and turns it into a type of digital fingerprint. This is stored in a central database along with address information. When the mail arrives at its destination, it is scanned again and the stored fingerprint is accessed for the address information.

---

[4]Koller, D., Trimble, J., Najbjerg, T., Gelfand, N., and Levoy, M., "Fragments of the city: Stanford's digital Forma Urbis Romae project," *Proceedings of the Third Williams Symposium on Classical Architecture, Journal of Roman Archaeology*, Suppl. 61, 2006, 237–252.

[5]Berezhnoy, I. E., Postma, E. O., and van den Herik, J., "Computerized visual analysis of paintings," in *Humanities, Computers and Cultural Heritage*, Royal Netherlands Academy of Arts and Sciences, 2005, 28–32.

Machine Vision

Machine vision is the application of computer vision to industry and manufacturing. Machine vision most often requires digital input/output devices and the use of networks to control other manufacturing equipment such as robotic arms. Common applications of machine vision include the inspection of manufactured goods such as food and pharmaceuticals. A machine vision system is composed of a series of algorithms incorporating image processing, pattern recognition, and specialized techniques such as fuzzy logic to create a sequential combination of tasks. An interesting example is the use of machine vision to inspect pizzas for topping percentages and distribution.[6] The percentage and distribution of toppings on a pizza are major features in the quality inspection of pizzas. As you can imagine, the inspection of pizzas isn't exactly an easy task, especially when compared to other tasks in machine vision, such as the surface inspection of industrial parts. Actual pizzas have different toppings, toppings have nonuniform color and shape, and some toppings have similar color appearance. Machine vision is also used in sizing and inspecting potatoes, detecting stones in soft fruit, finding defects on ceramics, visually grading fruit, detecting bones in processed poultry, locating contaminants in grain, and inspecting cream biscuits, to name but a few.

Film and CGI

Do they make any films without computers these days? Many films contain special effects to realize scenes, such as space travel, that cannot be achieved by live action or normal means. CGI, or *computer generated imagery*, is a common technique for creating visual effects using software such as Maya. Two-dimensional CGI was first used in 1973's *Westworld*. Examples of CGI techniques include *digital grading*, where parts of the original image are color-corrected. A detail that is deemed too dark in the original shot can be enhanced in this post-production process. For example, in *The Lord of the Rings: The Fellowship of the Ring*, digital grading was used to drain the color from Boromir's face as his character died. In 1993 Steven Spielberg's *Jurassic Park* used CGI to create realistic dinosaurs. For the battle between the Last Alliance and the forces of Sauron that introduces *The Lord of the Rings: The Fellowship of the Ring*,[7] an elaborate CGI animation system, called *Massive* (Multiple Agent Simulation System in Virtual Environment), was developed by Stephen Regelous that would allow thousands, or indeed millions, of individual animated "agents" (characters) in the program to act independently. The program uses fuzzy logic to enable every agent to respond individually to its surroundings. In addition to the artificial intelligence abilities of Massive, there are numerous other features, including cloth simulation, rigid body dynamics and GPU-based hardware rendering. This program has since been used in films like *The Chronicles of Narnia: The Lion, the Witch and the Wardrobe*, *King Kong*, *Eragon*, and *Happy Feet*.

---

[6]Sun, D-W., "Inspecting pizza topping percentage and distribution by a computer vision method," *Journal of Food Engineering*, 2000, Vol. 44, 245–249.

[7]http://www.lordoftherings.net/effects/launch.html

A Common Thread

What do all these systems have in common? They are computer systems, but more to the point, they involve the use of software, and software involves programming. Programming involves designing algorithms. Designing algorithms often involves thinking outside the box. We are living in a knowledge-based society, where the adage is that knowledge and know-how underpin the forces of growth and progress. Everyday we are barraged by an ever-increasing quantity of visual, textual, and audio information. The art of processing all this information involves various levels of automation. And automation involves programming.

What Programming Cannot Do

Not every problem can be solved by writing programs. Consider a TV show such as *Human Target*,[8] in which it is possible to press the "Enhance" button and have a low-resolution blob representing a reflection of a person's face in a window turn into a high-resolution image. Many shows do it: *CSI*, *24*, *Law and Order*, and *Numb3rs* all use magical software to enhance images. The reality, of course, is quite different. The foremost limitation of computer-based visual systems is that computers interpret numbers, yet we try to design algorithms that mimic the human visual system, a system with millions of years of evolutionary design, which works on dynamic images in real time. Consider the following photograph in front of the Louvre in Paris, which is 1725 by 1122 pixels, or approximately 2 megapixels, which is an appropriate resolution for a high-level security camera.

Extracting the face of the person who is approximately mid-center and 25 percent from the bottom, we obtain the accompanying 19 by 21 pixel image. From this image, it is impossible to recover the face of the person. There is just too much information missing. It is possible to approximate the person's facial features, but a positive ID is impossible—we can't recreate information that doesn't exist.

---

[8]"Lockdown" episode, 2010.

The Need to Compute

The idea behind programming is to solve problems. Humans achieved this unaided for millennia, but as problems became larger, or had to be solved in an expedited manner, something had to be invented to aid in computation. The first use of the term computer was recorded in approximately 1613, and it referred to a person who carried out calculations or computations. The history of computers can probably be split ideas along two lines: automated calculation and programmability. Many analog computers were invented to perform calculations, using mechanical, electrical, or hydraulic phenomena to model the problem being solved. One of the first mechanical computers may have been the Antikythera mechanism.[9] The Antikythera mechanism is an ancient mechanical analog computer designed to calculate astronomical positions. It was discovered by Valerios Stais, an archaeologist, in a shipwreck off the Greek island of Antikythera in 1900. It has been dated to 150–100 B.C. The infamous slide rule, developed in the 1600s, is a mechanical computer that was used as a calculation tool in science and engineering until the advent of the pocket calculator.

The caveat with many mechanical computers was that they were not programmable. In 1801, Joseph Marie Jacquard added paper punch cards to a textile loom as templates to allow intricate patterns to be woven automatically. The resulting Jacquard loom was an important milestone because it could be viewed as an early, albeit limited, form of programming. The first fully programmable mechanical calculator appeared in 1837, in Charles Babbage's analytical engine. Mechanical computers were used extensively during World War II for fire control systems and bombsights such as those manufactured by Norden.

The 1940s heralded the birth of the digital computer. In 1941, Konrad Zuse (1910–95), a German engineer and computer pioneer, developed the first functional tape-stored, program-controlled, electromechanical computer, the Z3. It was a binary calculator featuring programming with loops, but no conditional branches. The British Colossus[10] was designed by Tommy Flowers in 1943–44. The Colossus machines were digital, all-electronic, and reprogrammable by rewiring and were used to decipher teleprinter messages that had been encrypted using the Lorenz SZ40/42 machine.[11] ENIAC, short for Electronic Numerical Integrator and Computer,[12] was the first large-scale, electronic, digital computer capable of being programmed. ENIAC (1946) was developed by the U.S. Army for its Ballistics Research Laboratory for the purpose of calculating ballistic firing tables. ENIAC was a monster, weighing 27 tons, with a footprint of $63m^2$. ENIAC could perform 385 multiplication, 40 division, or three square root operations per second. More than six decades later, in November 2009, the Cray XT5 Jaguar at the Oak Ridge National Laboratory became the fastest supercomputer, using 224,256 cores to run at 1.75 petaFLOPS (FLoating point Operations Per Second), or 1.75×10^{15}. In comparison, ENIAC operated at approximately 500 FLOPS. The need for increased computational power has been driven by the increased size of data to process, and the increased need to process data quickly.

---

[9]D. J. de Solla Price, "An Ancient Greek Computer," *Scientific American* (1959): 60–67.

[10]J. Copeland, *Colosses: The Secrets of Bletchley Park's Code Breaking Computers* (Oxford, England: Oxford University Press, 2006).

[11]German cipher machines used during World War II.

[12]H. H. Goldstine and A. Goldstine, *The Electronic Numerical Integrator and Computer (ENIAC)*, 1946; reprinted in *The Origins of Digital Computers: Selected Papers* (Berlin and New York: Springer-Verlag, 1982), 359–73.

Evolution of Programming Languages

The first programming language, designed by Konrad Zuse between 1942 and 1946 was known as Plankalkül, German for "Plan Calculus."[13] During the ensuing years, a number of such systems were developed, often in some form of *machine language*, such as assembler. This culminated in the appearance of the first key programming language in the guise of Fortran. Fortran was developed in 1954–57 by John W. Backus and his team at IBM, its name a portmanteau of **formula** **trans**lation. This language was widely used by scientists to solve numerical problems. Fortran incorporated many ideas that formed the basis of modern languages, including data types such as integer, double precision numbers, and control structures such as **if**. In the years following the introduction of Fortran, programming languages proliferated. Sometimes new languages were created to correct deficiencies or to get additional capabilities. By 1971, there were approximately 148 different programming languages.[14] Some, like JOVIAL (Jules Own Version of the International Algorithmic Language), a language adept at handling scientific computations but designed for embedded systems, are still being used today. JOVIAL was developed in 1959 and the U.S. Air Force now uses it for applications such as the C-17 transport aircraft, E-3 Sentry AWACS, and F119 jet engines. COBOL, a language for business and finance, appeared in 1959, and currently comprises 80 percent of the world's business software. There may be 200 billion lines of code in existence with 5 billion lines added annually. Another language, ALGOL, or **ALGO**rithmic Language, was designed as a universal, machine-independent language and appeared in 1958. ALGOL became the blueprint for the way languages would evolve for the next three decades. ALGOL used bracketed statement blocks and was the first language to use *begin-end* pairs for delimiting them. After various incarnations of ALGOL, the programming language Pascal appeared, developed by Niklaus Wirth in 1970 and named in honor of mathematician and philosopher Blaise Pascal. In 1972, Ken Thompson and Dennis Ritchie introduced C. Pascal evolved into Modula-2 around 1978. Ada appeared in 1983, designed by a team led by Jean Ichbiah of CII Honeywell Bull, and used extensively in embedded and real-time applications for military and aerospace systems. By the early 1980s, extensions had been made to C to incorporate the idea of objects, evolving into Bjarne Stroustroup's C++ in 1983. In 1987, Larry Wall developed Perl (Practical Extraction and Reporting Language), a scripting language that has been described as the "duct tape of the Internet." The 1990s saw the introduction of Java by Sun Microsystems, a C-derivative language suited to network and Internet applications. Other languages that have evolved include Ruby, MATLAB, Lua, and Go. Ironically, many of these newer "interpreted" languages are actually themselves written in C.

---

[13]F. L. Bauer and H. Wossner, "The Plankalkül of Konrad Zuse: A Fore-Runner of Today's Programming Languages," *Communications of the ACM*, 15, no. 7 (1972): 678–85.

[14]J. E. Sammet, "Programming Languages: History and Future," *Communications of the ACM*, 15, no. 7 (1972): 601–10.

Structured versus Spaghetti Programming

Much of the programming prior to 1970 was what is now considered unstructured. It is often synonymous with the pejorative term *spaghetti code*, meaning a source code with a complex and tangled control structure. Languages such as Fortran were heavily reliant on programming structures such as **goto**. By the mid-1960s, programming pioneers such as Edsger W. Dijkstra were starting to become concerned about programming clarity, correctness, and structure. Dijkstra contended that modular, goto-less programs are more easily created and understood by humans. In 1968, he published a letter, "Go To statement considered harmful,"[15] in which he condemned the indiscriminate use of the goto statement. Instead, he advocated the use of procedures and conditional / repetition structures for program control. In the 1960s, Niklaus Wirth developed PL360, an assembly-like language incorporating the notion of blocks; procedures; and if, for, and while clauses. By 1968, the notion of incorporating structure in programming languages had been conceived. In 1969, Dijkstra wrote a set of notes, "Notes on Structured Programming,"[16] which helped develop the field and gave it its name. Primitive control structures put forward by Dijkstra included if-then-else (selection), and its degenerate form if-then, case-of (alteration), while-do, and repeat-until (two forms of repetition). He then described the idea of *stepwise refinement*. By 1970, Harlan D. Mills of IBM had proposed the use of block-structured format, "top-down" design, and indentation to make programs more readable. In 1971, Wirth published a paper, "Program Development by Stepwise Refinement,"[17] using the 8-Queens problem as an example, establishing stepwise refinement as core to structured programming. Mills published a paper in 1972 titled "Top Down Programming in Large Systems,"[18] which set forth a set of rules that lie at the heart of all modern structured programming:

- Do not use goto's.
- Develop the program top-down.
- Use a consistent set of indentation conventions.
- Modularize the program.

Wirth defined the Pascal programming language in 1969 as perhaps the first language to contain all the "good" control structures needed for structured programming.

---

[15]E. Dijkstra, "Go To Considered Harmful", Communications of the ACM, 11, no. 3 (1968): 147–48.

[16]E.W. Dijkstra, "Notes on Structured Programming", *Structured Programming*, O.J. Dahl, E.W. Dijkstra, C.A.R. Hoare (eds), (1972) 1–82

[17]N. Wirth, "Program Development by Stepwise Refinement", *Communications of the ACM*, 14, no. 4 (1971): 221–27.

[18]H.D. Mills, "Top-Down Programming in Large Systems," *Debugging Techniques in Large Systems*, ed. R. Rustin. Englewood Cliffs, N.J.: Prentice-Hall, (1971) 41–55.

Epilog

The first microprocessor had 2,200 transistors. In 1965, this amounted to about a dollar each. Four decades later, chips contain upwards of 1,000,000,000 transistors, at about 1/10000 of a cent each. Quite a transition, don't you think? Of course we have gone from computers calculating simple equations to computers pervading every aspect of our lives.

All things considered, the choice of programming language makes little difference on one's ability to solve problems. Some elements of C make it difficult to learn, but despite this it is still an inherently powerful language. Its creation has spurred the development of languages such as C++, Java, and C#. The similarity in many computing applications is that none of them are intrinsically simple. Simple for humans, maybe, but for computers they pose a challenge. They all contain a diversity of algorithms to deal with machine vision, databases, networking, pattern recognition, or computational intelligence. Before anyone was thinking of these applications, though, they were thinking of the elements of programming.

What Is Programming?

Let the machine do the dirty work.
—Kernighan and Plauger

Introduction

programming - n.

1. The art of debugging a blank sheet of paper (or, in these days of online editing, the art of debugging an empty file).

2. "Bloody instructions which, being taught, return to plague their inventor" ("Macbeth," Act 1, Scene 7).

3. A pastime similar to banging one's head against a wall, but with fewer opportunities for reward.

These lighthearted quotes aptly sum up the process of writing a program. Many people taking a programming class for the first time are terrified by the thought of writing code. But programming is so much more than just writing code. If taught properly, people who loathe the idea of learning programming become people who can write programs to solve problems.

The term *programming* refers to the process of analyzing a problem and deriving a solution in the form of a program. A *program* is a set of instructions that is executed to perform some task. The process of writing the statements using a *programming language* is termed *coding*. Often the distinction between these tasks blurs, and therefore we prefer to use *programming* to refer to the entire process. Programming can also be viewed from another angle: It is a process whereby a problem is analyzed and the solution is turned into a form that can be interpreted by a computer. Programming therefore offers a medium between humans and computers.

It's All About Rules

Some problems *seem* inherently easy, and they are—to humans, that is. Computers have a more difficult time discerning ideas. Consider the following example. Count the number of words in the following sentence:

```
You must unlearn what you have learned.
```

With any luck the result will be seven words. To come to this conclusion we would have to decide what a word is, that is, "a sequence of letters delimited by spaces." We have also learned that a sentence is a series of words terminated by a period, an exclamation mark, or a question mark. Consider now another example:

```
"These aren't the droids you're looking for."
```

Now the problem is complicated by the fact that two of the words have apostrophes. So the rule has to change to something like "a sequence of letters *including apostrophes,* delimited by spaces." Things become more complicated still with a sentence of the form:

```
"Do,or do not,there is no try."
```

Now, the rule has to be changed again to something like "a sequence of letters including apostrophes, delimited by spaces *or commas.*" Using that rule, you would indeed find eight words, instead of *six.* As you can clearly see, there are potentially *many* different circumstances with which to contend. We continue modifying the rules each time we encounter a problem. This seems easy for a human, because we process the words regardless of differences in punctuation. The "algorithm" in our minds is probably quite sophisticated, but we take it for granted, just as we dismiss the ability of our eyes to identify and track objects. So why do we need to make up rules?

Why indeed. Rules must be explicitly defined because computers can't think by themselves. They are not intuitive. They need to be told what to do. When they know what to do, they can definitely do it more expediently than humans. Take the trilogy *The Lord of the Rings,* by J. R. R. Tolkien. How long would it take to count the number of words in all 1,172 pages, which amounts to more than 450,000 words? I tried counting the words in one page, which took me 2 minutes. So, 1,172 pages would take me 2,344 minutes, or approximately 39 hours. A well-written program would probably take less than a minute to count an electronic version of this document, maybe even less.

The difference between humans and computers is that computers perform tasks precisely and in an identical manner every time. Humans aren't so well tuned. If we had to count all the words in *The Lord of the Rings,* we probably wouldn't last past a couple of hours, and we certainly would lose track numerous times and have to start over. More likely, we would just get bored and say forget it. Humans are better at multitasking, and this is probably why the human brain is much more powerful than a computer. While a computer's speed is a million times faster than a human's neural network, the brain has a larger number of processors compared to computers. Consider briefly all the things that the human body does simultaneously. *That* is multitasking. A program to count words may use the following rules:

1. A word is a series of alphabetic characters (both uppercase and lowercase) possibly containing an apostrophe, delimited by spaces.

   For example: **paint painter's DaVinci**

2. Words terminating a sentence may have a period, exclamation mark, or question mark at the end.

   For example: **DaVinci was a painter.**

3. If a word ends with a comma, semicolon, colon, or dash, separate the phrase into two or more separate words.

   For example: **The Last Supper, Mona Lisa**

4. Numbers are not words.

   For example: **1499 1902**

These rules are eventually converted to a series of *instructions* and implemented in a programming language. For example, although it is easy for a person to add the numbers 1 through 1000 together, it may take time using a simple calculating device such as a calculator. A program, however, can easily achieve the calculation using a few simple instructions:

```
sum = 0
for i = 1 to 1000
     sum = sum + i
```

The computer can perform this repetitive task accurately and efficiently. However, computers cannot think for themselves, in the sense that they are limited by the instructions given to them. They cannot think of a more efficient way of performing the calculation. A human might think outside the box and come up with the following equation:

$$1+2+3+\ldots+n = \frac{n(n+1)}{2}$$

Now the task is much simpler. To have the computer perform the same calculation requires the instructions to be changed:

```
sum = (1000 * (1000 + 1)) / 2
```

Solving Problems

Some tasks may be too trivial for a computer. Computers are adept at dealing with thousands of repetitions of the same problem. Tens of thousands of cheques are electronically processed by banks every day. Each cheque processed involves acquisition through scanning, performing handwriting recognition to acquire the signature, verifying this signature against one stored in a digital repository, and storing the cheque as a digital image. It might also involve processing the "security features" present on the cheque.

There are also problems of a more iterative nature. Take π, for instance. Calculating π is usually performed using an iterative formula such as the Gauss-Legendre algorithm. The current record expansion of π stands at 1,241,100,000,000 digits calculated by Yasumasa Kanada of Tokyo University in 2002. It was computed on a 64-node Hitachi supercomputer with one terabyte of memory. This machine carries out 2 trillion operations a second, which you must admit is quite fast.

Some problems are easier to derive algorithms for than others. The task of deriving π is quite easy to program, whereas converting Japanese script to English text is considerably more difficult. The reason is that the first problem can be stated explicitly as a sequence of operations, whereas the second operation cannot without a great deal of difficulty.

Some problems can be solved quickly by a computer, while others that appear simpler require more time. Consider the problems of searching a book for a particular word and searching a picture for Waldo.[1] It takes very little effort for a computer to perform the first task, because it is fairly linear. Take the book in electronic form and the word to find, and compare the word to each word in the book until a match occurs. Computers can do this uber-quickly. Humans less so. The second task, on the other hand, is relatively easy for humans, but not so for computers. Computers first must have an understanding of the object of their search. This is a task in itself. Then they have to actually find the object. Is the picture in colour? Is the scene complex? All these factors make searching for the image more difficult. When it comes to tasks such as vision, there is a great disparity between humans and computers. How can you describe Waldo in the context of a computer? If Waldo were always in the same pose, the task would be easier for a computer. It could take a copy of Waldo and "pass" it over the whole image; where they overlay is where Waldo exists. But this isn't the case, because Waldo can take a number of poses in a highly complex scene. You might design an algorithm that uses colour to find Waldo (red and white stripes), although more people than Waldo wear this pattern. In reality the problem of Waldo *could* be solved because the problem is fairly contained (i.e., there are known entities). Vision problems involving real-world scenes are much harder to decipher.

Whatever the problem is, to derive a solution you often have to think innovatively and look in fields beyond the problem domain to formulate ideas. Take, for instance, the task of logistics in the distribution of material. Individually, a courier company such as UPS has many trucks performing independent deliveries, but how do you know which route provides the most efficiency with respect to delivery time? For an idea of how to solve the problem, you may decide to look at collective insects such as bees and ants and a concept known as *swarm intelligence*. When ants gather food, they all walk off randomly, but after a while, food is located and the shortest route develops more or less instinctively. This route in turn attracts even more ants, leading to an efficient route. Place an obstacle in their way, and the ants will rediscover a new route. The same could be achieved for UPS delivery vans. By studying delivery addresses and routes taken by each van, a network of "shortcut routes" can be established, with the system having the ability to predict a new route should an existing route become temporarily unavailable.

---

[1]Martin Handford, *Where's Waldo?*, Candlewick Press.

A Language Is a Language Is a Language

Programming languages are languages. When it comes to the mechanics of the task, using a programming language is in many ways like learning to speak a human verbal or sign language. In both kinds of language, you must learn new vocabulary, syntax, and semantics (new words, sentence structures, and meanings). Moreover, both kinds of language require considerable practice to make perfect. There is, however, at least one important general difference that may strike you forcibly as you learn:

```
Programming languages lack ambiguity and vagueness.
```

Questions raised in English by sentences such as "I saw the man with a telescope" (Who had the telescope?) or "Take a pinch of salt" (How much is a pinch?) simply do not arise. In a programming language a sentence either means one thing or it means nothing!

Programming is fundamentally the same in any language. The constructs of programming such as decision and repetitive statements are the same. Only the syntax of the particular language makes it different. The *syntax* of a language is the set of allowed lexical elements and the set of rules used to combine the lexical elements into legitimate constructs. These lexical elements include operators (+, =), reserved words, function names, and variable names. In spoken languages, syntax is concerned with building valid sentences and paragraphs. In a programming language the syntax is concerned with building elements such as expressions and functions. The following sentence contains numerous spelling and punctuations errors, but its meaning can still be deciphered:

```
Tha kat saton, tha matt:
```

A compiler or interpreter is very strict about syntax. A single missing semicolon in a C program could cause a compiler failure. For instance in mathematics, the equation for the area of a circle might be expressed as:

$$area \leftarrow \pi r^2$$

If you wrote this in most programming languages, the compiler would most likely reject it for a number of reasons. First, it might consider the assignment symbol "$\leftarrow$" to be incorrect (i.e., it's not a part of the standard character set). It also has no idea what Greek letters are, so π would be a mystery (if you could even type it in the program!). Superscripts aren't allowed. But if you get something wrong, the compiler will usually produce a *syntax error*. More about these later. The structure of English is much more flexible, but rules about the structure of sentences *do* exist. For example consider the process of calculating the area of a circle, which can be described in C in the following manner:

```
area = 3.14159 * radius * radius;
```

If we leave the semicolon out at the end of the statement, the compiler will complain that there is a problem with the syntax, because it expects a semicolon at the end of the statement to terminate it. If it doesn't find things the way it expects to see them, the compiler will balk. The *semantics* of a language is the meaning given to its elements. Consider again the area of a circle. The equation for the area of a circle is πr^2. If the statement in the program were to become the equivalent of πr^3, or

```
area = 3.14159 * radius * radius * radius;
```

then this becomes a gaffe in the semantics. The compiler will compile the program with no problems, as there are no problems with the syntax. It's sort of equivalent to writing:

```
The cat sat on the hot tin roof.
```

Maybe it did, and in terms of syntax, it looks good. It has lost its meaning, though.

Languages are often designed with a specific use in mind, and some are better than others for dealing with certain problems. Each language provides slightly different functionality, so the language should match the problem. There are many different programming languages: FORTRAN, Pascal, Java, Python, Perl, Oberon, Modula-2, Lisp, Eiffel, Ada, ALGOL, Smalltalk, HTML, and Prolog. Consider the problem of calculating the area of a circle. It can be expressed in a similar fashion in a number of languages:

```
ALGOL        area := 3.14159*r*r;
FORTRAN      area = 3.14159*r**2
C/C++        area = 3.14159*r*r;
MATLAB       area = pi*(r^2);
Ada          area := 3.14159*(r)**2;
Pascal       area := 3.14159*r*r
Python       area = 3.14159*r**2
Java         area = 3.14159*r*r;
Ruby         area = 3.14159*r**2
```

As you can see, there isn't a great deal of difference between the nine languages.

"I Need a Droid That Knows Something about the Binary Language of Independently Programmable Moisture Vaporators"[2]

This statement may seem far-fetched, but one day we may have droids or robots with the capability of reprogramming other machines. One day, that is, not yet. Intelligence exhibited by artificial entities such as R2D2 and C-3PO is something called *artificial intelligence*. It is one of many fields in computer science that uses programming as the basis for expressing a solution. Deriving a solution involves a series of stages, a *life cycle* if you will. A life cycle contains five distinct phases:

1. Analyze the requirements.
2. Derive the specification.
3. Design the algorithm.
4. Implement the program.
5. Test the program.

There are a number of different models for the life cycle, but two of the most common are the *waterfall* and the *spiral*. Just as water flows only downhill, a *waterfall* model

---

[2]*Star Wars: A New Hope* (1977)

proceeds sequentially from phase to phase. However, although this seems like a reasonable model for constructing software, software is not built in the same way as ordinary construction. Bridges are built using a sequential process, and once they are completed they are rarely refined. Building software, however, is an evolutionary process, so the waterfall model is not the most appropriate. An alternative is the *spiral* model, in which each phase is revisited as many times as required as the software evolves.

Analyze the Requirements

Specifying the problem statement forces us to state the problem clearly and unambiguously to gain a clear understanding of what is required for its solution. For example, ponder the following requirements:

> `Compute the straight-line distance between two points in a plane.`

Devise the Specification

A *program specification* is a statement of the precise functions that are to be performed by a program. It involves analyzing the requirements and identifying the problems, inputs and outputs (I/O), and any additional requirements or constraints upon the solution. The problem of straight-line distance has two inputs, one for each point, and one output representing the distance between the two points. For the relationship between the two points, we can use:

> `The distance between two points is the hypotenuse of a right`
> `triangle. Using Pythagorean theorem, the distance can be cal-`
> `culated using:`

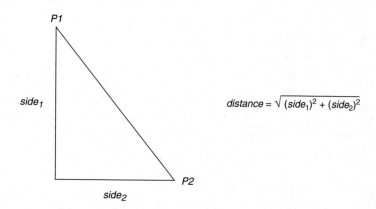

$$distance = \sqrt{(side_1)^2 + (side_2)^2}$$

Design the Algorithm

The next step involves designing the program. This is basically the point at which you decide what the program is going to do. This is normally expressed in terms of an *algorithm*. Here's a rough algorithm for the straight-line distance between two points:

1. Obtain values for the two points.
    - Consists of *x* and *y* coordinates for each point.
2. Compute the lengths of the two sides of the right triangle generated by the two points.
3. Compute the distance between the two points, which is equal to the length of the hypotenuse of the triangle.

Implement the Program

Write Code.   Now the bad news. You can't write programs in English, Latin, Italian, or Japanese. Well, they are more or less written *using* English, but not using English phrases. For example, you couldn't write a program using natural language, like this:

```
Input an electronic book.
Count the number of words in the book.
```

That would be nice, but it would imply that the computer has the ability to look at the phrase "count the number of words," and (a) interpret what a word is, and (b) devise a way of counting them. All by itself. Not really possible. No, you have to learn how to use a programming language.

We have all had experiences with languages. I remember learning German with its three genders for nouns. Consider the statement made by Mark Twain in his commentary "The Awful German Language": "It is either *der* (the) Regen, or *die* (the) Regen, or *das* (the) Regen, according to which gender it may turn out to be when I look." Thankfully programming is not as difficult as all this. There are certainly rules, but not to the extent of spoken languages. And the rules are not open to interpretation. Programming languages use English terms like "if," "for," and "end." Here's the program for the straight-line distance between two points:

```c
#include <stdio.h>
#include <math.h>

int main(void)
{
    double x1=1, y1=5, x2=4, y2=7;
    double side1, side2, distance;

    // Compute the sides of a right triangle
    side1 = x2-x1;
    side2 = y2-y1;

    // Compute the distance
    distance = sqrt(side1*side1 + side2*side2);

    // Print the distance
    printf("The distance is %.2f\n", distance);

    return 0;
}
```

Compile.   Writing the program is all good and fine. The problem now is that computers don't understand English text. Computers only understand groups of ones and zeros—the language of binary. You must *translate* the program in such a way that it can be understood by the computer. This process is known as *compiling* or *compilation*. The program that does the compiling is called a *compiler*. Go figure. If the compiler doesn't like what you've written, it will tell you and stop the compilation process. You may have to fix some problems with syntax, and try compiling again. Appendix F addresses the use of the gcc compiler.

Run the Program.   Once the compiler is happy with the your code, it will generate a program. Once you have a program, you can run it, or *execute* it. Both these terms just mean telling the computer to load the program and to abide by its instructions. Here's the output for the program for the straight-line distance between two points:

```
The distance is 3.61
```

Sometimes the compiler thinks what you've written is okay, but your program may not work because of some error in your logic. The process of fixing this is called *debugging,* which is covered in detail later.

Test the Program

The first time you run the program, enter some values to test it. It may work, or it may fail. Just because you removed things the compiler wasn't happy about doesn't mean that defects don't exist in the code. Maybe you got an equation wrong? Maybe the program tried to divide by zero? Did you make allowances for this in the program? Did you include input verification to check what people input? The example program didn't have any input, which makes it somewhat easier to test.

The Art of Coding

What is coding? Coding is the actual process of writing code. It may be the easiest part of programming and the part you'll spend the least amount of time doing—if you have designed a good algorithm. You probably actually spend more time debugging and testing code than you actually do writing it. Some portion of this book will deal with coding in the C programming language. C is just used as a conduit to explain the concepts of programming. Most of the knowledge learned in C can easily be transferred to other programming languages. One of the caveats of C is that it can be a complex language, partly because of its extensive use of symbols. The most basic program introduced to every student in just about every textbook is the "hello world" program. It does absolutely nothing except print the words "hello world" on the *standard output,* or screen.

```c
#include <stdio.h>

int main(void)
{

    printf("hello, world\n");
    return 0;

}
```

This is usually enough to scare some people away from programming. C programming is not as intuitive as other languages have been. Consider the same program in Pascal:

```
Program Hello (Input, Output);

Begin
    Writeln('hello, world');
End.
```

C uses the { and } instead of Begin and End, which doesn't seem very natural. Like anything, after a while using braces will come naturally.

Why Program in C?

Why not? No one ever contended that C is a language free of imperfections. Some people like imperfections such as shortcut operators. They call them "features." C was designed as a language to be *used,* and that makes it powerful. Languages like Pascal were designed for teaching language structures. Languages like Java were designed for a specific genre of applications (e.g., Web) and were not really designed for teaching. C also has pointers. Yes, I'll admit I don't like pointers. I consider them an element of the "dark side" and hence avoid them at all cost. Recursion is another topic that seems to be of little interest to some. But there may be some point in time where it is prudent to have knowledge of such concepts. Try to write a simple program to process images acquired on a camera attached to a probe approaching the outer reaches of the solar system, and you will soon realize that you have strict limitations on the amount of memory available and on the processing capabilities of the system itself. It might be that the software needs to be hard coded into the system and manipulate the video memory directly: This is an example of a good use of pointers.

A Brief History of C

In the beginning there was B. Well, actually there was BCPL[3] (Basic Combined Programming Language), a programming language designed by Martin Richards of the University of Cambridge in 1966. It was originally intended for use in writing compilers for other languages. B was designed by D. M. Ritchie and K. L. Thompson,[4] primarily for nonnumeric applications such as system programming, and appeared circa 1969. B was essentially a stripped down version of BCPL, which had one datatype: the computer *word.* Early implementations were for the DEC PDP-7 and PDP-11 minicomputers. The PDP-7 was introduced by DEC in 1965 as a less expensive alternative to the PDP-4, with a price tag of

---

[3]Richards, M., "BCPL—a tool for compiler writing and systems programming," *Proceedings of the Spring Joint Computer Conference,* 1969, Vol. 34, 557–566.

[4]Kernighan, B., "A tutorial introduction to the language B," http://cm.bell-labs.com/cm/cs/who/dmr/btut.htm

$72,000 for a minimal system. It had an 18-bit word length and 4K words as its standard main memory (equivalent to nine kilobytes), and it was upgradeable to 64K words (144 KB). Like its predecessors, input and output were conducted with a *teletypewriter*, also referred to as a *teletype* machine, a kind of electromechanical typewriter that was commonly used for communication, and a punched paper tape drive unit. In 1969, Ken Thompson wrote the first version of the UNIX operating system in assembler for the PDP-7.

The problem with B was that it was *typeless;* that is, it didn't have specific data types to deal with whole numbers, characters, and real numbers. So it couldn't properly handle floating-point operations. Ritchie used the PDP-11 with its 24K of memory and added types to B, which for a while was called NB for "New B."[5] More extensions and improvements were made to this language until the language had changed sufficiently to warrant a new name—C, being the letter directly after B in the alphabet. In 1973, Ritchie completed the core of C and then rewrote the entire Unix kernel using the language. To put this in perspective, a PDP-11 is functionally equivalent to a 15MHz CPU with 32K of memory. In 1989 the first ANSI (American National Standards Institute) standard C was defined, followed by C95 in 1995 and C99 in 1999. The version of C that was adopted as the ANSI standard in 2000 still hasn't really received full support. An ANSI standard just means that a panel of C experts get together and decide what "features" would be good in the next rendition of C. Sometimes features are borrowed from other languages such as C++. Note that presumed *bad* features are never removed. A compiler should be backwards-compatible, meaning that programs written in previous versions of the compiler should work in new versions. ANSI C is now supported by almost all the widely used compilers. Most of the C code being written nowadays is based on ANSI C. ANSI code is good because it makes code more portable (i.e., it makes it possible to move code to a different platform or compiler). And, hopefully, it works, though this isn't always the case.

What Is a Compiler?

There are two ways of creating a program. One is by *compiling,* the other by *interpreting.* A compiler is a program that translates text written in a computer language (the source language) into a program. A compiler takes a program in plaintext and translates it into a form that a computer can understand. The original plaintext form of a program is called *source code.* The final form of the program is called an *executable.* Sometimes a compiler will create an intermediary file called an *object code file.* This file is a shorthand form of the source code, created when the code is translated through a process called *parsing.* Source files end with a .c, whereas object files end with a .o. There are various kinds of compilers. Some, such as **Xcode,** are known as Integrated Development Environments (IDE) and incorporate an editor and compilation environment in one. Other compilers such as **gcc** (GNU Compiler Collection) are command-line-based compilers. We will use both these compilers to illustrate programming concepts. An interpreted language is a programming language whose programs may be executed from source form by an *interpreter.* Examples of interpreted languages include

---

[5]Ritchie, D., "The development of the C language," http://cm.bell-labs.com/cm/cs/who/dmr/chist.htmll

MATLAB and Python. Both a compiler and an interpreter are in themselves programs. In the case of C, there are interpreters such as Ch (www.softintegration.com) and compilers such as Pelles C, gcc, or Digital Mars C Compiler. The programs that compilers create are dependent on the operating system upon which they are created. For example, a program compiled using gcc in MacOS will not run under Windows XP. A program compiled in Windows XP will likewise not run under MacOS. Not all computers are created equal.

What Makes a Good Programmer?

What makes you a good programmer? A photographic knowledge of C, perhaps? Well, that may help you write code, but in the task of learning to program, the details of syntax and programming style play a relatively minor role. Wiedenbeck[6] suggests that the real determinants are a programmer's knowledge and skill and a "bag of tricks" filled through long experience. As knowledgeable as you *think* you are, you probably have a long way to go before you are a fluent and artistic programmer. You will learn programming best by doing it. There is no magic way by which you can become a programmer through osmosis. Find a problem, write an algorithm, code it, and then test and debug it. Eventually you will become good at it.

---

[6]Wiedenbeck, S., "Novice/expert differences in programming skills," *International Journal of Man-Machine Studies,* 1985, Vol. 23, No. 4, 383–390.

3

Programs = Algorithms + Code

The sooner you start to code, the longer the program will take.
—Roy Carlson

Introduction

Despite their impending intelligence, computers still have to be told what to do, how to do it, and when. Such direction is provided through a program, which is similar to a computer's genetic blueprint. A *program* is a series of characters, which when put in the right place, will produce the result you want. Stanley L. Englebardt puts it aptly in a 1965 *Popular Science* article:

> Computers are really very stupid multimillion-dollar collections of wires and transistors. Plug one in and it does nothing. Yell at it, curse, kick it—and still it remains mute. The reason: no instructions.

Programs in their simplest form are composed of algorithms and code. The algorithms are, as defined by NIST (National Institute of Standards and Technology), "a computable set of steps to achieve a desired result." The code is the physical rendering of this algorithm in a computable form using a programming language. Of course, the art of designing software is more complex than just designing algorithms and writing code, but everything has a beginning, and I suppose this is it.

Is the Dark Side Stronger? Tempting, It Is . . .

Many people introduced to programming think problems can be solved by diving straight into coding, a process known as *coding on the fly*. This may be okay for very small programs or for experienced programmers, but the best way is to properly design a solution. We are all guilty of directly implementing programs, but the caveat usually doesn't come until six months later when you look at the code and realize you don't know what's happening, or how. Then it's back to the drawing board.

One of the most common problems among novice programmers is that they rush to code the program before fully understanding what is required of the solution or properly designing an algorithm. The greatest side effects of rushing to code are (a) writing code that works but is aesthetically unappealing, and (b) embedding subtle defects into the code. Becoming a good programmer takes time. It involves taking the time to design an appropriate algorithm, writing code, and properly testing the code.

Top-Down Design

Once we have analyzed the requirements and derived a specification, we have to design the program, often achieved through a process called *top-down design*. It involves starting with a top-level algorithm design and successively refining the algorithm until it is at a sufficient depth to implement. Top-down design was promoted in the early 1970s by IBM researcher Harlan Mills and by Niklaus Wirth.

Take, for example, the task of automated license plate recognition. Traveling along a toll route such as the 407, Express Toll Route (ETR) in Ontario is seamless because of the lack of tollbooths. The 407 uses a combination of transponders and automatic number plate recognition (ANPR) systems. It is the world's first highway to feature such a system. ANPR uses *optical character recognition* (OCR) to process images of vehicle license plates. Current systems are capable of scanning number plates in about 1 second for cars traveling 160km/h. Most ANPR systems use five core algorithms for identifying a license plate:

1. *Plate localization*—responsible for finding and isolating the plate region on an image.
2. *Plate orientation and sizing*—compensates for the skew of the plate and adjusts the dimensions to the required size.
3. *Image normalization*—adjusts the brightness and contrast of the image.
4. *Character segmentation*—finds the individual characters on the plate.
5. *Optical character recognition*—identifies the individual characters on the plate.

Each of these tasks is divided into a series of subalgorithms. This is the top-down approach to algorithm design. For example, algorithm 4 in the previous list calls for the segmentation of the individual plate characters, whereby the license plate is segmented into its constituent parts. This algorithm may be split into the following subalgorithms:

a. *Image binarization*—transform the image from a grey image to a black-and-white image, a process known as *thresholding*.
b. *Noise removal*—suppress noise and unwanted spots.
c. *Separate characters*—detach characters that are joined.
d. *Isolate character regions*—create a locality for each character.

Consider the following examples. The first image represents the number plate after Step 2 in the main algorithm. The next image has been enhanced to improve the clarity of the characters (Step 3 in the main algorithm). The third image represents subalgorithm 4.a, which turns the gray scale image into a binary image. Since there is little noise and the characters are well separated, in this case subalgorithms 4.b and 4.c can be bypassed, moving directly to subalgorithm 4.d, which isolates each character region.

Now this image is passed on to algorithm 5, which performs the recognition of individual characters.

Algorithms

Algorithms have been around for a long time. A recipe is, in essence, an algorithm. It is a set of instructions on how to prepare or make something, especially a gastronomic dish. It includes:

- The required ingredients along with their quantity
- Equipment and environment needed to prepare the dish
- An ordered list of detailed preparation procedures

Here is an excellent recipe for carrot cake.

Ingredients:

> 1 1/4 cups brown sugar
>
> 3/4 cup vegetable oil
>
> 3 eggs
>
> 1 1/2 cups plain flour
>
> 1 1/2 teaspoons baking powder
>
> 1 teaspoon baking soda
>
> 1 teaspoon ground cinnamon
>
> 2 1/2 cups grated carrots
>
> 1/2–1 cup nuts (e.g., pecan, walnut), optional

Algorithm:

1. Preheat the oven to 350° F (180° C).
2. Combine sugar and oil in a bowl and beat for 2–3 minutes.

3. Add the eggs gradually and beat well.

4. Combine dry ingredients.

5. Sift dry mixture into the wet mixture and mix well.

6. Add carrots and nuts, and mix until just combined.

7. Pour the mixture into a loaf pan lined with nonstick baking paper.

8. Bake for 50–60 minutes.

9. Frost with a combination of icing sugar and lemon juice.

This is a fairly simple recipe, but the steps must be followed consistently, and we must use the correct amount of ingredients. If we don't, the cake will not turn out properly. If we add too much flour, the cake will be dry. If we don't add enough carrot, we won't be able to call it a carrot cake! Some ingredients are optional, or we could substitute, say nuts with sultanas. If we set the oven too high, the cake will burn; too low, it will take too long to bake. This is not overly different from crafting an algorithm and implementing it in a programming language. The ingredients of an algorithm are the information needed as input. The quantity may be described as the type of information, the equipment any structures needed to manipulate the information, and the ordered list the series of steps in the algorithm.

What Is an Algorithm?

An *algorithm* is a procedure (a finite set of well-defined instructions) for accomplishing some task that, given an initial state, will terminate in a defined end-state. The following diagram illustrates the notion of an algorithm. The algorithm for calculating the area of a circle takes two inputs (the radius of the circle and π) and provides one output. The algorithm in this case is a "black box"; that is, there is no regard to its internal workings. This is the topmost level of the design.

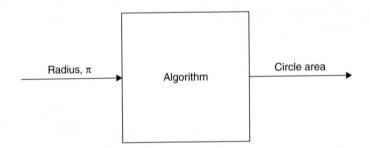

Characteristics of Algorithms

Algorithms have five properties.[1] These are the *input* to the algorithm, the *output* it yields, the *definiteness* of its steps, the *effectiveness* of its steps, and its *termination*. The first two are self-explanatory. Definiteness implies that an algorithm is unambiguously and precisely

---

[1]B. Meek, P. Heath, and N. Rushby, eds., *Guide to Good Programming Practice*, 2nd ed. (Chichester, England: Ellis Horwood, 1983).

defined: no doubt must exist. The challenge is, of course, that algorithms are always expressed first using natural language and, as such, are susceptible to uncertainty. Knuth defines *effectiveness* in *The Art of Computer Programming* (Vol. 1)[2] by saying that an instruction is effective if the operations it involves are of a succinctly basic nature to be performed using pencil and paper in a finite amount of time. A good example of this is the following instruction:

> Assign X the value of the largest real value less than 10.

This task is, of course, unattainable, since whatever value is chosen for X, a larger one may always be generated. If we choose X = 9.9999, then 0.99991 is larger and still less than 10, making the instruction ineffective. Termination is the property of an algorithm that assures it will end. Some algorithms, such as those containing an infinite loop, may never terminate.

History of Algorithms

The word *algorithm* comes from the name of the ninth century Persian mathematician Abu Abdullah Muhammad bin Musa al-Khwarizmi. The word *algorism* originally referred only to the rules of performing arithmetic using Hindu-Arabic numerals but evolved via European Latin translation of al-Khwarizmi's name into *algorithm* by the 18th century. The word evolved to include all definite procedures for solving problems or performing tasks. Let's start with the Babylonians. Babylonia was named for its capital Babylon, famed for its Hanging Gardens, situated in the southern region of Mesopotamia, which combined the territories of Sumer and Akkad. Babylonians wrote using cuneiform, a script that goes back to about 3000 BC. The Babylonians were well versed with the notion of mathematics using a base 60, or sexagesimal, numeral system.[3] From this system we derive the modern-day usage of 60 seconds in a minute, 60 minutes in an hour, and 360 (60 × 6) degrees in a circle. Less well known is that the Babylonians worked with *floating point* sexagesimal numbers. The Babylonian mathematicians were adept at arithmetic calculations, including algebraic equations. The caveat is that they had no real notation to express the algebra. Instead they used a step-by-step set of rules to represent each formula. On one ancient stone tablet, an approximation of the square root of 2 has been found, represented in sexagesimal notation as (1; 24, 52, 10) which is 1.41421296 in decimal form. This differs from the true value only by 0.0000006.

One of their interesting algorithms demonstrated knowledge of the Pythagorean theorem well before Pythagoras, as evidenced by this tablet translated by Dennis Ramsey and dating to c. 1900 BC:

> 4 is the length and 5 is the diagonal.
> > What is the breadth?
> > Its size is not known.
> > 4 times 4 is 16. 5 times 5 is 25.
> > You take 16 from 25 and there remains 9.
> > What times what shall I take in order to get 9?
> > 3 times 3 is 9. 3 is the breadth.

---

[2] D.E. Knuth, *The Art of Computer Programming:* Volume 1 Fundamental Algorithms, (Addison-Wesley, 1968).

[3] Knuth, D. E., "Ancient Babylonian algorithms," *Communications of the ACM*, 1972, Vol. 15, No. 7, 671–677.

This was possible due to their algorithms for factorization and deriving square roots. Many of these tablets ended in a phrase such as "This is the procedure," which implies that these Babylonian tablets are indeed genuine algorithms. Neat. One has to wonder if the ancient Babylonians weren't the first computer scientists.

Designing a Program

We briefly went through this in the previous chapter. Keep in mind this simple correlation: Good algorithm design comes with the ability to solve problems and experience. Let's go through the process by looking at devising an algorithm to calculate Euclid's greatest common divisor. Euclid of Alexandria (325–265 BC) was a Hellenistic mathematician considered by many to be the father of geometry. In his book *Euclid's Elements*, he described the Euclidean algorithm used to determine the "greatest common divisor" (GCD) of two integers, one of the oldest known algorithms. In 200 BC, Eratosthenes, an ancient Greek mathematician, developed an algorithm for finding all prime numbers up to a specified integer known as the "Sieve of Eratosthenes."

Analyze the Requirements

In order for a program to be designed, it has to be defined by means of its *requirements*. What is the program expected to do? Is this different from the intent of the customer? A problem can be well defined or it can be ill defined. Ill-defined problems are ambiguous, and their design is not well defined. The reality is that most programs start off in being ill defined. This is partially because there is a lack of understanding of the problem domain or the data to be used. The design of a program begins with a clear understanding of the problem, in the form of a written description. For example, the specification for the greatest common divisor (GCD) would include a description of what it is:

"The GCD of two positive integers is the largest positive integer that divides the numbers without a remainder."

Derive the Specification

Given two integers, x and y, and assuming x is greater than or equal to y, determine if y is zero. If it is, then x is the GCD. If it isn't, repeat the process using r, and the remainder after integer division of x by y. As an example, consider computing the GCD of 1,541 and 782, which is 23, using this process:

x	y	Description
1,541	782	Larger number is on the left, smaller on the right.
782	759	The remainder of 1,541 divided by 782 is 759.
759	23	Repeat the previous step, dividing 782 by 759, with a remainder of 23.
23	0	Repeat again. Since 759 is divisible by 23, we get a remainder of 0, and the algorithm terminates. The number on the left is the GCD = 23.

Design the Algorithm

From this we can formulate a simple algorithm. There are many ways of expressing the algorithm. One way is to simply express what we wish to accomplish as a series of steps in natural language.

1. Acquire two numbers, x and y.
2. Is x greater than y? If not, swap the two numbers, making x the larger.
3. Calculate the modulus, r, of x and y (i.e., the remainder when x is divided by y).
4. Test if y is zero.
   a. If y is zero, the algorithm ends, the GCD is x.
   b. If y is not zero, set x to the value of y, and assign y the value of r. Repeat step 3.

Code the Program

Euclid provides a good algorithm for computing because it can be used to illustrate varied algorithmic and programming principles. For example, an algorithm can be developed that is recursive:

```
int gcd(int x, int y)

{
    if (y == 0)
        return x;
    else
        return gcd(y, x%y);
}
```

or iterative:

```
int gcd(int x, int y)

{
    int temp, r;
    while (y != 0)
    {
        r = x % y;
        x = y;
        y = r;
    }
    return x;
}
```

The original algorithm as described by Euclid treated it as a geometric problem. It calculated a solution by repeatedly subtracting the smallest number from the largest number instead of using integer division.

```
int gcd(int x, int y)

{

    while (x != y)
        if (x > y)
            x = x - y;
        else
            y = y - x;
    return x;

}
```

All these algorithms have the same outcome but a different way of getting there.

Analyzing Problems

A common question is "Why is it important to do problem analysis?" One of the main reasons is that a precise statement of what is to be achieved is often the result of such analysis. The coding task is actually simplified if the problem is thoroughly analysed, and fixing the problem is facilitated should it be required.

A classic example involving problem analysis is the quadratic equation.[4]

The quadratic equation with real coefficients can be defined as:

$$ax^2 + bx + c = 0$$

The problem is to solve for any real numbers a, b, and c. If the value of a is zero, then the equation is not quadratic, but linear. We will consider the linear case first.

If in this case, b is also zero, then c must be zero and the case is trivial. That is, there are no roots.

If b is not zero, the solution is:

$$x = \frac{-c}{b} \tag{1}$$

In the quadratic case, there are three types of solutions, depending of the value of the *discriminant*, D:

$$D = b^2 - 4ac \tag{2}$$

Now, if $D > 0$, there is a pair of real solutions, given by:

$$x_1 = \frac{-b - \sqrt{D}}{2a} \quad \text{and} \quad x_2 = \frac{-b + \sqrt{D}}{2a} \tag{3}$$

In the case of $D = 0$, there is one solution:

$$x = -b/2a \tag{4}$$

---

[4]Sherman, P. M., *Techniques in Computer Programming*, Prentice Hall, 1970.

If $D < 0$, there is a pair of solutions, both of which produce a complex result, given by:

$$x_1 = \frac{-b - i\sqrt{-D}}{2a} \quad \text{and} \quad x_2 = \frac{-b + i\sqrt{-D}}{2a} \tag{5}$$

This provides all the information we need to start analyzing the problem. The way we have set out the constraints essentially provides us with a path for analysis. It is always important to remember that analysis itself may be an evolutionary process. There are a number of ways of expressing an analysis, but one of the easiest is probably listing the steps in point form. This has the added advantage of being in a format compatible with coding the solution. Here is the basic algorithm:

1. Establish the value of a. If the value of a is zero, proceed to step 2.
2. Establish the value of b. If the value of b is zero, the problem is trivial. If it is not zero, the solution is Eq. 1.
3. Evaluate the discriminant, D, using Eq. 2.
4. Analyze D:

   If $D > 0$, the solution is real, calculated using Eq. 3.

   If $D = 0$, the solution is singular, calculated using Eq. 4.

   If $D < 0$, the solution is complex, calculated using Eq. 5.

This global analysis has been formulated using four steps. We have treated every case of the quadratic, which is important in formulating a complete solution.

Problem-Solving Strategies

Among the common strategies that can be used in problem solving are trial and error, brute force, and divide and conquer.

Trial and Error

Trial-and-error is an age-old method of problem solving based on experience with no explicit use of insight or theory building. Trial and error is akin to finding someone's phone number in a phonebook with 1,000,000 entries by randomly selecting entries and seeing if they match.

Brute Force

The most simplistic approach to solving a problem is brute force. It involves systematically enumerating all possible candidates for the solution and chequing whether each candidate satisfies the problem's statement. Sometimes brute force is used in contexts such as searching. Brute force is akin to finding someone's phone number in a phonebook with 1,000,000 *unsorted* entries. Start at the first entry and cheque all the entries until the correct one is found. A good example is trying to match a fingerprint in a forensic database. The simplest way of matching a fingerprint is to try it against all the fingerprint images in the database until one matches. If you were using an AFIS (Automatic Fingerprint Identification System) to search a humble 10 million records using an algorithm that simply tries to match images, it might take a million seconds if you assume 10 images per second. That's approximately 278 hours! It may match the prints in one minute, or 277 hours, depending on where the print is located. Such systems analyze each fingerprint and identify *minutae*, or key points in each print, representing them as mathematical formulas called *feature vectors*. The algorithm then cheques the feature vector of the print against each fingerprint in the database to see which provides the best match.

Divide and Conquer

This approach to problem solving is based on partitioning a problem into a number of sub-problems, solving them each independently and combining their solutions to get a solution to the original problem. The sort of problems suitable for divide and conquer are often those capable of being solved in a recursive manner. Divide and conquer is akin to finding someone's phone number in a phonebook with 1,000,000 alphabetically *sorted* entries. If the name is Dijkstra, then you would find the entries starting with D, then those whose second letter is *i*, etc. For the fingerprint recognition problem, if the database of fingerprint feature vectors was sorted on some criteria, then the searching would definitely decrease in time.

Pseudocode

> Pseudocode: *n. a detailed yet readable description of what a computer program or algorithm must do, expressed in a formally styled natural language rather than in a programming language.*

Pseudocode is a way of expressing an algorithm in such a manner that it can be easily understood. In other words it uses a *natural* language. It does not use the syntax of any one particular language, but designers will sometimes borrow the appearance of a programming language with which they are familiar. Details are not important in pseudocode. Pseudocode is merely the plain English explanation of a piece of code. There is no real standard to writing; you can basically create your own if you like. Pseudocode is normally comprised of a series of statements that deal with sequence statements, such as input/output and assignments, selection statements (e.g., if), repetition statements (e.g., while, for), and block statements (begin-end). For example, a pseudocode representation of Euclid's algorithm (the iterative version) might look like:

```
INPUT x and y
IF x is not greater than y
    SWAP x and y
ENDIF
WHILE y does not equal 0
    CALCULATE r as the remainder of x divided by y
    SET x to the value of y
    SET y to the value of r
```

```
ENDWHILE
OUTPUT x
```

From this it is relatively easy to write the code. An example of how pseudocode differs from actual code follows. Regular code (written in C):

```
if (denominator != 0)
    divide(numerator,denominator);

else
    printf("Divide by zero error\n");
```

Pseudocode:

```
IF the denominator is not zero THEN

  DIVIDE the numerator by the denominator
ELSE
  SHOW a failure message for "divide by zero"
ENDIF
```

You don't have to use pseudocode, but it does provide a nice bridge between an abstract algorithm and the code itself. You might like to use flowcharts instead. Now let's look at the pseudocode for the quadratic equation.

```
INPUT a, b, and c

IF a is zero
    IF b is zero
        OUTPUT "no roots"
    ELSE
        CALCULATE Le = —c/b
        OUTPUT Le
    ENDIF
ELSE
    CALCULATE D = b2 — 4ac
    CALCULATE S = SQRT(ABS(D))
    CALCULATE A = 2a
    IF D is less than zero
        CALCULATE realx = —b/A
        CALCULATE imagx = S/A
        OUTPUT realx, imagx
    ELSE IF D is zero
        CALCULATE root = —b/A
        OUTPUT root
    ELSE IF D is greater than zero
        CALCULATE root1 = (—b+S)/A
        CALCULATE root2 = (—b—S)/A
        OUTPUT root1, root2
    ENDIF
ENDIF
```

An Ancient Math Problem

Many centuries ago in India a very smart man is said to have invented the game of chess. This game greatly amused the king, and he became so enthralled with it that he offered to reward the inventor with anything he wished, up to half his kingdom and his daughter's hand in marriage. Now the inventor of the game of chess was quite intelligent and not a little greedy. Not being satisfied with merely half the kingdom, he asked the king for the following gift:

> "Mighty King", he said, "I am but a humble man and would not know what to do with half of your kingdom. Let us merely calculate my prize as follows. Put onto the first square of the chessboard a single grain of wheat. Then onto the second square of the chessboard two grains, and onto the third square of the chessboard twice two grains, and so on until we have covered the board with wheat."

Upon hearing this the king was greatly pleased for he felt he had gotten off rather cheaply. He rapidly agreed to the inventor's prize. He called for a bag of wheat to be brought to him, and when it arrived he began counting out wheat. However, he soon used up the first bag and was not yet halfway across the board. He called for a second, and a third, and more and more, until finally he was forced to admit defeat and hand over his entire kingdom for lack of sufficient wheat with which to pay the inventor. Here's what part of the chess board would look like:

2^{16}	2^{17}	2^{18}	2^{19}	2^{20}	2^{21}	2^{22}	2^{23}
256	512	1024	2048	4096	8192	2^{14}	2^{15}
1	2	4	8	16	32	64	128

If you get to the 64th square, it would be 2^{63} or 9,223,372,036,854,775,808. That's over 9 quintillion grains of rice. Also, if you added all 64 squares of rice together, you would get enough rice to cover all of India knee deep in rice.

Now, we could solve this problem on paper, but we could also write a program to solve it. Let's start with the algorithm.

```
start with one grain of wheat
loop around 63 times
        each time we loop, multiply the grains of wheat by 2
```

Here is the pseudocode for the program:

```
INITIALIZE wheat to 1
FOR loop iterates from 1 to 63
    SET wheat to equal wheat × 2
```

The pseudocode translated into C code becomes:

```
int wheat, i;

int i;
long double wheat;
wheat = 1;

for (i=1; i<=63; i=i+1)
    wheat = wheat * 2;

printf("The king needed %.0f grains of wheat\n",
wheat);
```

It turns out that calculating it by hand isn't such a cool idea after all.

Algorithm Refinement

Algorithms are constantly refined, or improved. Remember in the first chapter how we looked at automated mail sorting? In almost thirty years, these systems have gone from single-line sorting based on town and postal code only on letters, to identifying all text and graphic objects on letters and parcels. Here's a brief history:

- 1978: single line (town and postal code)
- 1984: dual line (town, postal code, and street name)
- 1990: four-line (whole address)
- 1996: all-line reader (+ recipient address)
- 2000: ARTRead (all text and graphic objects)

As applications become more complex, algorithms must evolve. So by refining an algorithm, we are simply improving it. For example, an initial version of an algorithm to deal with recognition of postal addresses might only have been designed to deal with block letters. Once this is working, the algorithm could then be refined to deal with addresses written in cursive writing. An algorithm to process typewritten documents might first be designed to recognize the normal characters from a to z in lowercase and uppercase. It could later be refined to make full use of the extended character set and language specialties.

Flowcharting

It seems as though the concept of *flowcharting* isn't talked about much anymore. I suppose with the widespread adoption of what we term ALGOL-like languages, pseudocode is now used more to represent algorithms. Flowcharts are essentially a pictorial representation of an algorithm, or even code. Unless your problem is as simple as a series of equations, a flowchart is more valuable than a series of steps. Its value is due to its pictorial nature. A picture really is worth 1,000 words. For small programs, the concept of flowcharts helps define an algorithm. Apart from classic flowcharts, there are a number of variations: Nassi-Shneiderman diagrams, Ferstl diagrams, and Hamilton-Zeldin diagrams.

A classic flowchart consists of a number of boxes with directed lines interconnecting them. Statements of operations are placed within the boxes, and the directed lines leaving these boxes indicate the sequence in which the boxes are executed. Here's an example of a flowchart for the quadratic equation problem:

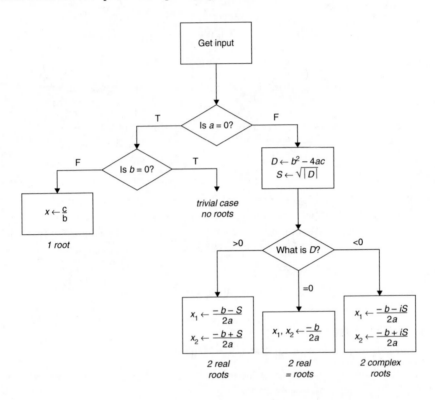

This flowchart only has three components:

- A *rectangular box*, which represents a contiguous sequence of instructions
- A *diamond-shaped box*, which represents a decision (in the simple case, it represents a binary decision)
- A series of *arrows* connecting the boxes to represent the flow of control. (There can be only one arrow flowing out of a rectangular box; that is, when a computer instruction finishes its execution, it can proceed to any one single next instruction or decision.)

Area of a Circle

Analyze Requirements

Given a radius, calculate the area and circumference of a circle.

Derive the Specification

The I/O diagram for this example is as follows:

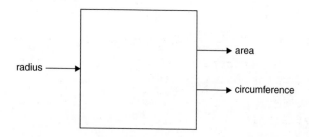

What information is needed to calculate both the area and circumference of a circle. The area and circumference of a circle can be calculated using for following formula:

$$area = \pi \cdot radius^2$$
$$circumference = 2\pi \cdot radius$$

Design the Algorithm

1. Obtain the value for the radius.
2. Calculate the value of the area.
3. Calculate the value of the circumference.
4. Output the values for area and circumference.

Implement the Algorithm

The next step involves converting the algorithm to a C program. The first part involves defining what variables are needed to store each of the values:

radius of the circle → **r** or **radius** or **Radius** or **rad**

the circumference of the circle → **c** or **circumference** or **Circumference** or **circ**

the area of the circle → **a** or **area** or **Area**

Do we need to use any math functions? No.
Do we need to use any constant values?

The value of π → 3.14159

We can't use Greek symbols, so we have to find a name for π: **PI** or **Pi** or **pi**

Express the mathematical equations as equations in C:

$$area = \pi \cdot radius^2$$

becomes:

```
area = PI * radius * radius;
```

$$circumference = 2\pi \cdot radius$$

becomes:

```
circumference = 2 * PI * radius;
```

The Code

```c
// A program to calculate the area and circumference of a circle
// given a value for the radius

#include <stdio.h>
#define PI 3.14159

void main(void)
{
    // Declare and initialize the variables
    double radius, area, circumference;

    // Obtain the value of the radius
    printf("Please enter the value of the radius in cm: ");
    scanf("%lf", &radius);

    // Calculate the area of the circle
    area = PI * radius * radius;

    // Calculate the circumference of the circle
    circumference = 2 * PI * radius;

    // Output the values
    printf("The area is %.2f cm^2\n", area);
    printf("The circumference is %.2f cm\n", circumference);
}
```

Test the Program

When you have finished writing the code, compile and run it.

```
Please enter the value of the radius in cm: 5
The area is 78.54 cm^2
The circumference is 31.42 cm
```

Make sure the answers are correct by calculating the results by hand.

Defensive Programming

To make the program more robust, consider adding elements to stop problems before they occur. For example, inputting a negative radius would not produce an error per se, but there is no concept of negative areas or circumferences. Maybe you could include the following code:

```c
printf("Please enter the value of the radius in cm: ");
scanf("%lf", &radius);
```

```
if (radius < 0)
    printf("A negative radius is invalid\n");
else {
    // Calculate the area of the circle
    area = PI * radius * radius;

    // Calculate the circumference of the circle
    circumference = 2 * PI * radius;

    // Output the values
    printf("The area is %.2f cm^2\n", area);
    printf("The circumference is %.2f cm\n", circumference);
}
```

This code will cheque to see if the radius is less than zero and output a message to that effect if it is. Otherwise, it will calculate the area and circumference. You could go further and use a loop to allow the user to re-input the radius without rerunning the program.

```
printf("Please enter the value of the radius in cm: ");
```

The following "infinite" **while** loop will read the input and cheque to see if it is less than zero. If it is, an error message is output and the loop continues, asking the user to input the value of the radius again. This continues until the value of radius is greater than or equal to zero. When this occurs, the **while** loop ends, and the area and circumference are calculated.

```
#include <stdio.h>
#define PI 3.14159

void main(void)
{
    // Declare and initialize the variables
    double radius, area, circumference;

    // Obtain the value of the radius
    while (1)
    {
        printf("Please enter the value of the radius in cm: ");
        scanf("%lf", &radius);
        if (radius < 0)
        {
            printf("Negative radii are unsuitable\n");
            continue;
        }
        else
            break;
    }

    // Calculate the area of the circle
    area = PI * radius * radius;
```

```
        // Calculate the circumference of the circle
        circumference = 2 * PI * radius;

        // Output the values
        printf("The area is %.2f cm^2\n", area);
        printf("The circumference is %.2f cm\n", circumference);
    }
```

Epilog

Algorithms have been around since the dawn of time, long before there was a special word to categorize them. Even Leonardo da Vinci designed algorithms. Klaus Schröer in his book "Ich aber quadriere den Kreis," suggests that da Vinci's work "Vitruvian man" is a recursive geometrical algorithm for the approximation of the squaring of a circle. Ulti-mately, the two most important elements to remember when designing an algorithm are a clear understanding of the problem to be solved, and an ability to "think outside the box," or look at a problem from a new perspective without preconceptions. Reliable algo-rithms are the core part of writing a good program. If you don't bother to design an algo-rithm and just go and code from your mind, it will be harder further down the track to decipher your program should something go amiss.

Exercises

Exercise 3.1

Before starting a hydropower-generation project, it is essential to calculate the amount of potential energy. The power of a dam can be calculated knowing the head and flow of the stream or river. The *flow* is the volume of water that can be captured and redirected to turn the turbine, and the *head* is the distance the water will fall on its way to the turbine. The larger the flow and the higher the head, the more energy is available for conversion to electricity. The P (kilowatts) can be calculated using the following equation:

$$P = \eta \rho g h Q$$

where

        η = turbine efficiency (0.0–1.0)
        ρ = density of the water (10^3 kg/m^3)
        g = gravitational constant (9.81 m/s^2)
        h = head of the water (metres)
        Q = volume of water flowing per second, m^3 per second

Efficiencies of around 70 percent can be expected, meaning that 70 percent of the hydraulic energy of the flowing water can be turned into mechanical energy spinning the turbine, with the remaining 30 percent lost. Energy is again lost in converting the mechanical energy into electrical energy and so a complete system has an efficiency of around 50 to 60 percent. For water flowing at one cubic metre per second from a head of one metre, the power generated is equivalent to approximately 10 kW assuming an energy conversion efficiency of 100 percent.

For example, a dam with a flow of 3m³, a head of 70 metres, and 60 percent efficiency will result in 1,236,060 kilowatts. Design an algorithm to represent the process of calculating the power generated in kilowatts. Illustrate the algorithm using pseudocode or a flowchart.

Exercise 3.2

Write an informal algorithm for one of the following:

(a) Making a cup of espresso.

(b) Toasting a piece of bread.

(c) Washing clothes.

Exercise 3.3

Consider a program that calculates all the numbers less than 1000 for which the sum of the cubes of the digits of the number is equal to the number itself. For example:

$$153 = 1^3 + 5^3 + 3^3$$

There are at least two approaches to deriving an algorithm for this problem—one is the *analysis* technique and is based on breaking the number down, and the second is the *synthesis* technique, which builds the number up. Try and derive algorithms for each.

Exercise 3.4

The *Montreal (QC) Gazette* examined in detail its own waste, using an ecological footprint assessment, and discovered some astounding facts. "The newsprint in one year's worth of *The Gazette*," explained the report, "consumes the equivalent of 186,816 trees. . . . To produce that much newsprint uses enough energy to heat 2472 homes for a year and enough water to fill 272 swimming pools, and emits as much carbon dioxide as 1500 cars."

The ecological footprint of a newspaper (assumed to weigh 0.3 kg) can be estimated by looking at two major resource inputs: processing energy and wood fibre.

- It takes 61 megajoules (MJ) of energy to produce one kilogram of paper. Therefore 61 MJ/kg $\times$ 0.3 = 18.3 MJ energy.

- The average wood fibre requirement for paper in Canada = 1.8m³/t.

Write an algorithm to calculate the ecological footprint of a newspaper, given an input that consists of the number of newspapers used per week.

It's All about Style

Any fool can write code that a computer can understand. Good programmers wrie code that humans can understand.

—Martin Fowler

Introduction

Some programmers never worry about style. There is a competition run every year called the "International Obfuscated C Code Contest," which simply implies that some programmers write code that is so confusing or opaque as to be difficult to perceive or understand. Sometimes these programs are termed *shrouded code*. The most infamous code from the competition is:

```
include <stdio.h>

main(t,_,a)char *a;{return!0<t?t<3?main(-79,-13,a+main(-87,1-_,
main(-86,0,a+1)+a)):1,t<_?main(t+1,_,a):3,main(-94,-
27+t,a)&&t==2?_+13?
main(2,_+1,"%s %d %d\n"):9:16:t<0?t<-72?main(_,t,
"@n'+,#'/*{}w+/w#cdnr/+,{}r/*de}+,/*{*+,/w{%+,/w#q#n+,/#{l,+,/n{n
+,/+#n+,/#;#q#n+,/+k#;*+,/'r :'d*'3,}{w+K w'K:'+}e#';dq#'l
q#'+d'K#!/+k#;q#'r}eKK#}w'r}eKK{nl]'/#;#q#n')){)#}w'){){nl]'/+#n';
d}rw' i;# ){nl]!/n{n#'; r{#w'r nc{nl]'/#{l,+'K {rw'
iK{;[{nl]'/w#q#n'wk nw' iwk{KK{nl]!/w{%'l##w#' i;
:{nl]'/*{q#'ld;r'}{nlwb!/*de}'c ;;{nl'-
{}rw]'/+,}##'*}#nc,',#nw]'/+kd'+e}+;#'rdq#w! nr'/ ') }+}{rl#'{n'
')# }'+}##(!!/")
<dl><dd>t<-50?_<H2>*a?putchar(31[a]):main(-
65,_,a+1):main((*a</H2>'/')+t,_,a+1)</dd></dl>
    :0<t?main(2,2,"%s"):*a=='/'⊤main(0,main(-61,*a,
"!ek;dc i@bK'(q)-[w]*%n+r3#l,{}:\nuwloca-O;m
.vpbks,fxntdCeghiry"),a+1);}
```

Even the most seasoned programmer will have a hard time trying to figure out what this code is doing. However, it is a legal C program that when compiled and run will generate the 12 verses of "The 12 Days of Christmas." It actually contains all the strings required for the poem in an encoded form inlined in the code.

Code like this is just plain *nasty*. The competition offers good examples of how NOT to program, in terms of style. There are, of course, features in any language that contribute to unreadability, but often the main cause of unreadable code is lack of *style*.

What Is Style?

One of the most important aesthetic attributes of a program is *readability*.[1] A program that is easy to read and understand is easier to test, maintain, and modify. Good programming style can't help fix an algorithm that is badly implemented, nor can it cure defects in a program. On the other hand, the best algorithm can be let down by poor style. Style is as important as other aspects of programming such as algorithm design, but is often neglected by novice programmers (and even some expert programmers!). Good style invokes a higher level of readability than poor style, making it easier to find problems in the code or to even understand what the code is doing. The latter is especially important if you are trying to decipher somebody else's ill-documented code (more on this later). I can't stress how important style is in programming. Having said that, the elements of this chapter are meant to guide you in the process of developing your own style. Some things are written in stone, but everything else is open to your own interpretation.

Facets of Style

Keep your code simple (do not write long-winded code):

- Make sure it is not unnecessarily complex.
- Write clear and precise code.
- Try to identify unclear or inelegant areas and improve them.

Outline your code:

- Outline and leave details to be filled in later.
- Create function prototypes but leave functions empty as a strategy to ensure program flow.
- Write the function code a piece at a time, and test it accordingly.

Do not create Swiss army knife functions:

- Have several specific functions rather than one bloated function.
- Break complicated functions into simple ones.

---

[1]Clifton, M.H., "A technique for making structured programs more readable," *ACM SIGPLAN Notices*, 1978, Vol. 13, No. 4, 58–63.

Indentation

Indentation is a popular technique for making control structures easier to read and is very important to the readability of a C program. Indentation is *not* a requirement of most programming languages. Rather, indentation is used to better convey the structure of a program to human readers. Some programming languages, such as Python, use indentation as a means of resolving structure instead of using braces or keywords. The most simple rule, first suggested by Leinbaugh in 1980, suggests that programmers *"indent statements from the control structure they belong to."*[2] The level of indenting represents the different layers of nesting. For example, if a **for** loop contains a compound statement, then all the statements in the compound statement should be indented the same amount. Consider the following sample code:

```
if (number % 2 == 0)
printf("Even\n");
```

Here the **printf** statement is part of the if structure. It is only executed if there is no remainder when number is divided by 2. So the printf statement should be indented, as follows:

```
if (number % 2 == 0)
    printf("Even\n");
```

How Many Spaces?

Miara and colleagues[3] undertook a study of indentation and program readability way back in 1983. They found that the level of indentation that seems to be optimal is between two and four spaces. As the number of spaces increases, the comprehension level decreases. If you use six spaces or more, the program is shifted so far to the right of the page that scanning the program becomes difficult. We consider two spaces to be too few, with the program becoming too compact. For convenience we suggest four spaces of indenting for each level of nesting. As an example below, a piece of code is shown with no, four, and eight spaces (the latter is equivalent to a tab).

Instead of (no spaces):

```
i = 0;
while (i < dx){
j = 0;
while (j < dy){
if (x[i][j] == 0)
x[i][j] = 1;
j = j + 1;
}
i = i + 1;
}
```

[2]Leinbaugh, D.W., "Indenting for the compiler," *ACM SIGPLAN Notices,* 1980, Vol. 15, 41–48.

[3]Miara, R.J., et al., "Program indentation and comprehensibility," *Communications of the ACM,* 1983, Vol. 26, No. 11, 861–867.

Use (four spaces):

```
i = 0;
while (i < dx){
    j = 0;
    while (j < dy){
        if (x[i][j] == 0)
            x[i][j] = 1;
        j = j + 1;
    }
    i = i + 1;
}
```

Don't use (eight spaces):

```
i = 0;
while (i < dx){
        j = 0;
        while (j < dy){
                if (x[i][j] == 0)
                        x[i][j] = 1;
                j = j + 1;
        }
        i = i + 1;
}
```

The sample code has three layers of indentation. A compiler doesn't care how many indents you use, if any at all! A compiler relies solely on the braces to determine a block structure. A programmer, on the other hand, relies heavily on the visual appearance of a program to decipher its structure.

Use Indenting Consistently

However, the usefulness of indentation diminishes when parts of a control structure are widely separated or heavily nested.

Instead of:

```
if (a_number % 2 == 0){
    evenS = evenS + 1;
    printf("Even numbers = %d\n", evenS);
}
else
    {
    oddS = oddS + 1;
    printf("Odd numbers = %d\n", oddS);
    }
```

Use:

```
if (a_number % 2 == 0) {
    evenS = evenS + 1;
    printf("Even numbers = %d\n", evenS);
}
else {
    oddS = oddS + 1;
    printf("Odd numbers = %d\n", oddS);
}
```

In the first example there are two inconsistencies: the positioning of the braces and the number of spaces used to indent. The second example uses both consistently.

Wrapping Lines

If an expression won't fit on a single line, split it: (a) after a comma or (b) after an operator. Make sure the new line is aligned with the beginning of the expression at the same level on the previous line. For example:

```
Good style:     humidex = air_T + ((5.0/9.0) *
                          (vap_P - 10.0));

Bad style:      humidex = air_T + ((5.0/9.0) * (vap_P
                          - 10.0));
```

The first is preferred because the break occurs after the inner parentheses. The second splits the inner parentheses.

Limiting Indenting

A sequence of **if-else-if** statements can quickly run off the side if indenting is practiced. For example:

```
if (expr1)
    statement1;
else if (expr2)
        statement2;
    else if (expr3)
            statement3;
```

It is better to express this in a linear form:

```
if (expr1)
    statement1;
else if (expr2)
    statement2;
else if (expr3)
    statement3;
```

Placement of Braces ()

There are various styles for the placement of braces, and no one is better than the other. It amounts to personal taste and an ability to use the style consistently. The first style is sometimes known as the BSD/Allman style (named after Eric Allman, the computer programmer who developed *sendmail*, a popular mail transfer agent). It puts the opening brace associated with a control statement on the next line, indented to the same level as the control statement. Statements within the braces are indented to the next level. The closing brace is aligned with the opening brace.

```
if (perC > 100.0)
{
    printf("The percentage should be 100 or less.");
    perC = 100.0;
}
```

In the second style, the opening brace for a compound statement associated with an **if, for, while,** or **do-while** is placed to the right of the line containing the statement's keyword.

```
if (perC > 100.0){
    printf("The percentage should be 100 or less.");
    perC = 100.0;
}
```

The closing brace appears in the same column as the first character of the control word. This form of indentation is sometimes termed *K&R style*, because it was used in the Kernighan and Ritchie book *The C Programming Language*.[4] The advantage of this form is that the opening brace doesn't require an extra line. The disadvantage is that it is more onerous to match braces. The caveat here lies with the **while** statement. This is one of those *bad features* of C. This is partly because the keyword **while** exists in two loops, the **while** loop and the **do-while** loop. Consider the following example:

```
do
{
    scanf("%d", &a_number);
    if (a_number != 0)
        x = log(a_number);
    else
        x = 0.0;
}
while (1);
```

Here it seems as though the **while** statement is not associated with the **do-while** loop, but is the start of a **while** loop. Putting the **while** statement on the same line as the closing brace helps differentiate the two.

```
} while (1);
```

---

[4]Kernighan, B. W., and Ritchie, D., *The C Programming Language*, Prentice Hall, 1988.

Ultimately C should have been designed using different constructs for the **do-while** loop, maybe the **repeat-until** that exists in other languages such as Pascal. Some have suggested a style that emphasizes the structured aspect of a language, for example:

```
while (x >= 0) {
    r = r + x;
    x = x - 1;
                  }
```

But this seems a little odd.

Another option is the *Whitesmiths style* (Whitesmiths was a software company that developed the first commercial C compiler). This style puts the opening brace associated with a control statement on the next line, indented. Statements within the braces are indented to the same level as the braces. For example:

```
while (x >= 0)
    {
    r = r + x;
    x = x - 1;
    }
```

The benefit of this style is that the alignment of the braces with the block emphasizes the fact that the entire block is conceptually a single compound statement.

The final style is known as *GNU style* and was made popular by Richard Stallman, the software freedom activist who launched the GNU Project (GNU is a recursive acronym for "GNU's Not Unix"; it is pronounced *guh-noo*, like *canoe*). GNU style puts braces on a line by themselves. The braces are indented by two spaces, and the contained code is indented by a further two spaces. For example:

```
while (x >= 0)
  {
    r = r + x;
    x = x - 1;
  }
```

Comments

An uncommented program is a travesty. Programs are read by humans. Computers don't really care what the program looks like, only that its syntax is correct. To have comments in a program *seems* self-evident, yet they are often excluded. Good comments are not easy to do since their purpose is to convey an understanding of the program. As designing a program is a cyclic process, it is foolish to wait until the program is finished to insert comments. If you can't describe what your algorithm does in plain English, you don't know what your program does! We consider two types of comments: preamble and explanatory. *Explanatory* comments explain any code that is not obvious simply by looking at it. Not every line of the program needs to be translated into English. A comment should not describe the operation of the statements. For example:

```
if (denominator != 0)
    fraction = numerator / denominator;
else
    fraction = 0.0;
```

We could have a comment such as

```
// Check if the denominator is not zero
```

However, it is not that good a comment because the person reading the code will be able to ascertain from the code what is happening. The code tells us *what* is being done, the comments should tell us *why* it is being done. A better comment might be the following:

```
// Set the value of fraction to zero if the numerator
 // is zero, avoiding a divide-by-zero error.
```

This tells us why we are checking if the denominator is zero. Do not just paraphrase the code.

The // (two slashes) style of comment, a C99 construct, should be used in most situations. Where ever possible, place comments above the code instead of beside it.

Here are some examples:

```
// Calculate the perimeter of a circle
Perimeter = 2.0 * pi * radius;
```

Comments can be placed at the end of a line when space allows, such as in the case of describing variables as they are created:

```
int r; // circle radius
```

Try NOT to use embedded comments of the form:

```
Area = /* of a circle */ pi * radius * radius;
```

Paragraphing

C source code can also be made more readable by creating cohesive paragraphs of code surrounded by black lines. The number of lines you use to separate each of these paragraphs should be consistent. For example consider the following code segment:

```
int w, j;
double a_number, f;
printf("Please enter a number: ");
scanf("%lf", &a_number);
w = (int)a_number;
f = a_number - w;
printf("The parts of %f are: %d and %f\n", a_number, w, f);
```

There are at least four "segments" of code in this grouping: variable declarations, input, assignment statements, and output. This grouping is somewhat cluttered and would be better served by separating each of the segments with a blank line. Remember, that the compiler doesn't care how many blank lines you add. It just ignores them.

```
int w, j;
double a_number, f;

printf("Please enter a number: ");
scanf("%lf", &a_number);

w = (int)a_number;
f = a_number — w;

printf("The parts of %f are: %d and %f\n", a_number, w, f);
```

Try to write only one statement per line. Using more can make code more confusing. For example:

```
a = 1; b = 2; c = a + b;
```

is better expressed as:

```
a = 1;
b = 2;
c = a + b;
```

White Spaces

The placement of blank spaces enhances the readability of C source code. Spaces improve readability by decreasing code density. Here are some guidelines for the use of space characters within code:

Use a single space after a comma between function arguments.

Good:	`scanf("%d%d",&a,&b);`
Better:	`scanf("%d%d", &a, &b);`

Use a single space between expressions in a control structure.

Good:	`for (i=0;i<100;i++)`
Better:	`for (i=0; i<100; i++)`

Try not to use a space after the parenthesis and function arguments

Good:	`scanf( "%d%d", &a, &b );`
Better:	`scanf("%d%d", &a, &b);`

Do not use spaces between a function name and parenthesis.

Good:	`scanf ("%d%d", &a, &b);`
Better:	`scanf("%d%d", &a, &b);`

Do not use spaces inside array brackets.

Good:	`x = vector[ index ];`
Better:	`x = vector[index];`

Use a single space before control flow structures.

Good: `for(i=0; i<100; i++)`
Better: `for (i=0; i<100; i++)`

Use a single space before and after relational operators.

Good: `if (i==j)`
Better: `if (i == j)`

Use a single space between operatora and operands.

Good: `area=pi*radius*radius;`
Better: `area = pi * radius * radius;`

The caveat with white spaces is that too much can dilute your code and actually make code unreadable.

A White Space Example

Let's look at a quick example of how white spaces can be improved in a program.

```
int vector[10],index,temp,found;

found=0;

scanf("%d",&temp);

for(i=0;i<10;i++)
    if(vector[i]==temp)
        found=1;
```

This program fragment works, but it is certainly not the most comprehensible from the point of view of readability. It may be more readable in this form:

```
int vector[10], index, temp, found;

found = 0;

scanf("%d", &temp);

for (i=0; i<10; i++)
    if (vector[i] == temp)
        found = 1;
```

Again, the compiler doesn't care how many white spaces you add to your program. It ignores them all.

Parentheses

Parentheses greatly improve the readability of a program. Leaving parentheses out of an equation makes correcting and reading the equation more difficult.

With too few parentheses	With extra parentheses
`A*B*C/(D*E*F)`	`(A*B*C) / (D*E*F)`
`A*B/C*D/E*F`	`(A*B*D*F) / (C*E)`
`A/B/C/D`	`((A/B)/C)/D`

Using Good Names

Good names make your program more readable. Consider the following example:

```
a = b * 1;
```

This is syntactically correct, but its meaning is opaque. Contrast this with:

```
area = breadth * length;
```

Here meaning is provided without having to write comments. A good name should be short, descriptive, and precise. Long names mean that everything becomes longer. Simple expressions become long and less readable. For example:

```
double sphere_surface_area, sphere_radius, pi;

sphere_surface_area = 4.0 * pi * sphere_radius *
sphere_radius;
```

This example is certainly descriptive, but the expression has become extremely long and awkward. A name should be descriptive, but this does not mean that it has to be long. Now consider:

```
double sphere_SA, sphere_R, pi;

sphere_SA = 4.0 * pi * sphere_R * sphere_R;
```

This example uses shorter words that are just as descriptive in the context they are being used. In this case the context is surface areas of geometric solids, so we have used standardized suffixes to denote characteristics such as surface area (SA) and radius (R). Where **sphere_SA** denotes the surface area of a sphere, **cylinder_SA** could similarly be used to denote the surface area of a cylinder. We could also have chosen suffixes such as **surfA, sArea**.

A good name is worth a paragraph of comments. Here are some general guidelines:

1. Variable names should start with a lowercase character. For example: **sphere_Radius, sphere_radius, sphereRadius**

2. Temporary variables should have short names that reflect the fact they offer temporary storage. For example, **temp** or **tempInt**.

3. The prefix *n* should be used with variables representing the number of objects. For example, **nBacteria, n_edges**.

4. Make all variable names either singular or plural. Identifiers should not only differ by the addition of the letter *s*. For example, **cell** and **cell_array** would be better than **cell** and **cells**.

5. Variables that are indices in a loop should be named or prefixed with **i, j, k,** etc.

6. Negative boolean names should be avoided! When these are coupled with a negation operation, you get a double negative, which can be hard to decipher. For example, if we have the variable **does_NotExist,** then **!does_NotExist** is a double negative. It is better to use something like: **exists.**

7. Avoid using a keyword for a variable name.

Why Not Use Uppercase?

You should use lowercase and uppercase characters consistently. C is *case sensitive*, which means that PI, pi, and Pi are all different. In C it is common practice to use uppercase for **define** statements and lowercase for variables and function names. Whatever you do, don't use a lot of uppercase. UPPERCASE is tantamount to YELLING. Consider the following program segment:

```
int W, J;
double A_NUMBER, F;

printf("PLEASE ENTER A NUMBER: ");
scanf("%lf", &A_NUMBER);

W = (int)A_NUMBER;
F = A_NUMBER − W;

printf("THE PARTS OF %f ARE: %d AND %f\n", A_NUMBER, W, F);
```

This code is not really that readable, and because C keywords are in lowercase, the effect is a less readable combination. It sort of looks like early FORTRAN or even COBOL.

Prettyprinting

Ledgard[5] first described the term *prettyprint* to denote a convenient shorthand for formatting the source code to enhance readability. In other terms it is called *code beautification.* Ledgard notes that ". . . prettyprinting is the spacing of a program to illuminate its logical structure." For example, consider the following segments of code:

```
if (a_number != 0)
    x = log(a_number);
else
    x = 0.0;

if (a_number != 0) x = log(a_number);
else x = 0.0;

if (a_number != 0) x = log(a_number);else x = 0.0;
```

All three programs compile in the same way, they just differ in white space. A code beautifier will convert these to a more aesthetically pleasing format. Utilities such as **Indent** can be used to automatically beautify your program. Such programs rearrange the

---

[5]Ledgard, H. F., *Programming Proverbs.* Hayden, 1975.

spacing and indentation of certain constructs to make the logical structure of the program appear more visually apparent. Should you use them? Maybe, but wait until you have a better understanding of the style before you go and automate it.

Epilog

At the end, the style you choose to use is up to you. The lessons and examples in this chapter are meant to provide you with some measure of grounding.

In 1974 Kernighan and Plauger wrote a book entitled *The Elements of Programming Style*,[6] which contains a numbers of "rules" we think aptly sum up how programming should be approached:

> Write clearly—don't be too clever.
> Say what you mean, simply and directly.
> Write clearly—don't sacrifice clarity for "efficiency."

Too many good programmers add too much complexity to their programs too soon, or they add fancy things. A word of advice: Don't. The reason some commercial software has become "bloatware" is because programmers have forgotten about the basics of how to right a "good" program. A program written in 400 lines may not necessarily be better than one using only 60 lines. There is a tendency to overwrite code by adding things that weren't in the specification or that seem "neat." There is also an affinity with writing obscure code that nobody else understands, partly because the programmer doesn't know what comments are. Most of these problems result from a combination of ill-advised algorithms and dubious coding practices.

Novice programmers often believe they are writing programs for computers. Experienced programmers begin to realize that they are writing programs for humans.

Exercises

Exercise 4.1

What does the following program do? Criticize the program from the point of view of style, and rewrite it incorporating elements of style.

```c
#include <stdio.h>
#include <math.h>
int main(void){
double a,b,ec;
printf("Semi-major axis:");
scanf("%lf", &a);
printf("Semi-minor axis:");
scanf("%lf", &b);
if(a>=b){ec=sqrt(a*a-b*b)/a;printf("E=%.5lf",ec);}
return 0;}
```

---

[6]Kernighan, B. W., and Plauger, P. J., *The Elements of Programming Style*, McGraw-Hill, 1978.

Exercise 4.2

What do the following statements represent? Rewrite the following code in a more understandable way:

```
bb = b * b;
a1 = a * c;
a2 = 4 * a1;
b1 = bb - a2;
b2 = sqrt(b1);
bottom = 2 * a;
top = -b + b2;
root1 = top / bottom;
```

Exercise 4.3

Increase the readability of the following program:

```
#include <stdio.h>

int main(void)

{
double ac_TON, hours, SEER, cost, OPcost;
printf("Size of air conditioner: ");
scanf("%lf", &ac_TON);
printf("Estimated hours of use per year: ");
scanf("%lf", &hours);
printf("Air conditioner efficiency (SEER): ");
scanf("%lf", &SEER);
printf("Cost per kWh ($/kWh): ");
scanf("%lf", &cost);
printf("Estimated annual operating costs: $%.2f\n", OPcost);
return 0;
}
```

It's a Bug's Life

If debugging is the process of removing bugs, then programming
must be the process of putting them in.
—Edsger Dijkstra

They've Shut Down the Main Reactor!

On September 21, 1997, the *USS Yorktown*, a U.S. Navy Ticonderoga class guided missile
cruiser, came to an abrupt standstill off the coast of Virginia. It seems that while trying to
manually calibrate a fuel valve in the 80,000hp propulsion system, a zero was entered in a
data field of the Standard Monitoring & Control System, resulting in a divide-by-zero
exception and subsequent failure of the propulsion system. It took more than
2 hours to restore electrical power. Failures like this occur largely because software is discontinuous. One millimeter of error in a jet engine component will cause a proportional
increase in failure rate. A corresponding small error introduced in software can be catastrophic or may have no noticeable effect.[1] In situations like this, when software goes hay-
wire, it is usually due to a software exception, or *bug,* a situation where a program deviates
from its intended behavior.

---

[1]Holloway, C. M., "Why engineers should consider formal methods," in *AIAA/IEEE Digital Avionics Systems*, 1997.

Practically everything from power plants to robotic milking systems to traffic lights and even the delivery of postcards requires some degree of control by software. The average passenger car now contains approximately 30 to 40 microprocessors controlling air conditioning, audio and video systems, and even critical functions such as braking systems and air bags.[2] More luxurious cars equipped with global positioning systems can have more than 100 microprocessors. The average car today contains approximately 35 million lines of code (LOC). With software that is so inherently complex, there is always a possibility of something going amiss. A *bug* in the most traditional sense of the word refers to some unwanted or unintended behavior of a program. The process of identifying the cause of symptoms and removing bugs is called *debugging.* Folklore suggests the first programming bug was discovered on September 9, 1947, when a Mark II programmable computing machine suddenly stopped.[3] An investigation established that a moth had shorted out one of the relay circuits.

Software by itself is not dangerous—it is an abstraction without the ability to produce energy and thus lead directly to a physical loss.[4] It is only when software is charged with controlling something (e.g., a robot) that complications arise. Software also tends to be changed frequently and "evolves" over time, but changing software without introducing undesired errors is difficult. The more changes made to the software the more "brittle" it becomes.

After programming for more than half a century, why are bugs still so prevalent in software? No programmer would consciously incorporate code such as:

```
if (divide_by_zero())
    shutdown_propulsion();
```

---

[2]Duvall, M., "Software bugs threaten Toyota hybrids," 2005, www.baselinemag.com

[3]Hopper, G. M., "The first bug," *IEEE Annals of the History of Computing*, 1981, Vol. 3, No. 3, 285–286.

[4]Leveson, N. G., "Systemic factors in software-related spacecraft accidents," *Space 2001 . . . the Odyssey Continues,* American Institute of Aeronautics and Astronautics, 2001.

The Impact of Software Failure

The most troublesome effect related to the existence of bugs is the increased incidence of avoidable defects that emerge after a product has been released. The aerospace industry, for example, has lost more than $1 billion since the mid-1990s in what might be attributed to problematic software. Examples include Ariane 5 (U.S. $640m, 1996), Mars Climate Orbiter (U.S. $328m, 1999), and Milstar (U.S. $800m, 1999). The proportion of time required for debugging programming errors in systems development has climbed from 25 percent in the mid-1960s[5] to more than 50 percent in the late 1990s.[6] Moreover, this is expected to increase as systems rely on ever larger and complex software. Consider, the case of software design for aerospace applications. Many systems, such as deep space missions and sorties to Mars, have increasing demands for autonomy and as such are becoming increasingly intricate: from 30,000 lines for Cassini (1997) to 120,000 lines for Mars PathFinder (1996) and 428,000 lines for Mars Exploration Rover (2003).[7] Holzmann[8] estimates that around 50 software errors remain in every 1,000 lines of recently written code, and code that has been thoroughly tested still contains 10. NASA has reduced the bug density by a modest amount from 8.1/1K of code in 1976 to 5.5/1K in 1990. Nonetheless, even using this low-ball figure the software aboard the Mars Exploration Rover harbors the possibility of containing up to 2,354 undetected software errors. NASA currently estimates a 40 percent chance of a critical software error during a mission containing 1 million lines of code. This ultimately affects robustness, which is significant considering that for projects like Mars Exploration Rover, entry, descent, and landing are all controlled by software. Hatton[9] estimates that perhaps 40 percent of software failures are statically detectable as faults; that is, they can be found *before* compiling the program. This usually results because of some language misuse that would fail in some context. As an example, consider ISO C, which lists 119 constructions of uncertain definition. Hatton also undertook a study of errors in scientific software and concludes that there are approximately 8 serious faults per 1,000 lines of code in C that are statically detectable in commercially released scientific software. Software errors occur due to a combination of programming errors and flaws in the software design process.

Not all the news is bad. One of the most successful software projects in terms of debugging is the "on-board shuttle group" who design software for the NASA space shuttle.[10] Their software takes a 120-ton shuttle with 4 million pounds of fuel aboard and lofts it into space, 100 miles up, automatically. But what makes it truly remarkable is the fact that the software never crashes and never needs to be rebooted. From 1994 to 1996, the software, all 420,000 LOC, contained just one error. Why are they so successful? Because they have a near-precise software design process designed to catch 85 percent of errors *before* formal testing even begins.

---

[5]Delaney, W.A., "Predicting the costs of computer programs," *Data Processing Magazine*, 1966, 32.

[6]Ward, R., "Beyond design: The discipline of debugging," *Computer Language*, 1998, 37–38.

[7]Regan, P., and Hamilton, S., "NASA's Mission Reliable," *IEEE Computer*, 2004, Vol. 37, No. 1, 59–68.

[8]Holzmann, G.J., "The logic of bugs," *Foundations of Software Engineering*, 2002, 81–87.

[9]Hatton, L., "The T-experiments: Errors in scientific software," *IEEE Computing in Science and Engineering*, 1997, Vol. 4, No. 2, 27–38.

[10]Fishman, C., "They write the right stuff," *Fast Company*, 1996/1997, No. 6, 95.

From Defects to Failures

Some programs fail, sometimes. In theory, a failure is created by a *defect* in the code, which generates a *fault* in the program state, which then propagates until it becomes an observable *failure*.[11] A failure is characterized as a system showing unexpected behavior at run time. Sometimes these failures are tied to inadequacies or limitations in the programming language. Hatton sums this up with the statement: "If a language contains a hole, programmers will fall into it. All languages contain holes."[12] More often than not, however, errors are associated with flaws in the algorithm design process. Defects are more commonly termed *programming errors*. Some are trapped by the compiler and relate more to deficiencies in the grammar.

It is obviously difficult to describe all the possibilities for programming errors that can permeate a program, but in deciding how to tackle a particular bug, it is often helpful to attempt to classify it. Often the best way for students to familiarize themselves with a programming construct is to compile a sample program. However, students often give very little consideration to the concept of programming errors. The first time they encounter an error, they are often puzzled as to how to proceed. Take, for example, the following simple C program, which calculates the square of a number:

```
1          #include <stdio.h>
2
3          void main(void)
4          {
5              int b;
6              printf("Enter a number: ");
7              scanf("%d", &a)
8              b = a * a;
9              printf("The square of %d is: %d\n",a,b);
10         }
```

A compiler such as Gnu C (gcc) might produce the following error message:

```
In function 'main':
7: 'a' undeclared (first use in this function)
8: syntax error before 'b'
10: warning: control reaches end of non-void function
```

To a novice programmer such feedback can be overwhelming and may lead to a number of questions:

- What does a warning imply?
- What does a syntax error mean?

---

[11]Cleve, H., and Zeller, A., "Locating causes of program failures," *27th International Conference on Software Engineering*, 2005.

[12]Hatton, L., "The T-experiments: Errors in scientific software," *IEEE Computing in Science and Engineering*, 1997, Vol. 4, No. 2, 27–38.

- Why is there a warning for the 10th line—it's just a curly brace?
- Why is there a syntax error before 'b'?

Other C compilers (Xcode) might offer a different error message:

```
main.c:8    error:parse error before 'b'.
```

Sometimes these errors are best described using some form of analogy: A *parse error* implies "to make sense of or comprehend." It's like the compiler saying, " I simply couldn't understand what you said *before* line 8." It is simply a syntax error.

The most confusing types of errors are those that don't produce any error messages. These are *logic* errors. Consider the following C program to calculate the sum of the numbers from 1 to 100:

```
1          #include <stdio.h>
2
3          void main(void)
4          {
5              int i=1, sum;
6              while (i <= 100)
7              {
8                  sum = sum + i;
9                  printf("%d\n", sum);
10             }
11         }
```

This program correctly compiles, but contains two logic errors, which only become apparent once the program is run. The first of these relates to the fact that the program contains an *infinite loop*, a situation where a loop continues processing its loop body endlessly. This would happen if the terminating condition in the loop definition is never met. In this case the error would be corrected by inserting the statement i = i + 1; after line 9. The second error may not be as apparent: The output produced is not correct, because the variable sum is not given an initial value, causing the statement **sum = sum + i;** to use a "garbage" number as its initial value. These are often the most difficult errors for students to resolve. There are situations when the operating system *masks* or disguises a runtime error by providing a confusing message. For example, an integer divide-by-zero error may be reported using the message: **"Floating exception (core dumped)."** A seasoned programmer will recognize this as being an error associated with a floating-point calculation that has caused a "core dump," essentially an image of the running program written to a file.

Compiler Errors

Compiler errors are messages that appear when a program is being compiled. They generally mean that something could not be understood by the compiler or was not considered correct syntax. Compilers generally provide two levels of messages: warnings and errors. A *compiler warning* indicates that something is gravely wrong, but not enough to stop compilation. Warnings should be corrected because they often lead to more serious problems that may not be so easy to find. As the compiler works on a source file, it expects to see sequences of characters that correspond to valid declarations, definitions, and so forth. If it finds something that doesn't conform to the language syntax, it will produce a compiler error. A compiler error indicates that something must be fixed before it can be compiled. Compiler errors are synonymous with syntax errors. A syntax error is caused when something that has been written does not conform to what the compiler considers proper formatting. It is analogous to a grammatical error in English. For example, a missing ";" or an extra "}" might lead to strange compiler error and warning messages. Often the place where the compiler complains is after the place where the defect exists. Compiler errors often present two difficulties for novice programmers:

- They frequently miss reporting an actual error on one line but get "thrown off track" and report errors on subsequent lines that are not truly errors.
- After encountering one true syntax error, compilers often generate many incorrect syntax error messages.

Runtime Errors

When a program is executed and something goes wrong it is termed a *runtime error* or *software exception*. There are two main types of runtime error: fatal errors and logic errors. A *fatal error* occurs when an executable crashes, due to memory faults or a stack overflow. A *logic error* is an error in meaning. A logic error occurs when the program simply doesn't do what it is suppose to do. The compiler does not detect these errors because they don't violate any rules. Examples of logic errors include infinite loop, off-by-one errors, and code inside a loop that doesn't belong there. An example is the case of the equality operator "==" in C. In C the expression **if (a = 0)** is perfectly legal and will not result in a compiler error. In fact the program will run, evaluating the condition as true while "silently" assigning *a* the value 0, rather than checking to see whether a "is equal to" 0. Logic errors are a special kind of semantic error, which also includes situations such as using uninitialized variables, dead code (code that will never be used), and certain type problems. A compiler can often bring these to your attention, but it must be told to do so explicitly (e.g., through warning and optimization flags).

One type of runtime error is *stack overflow*. A stack is a limited portion of memory used by a program (see Chapter 20 for more details). Stack overflow occurs when the stack is at capacity but an attempt is made to store something on the stack, causing it to *overflow*.

Syntax Error

A *syntax error* is a violation of the grammatical rules of a programming language. It's analogous to a grammatical error in English. If we write a line of C code containing a syntax error, the compiler does not know what we mean. A syntax error is sometimes called a *compile-time error* and is usually fatal, meaning that the C compiler cannot compile the source code. A warning, on the other hand, is usually just that.

How are they detected?

- Syntax errors are usually detected by the compiler.

Why do they occur?

- The syntax rules of C have been violated.

How do we eliminate syntax errors?

1. Start with the first error listed, try to correct it, and recompile the program. Sometimes many of the errors will disappear after one error is fixed.
2. If you are having trouble with a particular error listed for a specific line and are certain that the line is correct, then search for syntax errors in the lines above that line.
3. Repeat this process until all errors are eliminated.

Note: The compiler will generate error messages of the form:

```
test.c:6:11: error message
```

The first name relates to the name of the C program you are trying to compile. The first number (6) relates to the line number, and the second number (11), if it occurs, relates to how many characters along that line.

Syntax Warning

A *syntax warning* is a nonfatal error generated by the compiler when it has found that the syntax of some part of the code is valid but in a potentially erroneous way. Warnings should not be ignored, because they usually do indicate that something is wrong with the program, and it is likely to behave differently from what you would expect. Syntax warnings often lead to semantic errors.

How are they detected?

- Syntax warnings are usually detected by the compiler.

Why do they occur?

- The syntax rules of C have not been violated, but the compiler has built-in error checking for certain common programming errors.

Runtime Error

A *runtime error* occurs when a program is run (executed). When there are runtime errors in a C program, the compiler will compile the code. Most of the time runtime errors do not generate compiler warnings and are among the most common form of error. Runtime errors only occur when you run a program; thus, they can only occur if there is a program to run. That is, it must have compiled without syntax errors.

How are they detected?

- Runtime errors are usually detected by using the program. There are two types of runtime errors: *fatal* and *logic.*

Why do they occur?

- The syntax rules of C have been correctly followed, but the meaning of the code is incorrect (e.g., faulty algorithms, values calculated erroneously) or there has been an error in the way the program runs.

What is a fatal error?

- A fatal error occurs when the executable crashes (e.g., segmentation faults, bus errors).

What is a segmentation fault?

- A segmentation fault occurs when you try to access memory that your program is not allowed to use or that doesn't exist in the computer.
- These errors often occur due to improper use of arrays or pointers. For example, consider the following code:

```
#include <stdio.h>

int main(void)
{
    char dna[5];
    scanf("%s",dna);
    printf("%s\n",dna);
    return 0;
}
```

If you run the program and type "ATGCATGC" it works quite happily. It's overwriting some part of the memory with something it shouldn't be. But it doesn't cause a **"segmentation fault"** until you get to something like "ATGCATGCATGCATGCATG-CATGCATGC".

- Another example using pointers:

```
    int *p;
    *p = 1;
```

- Sometimes when a segmentation fault or other runtime error occurs, an image of the running program, called a *core file,* is generated. This process is called a core dump! A core file can be analyzed, but normally it should just be deleted.

Logic Error

A *logic error*, sometimes known as a *semantic error*, occurs when the program produces an unexpected and undesired outcome. A logic error is a violation of the rules of meaning of a programming language. Since a compiler only checks for the correct use of syntax, it is not able to check whether or not we have written code whose meaning is correct. When there are logic errors in a C program, the compiler will compile the code.

How are they detected?

- Logic errors are detected at run time.

Why do they occur?

- The syntax rules of C have been correctly followed, but the meaning of the code is incorrect (e.g., faulty algorithms, values calculated erroneously).

The Process of Debugging

Maurice Wilkes summed up debugging in 1949:

> As soon as we started programming, we found to our surprise that it wasn't as easy to get programs right as we had thought. Debugging had to be discovered. I can remember the exact instant when I realized that a large part of my life from then on was going to be spent in finding mistakes in my own programs."[13]

Many programmers confuse debugging and testing. If a program is not working correctly, then it needs to be debugged, so the process of debugging starts with evidence of program failure. If a program appears to be working correctly, then it is being *tested*. Sometimes, a program fails after it has been tested, and we will move back to the debugging stage. Testing determines that a failure exists, and debugging localizes the defect.

Debugging a program often is costly in terms of resources. An effort should be made to prevent bugs. First, avoid *questionable coding*. Don't use complex coding practices if simple ones will suffice. Second, never allow *data dependency*. Check data at input time to *ensure* that it is correct. Always complete logic decisions. If input is to be a 1 or 2, then don't just check for 1 and if false, assume 2. Check for both. Finally, never assume that the user will do anything correctly.

printf Debugging

The simplest form of program debugging uses appropriate output statements to automatically trace values of different variables at different stages of program execution. This can be achieved using debug "switches" and printf() debugging, for example:

---

[13]http://en.wikiquote.org/wiki/Maurice_Wilkes

```
#define debug 1

temp = 13.12 + 0.6215*airT-11.37*pow(windS,0.16);

if (debug)
      printf("%.2f",temp);

wind_chill = temp + 0.3965*airT*pow(wind_S,0.16);
printf("The wind chill is: %.2f\n", wind_chill);
```

In this example, if the value of debug is set to 1, then all the printf statements associated with the if (debug) statements will be performed, effectively outputting the value of the intermediary variable temp.

You can also use switch statements to prompt different debugging levels.

```
switch (debug)
{
      case 4: printf("high");
      case 3:
      case 2:
      case 1: printf("low");
      case 0: break;
      default: ;
}
```

Defensive Programming

Defensive programming, sometimes called *antibugging*, refers to the practice of writing a program in a manner in which errors are trapped.

Defensive programming is a preemptive process designed to help validate preconditions, postconditions, and invariants in a program by identifying sections of a program that could be encapsulated in a "self-checking" wrapper. This may involve checking arguments to a function for validity before execution of the body of the function of checking incorrectly constrained input. The latter relates to inspecting inputs for validity before processing continues. For example, two commonly overlooked errors relate to "divide-by-zero" and log(0). It is easy to use defensive programming to "rewrite" these functions.

```
double Log(double x)
{
    if (x == 0)
        return 0;
    else
        return log10(x);
}

double div(double n, double d)
{
    if (d == 0)
        return 0;
```

```
        else
            return n/d;
    }
```

This allows any errors relating to the calculation of log(0) to be trapped and handled in an appropriate manner well before it becomes a program failure at run time. It can also be used in situations where the programming language contains harmful constructs such as C's dangling-else problem. The "dangling else" is a common and subtle logic error found in the flow of control of a nested if statement. Since a compiler ignores indentation, it matches an else clause with the most recent unmatched then clause.

```
if (a > 0.0)
    if (a > maximum)
        maximum = a;
else
    minimum = a;
```

The following small change in the if statement—using braces to enforce an association—solves the problem.

```
if (a > 0.0){
    if (a > maximum)
        maximum = a;
}
else
    minimum = a;
```

Another example of defensive programming occurs in validating input. For example, what happens if **scanf** doesn't succeed in reading input? For example, consider the following code:

```
int a;
scanf("%d",&a);
printf("%d",a);
```

Now if a user enters the character *d* instead of an integer, we get the following result:

```
2147332096
```

A better way would be to create a function that checks the input and disposes of it if it isn't correct:

```
int get_int(void)

{
    int input;
    char c;

    while (scanf("%d", &input) != 1)
    {
        while ((c = getchar()) != '\n')
            putchar(c);
```

```
        printf(" is not an integer\n");
    }
    return input;
}
```

This function attempts to read an integer **(int)** into the variable input. If it fails to do so, it enters the body of the outer **while** loop. The inner **while** loop then reads the offending input and discards it, character by character. The function then prompts for the input again. The function persists until the user successfully enters an integer.

Defensive programming might advocate that an if-then statement should always be coded with braces, even when the then part contains only a single statement. It also encompasses techniques designed to resolve some common programming deficiencies, related primarily to (the lack of) proper programming style. Prevention is often better than the cure.

Assertions

Programs are bursting with assumptions. When you calculate n/d, you assume that d does not have value of zero. An assertion is an expression that should evaluate to true at a specific point in your code. If an assertion fails to evaluate to true, then a problem has been identified. It makes no sense to execute after an assertion failure. In C, you can incorporate the library **assert.h**, and write the expression you want to assert as the argument to assert, such as **assert (d > 0)**.

The **assert.h** library is comprised of a macro named **assert()**. It takes the value of an integer expression as its argument. If the expression evaluates as nonzero (false), the **assert()** macro writes an error message to standard output, and calls the **abort()** function, which terminates the program. The thought is to identify a location in a program where a certain condition should be true and use the **assert()** statement to terminate the program if the condition is not met. When assert fails, it typically displays the test that failed, the line number, and the name of the file. Consider the following example. It asserts that the denominator (b) is greater than zero before attempting to perform the division.

```
1       #include <stdio.h>
2       #include <assert.h>
3
4       int main()
5       {
6           double a, b, div;
7           printf("Enter two numbers: ");
8           scanf("%lf%lf",&a,&b);
9
10          assert(b > 0);
11          div = a / b;
12          printf("%f divided by %f is %f\n", a, b, div);
13
14      return 0;
15      }
```

The gcc compiler handles the assertion in the following manner:

```
Enter two numbers: 2 0
div.c:15: failed assertion 'b >0'
Abort trap
```

A similar outcome could be achieved using an **if** statement:

```
if (b <= 0)
{
    printf("b less than zero\n;
    abort();
}
```

This could also be incorporated in the form of a function:

```
#include <stdio.h>
#include <assert.h>

double safeDIV(double x, double y)
{
    assert(y > 0);
    return x/y;
}

int main()
{
    double a, b, div;
    printf("Enter two numbers: ");
    scanf("%lf%lf",&a,&b);

    div = safeDIV(a,b);
    printf("%f divided by %f is %f\n", a, b, div);

    return 0;
}
```

Exceptions

Some compilers offer extensions to the language that allows a program to acquire control when an event occurs that normally terminates the program. Acquiring control is known as an *exception*. Implementing an exception involves two ANSI functions: **setjmp** and **longjmp** found in the library **setjmp.h**. The function **setjmp** is called first and normally returns a value of zero, indicating to the program to execute the normal code. When the exception occurs, the **longjmp** function returns control to the location of **setjmp**. When **setjmp** is called by **longjmp**, the return value is controlled by an argument to **longjmp**. Consider the following program:

```
#include <stdio.h>
#include <setjmp.h>
```

```
jmp_buf env;

double div(double x, double y)
{
    if (y == 0)
        longjmp(env,3);
    else
        return x / y;
}

int main(void)
{
    double x, y, result;

    scanf("%lf%lf", &x, &y);

    if (setjmp(env) == 0)
    {
        result = div(x, y);
        printf("%lf\n", result);
    }
    else
        printf("Exception: divide by zero\n");
    return 0;

}
```

The variable **env** is where **setjmp** saves the current environment for **longjmp** to use later. It basically says, "remember where you are now, and store that place in **env**." When the main program executes, **setjmp** has a value of zero, so the **div** function is called. The value of **y** in **div** is tested to check if it has a value of zero. If it is zero, then an exception is thrown using **longjmp**; **longjmp** then says "go back to the place stored in **env**." Execution then skips to the **setjmp** call, **setjmp** returns the value 3, and the exception is handled through the error message. Exception handling is a great way of dealing with problems that could lead to a program crashing, but it is not for the faint-hearted.

Slicing

The concept of slicing was introduced more than two decades ago. With an initial program behavior (a variable associated with a particular statement), slicing reduces the program to a minimal form that still produces that behavior. Code not associated with the behavior is ignored, and the reduced program is termed a *slice*.

Slicing is based on the flow of information through a program. A slice of code with respect to a statement S and a variable v consists of those statements of the program that might affect the value of v at statement S. If the variable v in the output statement S contains an incorrect value, then the slice on v at S will contain the program fault causing the incorrect output value. This is true because program failures are indications of program faults and a slice on variable v with respect to statement S contains all statements that might affect the value of v at S. This is known as the slicing criterion and is often denoted {S, v}.

Dicing is the process of subtracting a slice on one set of variables at a statement from a second set of variables at the same or another statement. Slicing and dicing are code reduction methods. Some programming structures are more difficult to slice than others. Unstructured control flow (e.g., **goto** statements) are difficult, as are statements involving indirection, such as pointers.

There are several variations on slicing. Backward slicing is probably the most intuitive form of slicing. Here the slice is computed by working backward from the point of interest, finding all statements that can affect the specified variables at the point of interest and discarding all other statements. Forward slicing is the reverse of this. Here we work forward from the point of interest, identifying those statements that can be affected by changes to the specified variables. Chopping is another form of slicing that integrates both backward and forward slicing. Here two points of interest are chosen and the slice consists of those statements that allow a change from the source to the target. Backward slicing can assist in locating the parts of a program that contain an error, while forward slicing is used to predict the parts of a program that will be affected by a code modification.

In addition there are different strategies for calculating the slice, divided basically into static and dynamic slicing. Static slicing implies examining the code without actually running the program in question. Dynamic slicing analyzes the code while the program is running using specific input. Most forms of slicing are syntax preserving. This implies that they leave the syntax of the original program intact and simply remove statements to create a program slice.

An Example of Slicing

Consider the following example:

```
1          #include <stdio.h>
2          #include <math.h>
3
4          int main(void)
5          {
6                  double a, b, c, d, x1, x2;
7
8                  // Read input data
9                  printf("Enter the variables for the quadratic: ");
10                 scanf("%lf %lf %lf", &a, &b, &c);
11
12                 // Perform calculation
13                 d = sqrt(b * b - 4. * a * c);
14                 x1 = (-b + d) / (2. * a);
15                 x2 = (-b - d) / (2. * a);
16
17                 // Display output
18                 printf("\nx1 = %12.3e x2 = %12.3e\n", x1, x2);
19
20                 return 0;
21         }
```

We want to calculate a backward slice on the criterion $\{18, x2\}$. Statement 18 is a special case because the value of the variable x2 is not actually modified. Working backwards: Statement 15 modifies x2, but statement 14 does not; therefore, we add 15 to the slice, but remove 14. The value of d, calculated in statement 13, is used in statement 15, so this is also included in the slice. All three values input in statement 10 are used, as is statement 6. Statement 9 can be removed since it does not affect any of the variables in the program. The resulting slice (ignoring the core elements, (6 lines) of the program) therefore becomes:

```
6        double a, b, c, d, x1, x2;
10       scanf("%lf %lf %lf", &a, &b, &c);
13       d = sqrt(b * b - 4. * a * c);
15       x2 = (-b - d) / (2. * a);
18       printf("\nx1 = %12.3e x2 = %12.3e\n", x1, x2);
```

An Example of Backward Slicing

For another example of backward slicing, consider the C program fragment:

```
1        i = 10;
2        j = 12;
3        s = i / log(j);
4        t = s * j;
5        s = sqrt(i) + sqrt(j);
```

Now we want to calculate a backward slice on the criterion $\{5, s\}$, which is:

```
1        i = 10;
2        j = 12;
5        s = sqrt(i) + sqrt(j);
```

Dissecting this slice, it is easy to see that statement 4 cannot affect the value of s, so it is excluded from the slice. Statement 3 also has no effect upon the value of s, because although this statement revises the value of s, the value assigned is replaced in statement 5, essentially discarding the intermediary value. However, if we change statement 3 in the original fragment:

```
1        i = 10;
2        j = 12;
3        s = i / log(++j);
4        t = s * j;
5        s = sqrt(i) + sqrt(j);
```

we now have to include statement 3 in the program slice, because the value of the variable j is altered in the shorthand ++j (i.e., increase the value of j by 1, then calculate the log of this new value). The new slice would now look like:

```
1        i = 10;
2        j = 12;
3        s = i / log(++j);
5        s = sqrt(i) + sqrt(j);
```

An Example of Forward Slicing

When changes are made to a program, they can have a ripple effect through the program, possibly leading to unforeseen side effects and potential defects. This is where forward slicing plays a role in tracing these ripples to establish the regions of a program the changes will affect. Consider the following code, where a change is to be made in statement 2:

```
1        u = 6.7;
2        v = 4.1;
3        t = u * v;
4        alpha = exp(t);
5        if (t != 0)
6              alpha = sqrt(v);
```

Statement 2 assigns a value to the variable *j*. Any ensuing part of the program that relies on the value of *j* may behave differently after *j* is modified. The forward slice is given as:

```
3        t = u * v;
5        if (t != 0)
6              alpha = sqrt(v);
```

Statement 6 is included in the slice, as its execution is controlled by the logical expression t != 0, which is affected by the slicing criteria.

An Example of Static Slicing

In static slicing, the slicing criterion contains no information about the actual dynamic state of the program, so the slice represents the code for every possible execution pattern. Consider the following program to calculate the factorial and sum of a series of numbers:

```
1        scanf("%d", &n);
2        fact = 0;
3        sum = 0;
4        while (n > 1)
5        {
6              fact = fact * n;
7              sum = sum + n;
8              n = n - 1;
9        }
10       printf("%d %d", sum, fact);
```

The problem with this program is that the sum is always found to be zero. To locate the cause of this problem, we investigate a static slice of the form {6, fact}. The static slice is:

```
1        scanf("%d", &n);
2        fact = 0;
4        while (n > 1)
5        {
6              fact = fact * n;
```

```
8                    n = n - 1;
9          }
```

This shows that fact should be initialized to 1 rather than 0.

An Example of Dynamic Slicing

It is more often the case where a program will be executed one or more times during the testing phase (or so we would hope!). Instead of using a static slice, it would make more sense to construct a slice that takes advantage of the dynamic nature of input. A dynamic slice is constructed using the information from a static slice, in conjunction with information on a particular execution pattern. A dynamic slice of code with respect to a statement S, a variable v, and input i, consists of those statements of the program that might affect the value of v at statement S using input i. This is known as the dynamic slicing criterion and is often denoted {S, v, i}. Consider the dynamic slicing criterion for the example shown in the previous section {10, fact, n=1}, and the corresponding dynamic slice:

```
1          scanf("%d", &n);
2          fact = 0;
10         printf("%d %d", sum, fact);
```

It turns out that the loop on line 4 is never entered, so the value of fact relates to the values it was initialized with, which is zero. Of course 1! = 1, so the error can be identified much more quickly. Consider another program fragment:

```
1          m = 1.0;
2          scanf("%d", &n);
3          if (n%2 == 0)
4              m = m + n/2.0;
5          else
6              m = m - n/2.0;
7          printf("%f", m);
```

The dynamic slice for criterion {7, m, n=2} is:

```
1          m = 1.0;
2          scanf("%d", &n);
3          if (n%2 == 0)
4              m = m + n/2.0;
7          printf("%f", m);
```

The dynamic slice for criterion {7, m, n=3} is:

```
1          m = 1.0;
2          scanf("%d", &n);
3          if (n%2 == 0)
5          else
6          m = m - n/2.0;
7          printf("%f", m);
```

Just Plain Blunders

The word *blunder* is one of those nice words that means a spectacularly bad decision or action. I have seen it used in *The Elements of Programming Style* and feel that some programming faults are probably more aptly termed *blunders,* referring to things you didn't really mean to happen, they just did, and they usually aren't all that hard to fix. Two of the most common blunders are not initializing variables and being off by one.

Not Initializing Variables

Let's consider a program to calculate the harmonic series:

To implement this equation would require an upper bound n and a loop of some sort.

```
double harmonic;
int i;
for (i=1; i<=n; i=i+1)
    harmonic = harmonic + 1.0/i;
```

This simple program should work, if properly coded, but there is a small problem with this code. Can you see it? Look at the value of the variable **harmonic** inside the loop. It seems to be a successive sum of the various components of the harmonic series, up until *n*. But what happens when you run this program with the *n=4*. You get a result that doesn't exactly look right. Now try doing the math on paper, and compare answers.

If you now look through the code, you will notice that the variable **harmonic** has never been given an initial value. This is not a problem for most compilers, which will just assign **harmonic** a garbage number. This will be the initial value onto which the values of the harmonic series are added.

Off by One

These blunders normally occur somewhere where you decide to do something more than once. A great source of off-by-one errors is using a "greater-than" when a "greater than or equal to" is actually needed. Sometimes this is a matter of interpretation. For instance, if you have a statement of the form "a value of *x* between 1 and 100." Does this mean $1 \leq x \leq 100$ or $1 < x < 100$? Loops come to mind, as do arrays. Let's consider an example containing both.

```
int i, sum=0, rainfall[12] = {23,12,32,43,232};
for (i=1; i<=12; i++)
    sum = sum + rainfall[i];
```

Okay, so you go through the loop 12 times, or do you? Actually because arrays start at the index 0, you will end up processing array elements 1 through 12. However in C, array element 12 doesn't exist. It will work fine from **rainfall[1]** to **rainfall[11]**, but when it tries to access **rainfall[12]**, you will probably encounter some form of memory error. It is effectively trying to access an array element that doesn't exist. This is a classic off-by-one error. Fortunately, it's also relatively easy to fix. The **for** loop solution should be of the form:

```
for (i=0; i<12; i++)
    sum = sum + rainfall[i];
```

You would have had equally bad problems using a loop of the form:

```
for (i=0; i<=12; i++)
    sum = sum + rainfall[i];
```

That goes to show that most off-by-one errors have something to do with relational operators, or using <= instead of <.

Weird Errors

. . . 10 Seconds to Core Dump?

Some compilers, such as those on Unix systems, may produce something known as a *core dump* when a fatal exception occurs during run time. A core dump is a record of the raw, unstructured contents of one or more regions of working memory at a specific time. The name comes from core memory and the image of dumping a bulk commodity such as gravel or wheat. In essence, core dumps are multi-megabyte sized files, which you *could* examine if you wanted to.

A Bug by Any Other Name Is Still a Bug

These are weird bugs that actually exist! A *heisenbug* is a bug that disappears or alters its characteristics when it is researched. A *mandelbug*, named after fractal innovator Benoît Mandelbrot, is a bug whose causes are so complex that its behavior appears chaotic. A *Schroedinbug* is a bug that manifests itself apparently only after the software is used in an unusual way or seemingly at the point in time that a programmer reading the source code notices that the program should never have worked in the first place. At that point the program stops working entirely until the mysteriously now nonfunctioning code is repaired.

My Code Is Dead!

Dead or *unreachable code* is code that will never be executed. It manifests itself as variables that are declared but never used, functions that are never called, or code that is skipped because of a branch. Since the dead code is not executed, it is an error, often a logic error. Dead code is created by cavalier programmers. An easy way to create dead code is by use of a **goto** statement and labels. Here is an example:

```
goto process_image;
j = j + 1; // dead code here.
```

Since we have an unconditional branch to the label processing on the first line, the assignment statement on the second line can never be executed. A **return** statement can be used to make dead. code. Here is an example:

```
double div_0(double a, double b)
{
    if (b == 0)
        return 1;
    else
        return 0;
    return a/b; // dead code here.
}
```

The arithmetic expression **a/b** is performed after two **return** statements inside an **if-else**. Since the **if-else** combination will result in one of the **return** statements being executed, the final **return** statement becomes an *orphan*, because it is impossible to get to. That is, since code execution is linear, and there is no conditional expression wrapping the **return** statement, any code after the **return** statements cannot possibly be executed. When using some versions of gcc, you can use the compiler flag "**-Wunreachable-code**" to find dead code. For example, when compiling the above code in a complete program (with the dead code on line 11) using

```
gcc -Wunreachable-code deadcode.c
```

the compiler would return

```
deadcode.c: In function 'div_0':
deadcode.c:11: warning: will never be executed
```

Consider another example:

```
while (a != 0){
    index = index + a;
    r = r + log(vector[index]);
    continue;
    a = a - 1;
}
```

Here the statement **a=a−1** is never reached because the continue statement prior to it redirects the loop to its next iteration. The side effect of this is that the value of **a** is never decreased and the loop becomes infinite.

(e.g.) Finding Logic in Loops

Look at the following code:

```
int sum, i;
for (i=1; i<1000; i=i+1);
    sum = sum + i++;
```

What happens in this program? When we compile it there are no errors, but when we run the program, we get the following output:

−1881065780

Not exactly the answer we thought would appear, is it? If you look through the program, you will notice that the variable **sum** has never been set to zero, so it begins as garbage and on most systems accumulates more garbage with each successive call. It is easy to correct such as error *if* it is detected. This is a good example of a logic error. There are no rules in the compiler that specify variables need to be assigned a value before the program runs. From this we learn that if your program spits out a huge number, chances are you forgot to initialize a variable somewhere in your program. Let's change the declaration of sum to:

```
int sum=0, i;
```

Getting the right answer now? You're probably getting 1,000 right? Check a little closer. That semicolon at the end of the for statement is an empty statement. So everytime the loop executes, it is setting a new value for *i* and effectively doing nothing else. Once you delete it, the loop would work fine. Well, if there are two bugs, there is likely to be a third. Run it now, and the result is 250,000, which is a little short. Always check your answer! The third problem lies with the fact that the index variable *i* has been incremented within the body of the loop, effectively incrementing it twice! So the program is adding all the *odd* numbers from 1 to 999. The real answer is 499,500. Finding these sort of errors is by no means difficult, but it is time consuming.

Epilog

I will leave you with this thought.

"Every program starts off with bugs. Many programs end up with bugs as well. There are two corollaries to this: first, you must test all your programs straight away. And second, there's no point in losing your temper every time they don't work."—Z80 Users Manual

Chapter 5 Exercises

Exercise 5.1

Consider the following program. Identify the errors, and correct them.

```c
#include <stdio.h>

int main(void)
{
    double num, div;
    scanf("%lf%lf", num, &den);

    div = num % den;
    printf("%d", div);

}
```

What happens when the value of **den** entered is 0?

Exercise 5.2

Rainwater harvesting is the gathering, or accumulating and storing, of rainwater. Rain barrels are simply a storage tank for temporarily holding storm water. Storm water from a roof is diverted into a barrel connected to a downspout and stored for later use. To calculate the amount of rainfall needed to fill a rain barrel, we use the following information:

- Capacity of a rain barrel in gallons?
- Number of rain barrels?
- House dimensions in square feet?
- Portion of roof emptying into rain barrels (as a percentage)?

In order to perform the calculation, we need some additional information:

- 1 gallon = 231 cubic inches ? 0.1337 cubic feet.
- 1 square foot = 144 square inches.

Now the formula to calculate the number of inches required is

$$inches\_of\_rain = \frac{total\_barrel\_capacity}{roof\_surface\_area}$$

The total barrel capacity is calculated by multiplying the number of barrels by the capacity of a barrel by 231 to formulate the capacity in cubic inches. The roof surface area is determined by calculating the surface area of the building and multiplying it by the portion of the roof emptying into the rain barrels. Here is a solution for calculating the inches of rain needed to fill n rain barrels:

```c
#include <stdio.h>
#define cubicINgal 231
#define squareIN 144

int main(void)
{
    double rainB_cap, houseW, houseL, roofP;
    double rainB_capSUM, roof_SA, inches_rain;
    int n_rainB;

    printf("Capacity of a rain barrel (gallons)? ");
    scanf("%lf", &rainB_cap);
    printf("Number of rain barrels? ");
    scanf("%d", &n_rainB);
    printf("Width of the house (inches)? ");
    scanf("%lf", &houseW);
    printf("Length of the house (inches)? ");
    scanf("%lf", &houseL);
```

```
            printf("Portion of the roof emptying into barrels (%)? ");
            scanf("%lf", &roofP);

            // Calculate the surface area of the roof draining into
            // the barrels in square inches
            roof_SA = houseW * houseL * squareIN * (roofP / 100.0);

            // Calculate the total barrel capacity
            rainB_capSUM = n_rainB * rainB_cap * cubicINgal;

            // Calculate the number of inches of rain required
            inches_rain = rainB_capSUM / roof_SA;

            printf("There are %.2f inches of rain required.\n",
                   inches_rain);

            return 0;
    }
```

Several of the inputs have ranges of values that can be input. Values outside these ranges may cause the program to fail. Use defensive programming to add checks to the program to make sure all the input values are validated in some manner.

6

The Elements of C

I view the landslide of C use in education as something of a calamity.

—Niklaus Wirth

A C Skeleton

The most basic C program looks like this:

```
main()
{}
```

This program, when compiled, does nothing. That's right, nada, zip, zero. What it does do is illustrate the bare minimum required to code a C program. It essentially represents a skeleton program from which you can code bigger and better things. When the program runs, it calls the function **main**, which passes control directly back to the operating system because there is nothing to do. Every program has a core function called **main**. The set of parentheses following the main are used to contain arguments, or information you might want to *give* to the program. Lastly the braces { and }, sometimes referred to as curly braces or squiggly braces, are the *delimiters* for the program. Delimiters is a fancy word for start "{" and end "}." This is where the actual program instructions exist. If I compiled this program using a C99 compiler, however, I would get a warning of the form:

```
warning(1): Missing type specifier.
warning(2): Missing return value.
```

This program worked fine when Kernighan and Ritchie described it in the 1970s. Why not now? Things don't always work as they did in a previous rendition of C. It's complaining because the program doesn't return anything. What, you say? You didn't ask it to return anything. But that's programming languages for you; sometimes they just expect you to have put something there. In this case the compiler wants the program to return an *error level*. In some cases program X will execute program Y, and when Y ends, X expects some information back on how Y performed. Was the task completed successfully? Were there problems with some of the computations? This can be achieved by Y sending X an integer, which is then identified from a list maintained by X. Confused?

Consider the following example. Imagine you have a security system that consists of some software, which we will term the Intruder Processing System (IPS), and a series of wireless cameras attached to roving autonomous robots. The IPS processes still images captured from the remote cameras to look for differences, the presence of which denote possible intruders. Now the IPS captures images from the cameras by executing the program **captureImage(image)**, which acquires an image from a camera. When **captureImage(image)** ends, it returns a value to indicate whether the process was successful. If it returns a 0, IPS assumes everything is okay, and image contains the snapshot. If, however, **captureImage** returns a nonzero value, it might indicate that there were problems with the sensor, and no image capture was possible. This allows two programs to communicate with one another.

So to make our skeleton cover this situation, we expand our program to become:

```
int main()
{
    return(0);
}
```

The keyword **int** tells the program that an integer value is to be returned, and its value is 0, specified using the keyword **return**. You can use any type here, and it is based on the kind of information produced by the program. Typically though, **main** functions return integers. Notice the semicolon at the end of the return statement? The semicolon is like a period in a sentence; It *terminates* a statement. Also notice that the braces are now on lines by themselves and we have started using indentation. We'll talk more about data types later.

Now we may actually want our program to do something. Say, get some input, perform a calculation, and output something. That leads us to one of the oldest C programs and often the first introduced in any book on C:

```
#include <stdio.h>
int main()
{
    printf("hello, world");
    return(0);
}
```

The tradition of using the phrase "hello world" as a test message was influenced by an example program in the book *The C Programming Language,* by Kernighan and Ritchie. The book had inherited the program from a 1974 Bell Laboratories internal memorandum by Kernighan, "Programming in C: A Tutorial." In some respects "hello world" is somewhat of a Rosetta Stone. The Rosetta Stone is a stone of Egyptian origin that has writing in two languages, Egyptian and Greek, in three scripts, Hieroglyphic, Demotic Egyptian, and Greek. The presence of Greek was the key to deciphering the hieroglyphs. By comparing the same program written in different languages, it is possible to discern syntactic similarities between languages.

Now we have added two components to our skeleton. There is now a statement before the return statement in the main program. This **printf** causes the phrase "hello, world" to be output to a device known as the *standard output* (i.e., the screen). The first line in the program tells the compiler to include the header file **stdio.h.** This file contains information relating to the function **printf,** effectively telling the C compiler where to find it.

This is one of the more peculiar attributes of C. All programs have to include the file **stdio.h.** Without it you couldn't perform I/O, the acronym most commonly used to denote "Input/Output". Therefore the most basic C skeleton can be expressed as:

```
#include <stdio.h>

int main(void)
{
    return(0);
}
```

Preprocessing the Night Away

When you compile a C program, one of the first things it wants to do is something called *preprocessing.* This isn't really compiling, but it is a process unique to C compilers. The preprocessor more or less provides its own language, which can be a very powerful tool to the programmer. Preprocessor statements are the first things encountered in a C program and begin with a pound sign, #.

#include

This statement directs the processor to include code related to functions in a library. An example contained in nearly all programs is:

```
#include <stdio.h>
```

This directive allows us to use functions from the standard I/O library. When you compile the program, the preprocessor replaces the **#include** directive with the contents of the specified file. A library consists of commonly used program modules called *functions.* Examples of libraries in C include the math library **(math.h)** and string manipulation library **(string.h).** Each library has a standard header file whose name usually ends with the **.h** extension. If we don't include a library, the C compiler usually complains that it "can't find a function." We will discuss the various libraries as we encounter them. There are two forms of the **include:**

```
#include <filename>
#include "filename"
```

When the **filename** is enclosed in angle brackets "< >", the preprocessor looks in a predetermined place for the library. If it is enclosed by double quotes, the preprocessor searches the directory containing the source file. The latter is more commonly used for libraries created by the user.

#define

Sometimes we want to use something called a *symbolic constant.* It is basically used for substitution. When a program is compiled, each occurrence of a symbolic constant is replaced by its corresponding character sequence. The **#define** statement has the following general form:

```
#define SYMC value
```

where **SYMC** represents a symbolic name, and **value** represents the sequence of characters associated with that name. Note that there is no equal sign and it doesn't end in a semi-colon. Here is a commonly used example:

```
#define PI 3.141593
```

Now you can use the constant **PI** throughout the program without having to write the value of **PI** each time. So if you wrote a statement of the form:

```
area = PI * radius * radius;
```

when you compile the program, the compiler will swap all the instances of **PI** with the value 3.141593 before it starts actually compiling the code. The previous code becomes:

```
area = 3.141593 * radius * radius;
```

Here are some more examples of using **#define** to label constants:

```
// Speed of Light, m/s
#define c 2.99792e8

// Avogadro's Number mol^-1
#define Avogadro 6.022e23

// Acceleration of gravity m/s^2
#define charge_e 1.602177e-19
```

Why do we use **define?** It's not like the value of **PI** will change, or could it? What if you wrote a program where you used the value of **PI** 50 times. Later you wanted to increase the accuracy of your calculation by adding precision to **PI**. Want to search through your whole program and change every value of **PI**? Or, would you rather make a change of the following form:

```
#define PI 3.141592653589793238
```

Much easier. There are, however, three rules to ponder when using **#define:**

1. Do NOT use **#define** to customize the language
2. Do NOT force C to look like a different language.
3. Do NOT create replacements for C keywords.

For example, if we defined:

```
#define start int main(void)
```

little is gained in clarity, but much is lost in readability.

I'd Like to Comment About Comments

Comments are a mechanism in every programming language that are often ignored by programmers, both novice and expert alike. They are a mechanism to embed information within a program about the program. In other words comments help document code. The tricky bit is that most programmers never seem to get comments right. Some believe code should be extensively documented, while others believe that code should be written so it is self-explanatory. Comments should express the notion of *why* rather than *how*. If you have to explain that a **for** loop goes around 100 times, then maybe your code is just way too complex. Explaining how should be evident *in* the code. For example:

```
// This loop iterates 100 times
for (i=1; i<=100; i=i+1)
    printf("%d", i*i);
```

Ahhhhhh, really? Like I needed to know that. This advice from Steve McConnell (*Code Complete*) sums this up nicely:

> Good comments don't repeat the code or explain it. They clarify its intent. Comments should explain, at a higher level of abstraction than the code, what you're trying to do.

There is an exception to this rule, of course. If you figure out a really neat way of coding something, then you should explain it. If you don't, then nobody will be able to understand how it works, including yourself when you come back to it in two months!

There are two main types of comments: block and line.

Block Comments

Block comments use one sequence of characters to mark the start of a comment and another (usually the reverse sequence) to mark the end of the comment. This allows comments to extend over multiple lines. In C, this is the traditional way of creating comments, using the "/*" (slash-star) and "*/" (star-slash) sequences. Any text between the first "/*" and the next "*/" is ignored by the compiler. An example could be:

```
/* Calculate the area of a circle */
area = PI * radius * radius;
```

In C, you can't nest comments, so don't try it. Nesting comments essentially means creating comments within comments. Some languages allow this, C doesn't. Block comments are handy when you want to *comment-out* a piece of code for a short time. It saves deleting it and retyping it.

Some programming languages, notably Haskell, allow nested comments. Consider the following code:

```
/* Calculate the luminosity of the star
lumen = 3.36192 * pow(10.0,((140.0−2.0*absMag)/5.0));

/* Calculate the radius of the star */
radius = (1.0/(2.0*surfTemp*surfTemp))*sqrt(lumin/(pi*S_Boltzman));
```

What is wrong with this code? Nothing, you say? Look again a little closer. The first comment was erroneously not closed so the statement "lumen = . . ." gets crunched by a comment. This type of error is called a *runaway comment* and can be difficult to find. C won't allow nested comments, but watch out for these kinds of errors.

Line Comments

Line (or *end-of-line*) comments start with a comment delimiter and continue until the end of the line. C99 provides for line comments by using the // (double-slash) sequence. For example:

```
// Calculate the area of a circle
area = PI * radius * radius;
```

The type of commenting you decide to use is up to you. You can mix both types without any problems. We talk more about the *style* of commenting in the next chapter (when we address how many comments are enough).

 You can use comments to disable portions of code.

The Anatomy of a C Program

In the 1960s, E. Dijkstra proposed the use of a series of logical constructs from which any program could be formed. This was subsequently termed *structured programming*. A C program, or any program for that matter, is composed of a series of statements. A statement causes some definitive action to be carried out. Part of a program deals with creating containers to store information. Statements act upon the information within these containers. The containers are called *variables* and will be discussed in the next chapter. There are three basic types of structured constructs in C: sequence, condition, and repetition statements. In essence all modern languages provide similar constructs, although the keywords and punctuation may vary from language to language.

Sequence

Sequence refers to a series of programming steps followed in succession. For example:

```
printf("Enter a number");
scanf("%d", &n);
```

Condition

A *condition* provides the ability to select a series of instructions based on some logical decision. In C, this is usually provided by the **if** structure. For example:

```
if (n%2 == 0)
    printf("The number is even");
else
    printf("The number is odd");
```

Repetition

The structured construct of *repetition* provides the ability to repeat a series of instructions a number of times. In C, this is usually provided by looping structures such as **for**. For example:

```
for (i=1; i<=10; i=i+1)
    printf("%d\n", n*i);
```

Expression Statements

An expression statement consists of an expression followed by a semicolon. The semicolon is used to terminate the statement. For example:

```
area = PI * radius * radius;
```

The simplest statement of all is the empty statement, which looks like:

```
;
```

It does nothing. Nada. Zip. Zero. Nil. Zilch.

Compound Statements

A compound statement consists of several individual statements enclosed within a pair of curly braces { }. It starts with an opening brace {, ends with a closing }, and contains zero or more statements. In a compound statement the braces are used to group declarations and statements together into a *block*, so that they are equivalent to a single statement. This is where the term *block of code* comes from. The individual statements may themselves be expression statements, compound statements, or control statements. Unlike expression statements, there is no semicolon after the right brace that ends a compound statement. An example of a compound statement might be:

```
{
    circumference = 2. * PI * radius;
    area = PI * radius * radius;
}
```

Crawling Before You Walk

One of the caveats of learning to program is that sometimes you have to learn a little bit about something before you're ready to learn a lot. A case in point is I/O, which is short for Input/Output. Before you learn the intricacies of input and output, like how to read from a file and how to print to a string, you have to learn the basics. Without them, you won't be able to write even simple programs that will do anything. I mean, they will do something, but you won't know about it. Consider the following program:

```
#define PI 3.141593

int main(void)
{
```

```
        double area_C, radius;
        area_C = PI * radius * radius;
        return 0;
    }
```

This program will calculate the area of a circle. Or will it? What is the value of the variable **radius**? And what happens when the area is calculated and assigned to the variable **area_C**? The answer is that **radius** has no value, and even if it were to have a value (hard-coded perhaps?), when the program runs, NOTHING is output. So we have to add some I/O. If we were to add an input and an output statement, the program would now look like:

```
#include <stdio.h>
#define PI 3.141593

int main(void)
{
    double area_C, radius;
    scanf("%lf", &radius);
    area_C = PI * radius * radius;
    printf("The area is %f\n", area_C);
    return 0;
}
```

We will look at two functions here: **scanf** and **printf**. Both these functions allow us to communicate with a program. They are not the only I/O functions we can use in C, but they are among the most versatile. Ironically they are not part of the definition of C. That's why we have to include the **stdio.h** library. Before C was standardized, many of the functions for input and output were specific to the system on which the compiler was operating.

Input with scanf

The first statement is a **scanf**, pronounced *scan-eff.* The **scanf** function is used to acquire input from the *standard input,* which is usually the keyboard. The general form of a **scanf** statement is:

```
scanf(format_string, &arg1, &arg2, . . ., &argn)
```

Each **scanf** has two basic parts in its parentheses. The first is the **format_ string,** which refers to a character string containing certain required formatting information, sometimes known as the *conversion specifiers.* The second is **arg1, arg2,** etc., which are arguments that represent the individual input data items. Each format specifier consists of a percent sign (**%**), followed by a set of *conversion characters* that indicate the type of the corresponding data item. The two most useful conversion characters are those for integers and doubles:

```
%d   int
%lf  double
```

%lf stands for **long float,** which is synonymous with **double.** We'll talk more about conversion characters when we cover data types. The special operator used here is the ampersand, **&** (called the *address-of* operator). It tells the **scanf** statement where to store the double—that is, its address. If you leave it off, **scanf** won't know where to store the number. For example, consider the **scanf** statement in the previous code:

```
scanf("%lf", &radius);
```

There are two arguments in the **scanf.** The first is the format string (the string between the double quotes) essentially a placeholder for a double:

```
%lf
```

The format string "%lf" tells **scanf** what kind of data to store into the variable **radius.** The second argument is the variable **radius,** which denotes the place where the value input is to be stored:

```
&radius
```

This basically says to the **scanf:**

> "Read in a double number and store it in the address associated with the variable radius."

Output with printf

The second statement is the **printf,** pronounced *print-eff.* The **printf** function is used to provide output to the *standard output,* which is usually a screen. The general form of a **printf** statement is:

```
printf(format_string, arg1, arg2, . . ., argn)
```

The first argument is the **format_string,** which specifies how many pieces of data are to be output and how they are to be formatted. The formatting string is enclosed in double quotes and may contain text and/or conversion specifiers, similar to those found in **scanf** statements. Note that **printf** does *not* use the & operator. If you try and use it, you will most likely get junk printed out.

For example, consider the **printf** statement in the previous code:

```
printf("The area is %f\n", area_C);
```

There are two arguments in the **printf.** The first is the format string (the string between the double quotes):

```
The area is %f\n
```

It again uses a formatting string, with a **%f** conversion specifier. This says: (i) Output the text **"The area is"**; (ii) Look beyond the formatting string for the value to substitute for **%f,** in this case the value stored in **area_C;** and (iii) Output a **"\n",** which is a special code denoting a new line. The second argument is the variable **area_C,** which denotes the place where the value that is to be output is stored:

```
area_C
```

A conversion control sequence always begins with a % symbol and ends with a conversion character (e.g., *d, c*). Additional formatting characters can be placed between the % and the conversion character. You can definitely do more powerful things with *formatting strings*, such as left/right justification and character padding, but we shall learn these along the way.

 printf does not check the values it is given; it assumes they are correct.

Invisible Characters

Sometimes we want to print out characters we can't actually see, such as new lines and tabs. To do this we use special characters called an *escape sequence*, which is just a backslash "\", followed by a character. The two most commonly used in **printf** statements are:

\n   new line, the cursor drops to the start of the next line.
\t   tab, usually eight characters in length.

For example, if you use:

```
printf("Circle Area Calculation");
printf("Enter a radius:");
```

when this gets printed to the screen, what you will see is:

```
Circle Area CalculationEnter a radius:
```

What you probably wanted to see is:

```
Circle Area Calculation
Enter a radius:
```

To achieve this, you would write:

```
printf("Circle Area Calculation\n");
printf("Enter a radius:");
```

Two interesting escape sequences are:

\a   alert, provides an audible beep.
\b   backspace.

Printing Text

What happens when you actually want to print a quote? For example:

```
"Veni, vidi, vici"
```

In C, strings of text are enclosed in double quotes, but the quotes aren't actually part of the string. To print a quote mark, " you have to use the escape character again, \, for example:

```
printf("\"Veni, vidi, vici\"");
```

Making a Statement

Programmers often get *expressions* confused with *statements*. When we want to specify an action, we use a *statement*. This means that there is an effect, usually changing the state of a variable. The most common statement is the assignment statement. Consider the example from the previous program:

```
area_C = PI * radius * radius;
```

Here **area_C** obtains the value of the expression **PI * radius * radius** when it is evaluated. The previous value stored in **area_C** (if any, and in this case there isn't) is lost. Note also that the order in which statements are executed determines the results. For example:

```
i = i + 1;      and      j = 2 * i;
j = 2 * i;               i = i + 1;
```

These two groups of statements do not have the same effect. If we assume *i* has an initial value of 2, then the first statements yield **i=3, j=6**, whereas the second statements yield **i=3, j=4**.

Long Lines of Code

If a long line of code wraps around to the next line, the program will end up looking quite messy. To span a line of code over more than one line, use the continuation character, which is a backslash, \. Use continuation characters sparingly.

The Quadratic Equation

Now that we have done all the preliminary work for the quadratic equation in previous chapters, let's see what the actual code looks like.

```
#include <stdio.h>
#include <math.h>

int main(void)
{
    double a, b, c;
    double disc, A, sroot;
    double root, root1, root2, xreal, ximag;

    printf("Finding quadratic roots.\n");
    printf("Enter the values of a, b, and c: ");
    scanf("%lf%lf%lf", &a, &b, &c);
    printf("Equation: %.2f x%c + %.2f x + %.2f = 0\n",
        a,253,b,c);
```

```
    if (a == 0)
        if (b == 0)
            printf("No roots\n");
        else {
            root = -c / b;
            printf("Linear equation: root = %.2f\n", root);
        }
    else {
        A = 2 * a;
        disc = b * b - 4 * a * c;
        sroot = sqrt (fabs(disc));

        if (disc < 0) {
            xreal = -b / A;
            ximag = sroot / A;
            printf("Complex roots: root1 = %.2f+%.2fi\n",
                    xreal, ximag);
            printf("                        root2 = %.2f-%.2fi\n",
                    xreal, ximag);
        }
        else if (disc == 0) {
            root = -b / A;
            printf("Single root = %.2f\n", root);
        }
        else {
            root1 = (-b + sroot) / A;
            root2 = (-b + sroot) / A;
            printf("Real roots: root1 = %.2f\n", root1);
            printf("                    root2 = %.2f\n", root2);
        }
    }

    return 0;
}
```

The programs structure has three components: (i) variable declarations, (ii) a block of prompts and input statements, and (iii) a group of nested **if-else** statements that form the core structure of the program. It follows both the pseudo-code and flowchart outlined in Chapter 3.

Epilog

I want to briefly broach the notion of LOC, or *lines of code*. A few programmers have the notion that the more LOC, the better a program is. Hardly. LOC or source LOC (SLOC) are used as a measure of the magnitude of a program. For example, this program

```c
#include <stdio.h>
#define PI 3.141593

int main(void)
{
    double area_C, radius;
    scanf("%lf", &radius);
    area_C = PI * radius * radius;
    printf("The area is %f\n", area_C);
    return 0;
}
```

has 10 lines of code. However, functionality is less well correlated with SLOC: Skilled developers may be able to develop the same functionality with far less code, so one program with less SLOC may exhibit more functionality than another program.

Exercises

Exercise 6.1

A year on Jupiter (the time it takes Jupiter to make one full rotation around the sun) takes about 12 earth years. Write a program that converts Jovian years to earth years. Have the user specify the number of Jovian years. Allow fractional years.

Exercise 6.2

The area of a gable roof can be calculated using the length (L) and width (W) of the roof, and vertical height of the gable (H). To calculate the area of the roof requires calculating the length of the sloped roof (S) using the equation:

$$S = \sqrt{H^2 + (0.5W)^2}$$

Multiplying S by L gives the area of one-half of the roof. For example, if L = 10, W = 12, and H = 3, then S = 6.71, and the area of the roof equals 2(6.71L) = 134.2 ft2. Use this information to write a program to calculate the area of the gable roof.

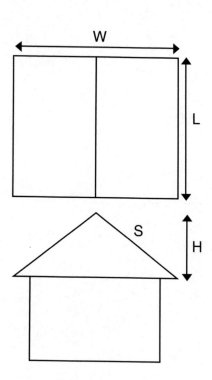

Exercise 6.3

Write a program for Exercise 3.4, the ecological footprint of a newspaper.

7

It's All about the Data

What's in a name? That which we call a rose by another name would smell as sweet.

—Shakespeare

Introduction

The terms *data, information,* and *knowledge* are overlapping concepts, with the main difference being the level of abstraction. Data by itself holds no meaning. The goal of programming is to interpret the data, the end result of which is information, which can in turn be used to derive knowledge. For example, consider the surface of the earth. It cannot be sensed directly; it can be understood only indirectly through the data it generates. If we take a satellite image of a region of the earth, as shown here, we now have a form of data. This data could be in various forms (e.g., infrared, photographs), which we can use to extract information. For example, we may wish to determine the amount of forest cover or the percentage of land use dedicated to buildings. This information, say on canopy cover, can then be used to identify regions for tree replanting. Canopy cover is then the thing about which we seek *information* through the various *data* we can obtain about it. Data is any perceivable thing from which information can be derived, that is, anything that humans and machines can sense—for example, obvious things such as words, numbers, images, and sound, as well as less discernible items such as color and magnetic state. In some cases, different forms of data can give the same information. For example, both a lightbulb and a candle produce light, which can be interpreted by lux meter, which provides a measure of luminance (SI unit). There are also different ways of interpreting data. The light intensity of both the candle and the lightbulb can be measured using lux, or foot-candles, which is "the luminance cast on a surface by a one-candela source one foot away" (1 foot candle = 10.764 lux). Data may be interpreted by different humans or different machines in different ways, depending on the type of algorithm used. The same information may result from different algorithms interpreting the same data.

Data and Memory

Programs are essentially about performing calculations and manipulating information. Information needs to be stored somewhere for a program to use it. Without being able to put a value in safekeeping, there would be no way of accessing the data for future reference. For example, in a simple calculator you enter a number, then an operator, then a second number (e.g., 4 + 7). Once you press the = key, you get an answer. However, the numbers 4 and 7 have now disappeared, with the only value in memory being the result: 11. More sophisticated calculators may let you store one or more values for future reference in *memory*. This is no different from storing information in a program. When you write a program, allocating memory is done transparently, so normally you don't worry about it. However, we briefly indulge this topic to provide you with a better understanding.

Most computers nowadays are 32-bit. This means they have 32-bit-wide internal registers and an address width of 32 bits. But what does this really mean? Initially most personal computers were 16-bit. How big is this? Imagine you have a standard 3-inch-by-3-inch yellow Post-It note. A 16-bit computer has 2^{16} memory locations, each of which represents:

$$\frac{\text{area of note}}{\text{memory size}} = \frac{75^2 \, \text{mm}}{2^{16}} = 0.086 \text{mm}^2$$

A 32-bit machine has an address that is double the width. This amounts to 2^{32}, or 4,294,967,296 addresses. Presuming we use the same size allotment for an individual memory location, this relates to approximately 368,640,000mm², which is about the area of 65,536 Post-It notes. Now imagine 64-bit machines with 2^{64} addresses. This relates to about 281,474,976,710,656 Post-It notes. That's about 1,583,297 km², or equivalent to covering an area the size of the six times the United Kingdom in Post-It notes. Put another way, a personal video recorder (PVR) with a disk of size 2^{32} could store 143 seconds of data, while a 2^{64} disk could hold 19,484 years of data (assuming 30 frames per second and 10^6 bytes per frame). For example, internal memory (RAM, or Random Access Memory) can be thought of as little storage boxes. Each of these boxes is capable of storing a certain amount of information (bytes). In a 32-bit system, these small boxes are 32 bits in size; in a 64-bit system, 64 bits.

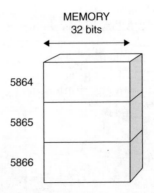

In this example the boxes represent pieces of memory, each 32 bits in size. The value 5864 represents the address associated with that particular piece of memory.

What Is a Variable?

A *variable* is essentially a storage location. You associate a name with it (an identifier) and a type (what sort of data do you want to store in it?). Then you can store a value in it. When you create a variable, a piece of memory is associated with it. When you run a program, it goes and selects the memory it needs to function.

Creating a Variable

Variables must be created before they can be used. This process is known as *variable declaration*. It essentially provides a compiler with information about how much memory should be allocated and how those bytes should be interpreted. A variable is created by giving it a name and associating a datatype with it. For example, when you create an integer variable of the form:

```
int area;
```

This essentially creates a variable identified by the name **area**, which is of type **int**; that is, it is capable of storing a whole number. An **int** on a 32 bit system is 4 bytes (32 bits) in size. At this point the contents of the variable are empty. Assume the first memory location in the following figure has the memory address **5864** and is given the name **area**.

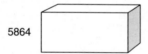

A variable declaration serves three purposes:

- It defines the name of the variable (identifier).
- It defines the type of variable (datatype).
- It provides a description of the variable.

A variable declaration has the following general form:

```
datatype identifier;
```

where *datatype* designates a valid C datatype and *identifier* a name.

Setting Initial Values

Declaration statements can also be used to store an initial value in a variable. When this is done, the variable is said to be *initialized*. For example, you could set the value of the variable **load** to 0 using the declaration:

```
double load=0.0;
```

Multiple Variables of the Same Type

When a group of variables has the same datatype, they can be grouped together using a single declaration statement. For example, the following four declarations:

```
double load;
double runoff;
double concBacteria;
double area;
```

can be replaced by a single declaration:

```
double load, runoff, concBacteria, area;
```

The space after each comma is inserted for readability, nothing more.

What's in a Name?

An *identifier* is the name given to a variable. When you're creating variables, you have a lot of latitude with respect to their names. The first element in naming variables is the length of the name. Shorter variables are good because they are easier to type, but often suffer a lack of innate meaning. It may also be difficult to distinguish single character identifiers. For example:

```
i, a, r
```

These are extremely nondescriptive. Contrast this with:

```
index, area, ratio
```

which are much more readable and still a reasonable size.

Identifiers in C

C has just a few rules to observe, which are essentially the same for variables, constants, and functions:

- The variable name must begin with a letter or an underscore (_).
- The variable may contain letters, underscores, or digits. It may not contain blanks, commas, or special characters such as &, #, ! or ?
- A variable name cannot be a keyword, sometimes called a reserved word.

C is also case sensitive, which means that it differentiates between lowercase and uppercase characters. So **PI**, **Pi**, **pI**, and **pi** are all different variables.

 Be careful! Look at these variable names:

```
NO15Y = NOISY + 1
```

What is wrong here? Probably nothing until you try to run it. Then it might dawn on you that both **NO15Y** and **NOISY** don't exist. You probably meant to write **NOISY**, and accidently got the O, I, and S mixed up with 0 (zero), 1 (one), l (lowercase L), and 5. Not unusual, it happens all the time. That's why we try to avoid uppercase characters, and specifically "O" and 0, "I" and 1/l, and "S" and 5. It's just not safe to use them.

One Hump or Two?

Camel case is the practice of writing compound words or phrases where the words are joined without spaces, and each word is capitalized within the compound. The name comes from the uppercase "bumps" in the middle of the compound word, suggestive of the humps of a camel. This practice is known by a large variety of names, including BiCapitalization, InterCaps, MixedCase. We can therefore write these identifiers as **AirTemperature, CircleArea,** and **CountOddNumbers.**

Word Boundaries

Sometimes in a program there is a need for descriptive identifiers, like "air temperature." Writing the words together, as in "circlearea," is not satisfactory because the names often become unreadable. Therefore C allows the use of the underscore, "_", character as a word-joiner. For example:

```
air_temperature, growth_rate, max_speed, dna_seq
```

When creating a two word variable name where the words can be put in any order, always put the more important word first. For example:

```
max_elevation instead of elevation_max
```

The Good, the Bad, and the Downright Ugly

With all that in mind, here are some examples of good (valid), bad (invalid), and ugly (just plain unattractive) identifiers:

Good	Bad	Ugly
area	3rd_entry	VELOCITY
temperature	the end	PLANCKs_constant
growth_rate	loge	AIR_SpEEd
c14	int	
electron_mass	%discount	
Planck	1stname	

Identifier Length

At one time, identifiers were limited to 31 significant characters. Consider these examples:

```
floccinaucinihilipilification123
floccinaucinihilipilification124
```

They are identical because the identifier is truncated at 31 characters. Now in C99, variables internal to a program can be 63 characters in length. Some compilers such as Pelles C allow identifiers a length of 4,095 characters. Regardless, you should keep identifiers to an appropriate length. Remember, the longer the identifier, the longer it takes to write it.

 Bacteria Growth

The number of bacteria, B, in a certain culture that is subject to refrigeration can be approximated by the equation

$$B = 300000e^{-0.032t}$$

where e is the irrational number 2.71828, known as *Euler's number*, and t is the time in hours that the culture has been refrigerated. Now we have to create some variables to hold information from this problem. Assuming the value of e can be calculated using a built-in function, we now have two variables to name B and t. B represents the number of bacteria, so we could name it any of:

    bacteria, NumBacteria, PopBacteria, nBacteria

The latter is a good choice, because the character **n** is commonly used to denote "the number of", either in uppercase or lowercase:

    NBacteria, nBacteria, N_bacteria

The other object, t, represents time in hours, so that's not as hard:

    time, Time, tHours

You could have chosen to just use **B** and **t**, and that's perfectly okay. Just remember that you will have to describe what the variables are. Using any one of the variable names described amounts to *self-commenting*. What about some not-so-ideal names for variables? Well, here are a few:

Number_of_Bacteria:	18 characters (too long)
B	too short, not descriptive
No_Bacteria	May imply there is no bacteria
Nbacteriainculture	Too confusing!

 Stormwater Runoff

As another example, consider the task of estimating stormwater runoff pollutant loads for urban areas. The equation to calculate annual load of bacteria is:[1]

$$L = 1.03 \cdot 10^{-3} \, RCA$$

where

L	=	annual load (billion colonies)
R	=	annual runoff (inches)
C	=	Bacteria concentration (#/100 ml)
A	=	area (acres)

[1]Schueler, T., "Microbes and urban watersheds," *Watershed Protection Techniques*, 1999, Vol. 3, No. 1, 551–596.

Now we essentially have four unknowns, or variables we have to give names. Here are some suggestions:

```
L  :  load_yr, yr_load, load
R  :  runoff_yr, yr_runoff, runoff
C  :  bacteria_conc, conc_bacteria, concBacteria
A  :  area, Area
```

For instance we may decide to use the following combination:

```
load, runoff, concBacteria, area
```

Keywords

Keywords, sometimes called *reserved words*, are words used by the compiler to construct a program. This means you can use them in your program, but you can't use them as variables. ANSI C has 32 keywords:

auto	double	int	struct
break	else	long	switch
case	enum	register	typedef
char	extern	return	union
const	float	short	unsigned
continue	for	signed	void
default	goto	sizeof	volatile
do	if	static	while

Type Systems

At this point it might be good to digress and discuss the *type systems* in languages. A type system is how a programming language classifies values and expressions into types. A *type* indicates a set of values that have the same behavior.

Static and Dynamic Typing

Types can be static or dynamic. Languages like MATLAB or Python have many different types, but when you look at a piece of code, nothing forces a variable to "be" (or to "point to") a piece of data of a particular type. For example, when you declare the following variable in MATLAB:

```
radius = 2;
```

the variable **radius** is typed as an integer. A subsequent re-declaration of the form:

```
radius = 4.593;
```

would make **radius** a floating point number. The previous typing and value would be lost. In languages like C, a certain variable will always be connected with a value of a certain, fixed type. For example:

```
int radius;
```

declares **radius** to be an integer and the subsequent assignment of a floating point number, **radius = 4.593** would result in **radius** storing the number 4, and discarding the rest. The first group of languages (where the type of everything is unknown when the program is compiled) has *dynamic* types, and the second group has *static* types. In dynamic typing, type checking is performed at run time, whereas with static typing it is performed at compile time. Dynamic types are good because the program source can be more flexible and compact. Static types are good because they allow certain errors in programs to be detected earlier.

Strong and Weak Typing

Types can be weak or strong. Many languages are strongly typed, which means that at any point in the program when it is running, the type of a particular piece of data is known. *Strong typing* implies that an operation on arguments that have the wrong type will not be allowed to succeed. Since a dynamically typed language does not have complete type information at compile time, it must, if it is strongly typed, keep track of the type of different values as it runs. Typically values are boxed together with information about their type value and type are then passed around the program together.

Weak typing means that a language will implicitly convert (or cast) types when used. Unlike the languages mentioned so far, C has weak typing. Some variables can point to different types of data, or even random areas of memory, and the program cannot tell what type of object is being referenced. Depending on the context within the program, the variable is assumed to point to some particular type, but it is quite possible—and a common source of confusing bugs—for this assumption to be incorrect. For example:

```
int x=3, y;
char ch='a';

y = x + a;
```

This converts the character **a** to its numeric (ASCII) representation, then adds it to **x**.

What Is a Datatype?

Remember when we said a variable had to have both an identifier and a datatype? The type of an object in C describes the way in which a chunk of memory is associated with a value. There are four basic datatypes in C: **int, float, double,** and **char.**

At the end of the day, many programs we write contain some form of numbers. If you want to steer a robot, you may deal with direction: 0 to 360 degrees of orientation, or maybe the length of a corridor. To determine the range of a Mars Rover, you have to calculate the amount of available energy, which equates to the storage capacity of the batteries and the charging capacity of the solar cells. To calculate mortgage payments in a financial institution, you have to input a whole series of values. You get the picture? Actually, even the pictures you take with your digital camera are nothing but combinations of numbers. To work with numbers, you must be able to store them. Now we could have one type of number to do everything, but it makes more sense to have different types of numbers for different applications.

Every piece of information is stored in C as a number, even characters. This may be somewhat difficult to fathom, because a keyboard is predominantly made up of symbols, whether they are numeric, punctuation, or alphabetical. But computers can't deal with an *A* the same way we do. Numeric datatypes rule the day. There are many numeric datatypes in C. Part of the role of this section is to differentiate between them and decide when it is most appropriate to use them. The type of data you choose is dependent on why you need it. If you need to store a year, you would most certainly use a whole number. If you need to store financial transactions, you would use a real number. Here are some visual representations of datatypes:

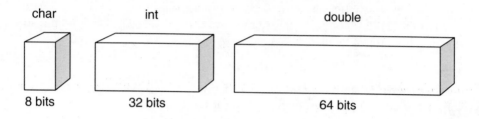

char	int	double
8 bits	32 bits	64 bits

Integers

Integers are the backbone of programming. They are *whole numbers* that allow for precise computations. Whole numbers have no fractional part. The core integer in C is the **int**. For example:

```
int prime;
```

This declares a variable named **prime** to store an integer. There are many benefits to using integers:

- Integers are precise: 1 + 1 is always 2.
- Integers require less storage than floating-point numbers.

From this, extensions can be created based on the length of the integer using datatype modifiers, and whether or not it has a sign.

The Long and Short of It

Integers in C can be of different sizes. This is important because there may be situations where we need to work with smaller or larger integers. Smaller integers take up less storage. Integers basically come in three sizes (apart from standard **int**s): **short, long** and **long long (C99)**. These are termed *size qualifiers* and denote different representation ranges of integers.

You have to be careful because not all systems represent these numbers in the same way. On many systems the range of **int** is actually the same as short **int**; on other machines, it is the same as **long int**. Below is a list of the ranges for **(signed)** integers on a typical 32-bit system:

```
short              -32768...32767
int                -2147483648...2147483647
long               -2147483648...2147483647
long long          -9223372036854775808...9223372036854775807
```

Constants that denote the limits of each range are usually found in the library file **limits.h** (usually in the *include* directory). This gives constants like **INT_MIN** and **INT_MAX**, which denote the lower and upper limits respectively. An example of a long integer is:

```
long int prime;
```

This declares a variable named **prime** to store a long integer, with any value from –2147483648 to 2147483647. Of course the keyword **int** is kind of redundant, so we get the same declaration just by using:

```
long prime;
```

A majority of programmers use this shorthand. In C99 somebody decided we needed even longer integers, so they designed the **long long,** which is intended to hold -2^{63} . . . $2^{63} -1$ integers.

NOTE: Unless you have a 64-bit system, a **long long** probably won't be of much use to you. Indeed it may have the same range as a normal **long**.

Signed

All integers come in two basic renditions: *signed* and *unsigned.* The former is the standard representation, in that the numbers they represent can be either positive or negative. The term **unsigned,** when used in conjunction with an **int,** denotes that the **int** can only hold positive values. For example:

```
unsigned int prime;
```

The **signed** version of integers has the same representational capacity as the **unsigned,** just all in the positive domain: 0.. 4294967295. You can also use **unsigned** by itself, as in:

```
unsigned prime;
```

Note that you can also specify that integers are to be **signed,** as in:

```
signed int prime;
```

but this is somewhat redundant as integers are signed by default; that is, it is equivalent to **int prime.** Below is a list of the ranges for unsigned integers on a typical 32-bit system:

```
int                     -2147483646...2147483647
unsigned int            0...4294967295
unsigned short          0...65535
unsigned long           0...4294967295
unsigned long long      0...2^64-1
```

Watch when assigning a negative quantity to an **unsigned** variable, or a large **unsigned** quantity to a **signed** variable. Both may be allowed by a particular compiler and result in a subtle mathematical error.

Why Do I Need More Than One Integer?

Why do I need more than one type of integer? Well, consider the problem of calculating factorials. The *factorial* of a natural number *n* is the product of all positive integers less than or equal to *n*. This is written as *n*!, a notation introduced by Christian Kramp in 1808, and is pronounced *n factorial*. The progression of factorials is:

```
1, 1, 2, 6, 24, 120, 720, 5040, 40320, 362880,
3628800, 39916800, 479001600, 6227020800,
87178291200, 1307674368000, 20922789888000,
355687428096000, 6402373705728000, 121645100408832000
```

As you can see, factorials grow really fast. If we want to calculate the 14th factorial, using an **int**, we couldn't because the largest value we can store as an **unsigned int** on a 32-bit system in Pelles C would be 4294967295, which is 236291379 digits too short! We can use the **long** type if we need to use numbers that **long** can handle and **int** cannot. If we don't need negative numbers, we could also use **unsigned long**. Similarly we could use **long long** if we need 64-bit integers.

When we want to calculate very large numbers, we have to use a large datatype.

Which Term Do I Use?

The number of terms used can get confusing very quickly. Below is a list of equivalent alternatives.

Common Type Specifier	Alternatives
int	signed int
short	signed short int, short int
long	signed long int, long int
long long	signed long long int, long long int
unsigned short	unsigned short int
unsigned long	unsigned long int
unsigned long long	unsigned long long int

As you can see, using the type specifier **unsigned long** is the same as **unsigned long int**.

Integers and I/O

To print different types of integers, we can use different type specifiers.

Integer type	printf	scanf
int	%d	%d
short	%hd	%hd
long	%ld	%ld
long long	%lld	%lld
unsigned int	%u	%u
unsigned short	%hu	%hu
unsigned long	%lu	%lu
unsigned long long	%llu	%llu

Floating Point Types

Integers are fine for some applications but sometimes you might need to use *real numbers*—that is, numbers with fractional components. For this you need floating point types. There are three basic types of floating point numbers in C: **float, double,** and **long double.** Considering that integers can also be represented in floating point form, how then do floating point numbers differ from integers? The answer lies in the way floating point numbers are represented inside the computer. An integer exists as a proper binary value. For example, the integer 24 is stored as 11000 in binary. A 32-bit integer is composed of 31 bits for the number and 1 bit for the sign (0 for positive, 1 for negative). Of course computers can't store floating point numbers in the same manner. Floating point numbers are stored using three components: a sign bit, a mantissa, and an exponent. A 32-bit **float** would look like this:

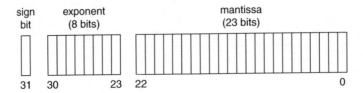

The *sign bit* stores the sign of the number: 0 for positive, 1 for negative. The *exponent* and *mantissa* are used together to create a mock-up floating point number.

A **float** represents a single-precision floating point number. Consider the following declaration of a **float** variable named **pi:**

```
float pi;
```

This declaration reserves sufficient space for one floating point number and tags the storage with the identifier *pi.*

The problem with **floats** is their limited precision. This means their accuracy is somewhat curtailed. To the rescue comes the **double,** which represents twice as much precision as a **float.** A **float** generally requires four bytes, a **double** requires eight bytes. Therefore a **double** precision number takes up two storage locations in memory. One of the reasons **double** is so commonly used is that many of the functions in the **math.h** library use dou-

ble values. Most modern systems provide 32-bit **float** storage and 64-bit **double** storage. That means both their exponent and mantissa are larger. A representation of a **double** is:

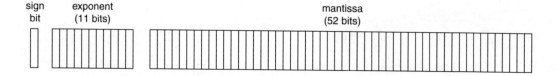

sign bit | exponent (11 bits) | mantissa (52 bits)

A **double** represents a double-precision floating-point number. Consider the following declaration of a **double** variable named **PI**:

```
double PI;
```

The third type of float, the **long double**, provides for even greater precision and range than a **double**. However, on many systems, including Windows, **double** and **long double** are synonymous. With all that in mind, here are some examples of valid and invalid floating point numbers:

```
Valid:      3.14159, 314.159e-2f, 0e0, 1.
Invalid:    3,14159, 3141549, .e0
```

Scientific Notation

Exponential (scientific) notation can also be used to represent floating point numbers. Numbers written using scientific notation have two components: a number called the *mantissa* followed by a power of 10 called the *exponent*. The character **e** or **E**, representing the exponent, is read as "times 10 to the power." For example:

```
253000.0    =    2.53e5    =    2.53E5
0.000034    =    0.34e-4   =    0.34E-4
```

Precision and Range

The possible values that a floating point type can be assigned are described in terms of attributes of precision and range. The term *precision* describes the number of significant decimal places that a floating value carries. A **float** has a precision of six significant digits:

$$0.d_1d_2d_3d_4d_5d_6 \times 10^n \qquad\qquad -37 \leq n \leq 38$$

A **double** has a precision of 15 significant digits. Consider the following declaration:

```
float pi;
double PI;
```

Now compare the precision of **pi** and **PI**, using a value of π to 20 decimal places:

```
pi = 3.14159265358979323846;
PI = 3.14159265358979323846;
```

If we print this value using:

```
printf("%.20f\n%.20lf\n",pi,PI);
```

we get:

```
3.14159274101257324218
3.14159265358979355369
```

Note how **pi**, the **float** variable, is accurate to 6 decimal places, whereas **PI**, the **double,** is accurate to 15.

The *range* describes the limits of the largest and smallest positive floating point values that can be represented in a variable of that type. The general ranges on a 32-bit system are:

```
float         10⁻³⁷ to 10³⁸
double        10⁻³⁰⁷ to 10³⁰⁸
long double   10⁻⁴⁹³¹ to 10⁴⁹³²
```

float $\qquad$ 10^{-37} to 10^{38}
double $\qquad$ 10^{-307} to 10^{308}
long double $\quad$ 10^{-4931} to 10^{4932}

However, most implementations of C guarantee only that **long double** is at least as precise as **double**.

Constants that denote the limits of each range are usually found in the **float.h** (usually in the *include* directory) header file. This gives constants like **FLT_MIN/FLT_MAX** and **DBL_MIN/DBL_MAX,** which denote the lower and upper limits of floats and doubles respectively. (There is also LDBL_MIN/LDBL_MAX for long doubles.)

Floating Point and I/O

The **printf** function uses the %f type specifier to print both **float** and **double** numbers and uses %e to print them in exponential form.

Floating point type	printf	scanf
float	%f, %e	%f, %e
double	%lf, %e	%f, %lf, %e
long double	%Lf, %Le	%Lf, %Le

How Big Are Floats Anyway?

Ever wondered how big a float or double is? I mean, how often will we ever need a number as large as 10^{4932} anyway? To fathom how small 10^{-37} is, consider that the mass of one electron is approximately 10^{-27} grams, and 10^{-37} is one ten-billionth of 10^{-27}. Pretty small, really. On the other hand, if you multiply the diameter of the Milky Way galaxy in kilometres by a trillion (1,000,000,000,000), the result is just one ten-thousandth of 10^{37}.

How Do **float** and **double** Differ?

The age-old question is how do **floats** and **doubles** differ? Suppose you are computing π^{100}. The influence of the number of significant digits used for π is the following. Using five significant digits for π gives

$$(3.1416)^{100} = 5.189061599 * 10^{49}$$

while using eight significant digits for π gives

$$(3.1415926)^{100} = 5.1897839464 * 10^{49}$$

The first estimate of π has five significant digits; however, $(3.1416)^{100}$ is accurate only for the first three digits.

Accuracy is reduced after numerous arithmetic operations. We can see a difference in the values calculated for log(7). Using precision = 10, with **float**, the natural log is

$$f = \log(7) = 1.9459100962$$

whereas with double

$$d = \log(7) = 1.9459101491$$

Does using one over the other really make a difference in terms of execution speed? Consider the following program:

```c
#include <stdio.h>
#include <time.h>

int main(void)
{
    long i;
    // Declare the time variables
    double ratio;
    clock_t t1, t2;

    ratio = 1./CLOCKS_PER_SEC;
    // Record the start time
    t1 = clock();

    for (i=0; i<100000000; i++)
    {
        // Math operations inserted here
    }
    // Record the end time
    t2 = clock();

    // Print out the difference, converting it
    // to seconds:
    printf("Time = %f", ratio*(long)t1 + ratio*(long)t2 );

    return 0;
}
```

Using a 100,000,000 iterations of an empty loop completes in ~0.234 s. One with basic float operations($*,/,-,+$) in ~1.265 s and the same functions with double in 1.265 s. The difference between double and float is therefore negligible.

To Infinity and Beyond!

In some respects the type of data used by your compiler is dependent on the machine you are using—the whole 32-bit versus 64-bit conundrum. Why? Because the size of a memory cell directly impacts the size of a number that can be stored.

There are limits associated with the size of numbers that can be stored by different datatypes. Most of the time, these limits are machine dependent because of different machine architectures. For example, most Intel-based systems have a 32-bit architecture. The range of integer values that can be stored in 32 bits is 0 through 4294967295, or -2147483648 through 2147483647. Conversely if you run the same program on a system with only a 16-bit processor, the number range would be -65536 through 65535, so the program might fail. Here's the whole gamut of numbers in C:

Type	Bits	Range
short	16	$-32768 \rightarrow 32767$
unsigned short	16	$0 \rightarrow 65535$
int	32	$-2147483648 \rightarrow 2147483647$
unsigned int	32	$0 \rightarrow 4294967295$
long	32	$-2147483648 \rightarrow 2147483647$
unsigned long	32	$0 \rightarrow 4294967295$
long long	64	$-9223372036854775808 \rightarrow 9223372036854775807$
unsigned long long	64	$0 \rightarrow 18446744073709551615$
signed char	8	$-128 \rightarrow 127$
unsigned char	8	$0 \rightarrow 255$
float	32	$1.175494e\text{-}38 \rightarrow 3.402823e38$
double	64	$2.225073e\text{-}308 \rightarrow 1.797693e308$
long double	128	$3.362103e\text{-}4932 \rightarrow 1.189731e4932$

Characters

Characters are actually integers. Confused? Well, remember that computers deal with binary numbers, so characters can't directly be represented inside a computer, but they can be epitomized by numbers. C provides a datatype called **char,** often pronounced *car,* to store characters. It is essentially one byte in length. For example,

```
char c;
```

declares the variable **c** to be a character. A **char** can store the values –127 to 128. Here's where it gets tricky. When we assign a value to the variable **c**, say for instance:

```
ch = 'A';
```

we are assigning an uppercase letter *A* to the variable **ch.** A single letter contained between single quotes is a C character constant. Note, don't use **A,** or it will try to assign a string to

ch. But we are not actually assigning a letter. This assignment statement assigns the "number" associated with the character "A" to the variable **ch.** The compiler looks up "A" in the ASCII table and finds the number associated with it. In this case the number is 65. So it stores the value 65 in **ch.** Just to prove a point, try the following:

```
printf("Letter %c : ASCII %d\n", ch, ch);
```

You should get:

```
Letter A : ASCII 65
```

The standard ASCII table runs from 0 to 127. Some common codes include:

```
48→57      The numbers 0 to 9
65→90      The uppercase letters A to Z
97→122     The lowercase letters a to z
```

We can also use **unsigned char,** in which case the range of values increases from 0 to 255. To input and output characters, we use the %c type specifier. More on that later.

Bacteria Growth/Runoff

Going back to our bacteria example, we now want to assign types to our variables. Let's deal with **tHours** first. It is most likely that the number of hours entered won't be an exact number, so let's make **tHours** a **double.** Now because the number of bacteria calculated won't be a whole number either, you are at a bit of a conundrum. Do you represent the answer as a whole number or a fractional number? Statistics like birth rates are always expressed as a fractional number, so you can use a double as well. For instance, the estimated birth rate in Canada in 2006 is 10.78 births/1,000 population. So we can declare our variables as follows:

```
double tHours, nBacteria;
```

Now consider the water runoff problem. What type of datatype do we assign to the variables? Most calculations involving data like water runoff are performed using floating point numbers, so they should all be **doubles:**

```
double load, runoff, concBacteria, area;
```

The Life of Variables (or, What Is Scope?)

Variables, unlike matter, can be created and destroyed. Variables have lives, or a time period in which they exist. By *existing* we mean they are stored in memory. Not all variables exist for the entire life of the program. The *scope* of an object is the region of the program in which statements may refer to that object or change its contents. The scope of an object runs from the point it is declared. In the following example, the scope of the variable **y** is below line 3. It would not be possible to change the assignment statement of line 2 to read **x=y,** because **y** is not created until line 3.

```
1   int x;
2   x = 1.2;
3   int y;
```

Global Variables

Sometimes variables are maintained in a region of the program where they are visible to the whole program. Such variables are said to be *global*. The variable x in the following code segment is considered global. It is declared in the region following the preprocessor statements, but before the main function is declared. The whole program has access to this variable.

```
1   #include <stdio.h>
2
3   int x;
4
5   int main(void)
6   {
7       return 0;
8   }
```

In general you should avoid using global variables due to the fact that they can potentially be modified from anywhere in the program. The value of a global variable could change unexpectedly, resulting in a subtle error that can be extremely difficult to locate, since the offending line could be anywhere in the program.

Hiding Variables

Sometimes a variable may be "hidden" by the scope of a local declaration inside a block. Take the following code segment for example:

```
1   int x=7; // Global x
2   {
3       double x = 1.2,y; // Local x
4       y = x;
5   }
```

Here the global x defined on line 1 is made "invisible" by the local scope of x defined on line 3. Therefore y is assigned the value of the local x (1.2). Scope is nothing to be scared about. You just have to watch where you create similar variables.

Scope and Functions

Scope is also important in functions. Take, for example, the following code:

```
1   double is_odd(int numI)
2   {
3       if (numI%2 == 1)
4           return 1;
```

```
5        else
6            return 0;
7    }
8
9    int main(void)
10   {
11       int odd, numO=2;
12       odd = is_odd(numO);
13       return 9;
14   }
```

The scope of the variable **numO** in the main program is the main program (lines 11–13), while the scope of the variable **numI** in the function **is_odd** is inside the function (lines 1–6). When the function **is_odd** is invoked, the variable **numI** is created to store the incoming number to check. When the function is destroyed, so too is **numI**. These two variables exist in different realities. You cannot access **numO** within **is_odd**, nor can you access **numI** in the main program.

Block Structure

Consider the following diagram illustrating block structure. The outermost block here is defined as level 0 and denotes a global scope. The next level is defined as level (i + 1).

Variables Defined in Block	Are Accessible in Blocks	Scope Level
A	A,B,C,D,E	0
B	B	1
C	C,D,E	1
D	D	2
E	E	2

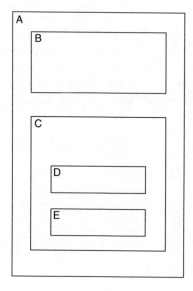

C allows you to give two variables the same name, provided they have different scopes. If they are declared in two different blocks, they will not conflict. A variable declared within a block cannot be accessed outside that block.

Assigning a Value

Once they have been created, variables can be assigned a value. This can be achieved by obtaining input through the keyboard, or explicitly assigning the variable a value:

```
int area;
area = 37;
```

This statement assigns the variable **area** the value 37.

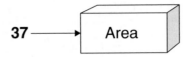

This value is now stored in the piece of memory assigned to the variable **area**. More on this in the next chapter.

Why So Many Numbers?

So why do we need so many numeric types? Looking at a real example will help solve the riddle. A 12 megapixel camera can create digital photographs that are 4000 × 3000 pixels in size. If we took only monochrome images, with 256 shades of gray, we could store the image as an **unsigned char**, using 1 byte per pixel, or 12,000,000 × 1 = 12 megabytes. Store the image using an **int**, and it becomes 12,000,000 × 4 = 48 megabytes. As a **double**, 12,000,000 × 8 = 96 megabytes. All this assumes no form of image compression (which helps shrink images by reducing redundant information). This is why images are usually stored as the smallest integer available. A color image is normally stored as three 1-byte layers for red, green, and blue (RGB), hence 3 bytes per pixel for 36 megabytes per 12 megapixel image.

Is having more than one numeric type necessary? Consider **int** versus **double**:

- Operations involving integers are faster.
- Less storage space is needed for integers.
- Operations with integers are always precise.
- There is some loss of accuracy with floating point numbers.
- Floating point values can represent a much larger range of values than integers can.

What's Your Address?

Every variable has three characteristics associated with it: (1) the value stored in the variable; (2) the address of the variable, and (3) the datatype. The address of the first memory locations is used to store the variable's contents. How many variables are used depends on the variables' datatypes. If you so desire, you can print the address of a variable using the type specifier **%p**. For example:

```
int num = 42;
printf("%d %p\n", num &num);
```

The result is (gcc)

```
42 0x2a
```

Calculating the `sizeof` a Variable

Sometimes it is convenient to determine the amount of storage allocated for a datatype. C provides this in the way of the **sizeof()** operator, which returns the number of bytes of a variable. On any C language implementation compliant with any C standard ever written, **sizeof(char)** is exactly one, whether **char** is 8, 16, 60, or 64 bits. For example,

```
double x;
printf("%i\n", sizeof(x));
```

prints out a value of 4 bytes, which = 4 × 8 = 32 bits.

Storage Classes

C offers a number of different ways to store an object, collectively called *storage classes*. The storage class specifiers are **auto, extern, register,** and **static.**

auto

This class does nothing and serves no real purpose. The implication is, "You don't need to remember this."

extern

Sometimes global variables can be defined in a form called an *allusion*. An allusion informs the compiler that a variable of a specified type exists but has been defined elsewhere. For example, the following code contains an allusion to variable **PI**:

```
int main(void)
{
    extern PI;
}
```

Here the term **extern** tells the compiler that the variable **PI** is external to the current program (usually another file somewhere). We'll cover this a little later in the chapter on functions.

register

The keyword **register** suggests to the compiler which variables should be kept in one of the microprocessor registers. It is a way to optimize a program. Don't worry about this.

static

A program doesn't usually keep track of the value of a variable after the function it lives in ends. The keyword **static** retains a variable's value after a function is done.

Qualifying Types

Type qualifiers are sort of like adjectives, but instead of telling you something about a noun, they do the same with variables. They do not modify the underlying storage or representation of an object but tell the compiler something about how that object will be used. There are three type qualifiers: **const, restrict,** and **volatile**. The latter two are more advanced topics, so I won't go beyond a brief description here. The **volatile** qualifier instructs the compiler to ensure that all accesses to the qualified object actually occur. We normally associate the term **volatile** with variables whose value could change unexpectedly. An example of this is global variables used in a multithreaded application. The **restrict** type qualifier is used with pointers.

I Want My Variable to Be Constant

The **const** qualifier is used to tell the C compiler that the variable value cannot be changed after initialization. For example, in

```
const double pi=3.14159265;
```

pi cannot be changed at a later time within the program. Of course **#define** does a fine job of defining constants, so **const** isn't all that useful. The **const** qualifier is a promise that the programmer won't try to modify something through a given value. It is *not* a constant, per se.

 # The Quadratic Equation

Going back to the program to calculate the quadratic equation, let's look at the part of the program dealing with the data. The first thing we know from the algorithm is that there is a series of values input into the program and another series calculated from these values. The equation requires three coefficients as input: **a, b,** and **c.** This is a case where it might be practical to leave these as they are and not give them specific identifiers, although we could tag them with the suffix _coeff if we wanted.

```
double a, b, c;
```

Next we will split up the quadratic equation into smaller pieces.

$$x = \frac{-b \pm \sqrt{b^2 - 4ac}}{2a} \left\}\begin{array}{c} D = b^2 - 4ac \\ A = 2a \\ sroot = \sqrt{D} \\ x = \frac{-b \pm sroot}{A} \end{array}\right.$$

This makes the calculations easier and provides us with a few more pieces of data for which to make variables. In this case:

```
double disc, A, sroot;
```

Note that we have changed D to **disc** just to make it more readable. Now we also need some storage for the roots that are calculated. Recall that our algorithm allows for five scenarios:

1. No roots: No variable needed
2. A linear equation: **root**
3. A single root: **root**
4. Two real roots   **root1, root2**
5. Two complex roots: **xreal, ximag**

These are declared as:

```
double root, root1, root2, xreal, ximag;
```

Now we can perform the input functions to obtain the values for **a, b,** and **c:**

```
printf("Finding quadratic roots.\n");
printf("Enter the values of a, b, and c: ");
scanf("%lf%lf%lf", &a, &b, &c);
printf("Equation: %.2f x%c + %.2f x + %.2f = 0\n",
       a,253,b,c);
```

The first two **printf** statements are informative only, prompting the user for the information. The **scanf** actually reads the three coefficients into their corresponding variables. The last **printf** outputs a rendition of how the equation would look. Notice that the second type specifier in the formatting string is a **%c,** and its corresponding argument is the value 253. On most systems this will print the equation using a special superscript 2 to signify squared. The output would look like:

```
Finding quadratic roots.
Enter the values of a, b, and c: 2 4 -30
Equation: 2.00 x² + 4.00 x + -30.00 = 0
```

Epilog

Information overload, right? You'll get used to using the correct datatype for the correct information and selecting appropriate names. Practice makes perfect. The preference for the use of floating point numbers is just to stick with **double**. Forget **float**. After a while you will realize that **int, char,** and **double** may be the datatypes you use the most.

Exercises

Exercise 7.1

To estimate the temperature in a freezer in degrees Celsius given the elapsed time (hours) since a power failure, we can use the formula

$$T = \frac{4t^2}{t+2} - 20$$

where t is the time since the power failure. Write a simple program to estimate T. Your program should prompt the user to enter the length of time since the start of the power failure in whole hours and minutes. Note that the program will need to convert the elapsed time into hours. For example, if the user entered 2 30 (2 hours, 30 minutes), the program would need to convert this to $t = 2.5$. Make sure your program is readable, including appropriate comments, and incorporates aspects of usability in the text prompts to the user.

Exercise 7.2

The efficiency of air conditioners is often rated by the Seasonal Energy Efficiency Ratio (SEER) as defined by the Air Conditioning and Refrigeration Institute. The higher the SEER rating of a unit, the more energy efficient it is. The SEER rating is the BTU (British thermal unit) of cooling output during a typical cooling season divided by the total electric energy input in watt-hours during the same period.

To calculate what it costs to operate an air conditioner on a yearly basis, four pieces of information are needed:

1. Size of the air conditioner in tons (12,000 BTUs)
2. Estimated number of hours used per season
3. Air conditioner efficiency (SEER)
4. Cost per kWh ($/kWh)

The formula to calculate annual operating costs (AOC) is

$$AOC \frac{\frac{Tons * 12000}{SEER}}{1000} * Hours * Cost\_kWh$$

Using the program skeleton given in Exercise 4.3, write the portion of the program that performs the calculation. Test your program using the following information:

Tons = 10

Hours of use = 700

SEER = 13

Cost per kWh = 0.09.

Operating costs = $581.54

Operators and Expressions

Use the good features of a language, avoid the bad ones.
—Kernighan and Plauger

Introduction

Just like humans, C has expressions. In the case of C, however, *expressions* are meaningful combinations of constants, variables, and function calls. The expression may consist of a single entity, such as a constant or variable, or it may consist of some combination of such entities interconnected by one or more *operators*. Expressions can also represent logical conditions that are either true or false.

What Are Operators?

Operators are the glue that bind expressions together. General expressions are formed by joining together constants and variables (operands) via various operators. Operators are composed of one or more special characters, such as < and <=. If an operator is composed of two characters, they must not be separated by a space (e.g., <=, not < =). The *relational*, *equality*, and *logical* operators all operate on expressions and yield either int value 1 (true) or int value 0 (false). In C, *false* is represented by any zero value and *true* is represented by any nonzero value. All these operators are used in expressions of the form:

```
expr1 op expr2
```

where **op** is a relational, equality, or logical operator.

Unary Operators

In mathematics, a unary operation is an operation with only one operand. It's basically the same in C.

Binary Operators

Binary operators work on two operands (*binary* here means two operands, not in the sense of base-2 arithmetic). The basic binary operators are:

```
+      addition
−      subtraction
*      multiplication
/      division
%      remainder, also called "modulo"
&&     logical AND
||     logical OR
<      less than
>      greater than
<=     less than or equal
>=     greater than or equal
==     equals
!=     does not equal
?      conditional operator
```

Being Positively Negative

The most common unary operator is the unary minus (negative), which occurs when a numerical constant, variable, or expression is preceded by a minus sign. Note that the unary minus is distinctly different from the arithmetic operator (–) that denotes subtraction, since the latter operator acts on two separate operands. For example:

```
x = −12;
```

This assigns the value –12 to the variable *x*. You could use + to denote a positive number, but numbers are positive unless you define them as negative, so adding a + is just redundant. These operators can be applied to any integer or floating point variables.

Assigning Values to Variables

When a C compiler sets aside storage for a variable, it fails to do one thing—initialize the variable. It's your responsibility to give the variable a value. As we saw previously, one way of doing this is assigning a value when you declare the variable:

```
double pi=3.14159;
```

This assigns the value 3.14159 to the variable **pi** within the declaration statement. In an assignment statement, the value of a variable is replaced with the value of an expression. For example:

```
pi = 3.14159;
```

Aside from initializing variables, assignment statements are also used to change a variable's contents. For example:

```
area = 0;
area = pi * radius * radius;
```

The first assignment statement sets the variable **area** to zero. The subsequent assignment statement overwrites the stored value of **area** (0) with the value calculated by the expression on the right hand side of the assignment statement.

Assignment Operators

The assignment operator in C is the equals operator, =. It is used to change the value of a variable. For instance, the expression:

```
PI = 3.14159;
```

causes the floating point value 3.14159 to be assigned to the variable **PI**. Multiple assignments are permissible in C. For example:

```
i = j = k = 4;
```

causes the integer value 4 to be assigned to **i**, **j**, and **k**, simultaneously (actually it assigns 4 to **k**, then the value in **k** is assigned to **j**, then the value in **j** is assigned to **i**). Assignment operators are really just binary operators. Here are some examples:

```
velocity = distance / time;
force = mass * acceleration;
count = count + 1;
```

Arithmetic Operators

There are four main arithmetic operators that should be familiar:

+   addition
–   subtraction
*   multiplication
/   division

Note that there is no built-in exponentiation operator in C. Some languages use the caret operator: ^. But it seems this functionality was left out of C! Instead, there is a library function (**pow**) that carries out this operation. For example:

x^2 is expressed as x * x or pow(x,2)

Operation	C Operator	Algebraic Expression	C Expression
addition	+	$x + 7$	x + 7
subtraction	–	$x - y$	x − y
multiplication	*	xy	x * y
division	/	$x \div y$	x / y
modulo	%	$x \bmod y$	x % y

Division

For the first three operators, there is no real difference from their mathematical equivalents. However, the division operator has two personalities. The difference lies in the way it handles integer division and floating point division. In an integer divide, the result is truncated; that is, the fractional part is discarded. For example:

```
17/10 = 1
```

This basically asks, "How many times does 10 fit into 17 exactly?" This is where we have to be a little careful, as integer division will always return just the result with no remainder. Here are some other examples:

```
15/3 = 5      16/3 = 5      17/3 = 5
3/15 = 0      0/4 = 0       4/0 = undefined
```

A quick note on the last example. As in mathematics, divide-by-zero has no meaning, so a calculation of this form will usually trigger an error of some sort. If either the divisor or the dividend is a floating point number, a floating point division is performed. For example:

```
17.0/10.0 = 1.7
```

Modulo

A special operator provided in programming languages is the *modulo* operator. It only operates on integers. The modulo operation calculates the integer remainder of the result of dividing the first operand by the second. For example:

```
5 % 4 = 1      7 % 5 = 2      15 % 0 = undefined
15 % 5 = 0     8 % 5 = 3
```

ANSI C doesn't define a result if either of the operands is negative.

Parentheses

Parentheses are used as punctuators to clarify or change the order in which operations are performed. For example, a mathematical equation of the form

$$a = \frac{b}{c + d}$$

could be expressed in C as

```
a = b / c + d;
```

but the answer would be wrong because the division is performed before the addition. Using parentheses, we can force the compiler to evaluate the expression in the proper sequence:

```
a = b / (c + d);
```

Relational Operators

There are four relational operators in C:

<	less than
>	greater then
<=	less than or equal to
>=	greater than or equal to

They compare entities on the basis of quantity. Note that two of the operators are <= and >=, which are synonymous with the ≤ and ≥ respectively in math.

Consider a relational expression such as **a<b.**

If **a** is less than **b,** then the expression has the **int** value 1, which is thought of as being *true.* If **a** is not less than **b,** then the expression has the **int** value 0, which is thought of as being *false.* Let **a** and **b** be arbitrary arithmetic expressions. The following table shows how **a–b** determines the value of expressions.

a–b	a < b	a > b	a <= b	a >= b
positive	0	1	0	1
zero	0	0	1	1
negative	1	0	1	0

Equality Operators

The equality operators are used for determining if two entities are equal or not. There are two equality operators in C:

==	equal
!=	not equal

They are synonymous with the symbols = and ≠ respectively in mathematics. Note that the equality operator == is two equals signs, which differs from the single = used in assignment expressions. These operators compare entities on the basis of quantity. The following table shows how **a–b** determines the value of expressions.

a–b	a == b	a != b
zero	1	0
nonzero	0	1

Consider a statement of the form:

```
(a_number % 2) == 0
```

This expression basically asks, "Is the value obtained by calculating **a_number** modulo 2 equal to zero?" If it is, then the expression generates a value of 1, signifying the result is true. If not, the value is 0, representing a result of false. In this case the expression

```
a_number % 2
```

calculates whether a number is divisible by 2, which, if true, denotes that **a_number** is an even number. The same could have been achieved using the statement:

```
(a_number % 2) != 1
```

which says that **a_number** is an even number if the remainder **is not** 1.

 Remember that == asks the question "are they equal?" and = means "equals".

Logical Operators

The relational and equality operators are used to form *logical* expressions, which represent conditions that are either true or false. There are three logical operators in C:

&&	logical AND
||	logical OR
!	logical NOT

The logical operators act on operands that are themselves logical expressions. The net effect is to combine the individual logical expressions into more complex expressions that are either true or false. For instance, the expression:

```
(i >= 0) && (i <= 1000)
```

is true if the value of **i** is greater than or equal to 0 *and* the value of **i** is less than or equal to 100. Otherwise it is false.

AND

The result of a logical AND operation is only true if both operands are true. It has the general form

```
expression1 && expression2
```

which evaluates to 1 (true) if *both* expressions are 1 and otherwise evaluates to 0 (false). For example,

```
perc >= 0 && perc <= 100
```

returns true if the value stored in the variable perc is *both* greater than or equal to 0 AND less than or equal to 100.

OR

The result of a logical OR operation is only false if both operands are false. It has the general form

```
expression1 || expression2
```

which evaluates to 1 (true) if either or both expressions are 1 and otherwise evaluates to 0 (false). For example,

```
perc < 0 || perc > 100
```

returns true if the value stored in the variable **perc** is either less than 0 OR greater than 100.

The following table shows the value of expressions for && and ||.

a	b	a && b	a || b
0	0	0	0
0	1	0	1
1	0	0	1
1	1	1	1

NOT

C also includes the unary operator ! that negates the value of a logical expression. That is, it causes an expression that is originally true to become false and vice versa. This operator is referred to as the logical *negation,* or complement or logical NOT. It has the general form

```
!expression
```

which evaluates to 1 (true) if the expression is 0 and otherwise evaluates to 0 (false). For example, the expression **!(k == 4)** is true if the value of **k** is not equal to 4 and false otherwise. Actually, though, it is easier to write:

```
(k != 4)
```

C99 Word Forms!

C99 now lets you use keywords instead of the cryptic symbols to represent logical operators. This adds a little more readability to code. To use this on many compilers, you have to use the **iso646.h** library:

&&	→	and
||	→	or
!	→	not

This means that you can effectively rewrite

```
if (n >= 0 && n <= 1000)
```

to become

```
if (n >= 0 and n <= 1000)
```

What to Avoid

Sometimes you will encounter mathematical phrases expressed of the form:

$$1 < x < 100$$

Programmers make the mistake of converting this expression as they see it:

```
if (1 < x < 100)
```

This expression would work fine if the value of **x** is 27, but that's mostly because 27 is greater than 1. This expression is evaluated as follows: The expression 1 < x is evaluated first. Because 27 is greater than 1, this expression evaluates to 1 (true). Next the second half is evaluated 1 < 100. It essentially replaces the first portion of the expression with the evaluated value, in this case 1. 1 is always less than 100, so the entire expression evaluates to true. This works.

Now try with a value such as 107:

1 < 107 evaluates to 1 (true)
1 < x < 100 becomes 1 < 100 which evaluates to 1 (true)

However, 107 is certainly not greater than 1 and less than 100. To fix this, you would have to split the expression up into two expressions of the form:

```
if (x > 1 && x < 100)
```

Now the expressions are evaluated independently, with both expression needing to evaluate to true for the entire expression to be true. The && is a logical operator that joins the two expressions.

Shortcut Operators

C offers some additional "shortcut" operators designed to make programs more compact. Compactness is certainly a virtue, but beginners should avoid their use until they fully understand the behavior of these operators. In most cases shortcut operators serve to make code obscure. This is compounded by the fact that it seems such code is very rarely properly documented. Just say no.

Compound Assignment Operators

The most commonly used shortcut operators are the *compound assignment operators*. There are instances when assignment expressions are of the form:

```
sum = sum + i/100.0;
```

Such statements use the same variable on both sides of the assignment operator. Such statements can be rewritten using the following assignment operators:

```
+=   -=   *=   /=   %=
```

This means the previous expression could be rewritten in the form:

```
sum += i/100.0;
```

These operators aren't so bad, but only use them if you understand them.

Increment/Decrement Operators

More confusing are the *increment* and *decrement* operators. These are special operators used only in the case where a variable is either increased or decreased by one. The increment and decrement operators are ++ and -- respectively. Using the increment operator ++, the expression i = i + 1 can be replaced by the expression ++i. Examples of the increment operator are:

```
count = count + 1   →   count++
```

The caveat with these operators is that there are two forms of each operator: *prefix* and *postfix*. When ++ appears before a variable, it is called a prefix operator; when it appears after a variable, it is a postfix operator. And naturally they behave very differently—well, sort of. When using an expression such as ++i or i++ by itself, both these expressions correspond to the longer expression i = i + 1. The difference occurs when a prefix or postfix operator occurs within an assignment expression. For example, the expression

```
index = ++n
```

does two things in one. The value of n is first incremented by one, and then the new value of **n** is assigned to the variable **index**. Hence, the statement **index = ++n** is equivalent to the two statements:

```
n = n + 1;      / Increment n by 1
index = n;      // Assign n's value  to index
```

The expression **index = n++** does the opposite. The value of **n** is first assigned to **index**, and then the value of **n** is incremented by one. Hence, the statement **index = n++** is equivalent to the two statements:

```
index = n;      // Assign n's value to index
n = n + 1;      // Increment n by 1
```

I know, now you're thinking is it possible to perform: ++n++? Fortunately no, the compiler should catch this. Thankfully it doesn't allow ++(n++) either! I strongly suggest avoiding these operators until you have a clear understanding of how they behave. Why? Because they cause something called *side effects*. If you're interested in this, we'll talk more about it in the chapter on the dark side of programming.

   Clarity is more valuable than compactness!

Setting a Precedent

Arithmetic expressions in programming languages sometimes differ from the way we want to intuitively write them. For example, the quadratic equation:

$$x = \frac{-b + \sqrt{b^2 - 4ac}}{2a}$$

could be written as

```
x = -b+sqrt(b*b-4*a*c)/(2*a)
```

But is this right? No, because programming languages engage a little-known concept called *precedence*. Precedence just means that the compiler scans the expression and decides which operations to perform next. Precedence has parallels in the animal kingdom. When a lion on the plains feeds, there is a hierarchy of other animals that wait in line to feed after the lion has finished. A lion has precedence over a hyena, which has precedence over a vulture, etc. In C (as in most languages), * and / have a higher precedence than + and –. In other words, they get fed first. So in the previous equation, the square-root operation is performed first, followed by the division by 2, then the multiplication by **a**, and finally the addition of **–b**. That means something isn't right here.

If we use the following values, **a=3**, **b=10**, and **c=2**, we get an answer of **r = 3.08**. The real answer, however, is **r=–0.21**. To alleviate this problem, we could separate the equation into subequations, or we could use parentheses. This gives us:

```
x = (-b+sqrt(b*b-4*a*c))/(2*a)
```

Parentheses avoid ambiguity. Use as many as you need to make an equation clear.

Operator	Execution Order
expr++ expr—	left to right
unary + unary — ! ++expr	right to left
— expr sizeof()	
* / %	
+ —	
< > <= >=	left to right
== !=	
&&	
||	
= += —= *= /= %=	right to left

The main message here is: Don't rely too heavily on precedence. For instance, instead of writing

```
i + j == 3 && i * 1 >= 5
```

and relying on the fact that arithmetic operators have precedence over relational and equality operators, which, in turn, have precedence over logical operators, it is better to write

```
((i + j) == 3) && (i * 1 >= 5)
```

Building Equations through Expressions

One of the most common uses for expressions is to build equations, or rather to translate mathematical equations to C expressions. Part of the challenge in solving a problem is expressing mathematical equations in a form with which a language can work. Even though assignment statements sometimes resemble mathematical equations, the two notions are distinct and should not be confused. For example, the mathematical equation

$\chi + 2 = 0$

does not become an assignment statement when you type

x + 2 = 0;

The left side of the equal sign is an expression, not a variable, and this expression may not be assigned a value. Consider the following mathematical expressions:

$y = mx + c$
$a = \pi r^2$

The problem here is that some algebraic constructs just aren't available in programming languages. If we were to write

y = mx + c;
a = πr^2

the term **mx** would be interpreted as a variable called **mx**. π is a Greek letter and, as such, can't be the name of a variable, so we can't use it in an expression. Finally r^2 doesn't work because there are no superscript operators in C (or any language for that matter). There are nuances to translating equations that just have to be experienced. The following list shows commonly used algebraic/mathematical symbols and their C equivalents.

Algebraic	Meaning	C Equivalent(s)
mx	Multiply m by x.	m * x
r^2	r to the power of 2	r * r, pow(r,2)
x^y	x to the power of y	pow(x,y)
π	Pi	PI, Pi, pi
$\sqrt{x}$	Square root	sqrt(x)
$x^{1/4}$	x to the power of 1/4	pow(x,0.25)
e^x	Exponential of x	exp(x)
e	Base of the natural logarithm	exp(1)
$\pm$	Plus or minus	Create 2 equations
$\neq, <>$	Does not equal	!=
$\geq$	Greater than or equal to	>=
$\leq$	Less than or equal to	<=
$x \div y, x/y$	Divide x by y	x/y
$\lvert x \rvert$	Absolute value of x	fabs(x)
$=$	Is equal to	==
$\ln x$	Natural logarithm	log(x)
$\mathrm{Log}\, x$	Base 10 logarithm	log10(x)

(e.g.) Quadratic Equation

Consider the example of converting the quadratic equation:

$$x = \frac{-b + \sqrt{b^2 - 4ac}}{2a}$$

In order to translate this it is best to split it up into sections. The first thing you will notice is that the left-hand side of the equation is *x*. This implies the variable to which the value of the quadratic is assigned could also be called *x*. Right? Well, there is a slight complication in that the equation *also* contains a ± symbol, which says that there are two possible equations. Let's create two variables, **x1** and **x2**. In C we would have expressions of the form:

```
x1 = ;
x2 = ;
```

That's a nice start. Now look at the part of the equation after the ±: $\sqrt{b^2}$ – *4ac*. The square root must be expressed in C using the **sqrt** function. So it becomes: **sqrt(b²–4ac)**. Now **b²** also can't be expressed in C, so we change this to **b * b**. Now our equation looks like sqrt(b*b–4ac). Finally, the term **4ac** must be expressed as **4*a*c**, so now the equation looks like **sqrt(b*b–4*a*c)**. We have:

```
x1 = sqrt(b*b—4*a*c);
x2 = sqrt(b*b—4*a*c);
```

Adding the expression –b± gives:

```
x1 = —b + sqrt(b*b—4*a*c);
x2 = —b — sqrt(b*b—4*a*c);
```

Now we just have to add the denominator, **2a**, which equates to **2*a** in C:

```
x1 = —b + sqrt(b*b—4*a*c) / 2*a;
x2 = —b — sqrt(b*b—4*a*c) / 2*a;
```

Right? Well, not quite. The way those silly precedence rules work, if we left this equation as is, it would perform the calculations (for **x1**) in the following manner:

1. **sqrt(b*b–4*a*c)**
2. **/ 2**
3. ***a**
4. **Add the result to –b**

Not quite what we had planned. To fix it, add some parentheses:

```
x1 = (—b + sqrt(b*b—4*a*c)) / (2*a);
x2 = (—b — sqrt(b*b—4*a*c)) / (2*a);
```

Now the order of calculations (for **x1**) are:

1. **sqrt(b*b–4*a*c)**

2. **Add the result to –b**
3. **Calculate 2*a**
4. **Divide the result of 2 by the result of 3.**

Great! There are, of course, still a couple of changes you could make to have it seem more efficient. Both expressions contain equations that appear twice:

```
sqrt(b*b—4*a*c)   and   (2*a)
```

We could calculate these only once, and store the value in a *temporary* or *intermediary* variable.

```
d = b*b—4*a*c;
z = 2*a;
x1 = (—b + sqrt(d)) / z;
x2 = (—b — sqrt(d)) / z;
```

Swapping Values

Now consider the task of swapping the values in two variables. We could just write:

```
i = j;
j = i;
```

Will this work? No. What happens here is that the value stored in the variable **i** is over-written with the value of **j**. In the next line, the value of **j** is overwritten with the value stored in **i**, which just happens to be the same value. To properly swap two variables, we have to introduce a new temporary variable, which we might call **temp** to store the initial value of **i**.

```
temp = i;
i = j;
j = temp;
```

 ## Bacteria Growth

Now we can actually start doing some calculations. Lets look again at the number of bacteria growing in a culture, represented by the equation:

$$B = 300000e^{-0.032t}$$

The algorithm for this is relatively simple:

1. Input the time in hours.
2. Calculate the number of bacteria using the equation given.
3. Output the results.

In the previous chapter we decided to use the variables **nBacteria** and **tHours** to represent B and t respectively. Now let's translate the equation. Don't concern yourself too much with the mathematical functions. We'll go over them in the next chapter. The presence of e implies the use of the **exp** function from the math library, **math.h**. We want to calculate e "to the power of" $-0.032*t$, which becomes:

```
exp(—0.032 * tHours)
```

Now we add in the rest of the equation, resulting in an expression of the form:

```
nBacteria = 300000 * exp(—0.032 * tHours);
```

Our program now looks like:

```
#include <stdio.h>
#include <math.h>

int main(void)
{
    double tHours, nBacteria;

    nBacteria = 300000 * exp(—0.032 * tHours)

    return 0;
}
```

Of course, as it stands, our program has no I/O, so it won't really work. Let's add some code to input the time in hours:

```
printf("How many hours have elapsed? ");
scanf("%lf", &tHours);
```

Moreover, we might actually want to produce some output:

```
printf("The number of bacteria is %.2f", nBacteria);
```

Our final program looks like:

```
#include <stdio.h>
#include <math.h>
int main(void)
{
    double tHours, nBacteria;

    printf("How many hours have elapsed? ");

    scanf("%lf", &tHours);

    nBacteria = 300000 * exp(—0.032 * tHours)
    printf("The number of bacteria is %.2f", nBacteria);

    return 0;
}
```

Exercises

Exercise 8.1

You have probably seen movies in which giants ants or bees take over the world. If you are truly worried about mutant ants, rest assured that they could never exist. Insects, humans, and most other beings are subject to a principle called the *square-cube law*, first demonstrated in 1638 in Galileo's *Two New Sciences*. If an animal were scaled up by a considerable amount, its muscular strength would be severely reduced since the cross section of its muscles would increase by the square of the scaling factor, whereas its mass would increase by the cube of the scaling factor. As a result, cardiovascular functions would be severely limited. In the case of flying animals, their wing loading would be increased if they were scaled up, and they would have to fly faster to gain the same amount of lift. Because of this, the giant insects, spiders, and other animals seen in movies are unrealistic, as their sheer size would force them to collapse. The exceptions are giant aquatic creatures, as they are supported by water. The square-cube law is defined by the following equation:

$$v_2 = v_1 \left(\frac{l_2}{l_1}\right)^3$$

where v_1 is the original volume, v_2 is the new volume, l_1 is the original length, and l_2 is the new length. Write a program to prompt the user for the appropriate data and calculate the new volume.

Exercise 8.2

Write a program for Exercise 3.1 for calculating the power of a dam.

Exercise 8.3

The *body surface area* (BSA) is the calculated surface area of the human body. The BSA is used as an indicator of metabolic mass. For example, the cardiac index is a measure of cardiac output divided by the BSA, providing a better approximation of the required cardiac output. There are various formulas for calculated the BSA. One formula is that of Du Bois and Du Bois (D. DuBois and E. F. DuBois, "A Formula to Estimate the Approximate Surface Area if Height and Weight Be Known," *Archives of Internal Medicine*, 17 (1916): 863–71):

$$BSA(m^2) = 0.007184 \times weight(kg)^{0.425} \times height(cm)^{0.725}$$

Write a program to prompt the user for the appropriate information and calculate the BSA. Make sure your program is readable, including appropriate comments, and incorporates aspects of usability in the text prompts to the user.

Hey, Do the Math!

. . . one of the main causes of the fall of the Roman Empire was that, lacking zero, they had no way to indicate successful termination of their C programs.

—Robert Firth

Introduction

In this chapter we will cover some of the issues relating to the use of numbers in programming.

Number Conversions

One of the caveats of working with numbers in any programming language occurs when you mix the types of the numbers, such as using integers with floating point numbers in the same expression. The caveat is conversion and occurs in assignment statements or when calling a function. Sometimes the results are not as expected. For example, consider the following code fragment:

```
int x=6, y=4;
double div;

div = x / y;
```

This expression results in an incorrect value stored in **div**. As both **x** and **y** are **ints**, integer division is performed, resulting in an **int**. The integer division is performed *before* the conversion. The conversion is somewhat redundant, effectively converting 1 to 1.0. There are two forms of type conversion in C. One is *implicit* conversion (as shown in the previous example), the other is *explicit* conversion. This process is sometimes called *typecasting*.

Implicit Conversion

Implicit implies that the conversion is performed automatically. It is sometimes termed *coercion*. Consider the previous example with the roles reversed:

```
double x=6.0, y=4.0;
int div;

div = x / y;
```

The variable **div** acquires the value 1, because the right side of the assignment statement is a **double** expression, whereas the left side is an **int**. When **div** acquires the value, 1.5 is coerced to an integer, effectively truncating the fractional components. This behavior occurs anytime a comparison or assignment is performed. In the previous example, there is a loss of information in a conversion from type **double** to type **int** if the value of the expression x/y is larger than **div** can hold. Note that converting from an **int** to a **double** can also cause problems, due to the fact that floating point values are not capable of holding integer values precisely.

Explicit Conversion

In some situations we wish to force a conversion. This is the role of explicit conversion, sometimes known as *casting*. Consider the original example again, now containing a cast:

```
int x=6, y=4;
double div;

div = (double)x / y;
```

The cast here is the expression **(double)**, which is essentially a type enclosed in parentheses. This takes the value of the variable **x**, converts it to a **double**, then proceeds to perform the division operation, which is now effectively, 6.0/4, the result of which will be a floating point value. Now that the right side of the assignment statement is a **double**, the variable **div** can be assigned the value 1.5. The general form of a cast is:

```
(type) expression
```

This converts the value of the **expression** to a different type. However, we have to be careful how we formulate a cast. For example:

```
div = (double) (x / y);
```

This will result in the expression **(x/y)** being calculated first, resulting in a value of 1, as integer division is performed. This is the value converted to a **double**, so the result stored in **div** is 1.0. There are, of course, many valid ways of using casts:

```
div = (double)x / y;
div = x / (double)y;
div = (double)x / (double)y;
```

All give the same result.

Numerical Errors

All numbers are *not* created equal. Divide 1.0 by 3.0 on a calculator and you will get 0.33333333, depending on how many digits the display can handle. Multiply this by 3, and you invariably get 1.0. The same may or may not happen when programming; actually, more likely it will not happen. Integers are probably the most precise numeric datatype. When you compare two integers, they are either equal or not. They are discrete values and one differs from the other by exactly 1. In contrast to this, floating point numbers are not discrete, but continuous. As such they are subject to more "inadequacies" than integers. There are two basic forms of numerical error: *representational* errors and *computational* errors. Many of the problems encountered with numbers occur due to inadequacies in computation. Some of these are by no means restricted to floating point numbers. Keller[1] describes such an error in the NASA space shuttle software. A round-off in a floating point number propagated into a logical comparison of floating point values, which led to a robot arm falling into the wrong quadrant: 360–0.000001° instead of 360+0.000001°.

Why 1/3 + 1/3 + 1/3 ≠ 1.0?

One thing you have to remember is that not all numbers can be stored exactly using floating point representation. Consider the following example:

```
#include <stdio.h>

int main(void)
{
    double z,y;
    z = 1.0/3.0; /* one third */
    y = 1.0 — z — z — z; /* should be zero */
    printf("%20.18le\n",y);
    return 0;
}
```

The result is **1.110223024625156540e–16**. That's pretty close to zero, but not exactly zero! Now the result may be different depending on the computer on which it is run, but it's no surprise considering that 1.0/3.0 cannot be represented exactly as a floating point number. Now if you try:

```
y = 1.0 — 3 * z;
```

You will get zero.

---

[1]Keller, T. W., "Achieving error-free man-rated software," *International Software Testing Analysis and Review Conference*, 1993.

Some Numbers Are Precise, Others Just Aren't

That's just the way it is. For example, numbers such as 1/2 and 2/5 are precise. Indeed, *any* fraction with a denominator containing factors of 2 or 5 can be precisely represented. *All* others are imprecise. This is understandable for numbers such as 1/3, because the answer is 0.3333333 recurring infinitum. The more 3s you add to the end, the more accurate the approximation becomes. But it is still an approximation. Less easy to see with 1/10, because the answer here is 0.1. The problem lies not with the numbers themselves, but in the conversion to binary. All numbers have to be converted to binary in the inner workings of the CPU because that's how they are processed.

For example:

```
1/2=0.5, 1/5=0.2, 7/10=0.7, 9/20=0.45, 3/25=0.12
```

If the denominator contains some factor other than 2 or 5, then the number cannot be represented exactly in the decimal number system. For example:

```
1/3 = 0.3333 . . ., 1/7 = 0.142857 . . . . 1/24 =
0.041666. . ., 1/35 = 0.0285714 . . .
```

Unfortunately, most decimal fractions cannot be represented exactly as binary fractions. A consequence is that, in general, the decimal floating point numbers we enter are only approximated by the binary floating point numbers actually stored in the machine. Now 1/10 cannot be represented accurately because no matter how many base 2 digits you're willing to use, the decimal value 0.1 cannot be represented exactly as a base 2 fraction. In base 2, 1/10 is the infinitely repeating fraction

```
0.000110011001100110011001100110011001100110011 . . .
```

You can see a repeating base of **1001**. Stop at any finite number of bits, and you get an approximation. This is why we see things like:

```
0.10000000000000001 or 0.0999999999999998
```

The consequence of this is that summing ten values of 0.1, may not exactly yield 1.0:

```
int i;
double sum=0.0, frac;

frac = 1.0/10.0;
for (i=1; i<=10; i=i+1)
    sum = sum + frac;
printf("%f\n", sum);
```

This is extremely problematic when you try to compare such numbers. More on this later.

Conversion of Fractions Is a Binary Conundrum

Conversion to binary can be achieved by taking the fractional component, multiplying by 2 and taking the most significant bit. Repeat this until the remainder is zero. For example:

$$0.75_{10} \quad = ?_2$$
$$0.75 \times 2 \quad = 1.50 \rightarrow 1$$
$$0.50 \times 2 \quad = 1.00 \rightarrow 1$$
$$= 0.11_2$$

$$0.11_2 = ?_{10}$$
$$0.1 \quad = 2^{-1} + 2^{-2}$$
$$= 0.5 + 0.25$$
$$= 0.75_{10}$$

Not so nice for 0.3:

$$0.3_{10} \quad = ?_2$$
$$0.3 \times 2 = 0.6 \rightarrow 0$$
$$0.6 \times 2 = 1.2 \rightarrow 1$$
$$0.2 \times 2 = 0.4 \rightarrow 0$$
$$0.4 \times 2 = 0.8 \rightarrow 0$$
$$0.8 \times 2 = 1.6 \rightarrow 1$$

$$. . .$$
$$= 0.0100110011001 . . ._2$$

$$.010011001_2 = ?_{10}$$
$$= 0^{-1} + 2^{-2} + 0^{-3} + 0^{-4} + 2^{-5} + 2^{-6} + 0^{-7} + 0^{-8} + 2^{-9}$$
$$= \frac{1}{4} + \frac{1}{32} + \frac{1}{64} + \frac{1}{512}$$
$$= 0.298828125_{10}$$

Representational Error

The difference between the true value of a floating point number and its representation is termed *representational error*. Both **float** and **double** are representations for floating point numbers, but with differing degrees of precision. Consider the following code fragment:

```
double x;
float y;

x = 3.14159;
y = 3.14159;

if (x == y)
    printf("%f %f\n", x,y);
```

The result will be that nothing gets printed, because **x** and **y** have differing precision, and the equality operator == tests for exact equality. Another case of representational error occurs during computation. Consider this code fragment:

```
double x, y;

x = 1.0/3.0;
y = x + x + x;

if (y == 3.0)
    printf("Equal");
```

The question must now be asked as to how to determine whether two floating point numbers really are equal. As the previous example shows, even though we know that 1/3*3 should equal 1.0, the == operator tests for exact equality. Since floating point values may be imprecise, the operators == and != cannot be used effectively on **floats** and **doubles**. To get around this we actually have to calculate the difference of the two numbers and compare this value against a preset epsilon value. This is sometimes termed an *approximate comparison.* Let's rework the code fragment:

```
double epsilon = 1.0e-5;
double x,y;

x = 1.0/3.0;
y = x + x + x;

if (fabs(y-3.0) < epsilon)
    printf("Equal");
```

This **if**-statement basically calculates the absolute value of the difference using the floating point absolute value function **fabs,** and checks to see if this value is less than epsilon.

Accuracy versus Precision

Very few textbooks of any sort address these two issues. Yet when designing algorithms that use numbers, they are of prime importance. Precision represents *tightness of specification,* whereas accuracy represents *correctness.* The mirror for the Hubble space telescope was ground with great precision but was not accurate. The primary mirror had been ground to the wrong shape. The mirror was barely 2 micrometers out from the required shape, but the difference was catastrophic, introducing severe spherical aberration (one micrometer is 1×10^{-6}m).

Floating Point Precision

Precision can be simulated using the following code:

```
double x   = 20000.0;
double y   = 0.01;

x += y; /* adds 0.01 */
printf("x = %30.15lf\n",x);
y /= 100;
x += y; /* adds 0.0001 */
printf("x = %30.15lf\n",x);
y /= 100;
x += y; /* adds 0.000001 */
printf("x = %30.15lf\n",x);
y /= 100;
x += y; /* adds 0.00000001 */
printf("x = %30.15lf\n",x);
y /= 100;
x += y; /* adds 0.0000000001 */
```

```
printf("x = %30.15lf\n",x);
y /= 100;
x += y; /* adds 0.000000000001 */
printf("x = %30.15lf\n",x);
```

The results aren't quite what a mathematician would expect: We've got 15 significant digits of accuracy guaranteed by our compiler, but we've displayed the results to 20 significant figures. The last 5 should, of course, be regarded with suspicion. Notice that the final addition has made no difference to the stored number. Expected results are shown in parentheses.

```
x = 20000.009999999998399 (20000.01)
x = 20000.010099999999511 (20000.0101)
x = 20000.010100999999850 (20000.010101)
x = 20000.010101010000653 (20000.01010101)
x = 20000.010101010098879 (20000.0101010101)
x = 20000.010101010098879 (20000.010101010101)
```

Try doing the same operations using **float** instead of **double**. Here the number of significant digits is 6.

```
x = 20000.009999999776483 (20000.01)
x = 20000.009865624997474 (20000.0101)
x = 20000.009766625000339 (20000.010101)
x = 20000.009765635000804 (20000.01010101)
x = 20000.009765625098225 (20000.0101010101)
x = 20000.009765625000000 (20000.010101010101)
```

Every time you perform an arithmetic operation, you introduce an additional error of at least ε. Kernighan and Plauger sum this up quite nicely: "Floating point numbers are like piles of sand; every time you move one you lose a little sand and pick up a little dirt."[*]

Round-off Error

A *round-off error*, also called *rounding error*, is the difference between the calculated approximation of a number and its exact mathematical value. Round-off errors occur because our number crunching programs are often limited in the precision with which they represent the quantities used in numerical calculations. A good example is the use of π in calculations. Many times π is approximated as 3.14159, where the real value of π is 3.14159265358979323846 and on and on, which leads to an error of 0.00000265358979323846. That may not seem overly significant until we try to do complex calculations that rely on the value of π. Rounding errors occur because somewhere a numerical quantity is being rounded up or down. For example π might be round down at the fourth digit to 3.14, (because 1<5), or round up at the fifth digit to 3.1416 (because 5 >= 5). Here's another good example: Suppose we invest $1,000 at 5 percent interest, compounded daily. How much money will we end up with after 1 year? If the bank computes the value correctly, we should end up with $1051.27.

Using the program from Case Study 15 with $1000.0 at 5% interest for 1 year with 365 periods in the year we get:

```
$1051.2674964675
```

---

[*]Kernighan, B. W., Plauger, P. J. *The Elements of Programming Style*. McGraw-Hill, 1978, p. 117.

Suppose, instead, that the bank stores our balance as an integer (measured in pennies). At the end of each day, the bank calculates our interest and rounds the result to the nearest penny. Then the result is:

$1051.10

We have effectively been cheated out of 17 cents. The error of not storing the fractions of a penny accumulate and can eventually become significant, even fraudulent.

Truncation Error

A *truncation error* occurs when the number of digits right of the decimal point is reduced by discarding the least significant digits. For example if we truncate π to three decimal places we get the value 3.141. Truncation can be done using the **floor** or **trunc** (C99) functions, but it can also occur when a floating point number is coerced into an integer. For example:

```
double pi=3.14159, radius=2.0;
int area;
area = pi * radius * radius;
```

The right side of the expression evaluates to 12.56636. However, because **area** is an **int,** the value **12.56636** is truncated to **12** as it is assigned to **area.** Now let's go back to the interest example. Suppose instead the bank rounds down to the nearest penny at the end of each day, effectively truncating the number. Now the result is:

$1049.40

We have been cheated out of $1.87, which is even worse than rounding.

Catastrophic Cancellation

Catastrophic cancellation is an overwhelming loss of precision when small numbers are computed from large numbers by addition or subtraction. For example, consider the following snippet of code:

```
double x1 = 5.000000000000004;
double x2 = 5.000000000000000;
double y1 = 5.00000000000004;
double y2 = 5.00000000000000;
double z;

z = (y1 - y2) / (x1 - x2);

printf("%.10f", z);
```

When we actually run this program, we get a value of 9.0. That is not exactly the right answer. If we look at the separate components of z, we get

```
(y1-y2) = 0.0000000000003996803
(x1-x2) = 0.0000000000000444089
```

where the problems of loss of precision are real. Change the value of z to

```
z = (4.0/10000000000000.0)/(4.0/100000000000000.0);
```

and we actually get the real answer: 10.0. So subtraction is the culprit!

Successive Additions

A common task involves summing a series of values, which can lead to accumulated round-off error. The difficulty arises when small numbers are added onto an increasingly large partial sum. To understand this, consider the following code, which sums 0.001 ten thousand times using a **float** variable **sum**:

```
float sum = 0.0;
for (i=1; i<=10000; i=i+1)
    sum = sum + 0.001;
```

This gives us a result of 10.000411. The process produces more accurate results by calculating sub-sums and then adding these together. Consider instead calculating the sum of 50 groups of 200 values of 0.001:

```
float sum = 0.0, SBsum;
for (i=1; i<=50; i=i+1){
    SBsum = 0.0;
    for (j=1; j<=200; j=j+1)
        SBsum = SBsum + 0.001;
    sum = sum + SBsum;
}
```

This gives a result of 10.000009, which is smaller than the previous result.

Overflow and Underflow

The term *overflow* is used to denote a condition whereby the result of an operation becomes larger than the representation of the numeric type. This occurs for both integer and floating point types and is a condition that cannot be tagged by the compiler. Imagine that you have a very large number in "fluid" form in cylinder A, and you try to store the contents of this cylinder in a smaller cylinder B. Here cylinder A holds 230 digits, and cylinder B 45 digits. If you try to pour the entire number into cylinder B, eventually the "fluid" number would overflow cylinder B. This is essentially what occurs in memory.

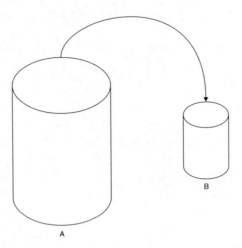

Integer Overflow

Computations that cause integer overflow are more common than not. When integer overflow does occur, it is most commonly noticed when the number presented is not exactly what is expected! Take for example the task of calculating a series of factorials, using **int** in the following code fragment:

```
int i, fact=1;
for (i=1; i<=20; i=i+1)
{
    fact = fact * i;
    printf("%d\n", fact);
}
```

On a 32-bit system **(INT_MAX = 2147483647)**, the following output is obtained:

```
 1     1
 2     2
 3     6
 4     24
 5     120
 6     720
 7     5040
 8     40320
 9     362880
10     3628800
11     39916800
12     479001600
13     1932053504
14     278945280
15     2004310016
16     2004189184
```

```
17   −288522240
18   −898433024
19   109641728
20   −2102132736
```

The problem lies that when 479001600 is multiplied by 13, the answer is 6227020800, which is larger than the maximum representation of an **int** (2147483647). The computation then actually cycles through the **INT_MAX** twice, with the remaining sum being 1932053504. The number is wrapped around, or "overflows." The program will, however, keep running with a faulty number that is not near being correct. To fix this problem, increase the representation for **fact** to **long long**. Now the results look like:

```
1
2    2
3    6
4    24
5    120
6    720
7    040
8    40320
9    362880
10   3628800
11   39916800
12   479001600
13   6227020800
14   87178291200
15   1307674368000
16   20922789888000
17   355687428096000
18   6402373705728000
19   121645100408832000
20   2432902008176640000
```

Floating Point Overflow

The notion of wrapping is unique to integers. Floating point numbers deal with overflow in a much more eloquent way. The IEEE floating point standard defines a special term, denotes **Inf**, which is short for infinity and results when overflow occurs. For example, if we change the factorial code fragment to use a **double**:

```
int i;
double fact=1.0;

for (i=1; i<=200; i=i+1)
{
    fact = fact * i;
    printf("%f\n", fact);
}
```

When we run this, we get a value of **Inf**.

Underflow

Underflow is the opposite of overflow. It occurs when the magnitude of a number falls below the smallest number that can be represented. This only occurs for floating point numbers.

To Infinity and Beyond

The term **Inf** does not actually mean the result is infinite. It simply means it is too large to represent, and this occurs fairly quickly with factorials because they grow extremely quickly. A value of **Inf** also occurs when a nonzero floating point number is divided by zero, or an attempt is made to calculate **log(0.0)**. In other situations, when no exact representation of a number exists, the term **NaN** is printed. **NaN** is short for "Not a Number." This can occur if zero is divided by zero, or an attempt is made to calculate the **sqrt(–1.0)** or **log(0.0)**.

Math Library Functions

Most programming languages provide some simple mathematical functions, not dissimilar to those found on a calculator. I suppose they figure you really wouldn't want to program these yourselves (but you could, of course!). The C math library is contained in the header file **math.h**. It contains the following standard functions:

Trigonometric	Log/e	Mathematical
acos	exp	fmod
asin	log	fabs
atan	log10	pow
atan2		sqrt
cos		modf
cosh		frexp
sin		ldexp
sinh		
tan		
tanh		

A program that makes use of the C math library would contain the statement:

```
#include <math.h>
```

Note that if you are using the **gcc** compiler, some versions of Unix require you to specify the –lm option when compiling. For example:

```
gcc –lm test.c
```

If you don't include it, the compiler goes nuts because it can't find the math library (which is odd because you have told it to use it, and it can find all the other libraries just fine!).

Trigonometric Functions

There is evidence that the Babylonians first used trigonometric functions, based on a table of numbers written on a Babylonian cuneiform tablet, Plimpton 322 (circa 1900 BC). Most modern programming languages provide a basic assortment of trigonometric functions. In C this includes the standard trigonometric functions:

```
cos(d)      cosine of d
sin(d)      sine of d
tan(d)      tangent of d
```

the inverse trigonometric functions:

```
acos(d)       arc cosine of d (in range 0 to pi)
asin(d)       arc sine of d (in range –π/2 to π/2)
atan(d)       arc tangent of d (in range –π/2 to π/2)
atan2(d1,d2)  arc tangent of d1/d2 (in range –π to π)
```

and the hyperbolic trigonometric functions:

```
cosh(d)       hyperbolic cosine of d (cosh)
sinh(d)       hyperbolic sine of d (sinh)
tanh(d)       hyperbolic tangent of d (tanh)
```

In the body of the program, a statement like

```
x = cos(y);
```

would cause the variable **x** to be assigned a value that is the cosine of the value of the variable **y**. With one exception **(atan2)**, all of these functions take a **double** argument and return a **double** result. The function **atan2** takes two **double** arguments.

What About These Crazy Radians?

Note that all the trigonometric and hyperbolic functions take a value in radians as input. A *radian* is a unit of plane angle, represented by the symbol **rad**. Basically $2\pi\text{rad} = 360°$, therefore:

$$\pi \text{ } radians = 180°$$

$$1 \text{ } radian = 57.2957795°$$

Strangely enough, C doesn't provide a function such as **deg2rad** to convert degrees to radians, but it is easy enough to do. You can achieve this using the following equations:

$$degrees = radians \cdot \frac{180°}{\pi} \qquad radians = degrees \cdot \frac{\pi}{180°}$$

Converting these two equations yields:

```
rad = (PI / 180.0) * deg;
deg = (180.0 / PI) * rad;
```

The conversion from degrees to radians can be achieved with following simple code:

```
printf("Enter a values in degrees: ");
scanf("%lf", &deg);
rad = (PI / 180.0) * deg;
printf("%.2f degrees is %.2f radians\n", deg, rad);
```

I Want to Create My Own Sine!

It takes all kinds, I suppose. If you don't trust the sine function provided by C, you can create your own. It's not really that hard. Just use the series:

$$\sin x = x - \frac{x^3}{3!} + \frac{x^5}{5!} - \frac{x^7}{7!} + \dots \sum_{n=0}^{\infty} \frac{(-1)^n x^{2n+1}}{(2n+1)!}$$

We might try to do this when we're doing loops. Of course, there are similar expressions for **cos** and **tan**.

How Many Logs Do We Need?

The following library functions deal with exponential and logarithmic calculations. Each of these functions returns a **double**. The three most commonly used functions in this category include:

`exp(d)`	exponential of d
`log(d)`	natural logarithm of d
`log10(d)`	logarithm (base 10) of d

Don't get the logarithmic functions confused—there are two of them. The first, the *natural* logarithm, usually represented by **ln**, is represented in C by:

```
z = log(x);
```

The *base 10* logarithm, usually represented by **log,** is represented in C by:

```
z = log10(x);
```

In both cases errors occur if x ≤ 0. Also the function e^x, where **e** is the base for natural logarithms, or approximately 2.718282, is represented in C by:

```
z = exp(x);
```

Don't get this confused with scientific notation (e.g., 3.3479e7 implies 3.3479×10^7).

Ceilings and Floors

These aptly named functions work to prune a floating point number. Both take a **double** as the arguments and return a **double** as the result.

```
ceil(d)        the smallest integer that is not less than d.
floor(d)       the largest integer that is less than, or equal to, d.
```

For example:

```
x = ceil(5.7);
```

results in *x* being assigned the value 6. Conversely:

```
x = floor(5.7);
```

results in *x* being assigned the value 5.

Mathematical Functions

The remaining mathematical functions are just the simple ones:

`fabs(d)`	Returns the absolute value of d (double)
`abs(d)`	Returns the absolute value of d (int)
`pow(x,y)`	Returns x raised to the power y
`sqrt(d)`	Returns the square root of d
`modf(x,&y)`	Splits a floating point value into integer (y) and fractional parts
`frexp(x,y)`	Breaks down a floating point value into mantissa and exponent
`ldexp(x,y)`	Creates a floating point value from the mantissa (x) and exponent (y)
`fmod(x,y)`	Returns the remainder of two floating point values

sqrt

Calculates the square root of a number. For example:

```
z = sqrt(2.0);
```

This calculates $\sqrt{2.0}$, which is 1.414214.

pow

In most programming languages the ^ (caret) symbol is used to "raise the power to," as in 2^10. This is not so in C. Instead, you can use the **pow** function. For example:

```
z = pow(2.0,10.0);
```

This raises the value 2 to the power of 10, which is the exponent. The result is stored in the double variable z=1024.0.

Is **sqrt(x)** the same as **pow(x,0.5)**? Yes, but they differ in the time it takes to perform the calculation. If we perform one million of each, **sqrt(x)** will take 0.125 seconds, whereas **pow(x,0.5)** takes 0.546 seconds. I know, you're going to say that it's about a significant a difference as the timing in the Olympics. True, but over billions of calculations it does make a difference. More about this later.

abs & fabs

The absolute value of a number is its positive value. For example,

```
z = abs(-19);
```

produces the value 19. However, try this with a floating point number and you will get gibberish returned. Finding the absolute value of a floating point number is achieved analogously using the **fabs** function.

modf

The **modf** function effectively splits a floating point number into its whole number and fractional parts. For example,

```
zf = modf(5.7,&zi);
```

returns 5.0 in **zi** and assigns the value 0.7 to the variable **zf**.

fmod

The **fmod** function (not to be confused with **modf**) effectively operates in the same way for floating point numbers as % works for integers. For example,

```
z = fmod(5.7,2.3);
```

returns the value 1.1, as 2.3 fits into 5.7 twice, with a remainder of 1.1.

frexp & ldexp

Two lesser known exponential functions are **frexp** and **ldexp**. The function **frexp** breaks down a floating point value into mantissa and exponent and has the following form:

```
z = frexp(x,&e);
```

It takes two arguments, the first a **double**, the second a pointer to an **int**. The function converts x into a fraction multiplied by a power of 2. The fractional part is returned by the function, the exponential value is stored in the object pointed to by **e**. The function **ldexp** creates a floating point value from the mantissa (x) and exponent (e) and has the following form:

```
z = ldexp(x,e);
```

It takes two arguments, the first a **double**, the second an **int**. The function multiplies x by 2 to the power of **e**.

C99 Functions

The latest specification for C, C99, has included a multitude of new math functions:

```
acosh, asinh, atanh, exp2, expm1, ilogb, log1p, log2,
logb, scalbn, scalbln, cbrt, hypot, erf, erfc, lgamma,
tgamma, nearbyint, rint, lrint, llrint, round, lround,
llround, trunc, remainder, remquo, copysign, nan,
nextafter, nexttoward, fdim, fmax, fmin, fma
```

Here's a brief overview of the more useful ones:

`exp2(d)`	Calculates 2 raised to the power of d `z = exp2(8.0);` Yields z = 256
`cbrt(d)`	Calculates the cube-root of d. `z = cbrt(8.0);` Yields z = 2.0
`hypot(x,y)`	Calculates the hypotenuse, or $\sqrt{x^2 + y^2}$ `z = hypot(3.0,4.0);` Yields z = 5.0
`round(d)`	Rounds a floating point number to the nearest integer. `z = round(3.14159);` Yields z = 3.0
`trunc(d)`	Truncates a floating point number. `z = trunc(5.895784);` Yields z = 5.0
`fdim(x,y)`	Calculates the positive difference between x and y. `z = fdim(5.6,3.7);` Yields z = 1.9
`fmax(d)`	Returns the largest value of x and y. `z = fmax(5.6,3.7);` Yields z = 5.6
`fmin(d)`	Returns the smallest value of x and y. `z = fmin(5.6,3.7);` Yields z = 3.7

Classification macros include:

```
fpclassify, isfinite, ifinf, isnan, isnormal, signbit
```

Comparison macros include:

```
isgreater, isgreaterequal, isless, islessequal, isless-
greater, isunordered.
```

I'm not going to delve into the intricacies of these here. Just know that they exist and you can use them. It is best to check specific compiler documentation.

Need a Piece of π?

Some books make explicit mention of the constant defined for π in **math.h: M_PI**. That constant is not standard, so it may not actually exist. If you need pi, you'll have to define it yourself, or compute it with 4atan(1.0) or acos(−1.0).

```
#define PI 3.141592653589793238
```

Epilog

Numbers are inherently powerful, but have to be used with caution. Remember, integers are precise, but floating point numbers are not inherently so.

Exercises

Exercise 9.1

Write a program to do each of the following:

Sum (1.0/10.0) 10 times.

Sum (1.0/100.0) 1 hundred times.

Sum (1.0/1000.0) 1 thousand times.

Sum (1.0/10000.0) 10 thousand times.

Sum (1.0/1000000.0) 1 million times.

Here is some code to use, where **N** is the number of times the loop should iterate:

```
double sum=0.0;
for (i=1; i<=N; i=i+1)
      sum = sum + (1.0/N);
```

How close are the results to unity? Why are some results not exact?

Exercise 9.2

German mathematician and scientist Carl Friedrich Gauss (1777–1855) first presented an algorithm for calculating the date of Easter Sunday in 1800. He used the following equations:

$a = y \bmod 19$

$b = y \bmod 4$

$c = y \bmod 7$

where *y* denotes the year, and the function **mod**, the remainder of integer division. Then calculate

$d = (19a + m) \bmod 30$

$e = (2b + 4c + 6d + n) \bmod 7$

For the Julian calendar (used in Eastern churches), $m = 15$ and $n = 6$. For the Gregorian calendar (used in Western churches), *m* and *n* are calculated as follows:

$k = \text{floor}(y\ /\ 100)$

$p = \text{floor}((13 + 8k)\ /\ 25)$

$q = \text{floor}(k\ /\ 4)$

If $d + e < 10$, then Easter is on the $(d + e + 22)^{th}$ of March, and otherwise on the $(d + e - 9)^{th}$ of April. The following exceptions must be taken into account for the Gregorian calendar:

- If $d = 29$ and $e = 6$, replace April 26 with April 19.
- If $d = 28$, $e = 6$, and $a>10$, replace April 25 with April 18.

Write a program to calculate the date of Easter, given the Gregorian year.

Exercise 9.3

Deflection is the physical sagging or deformation of a beam under load.

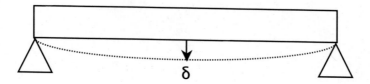

The maximum (midspan) deflection for a beam simply supported at the ends can be expressed using the following equation:

$$\delta_{max} = \frac{5wl^4}{384EI}$$

where

δ is the maximum deflection (*m, mm, in*)
w is the uniform load (*N/m, N/mm, lb/in*)
l is the length of the beam (*m, mm, in*)
E is the modulus of electricity (*Pa [N/m², N/mm², psi*)
I is the moment of inertia (*m⁴, mm⁴, in⁴*)

Note that the variables are given with three sets of units. Write a program to calculate the maximum deflection in a beam. Test your program by calculating the maximum deflection of a wooden joist (southern pine, $E = 1,400,000$ psi), with the following criteria: A 2 × 12 ($I = 178$ in.^{4}) floor joist that spans 16ft (192 in.); a live load of 40 psf, a dead load of 10 psf, and 16-in. joint spacing.

$$\delta = \frac{5w(192)^4}{(384)(1400000)(178)} = 0.071w$$

$$40\text{psf}/144\text{in}^2 = 0.277\text{psi}$$

The joints are spaced at 16 in. so each joist carries the load of a 16-in. width of floor. The applied load of each joist is then 16 × 0.277 = 4.44 lb/in. Therefore, the maximum deflection is

$$0.071 \times 4.44 = 0.315 \text{ inches}$$

Write a program to calculate the maximum midspan deflection of a beam.

10

Time to Make a Decision
Avoid unnecessary branches.
—Kernighan and Plauger

Introduction

Humans make decisions on a daily basis. Systems must also make decisions, albeit in the guise of algorithms. Decision, selection, or conditional statements, as they are often referred to, are the basic logical structures of programming. A conditional statement resembles a fork in the road. There are at least two paths that may be taken and one must be chosen. Take, for example, a navigation system on a robot investigating inaccessible nuclear reactors. If a robot encounters an obstacle, then it might stop to consider its prospects for movement. We could formulate a decision statement in pseudocode of the form:

```
IF an obstacle is encountered
     THEN stop
```

We could also include the case where there is no obstacle:

```
IF an obstacle is encountered
     THEN stop
     ELSE keep moving forward
```

This statement allows the robot to perform one of the actions, but not both, which would be infeasible unless the robot were capable of cloning or splitting itself. The basic construct of this statement first checks to see if an obstacle exists. If this condition is satisfied, then the robot stops. Otherwise, if the condition is not satisfied, the robot continues moving. Are there more alternatives for the robot than just stopping? The robot could turn left, turn right, or turn around and go back. Now there are three decisions to be made, but a basic if-statement only allows two choices. This is where some form of nested decision statement makes sense.

```
IF an obstacle is encountered AND the left is clear
     THEN turn robot left
```

161

```
ELSE IF an obstacle is encountered AND the right is clear
      THEN turn robot right
ELSE backtrack the robot
```

Decision statements answer questions, and all but the simplest programs have some form of decision making involved. There is no *maybe* in programming. C has two decision statements: the **if** statement and the **switch** statement.

if Statement

The **if** statement is the simplest form of conditional statement used in C (or any other language for that matter). The idea of a conditional statement in the form **IF THEN ELSE**, was introduced in ALGOL 60. It is a branching or selection statement because it provides a junction within the program. In C, the **if** statement is often termed an **if-else** statement, with the **else** portion dealing with an alternative to the desired solution. The general syntax of the **if** statement is:

```
if (expr)
     statement;
```

This is a one-way, or *unary* decision. If the *expr* evaluates to nonzero (true), the statement is executed. Otherwise it is skipped. The statement can either be a single statement or a single compound statement or block. The meaning, or semantics, of this **if** statement is as follows:

> If the expression is true, execute the statement; otherwise pass control to the statement *after* the if statement.

The flow diagram for an if statement is given as follows:

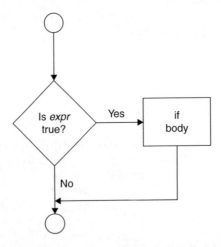

Consider the following example:

```
if (a_number % 2 == 0)
     printf("%d is an even number\n", a_number);
```

Here the **printf** statement is executed if the remainder of **a_number** divided by 2 is 0.

 We can use the **&&** operator to test for ranges. For example, to test that a variable **perc** is in the range 0 to 100, we could write:

```
if (perc >= 0 && perc <= 100)
```

Or we can also check for outliers. For example, to test that a variable **perc** is outside the range 0 to 100, we would use the **||** operator:

```
if (perc < 0 || perc > 100)
```

if-else Statement

If we wanted to provide an alternative, we could use a *binary* decision of the form:

```
if (expr)
    statement1;
else
    statement2;
```

If the *expr* evaluates to nonzero (true), **statement1** is executed. If *expr* is false (0) **statement2**, following the **else**, is executed. The statements can again be simple or compound. Note if we want to use more than one statement between the **if** and **else**, we must enclose it in a compound statement. The flow diagram for an **if-else** statement looks like this:

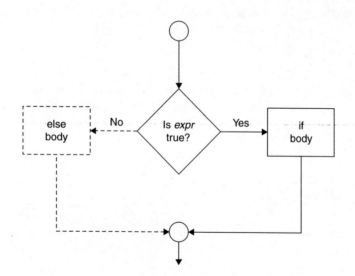

The meaning of this **if** statement is as follows:

```
If the expression is true, execute the code statement1; oth-
erwise, pass control to the code in statement2.
```

Returning to the example of expressions to determine whether a number is even, we elaborate on designing an **if** statement to print out whether a number is even or odd.

```
if ((a_number % 2) == 0)
    printf("%d is an even number\n", a_number);
else
    printf("%d is an odd number\n", a_number);
```

This simple **if-else** statement first determines if a remainder occurs when **a_number** is divided by 2. If there is no remainder, a message states that the number is even, otherwise, another message states it is odd.

Both the **if** and the **else** parts of the **if-else** statement permit a single statement. However, it is possible that this statement can be a single compound statement. For this we use the following syntax:

```
if (expr)
{
    statement1;
    statement2;
    statement3;
}
else
    statement4;
```

Notice that semicolons *do not* go after the curly braces that end the **if** part. Notice also how we used indentation to make the structure of the statement more clear.

Nested `if-else` Statement

As we have already seen, an **if** statement can contain simple or compound statements. Any valid C statement can be used, including other **if-else** statements. The inclusion of one or more **if** statements within an existing **if** statement is called a *nested* **if** statement. The concept of *nested* structures is derived from the Matryoshka doll, a Russian nested set of dolls of decreasing sizes placed one inside another.

```
if (expr1)
    if (expr2)
        if (expr3)
            statement1;
```

This code basically says if **cond1** is true, then if **cond2** is true, then if **cond3** is true, perform **statement1**. There is, of course, another way of writing this, using logical operators:

```
if (expr1 && expr2 && expr3)
    statement1;
```

Dangling Else

The *dangling* **else** is a well-known problem in many programming languages, where a well-defined structure becomes ambiguous. Consider the two pieces of code:

```
if (expr1)
    if (expr2)
        statement1;
    else
        statement2;
if (expr1)
    if (expr2)
        statement1;
else

    statement2;
```

Both of these code fragments are essentially the same. Remember, C does not use indentation to demarcate programming structure, so the indentation is irrelevant as far as the compiler is concerned. Whether the indentation exists or not, the **if** statement is compiled by associating the *last* **else** with the closest unpaired **if**. So the code in fragment 1 represents the actual syntax interpreted by C. If the intent was the code in fragment 2, then it must be rewritten. The addition of a compound statement associates the **else** statement with the first **if** statement.

```
if (expr1){
    if (expr2)
        statement1;
}
else
    statement2;
```

if-else Chain

There are situations where a value must to be checked against a series of values, with corresponding actions taken. This form of a nested **if** statement is referred to as an **if-else** *chain*. Each condition is evaluated in order, and for the first statement that is true, the corresponding statement is executed. The remaining statements in the chain are bypassed. The last statement is effectively the default statement.

```
if (expr1)
    statement1;
else if (expr2)
    statement2;
else if (expr3)
    statement3;
```

```
else if (expr4)
    statement4;
else
    statement5;
```

if and && Equivalents

Using a range such as:

```
if ((i >= 0) && (i <= 100))
    printf("valid percentage");
```

is equivalent to

```
if (i >= 0)
    if (i <= 100))
        printf("valid percentage");
```

Of course, it doesn't work so well if there is an **else** statement:

```
if ((i >= 0) && (i <= 100))
    printf("valid percentage");
else
    printf("percentage is not valid");
```

is equivalent to

```
if (i >= 0)
    if (i <= 100))
        printf("valid percentage");
    else
        printf("percentage is not valid");
else
    printf("percentage is not valid");
```

e.g. Even/Odd Numbers

There is one caveat with the even/odd numbers example, and it involves a third state, which illustrates that sometimes you have to delve a little deeper to uncover all the modes of a solution. What happens when **a_number** equals 0? Is zero an even number? By default it is, because 0 divided by 2 results in a remainder of 0. However, we may wish to expand the decision statement to account for this mode. A sample solution is:

```
if (a_number == 0)
    printf("%d is zero\n",a_number);
else if ((a_number % 2) == 0)
    printf("%d is an even number\n", a_number);
else
    printf("%d is an odd number\n", a_number);
```

Notice that our check to identify if **a_number** is zero is the first portion of the **if-else** tower. This way the problem of zero is dealt with first. If we were to put this statement last, for example,

```
if ((a_number % 2) == 0)
    printf("%d is an even number\n", a_number);
else if ((a_number % 2) == 1)
    printf("%d is an odd number\n", a_number);
else
    printf("%d is zero\n",a_number);
```

the logic would fall into the trap of again acknowledging that zero is an even number, because the first expression is the first that evaluates to true. The default else is never reached, and hence becomes what is known as *unreachable code*. Regardless of whether a number is odd, even, or zero, the program will never execute the last **printf** statement.

Avoid the use of unnecessary branches. Don't write code like this:

```
if (a_number % 2 == 0)
    printf("The number is even");
else
    ;
```

The **else** statement and the accompanying semicolon are *superfluous*, a fancy word for *not needed*.

`switch` Statement

The **switch** statement provides an alternative to the **if-else** chain for cases that compare the value of an integer expression to a specific value. It began its life in the **case** statements of Pascal.

```
switch (expr)
{
    case lab1: statement1;
    case lab2: statement2;
    case lab3: statement3;
    case lab4: statement4;
    ...
    case labn: statementn;
    default: default_statement;
}
```

Here the value of *expr* is matched against each case label *(labx)*. If a given **case** is matched, control is transferred to the first statement after the label. As with **if** statements, the **statement** can be either a single statement or a compound statement. Notice that the body of the **switch** statement is a compound statement. This is how the switch statement works:

1. Evaluate a **switch** expression.
2. Go to the **case** label having a constant value that matches the value of the expression found in step 1. If a match is not found, go to the **default** label; if there is no **default** label, terminate the **switch.**
3. Terminate the **switch** when a **break** is encountered, or by "falling off the end."

The **default** statement performs some standard action when none of the labels match. The flow diagram looks like:

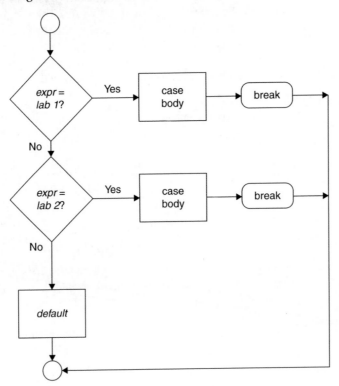

How to Break `switch`

Here is a silly example (silly because we probably wouldn't write code that looks like this):

```
1    switch (a_number)
2    {
3         case 0:printf("even");
4         case 1:printf("odd");
5         case 2:printf("even");
6         case 3:printf("odd");
7         case 4:printf("even");
8    }
```

If the value of **a_number** is 2, then control is passed to "case 2" and the word **"even"** is printed out. But there is a *side effect* here. What actually gets printed is:

```
even odd even
```

This is because of something called *falling-through*, or *follow-through*. This code doesn't have any way of stopping control going to the next statement, so when it finishes printing **even**, it flows through to the code on line 6, ignores the case label, and prints **odd**, then to the code on line 7, which prints **even**. To stop this from happening we have to use a **break** statement after each line. This passes control to the next statement *after* the **switch**. For example, rewriting the previous code gives:

```
1    switch (a_number)
2    {
3         case 0:printf("even");
4              break;
5         case 1:printf("odd");
6              break;
7         case 2:printf("even");
8              break;
9         case 3:printf("odd");
10             break;
11        case 4:printf("even");
12   }
```

Notice that the last **case** doesn't need a **break** because it is the last statement in the **switch**. Also note that although there are two statements after each **case** label, they do not have to be enclosed in a compound statement. **break** *is a part of* **switch**. Another way of writing this using a **switch** statement would be:

```
1    switch (a_number)
2    {
3         case 0: ;
4         case 2: ;
5         case 4:printf("even");
6              break;
7         case 1: ;
8         case 3:printf("odd");
9    }
```

Here we have actually used the *falling-though* to our advantage. Regardless of whether **a_number** has a value of 0, 2, or 4, it prints **"even"** and then passes control to the next statement after the **break**. The single semicolon (empty statement) on lines 3 and 4 allows falling-through to the statement on line 5. The empty statement on line 7 flows though to the statement on line 8. This code illustrates a point, but it may be better to use the code defined using the **if** statement.

Where **switch** Doesn't Work

We can't use a **switch** statement if our choice is based on evaluating a floating point variable or expression. Nor can we use a **switch** for ranges. For example, it is easy to use:

```
if (perc >= 0 && perc <= 100)
```

However, using a **switch** would involve setting up case labels for each integer in the range 0 to 100. It would look like this:

```
switch (perc)
{
    case 0: ;
    case 1: ;
    case 2: ;
    case 3: ;
    ...
    case 100: statement;
}
```

Whoa! That's not really great coding.

Ordered Numbers

This code snippet determines if three numbers are in a given order—that is, if they are ordered or sorted. The numbers are considered ordered if they increase in value or decrease in value. For example the set {9,17,23} are ordered, {4, 37, 19} are not. If two numbers are equal, they are always considered ordered. Let the three numbers be represented by *a*, *b*, and *c*. First compare *a* and *b*. If they are equal, then the set is ordered, regardless of the value of *c*. For example, {9,9,17} and {23,23,8} are both ordered. If *a* does not equal *b*, we compare *b* and *c*. If *b* bears the relation to *c*, that *a* bears to *b*, the set is ordered. Furthermore, if all three numbers are equal, then the set is always ordered.

The algorithm can be described as:

1. If $a = b \rightarrow$ the set is ordered
2. If $a > b$ and $b >= c$, the set is ordered.
3. If $a > b$ and $b < c$, the set is not ordered.
4. If $a < b$ and $b <= c$ the set is ordered.
5. If $a < b$ and $b > c$, the set is not ordered.

Now here's the equivalent coded using a series of **if** statements:

```
if (a == b)
    ordered = 1;
if (a > b && b >= c)
    ordered = 1;
```

```
if (a < b && b <= c)
    ordered = 1;
if (a > b && b <= c)
    ordered = 0;
if (a < b && b >= c)
    ordered = 0;
```

That is all very nice, but there is a shorter and more convenient way of writing this:

```
if ((a == b) || (a > b && b >= c) ||
                (a < b && b <= c))
    ordered = 1;
else
    ordered = 0;
```

 ## = instead of ==

One of the most common coding errors that occurs with **if** statements in C is the use of an assignment operator, =, in place of the relational operator ==. Unfortunately, the use of an assignment operator will not flag an error, partially because *any* expression can be used in an **if-else** statement. For example, consider the statement:

```
if (divisor = 0)
    result = 0;
else
    result = number / divisor;
```

This statement always results in a value of number/divisor being generated, regardless of the initial value of the variable **divisor**. The reason is that divisor is set to zero, which is false in C, so the statement associated with the else is invoked. Even when divisor's value is zero, the statement associated with the *if* is never invoked. The correct expression to determine the value in **divisor** is:

```
if (divisor == 0)
    result = 0;
else
    result = number / divisor;
```

 ## Humidity

Let's look at the case study on calculating the humidex. You may wonder why we care about humidity? Well, the body attempts to maintain a constant temperature of 37° C at all times. In hot weather, the body produces sweat, which cools the body as it evaporates. As the humidity or the moisture content in the air increases, sweat does not evaporate as readily. Sweat evaporation stops entirely when the relative humidity reaches about 90 percent. Under these circumstances, the body temperature rises. The Weather Service of Environment Canada uses humidex numbers to inform the public when conditions of heat and humidity are possibly uncomfortable. Environment Canada provides the following guide as a measure of discomfort according to humidex:

Humidex Range	Degree of Comfort
20–29° C	*comfortable*
30–39° C	*some discomfort*
40–45° C	*intense discomfort*
above 45° C	*dangerous discomfort*
above 54° C	*heat stroke imminent*

Let's see if we can incorporate some feedback on these measures into our program using an **if** statement. Basically we have been given ranges to work with and a message associated with each range. We can use an **if-else** chain of the form:

```
if (humidex >= 20 && humidex <= 29)
    printf("It is comfortable.\n");
else if (humidex >= 30 && humidex <= 39)
    printf("There is some discomfort.\n");
else if (humidex >= 40 && humidex <= 45)
    printf("There is intense discomfort.\n");
else if (humidex > 45 && humidex <= 54)
    printf("There is dangerous discomfort.\n");
else if (humidex > 54)
    printf("Heat stroke is imminent.\n");
```

(e.g.) The Quadratic Equation

Now we can look at the final bit of the quadratic equation program, which deals with calculating the roots. Remember what the pseudocode looked like:

```
IF a is zero
    IF b is zero x and y
        OUTPUT "no roots"
    ELSE
        CALCULATE Le = —c/b
        OUTPUT Le
    ENDIF
ELSE
    CALCULATE D = b² — 4ac
    CALCULATE S =   SQRT(ABS(D))
    CALCULATE A = 2a
    IF D is less than zero
```

```
        CALCULATE realx = –b/A
        CALCULATE imagx = S/A

        OUTPUT realx, imagx
    ELSE IF D is zero
        CALCULATE root = –b/A
        OUTPUT root
    ELSE IF D is greater than   zero
        CALCULATE root1 =     (–b+S)/A
        CALCULATE root2 =     (–b–S)/A
        OUTPUT root1, root2
    ENDIF
ENDIF
```

This is what we now have to translate into C.

```c
if (a == 0)
    if (b == 0)
        printf("No roots\n");
    else {
        root = –c / b;
        printf("Linear equation: root = %.2f\n", root);
    }
else {
    A = 2 * a;
    disc = b * b – 4 * a * c;
    sroot = sqrt(fabs(disc));

    if (disc < 0) {
        xreal = –b / A;
        ximag = sroot / A;
        printf("Complex roots: root1 = %.2f+%.2fi\n",
                xreal, ximag);
        printf("                root2 = %.2f–%.2fi\n",
                xreal,  ximag);
    }
    else if (disc == 0) {
        root = –b / A;
        printf("Single root = %.2f\n", root);
    }
    else {
        root1 = (–b + sroot) / A;
        root2 = (–b + sroot) / A;
        printf("Real roots: root1 = %.2f\n", root1);
        printf("             root2 = %.2f\n", root2);
    }
}
```

The core algorithm outlined in the pseudo-code uses a series of nested **if-else** statements. The first **if-else** statement deals with whether or not a is zero. If **a = 0**, then control is passed to another **if-else** pairing, to check whether or not b is zero. If **b = 0**, then there are no roots; otherwise (a = 0, b ≠ 0), there is a single root. If **a ≠ 0**, then the discriminant (**disc**) is calculated and checked using an **if-else** chain. If the value of **disc** is less than zero, the roots are complex; if the value of **disc** is equal to zero, there is a single root; otherwise (the default value is greater than zero), there are two real roots. The result is a tiered group of **if-else** structures and associated compound statements.

So now when we run the whole program, this is what the output looks like:

```
Finding quadratic roots.
Enter the values of a, b, and c: 2 4 −30
Equation: 2.00 x² + 4.00 x + −30.00 = 0
Real roots: root1 = 3.00
            root2 = 3.00
```

Epilog

The syntax of an **if** statement doesn't really change much in other languages. There always has to be a way to make decisions. The **switch** statement in C is often harder to use. One would question whether it would be useful at all without the **break** statement. That aside, it would be more functional if it allowed ranges of integers.

Exercises

Exercise 10.1

The relationship between energy release rate and the average flame height (the point at which the top of the flame exists 50 percent of the time) is given by the following equation:

$$HRR = \frac{79.18 H_f^{5/2}}{k}$$

where HRR is the energy release rate in kilowatts, H_f is the flame height in metres, and k is the wall effect factor. For example, $k = 1$ when there are no nearby walls, $k = 2$ when the fuel package is at a wall, and $k = 4$ when the fuel package is in a corner.

For example, in the centre of a room with a flame height of 2 m:

$$HRR = \frac{79.18 \times 2.0^{5/2}}{1.0}$$

So the energy release rate is 447.91 kilowatts. The same fire against a wall is

$$HRR = \frac{79.18 \times 2.0^{5/2}}{2.0}$$

Here the energy release rate is 223.95 kilowatts. Write a program that calculates the energy released from a fire given the flame height and wall effect factor. Prompt the user with choices for the wall effect factor and set the variable **wall_effect** to the appropriate value.

Exercise 10.2

Extend the Easter Sunday program of Exercise 9.2 to allow the user to choose between Gregorian or Julian calendars.

Exercise 10.3

As temperatures fall and the wind begins to howl, we begin hearing about the dangers of "wind chill." The wind chill factor, W, is reported by meteorologists during winter. W is an equivalent temperature that accounts for the increased chilling effects of wind on a human body. The wind chill factor combines the temperature and wind speed to tell you how cold the wind makes it "feel." In 2001, a new formula was derived, based on a model of how fast a human face loses heat and incorporates modern heat transfer theory—that is, the theory of how much heat is lost by the body to its surroundings during cold and windy days (the face is the part of the body most often exposed to severe winter weather). It must be noted that although the wind chill factor is expressed on a temperature scale, it is not a temperature; it expresses a human sensation. There are two formulas used by Environment Canada:

1. $W = 13.12 + 0.6215T_{air} - 11.37V_{10m}^{0.16} + 0.3965T_{air}V_{10m}^{0.16}$

2. $W = T_{air} + [(-1.59 + 0.1345T_{air})/5]V_{10m}$

where W is the wind chill factor based on the Celsius temperature scale, T_{air} is the air temperature in degrees Celsius, and V_{10m} is the wind speed in km/h at 10 meters. The first equation is used when the temperature of the air is $\leq 0°C$ and the wind speed is ≥ 5 km/h. Then second equation is used when the temperature of the air is $0°C$ and the wind speed is > 0 km/h, but < 5 km/h.

Write a program to calculate the wind chill, prompting the user to provide the wind speed and air temperature and applying the appropriate equation.

11

Going Loopy

Endless Loop: n., see Loop, Endless.

Loop, Endless: n., see Endless Loop.

—Random Shack Data Processing Dictionary

Introduction

Humans are, by nature, repetitive beings. Watch the *Star Trek: The Next Generation* episode "Cause and Effect," and you will quickly understand what a loop is as the Enterprise is caught in a causality time loop. There are also times when programs must do a task more than once. If the repetition is limited to some countable number of recurrences with a foreseeable end, it is called a *loop*. And if, at least in the perception of the individual who is experiencing a certain situation, there is no end in sight, then one is talking about endless or infinite loops. All of the above can be desirable or not. There are many reasons for using a loop in an algorithm:

1. Doing something more than once
2. Interactive input within a loop (e.g., summing *n* input numbers)
3. Selection within a loop (even/odd)
4. Evaluating functions with different parameters (square-root, temperature)
5. Calculating a series (e.g., Fibonacci)
6. Making choices from menus

What Is a Loop?

A *loop* is a programming structure that allows a program to repeat a group of statements any number of times or until some loop condition occurs. A loop is useful, because we don't want to have to write the same statement multiple times. Consider the following example, whereby we are summing the first 10 odd numbers:

```
int sum = 0;
sum = sum + 1;
```

```
sum = sum + 3;
sum = sum + 5;
sum = sum + 7;
sum = sum + 9;
sum = sum + 11;
sum = sum + 13;
sum = sum + 15;
sum = sum + 17;
sum = sum + 19;
```

This is somewhat tedious. Imagine how wearisome it would become if we had to do this with the first 1,000 odd numbers, or the first 1,000,000? Consider then the alternative using a loop:

```
int i, sum = 0;
for (i=1; i<=19; i=i+2)
    sum = sum + i;
```

Now the task is achieved in two lines instead of ten. And if we want to change the number of odd numbers to sum, we just have to change one term in the loop. Say we want to sum the first 1,000 odd numbers instead. All we have to do is change the 19 to 1,999. So instead of using 1,000 lines of code, we are still using only two.

Iterative Refinement

Some problems are *iterative*. By this we mean that an answer is derived through a process of refinement. Start with an initial estimate and continue refining the solution until an optimum value is reached. Consider the problem of calculating the square root of a positive number. The iterative formula for this process is given by:[1]

$$x_{i+1} = \frac{1}{2}\left(x_i + \frac{A}{x_i}\right) \tag{1}$$

where x_i is the ith estimate of the square root of A, which is a positive number. An initial estimate x_1 is made of $\sqrt{A}$, and a new estimate x_2 is calculated from the formula. The process continues until a sufficiently accurate value is derived. The accuracy can be tested by comparing its square with A. When the difference is less than a tolerance E, the iteration can stop. The difference can defined by:

$$D = \left|A - (x_i)^2\right| \tag{2}$$

The value i in the formula is termed an *index* value.

1. Assign an initial value for the index, $i=1$
2. Assign an initial estimate to x_i.

---

[1]Sherman, P. M., *Techniques in Computer Programming*, Prentice Hall, 1970.

3. Perform the calculation specified by Eq. 1, calculating x_{i+1}
4. Increment the index, $i = i + 1$
5. Calculate the difference, D, using Eq. 2. If $D >= E$, continue to step 2. Otherwise, stop.

This is an excellent example of iteration. If a task involves iteration, it means loops.

The Basic Elements

A loop has three basic elements:

1. A loop initialization
2. A loop body, where the index is modified
3. A loop continuation condition

A loop is controlled by a variable called a *loop index,* or control variable. As you will see, most loop indices have simple identifiers associated with them. Good examples include **i, j,** and **k.** Now you'll wonder that they aren't very descriptive, but that's okay. Since they may be used in many places in a loop, it's nice to keep them simple. For example if you decided to use a loop index called **loop_index** in a **for** loop it would look like:

```
for (loop_index=1; loop_index<=100; loop_index0++)
```

It is much less confusing and more readable to simply use **i:**

```
for (i=1; i<=100; i++)
```

In C there are three forms of loops: **for, while,** and **do-while.**

How Do I Know When I Need a Loop?

We commonly encounter two types of loops when we want to repeat something: counting loops and conditional loops. *Counting loops* are used when it can be determined before loop execution how many loop repetitions will be needed. *Conditional loops* are used when a loop should be repeated until a desired condition is met. You can use the following algorithm to determine if you need a loop:

```
IF any steps in the algorithm are repeated.
    THEN
        IF the number of times is known
           THEN use a counting loop
           ELSE use a conditional loop
        ENDIF
    ELSE no loop is required
ENDIF
```

`for` Loop

The quintessential loop in C (and many languages for that matter) is the **for** loop. It is used in situations where the number of passes through a loop is known in advance. The general form of a **for** loop is:

```
for (expr1; expr2; expr3)
    statement;
```

where **expr1** is used to initialize some parameter (the control variable, or index) that controls the looping action, **expr2** represents a condition that must be true for the loop to continue execution, and **expr3** is used to modify the value of the control variable initially assigned by **expr1**. The semantics of a **for** loop are as follows: First **expr1** is assessed, and the loop index is initialized. Next **expr2** is evaluated. If the expression evaluates to zero, the **for** loop is exited and control is passed to the statement following the **for** loop. If **expr2** is nonzero, **statement** is executed. After **statement** is executed, **expr3** is evaluated. This is normally some form of index modification. The **for** statement then loops back to evaluate **expr2** again. This continues until **expr2** evaluates to zero. Note that, **expr2** is evaluated and tested at the beginning of each pass through the loop, whereas **expr3** is evaluated at the end of each pass. If the loop-continuation condition is initially false, the body portion of the loop is not performed.

statement can be either an empty statement, a single statement, or a series of statements enclosed in a block. For example a compound statement would look like:

```
for (expr1; expr2; expr3)
{
    statement1;
    statement2;
    statement3;
}
```

Here is what the **for** loop looks like as a flow diagram:

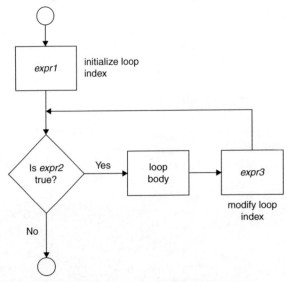

Here are some examples of **for** loops:
Vary the control variable from 100 to 1 in increments of –1 (decrements of 1).

```
for (i=100; i>=1; i=i-1)
```

Vary the control variable for 3 to 33 in increments of 3.

```
for (i=3; i<=33; i+=3)
```

Vary the control variable from 20 to 2 in steps of –2.

```
for (i=20; i>=2; i-=2)
```

Note that there are many ways to write the same **for** loop:

```
for (i=1; i<=100; i=i+1)
for (i=1; i<101; i=i+1)
for (i=1; i<=100; i++)
```

They are all the same, just written differently.

(e.g.) **Summing Numbers I**

```
int i, sum=0;
for (i=1; i<=100; i=i+1)
    sum = sum + i;
```

The variable **i**, defined as an **int**, is the loop index. The first part of the loop, **i=1**, sets **i** to an initial value of 1. This is done only once, when the loop is initiated. The next expression, **i<=100**, controls the loop. This basically says that the loop repeats as long as the variable **i** has a value less than or equal to 100. When **i** becomes 101, the loop terminates. If the expression is true, the loop body is executed, in this case the statement **sum = sum + i**. Finally the expression **x=x+1** is executed. It increments the loop variable **i** by 1.

Intrinsic Declaration

C99 lets you actually declare a variable within **expr1** of a **for** loop. An index variable declared in such a manner has its scope (life) limited to the block of code controlled by the **for** loop (i.e., between the curly braces). The **for** loop illustrated previously could be rewritten:

```
int sum=0;
for (int i=1; i<=100; i=i+1)
    sum = sum + i;
```

Here the type **int** is used in **expr1** to give **i** a type. Outside the loop, **i** is unknown. Here's another example to illustrate the scope of this loop index:

```
int p = 10;
printf("Pre-loop p = %d\n",p);
for (int p=1; p<3; p++)
    printf("loop: p = %d\n",p);
printf("Post-loop p = %d\n",p);
```

How does this work?

```
Pre-loop p = 10
loop: p = 1
loop: p = 2
Post-loop p = 10
```

The **p** declared in the **for** loop is "alive" until the end of the loop and hides the initial **p**. But after execution leaves the loop, the original **p** becomes visible again.

Omitting Parts

Any of the three expressions in a **for** loop can be omitted, although the semicolons must remain. If **expr1** is omitted, the loop index must be initialized elsewhere:

```
i = 1;
for ( ; i<=100; i=i+1)
    sum = sum + i;
```

expr3 can be omitted if the control variable is altered by statements in the body of the for loop:

```
for (i=1; i<=100;){
    sum = sum + i;
    i = i + 1;
}
```

The expression used for **expr3** can be any mathematical expression that can be evaluated. This expression acts like a stand-alone C statement at the end of the body of the **for** loop. Therefore, the expressions

```
i = i + 1
i += 1
++i
i++
```

are all equivalent in incrementing the value of **i** by 1.

Overstuffed **for** Loops

The comma operator "," can be used to combine statements in a **for** statement. For example, the statement

```
for (i=1, j=0; i<100; i=i+1, j=j+5)
```

is perfectly legal. This statement causes the variable **i** to increment by one and the variable **j** to increment by 5, all in one loop.

Can You Change the Loop Index Inside the Loop Body?

Yes, but the practice is *not recommended.* A loop index is used to control the loop, so its value should be changed in the modification expression, not in the loop body. The following loop is "correct," but would cause an infinite loop:

```
for (k=1; k<3; k=k+1)
    k = 1;
```

while Loop

The second most common loop is the **while** loop. It is used in situations where the number of repetitions of a loop is unknown. The general form of a **while** loop is:

```
while (expr)
    statement;
```

The semantics are as follows: First **expr** is evaluated. If the value returned is nonzero, **statement** is executed. After the execution has been completed, control returns to the top of the **while** statement, and the process is repeated. This continues until **expr** evaluates to zero (false). Note that **statement** can be a single statement, or a series of statements enclosed in a block. For example:

```
while (expr)
{
    statement1;
    statement2;
    statement3;
}
```

Here's an example flow diagram:

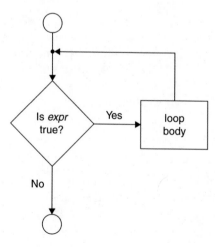

The major difference between the **for** loop and the **while** loop is that the former is pretty well self-contained. All the parts needed—index initialization, conditional expression, and the index modification—are included. In the **while** loop, only the conditional expression used to terminate the loop is included (equivalent to **expr2** in the **for** loop). As long as the conditional expression remains true, the loop will repeat. An equivalent to the **for** loop would be:

```
expr1;
while (expr2)
{
    statement;
    expr3;
}
```

where **expr1** is used to initialize some parameter (called a *control variable*, or *index*) that controls the looping action, **expr2** represents a condition that must be true for the loop to continue execution, and **expr3** is used to modify the value of the control variable initially assigned by **expr1**.

(e.g.) **Summing Numbers II**

Let's look at the summation process we did using a **for** loop and modify it for a **while** loop:

```
int i, sum=0;
i = 1;
while (i <= 100)
{
    sum = sum + i;
    i = i + 1;
}
```

First the expression **i <= 100** is evaluated. Since the current value of *i* is 1, the expression is true, causing execution of the statements between the braces. The variable **sum** is assigned the old value of **sum** plus the value of **i**. The variable **i** is incremented by assigning it the old value of **i** plus 1. The loop has now been processed once. Now the program reevaluates the expression **i <= 100**. Since **i <= 100** is still true, the loop is executed again. This process continues until **i** has the value 101, when expression **i <= 100** becomes *false.*

do Loop

The least known loop in C is the **do-while** loop. It is used in situations where the number of passes through the loop is known in advance, and the loop must execute *at least* once.

That's essentially what differentiates it from a **while** loop. A **while** loop may never execute, whereas a **do-while** will always execute at least once. The general form of a **do** loop is:

```
do {
      statement;
} while (expr);
```

where **expr** represents a condition that must be true for the loop to continue execution. The semantics are as follows: First **statement** is executed. After the execution has been completed, **expr** is evaluated. If the value returned is nonzero, control returns to the top of the **do** statement, and the process is repeated. This continues until **expr** evaluates to zero (false). Again, as with the **for** and **while** loops, **statement** can be a single statement or a series of statements enclosed in a block. For example:

```
do {
      statement1;
      statement2;
      statement3;
} while (expr);
```

(e.g.) **Summing Numbers III**

Let's look again at the summation process:

```
int i, sum=0;
i = 1;
do {
     sum = sum + i;
     i = i + 1;
} while (i <= 100);
```

This works fine as long as **i** has an initial value less than or equal to 100. If **i** has the value 101, for instance, then the value of **sum** will be 101, because the loop will have executed at least once. The order of evaluation is more important here, too. For instance, if we interchange the fourth and fifth lines, as in

```
int i, sum=0;
i = 1;
do {
     i = i + 1;
     sum = sum + i;
} while (i <= 100);
```

the result would be that sum has the value 5,150 instead of 5,050. This is because the loop is now incrementing **i** before it is added to **sum**, effectively summing the values 2 to 101. The flow diagram is shown here:

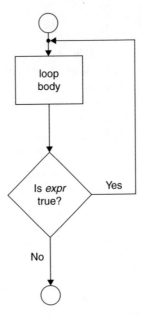

do or while, There Is No Try!

What are the differences between **while** and **do-while** loops, and why would you choose one over the other? The major difference between the two loops is that, in the **while** loop, the expression is tested first, and if the expression result is false, the loop body is not executed. However, in the **do-while** loop, the loop body is always executed once. After that, the expression is tested; if the test result is false, the loop body is not executed again. **do** loops are commonly used in creating menus, where the menu has to be displayed at least once.

Loop d' Loop with Nested Loops

In certain situations it is appropriate to use a loop inside another loop. Such a loop is called a *nested loop* and is similar in concept to a nested **if** statement. A nested loop is executed, essentially, from the inside out. Each loop is like a layer and has its own loop index, its own loop expression, and its own loop body. In a nested loop, for each value of the outermost counter variable, the complete inner loop will be executed once. For example:

```
int i, j, sum;
for (i=1; i<=4; i=i+1){ // outer loop
    sum = 0;
    for (j=1; j<=3; j=j+1) // inner loop
        sum = sum + i * j;
}
```

Here, **i** is the outer loop index and **j** is the inner loop index. The outer loop is executed four times, with **i** = 1,2,3,4. For each **i** value, the inner loop is executed three times. Since **j**=1,2,3, the inner loop is executed three times. The statement involving calculating the sum is effectively executed 4×3, or 12 times. Here is a breakdown of what the values are for each loop index and the sum:

```
loop
1          i=1,  j=1,  sum=1
2          i=1,  j=2,  sum=3
3          i=1,  j=3,  sum=6
4          i=2,  j=1,  sum=2
5          i=2,  j=2,  sum=6
6          i=2,  j=3,  sum=10
7          i=3,  j=1,  sum=3
8          i=3,  j=2,  sum=9
9          i=3,  j=3,  sum=19
10         i=4,  j=1,  sum=4
11         i=4,  j=2,  sum=12
12         i=4,  j=3,  sum=24
```

Most compilers allow 15 levels of such nesting. But honestly if code has more than three or four levels of nesting, it is probably too complex.

What nesting patterns for looping control structures are allowable? Anything, really. It mostly depends on the algorithm being designed. Here are some examples:

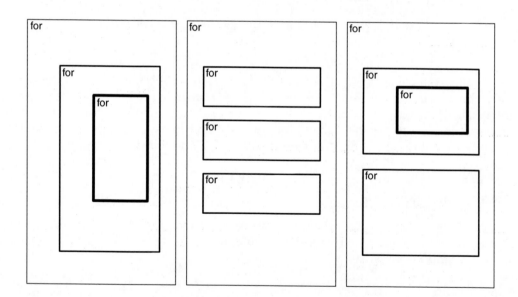

Darker lines denote a deeper level of nesting. These examples show nested **for** loops, but you are by no means restricted to nesting one form of loop. You could also nest a **for** loop inside a **while** loop inside another **for** loop.

Cracking Loops with `break`

We have already met the **break** statement in connection with the **switch** statement. In that context it eliminates *fall-through* between **case** statements, effectively terminating the **switch** statement prematurely. With respect to loops, the **break** statement causes an exit from the innermost enclosing loop. The general form of a **break** statement is:

```
break;
```

It provides an early exit from **for, while,** and **do** loops (and the **switch** statement). Here's an illustration of what happens:

```
while (expr)
{
    statements
    break;
    more_statements
}
```

For example:

```
1    double x;
2    while (1)
3    {
4        scanf("%lf", &x);
5        if (x < 0.0)
6            break;
7        printf("The square root is: %f\n", sqrt(x));
8    }
9    // break jumps to here
```

In this example, a test for a negative argument is made (on line 5), and if the test is true, a **break** statement is used to pass control to the statement immediately following the loop (line 9). What would otherwise be an infinite loop is made to terminate upon a given condition tested by the **if** expression. Care should be taken when using **break** statements because they cause a discontinuous jump to a new position in the program.

`continue` Looping

The **continue** statement causes the current iteration of a loop to stop and the next iteration to begin immediately, effectively bypassing the remainder of the loop. The general form of a **continue** statement is:

```
continue;
```

It allows for a loop to continue. It applies only to loops, though, not to **switch.**

Here's an illustration of what happens:

```
while (expr)        ◄───────────┐
{                               │
    statements                  │
    continue; ──────────────────┘
    more_statements
}
```

For example:

```
1   double x, sum;
2   int count, n=10;
3   while (count < n)
4   {
5       scanf("%lf", &x);
6       if (x > —0.01 && x < 0.01)
7           continue;
8       count = count + 1;
9       sum = sum + x;
10      // continue jumps to here to begin the next
11      // iteration
12  }
```

In the preceding example, a test for a small number is made on line 6, and if the test is true, the **continue** statement is used to pass control to the next iteration of the loop (line 3).

Loops and Validity Checking

do-while loops can be used successfully to provide an iterative way of validating input. For example, in one of the case studies we design a program that calculates radioactive decay. However, if the user enters an number that is outside the bounds of the equation, it may result in an erroneous output. How do we solve this problem? Through input validity checking. *Validity checking* is a process whereby information is validated when it is entered. It is a form of defensive programming discussed earlier. For example, consider the following code:

```
printf("Enter the percentage of X remaining: ");
scanf("%lf", &perC);
```

If the value of the variable **perC** is greater than 100, the equation will not function as expected. A better solution would be to use a loop to filter the input. This code could be rewritten in the form:

```
do {
    printf("Enter the percentage of X remaining: ");
    scanf("%lf", &perC);
} while(perC < 0 || perC > 100)
```

This **do** loop will iterate at least once. If the value entered is outside the range 0 to 100, then the loop will continue iterating until a value between 0 and 100 is entered.

Infinite Loops

We talked to some extent about infinite loops in the chapter on debugging. Unintentionally introduced into a program, they can cause the program to loop endlessly, which isn't too hard to figure out because your program will go nowhere.

Infinite loops are represented quite clearly in nature. The cycle of water rains down from clouds, forms rivers and oceans, and then evaporates just to form clouds again. The Earth's movement around the sun causes day to night and then day again continuously. Consider the following light-hearted algorithm:

```
earth = 1;
while (earth)
     rotate(earth);

function rotate(planet)
start
     day(planet);
     night(planet);
end
```

Here the algorithm just continues to rotate the Earth while the Earth exists (or is true). If the Earth becomes false, the loop stops. Here the Earth will always be true, so the loop goes on for infinity (well, at least for another 4 to 5 billion years, anyway). A good physical example of infinite loops are scratches on a vinyl record that cause it to play a scrap of tune over and over again.

Loops of the undesirable kind are generally hard to stop. Some loops show a tendency to degenerate into really nasty things, namely *vicious circles* or *deadlocks*. Vicious circles are loops that, from one cycle to the next, produce a situation that is worse in comparison to the previous state. Deadlocks are processes that have come to an unwanted standstill due to some mutually contradicting requirements or counteracting forces that balance each other out. Sometimes, however, it is beneficial to use infinite loops in your algorithm.

The code in the previous section on validity checking does not alert the user to the cause of the new request. This can be remedied by altering the code:

```
do {
     printf("Enter the percentage of X remaining: ");
     scanf("%lf", &perC);
     if (perC < 0 || perC >   100){
          printf("An invalid percentage was entered\n");
          printf("Please enter a number in the range");
          printf(" 0 to 100\n");
     }
     else
          break;
} while(1)
```

This turns the **do-while** loop into a *controlled infinite loop.* If the percentage entered is still outside the bounds, an error message is output, and the user is asked to reenter the percentage. Otherwise a **break** statement is used to exit the loop. Here are the three most common ways to write infinite loops:

```
while(1)              do {                 for(;;)
{                                          {
}                     } while(1);          }
```

Pseudo-Infinite Loops

A *pseudo-infinite loop* is a loop that appears infinite but is really just a very long loop. It is usually due to some impossible termination condition. Consider this example:

```
unsigned int i;
for (i = 1; i > 0; i=i+1)
{
    ...
}
```

It appears that this will go on forever, but in fact the value of i will eventually reach the maximum value storable in an unsigned **int** and adding 1 to that number will wrap-around to 0, breaking the loop. The actual limit of i depends on the details of the system and compiler used.

Translating Summations

One of the best illustrations in the use of loops is when translating summations in equations. A summation is expressed mathematically in the form

$$S = \sum_{i=1}^{n} i^2$$

which literally means: "Sum the values of i squared such that i varies from 1 to *n.*" If we were to write a loop to do this, it might look like:

```
for (i=1; i<=n; i=i+1)
{
    S = S + (i * i);
}
```

Perfect Numbers

Perfect numbers are whole numbers that equal the sum of all their whole number divisors less than themselves. For example, 6 has the divisors 1, 2, and 3; the sum 1+2+3=6. So, 6 is a perfect number. On the other hand, 12 has the divisors 1, 2, 3, 4, and 6; the sum 1+2+3+4+6=16. So, 12 is not perfect. What we want to do is design a program to determine all the perfect numbers less than 1,000.

The Algorithm

1. Start with a number, p=1, sum=0.
2. Check to see is p is divisible by all numbers less than it.
   i.e. x: 1→p-1
      a. If p is divisible by x, add x to sum.
      b. Repeat step 2.
3. Check if the value of sum equals p.
      a. If yes, then p is a perfect number.
      b. If no, then p is not perfect.
4. Increment p
5. Repeat step 2.

There are in essence two loops here: (1) a cycle through the numbers 1 to 1,000 represented by p, and (2) for each of these numbers a cycle through the numbers 1 to **p-1** to see which are divisible.

The Program

```
#include <stdio.h>
void main(void)
{
    int i, j, perfect;
    for (i=1; i<=1000; i++)
    {
        perfect = 0;
        for (j=1; j<i; j++)
        {
            if (i%j == 0)
                perfect = perfect + j;
        }
        if (perfect == i)
            printf("%d is a perfect number\n", perfect);
    }
}
```

Code Walkthrough

First we define three variables:

```
int i, j, perfect;
```

The first two act as loop indices, and the latter is used to store the value of the perfect number. Now we can set up the loop that checks for all perfect number less than 1,000. We can use a **for** loop, because we know how many iterations the loop has to process. This loop sets the loop counter to 1 initially, checks to see if **i** is less than 1,000, performs the statements in the body of the loop and then increments the loop counter by 1. It allows us to check each number from 1 to 999.

```
for (i=1; i<1000; i++)
{
    perfect = 0;
    for (j=1; j<i; j++)
    {
        if (i%j == 0)
            perfect = perfect + j;
    }

    if (perfect == i)
        printf("%d is a perfect number\n",perfect);
}
```

The statements in the body of the loop can be handled next. The first of these sets the variable **perfect** to zero. This occurs each time the loop iterates, since to check each number from 1 to 1,000 to verify if it is perfect, you have to reset the variable storing the sum of divisions.

```
perfect = 0;
```

Next we create an inner loop, using the variable **j** as the loop counter. It is set to 1 initially, with an upper bound of "less than **i**." If we are checking the number 6 to see if it is a perfect number, the values of **j** for the loop will be **j = 1 to 5 (j<6).**

```
for (j=1; j<i; j++)
{
    if (i%j == 0)
        perfect = perfect + j;
}
```

Inside the second loop, we use an **if** statement and an expression involving the modulo operator to check if there is a remainder when **i** is divided by **j**. If there is no remainder, then **j** is a divisor of **i**, so we can add the value of **j** to the value stored in the variable **perfect**.

```
if (i%j == 0)
    perfect = perfect + j;
```

When we have finished checking all the values of **j**, we check to see if the calculated value stored in the variable **perfect** equals the value stored in the variable **i**. If they are both the same, then **i** is a perfect number.

```
if (perfect == i)
    printf("%d is a perfect number\n",perfect);
```

Testing the Program

Let's test some numbers:

```
i = 6, j = 1, 2, 3, 4, 5
perfect = 0
```

```
    i = 1:
    if (6%1 == 0) //TRUE because 6 is divisible by 1
        perfect = 0 + 1; // EQUALS 1

    i = 2:
    if (6%2 == 0) //TRUE because 6 is divisible by 2
        perfect = 1 + 2; // EQUALS 3

    i = 3:
    if (6%3 == 0) //TRUE because 6 is divisible by 3
        perfect = 3 + 3; // EQUALS 6

    i = 4:
    if (6%4 == 0) //FALSE because 6 is not divisible by 4

    i = 5:
    if (6%5 == 0) //FALSE because 6 is not divisible by 5
```

The final value of perfect = 6, and because **perfect = i,** 6 is a perfect number.

Epilog

The loop evolved from the complex and tangled world of control structures found in languages prior to 1970, especially one using many GOTO's, exceptions, or other "unstructured" branching constructs. If you've never heard of goto, then forget I mentioned it. If you have heard of goto, then "you have never heard of goto." Loops pervade nearly every algorithm. When we are spell checking a document, we are using a loop whose length is the number of words in the document. When cars drive through the gantries of a toll route the camera that acquires images of the number plate work in a cycle, continuously taking images, maybe in the form of an infinite loop? An iPod uses a loop to play all the songs in an album, and a furnace uses a loop to control when it heats, and when it sits idle.

Exercises

Exercise 11.1

Pascal's triangle is a geometric arrangement of the binomial coefficients in a triangle named after Blaise Pascal. Notice that the edges of the triangle are occupied by the digit 1, and that each number is the sum of the two numbers immediately above it.

$$1$$
$$1 \quad 1$$
$$1 \quad 2 \quad 1$$
$$1 \quad 3 \quad 3 \quad 1$$
$$1 \quad 4 \quad 6 \quad 4 \quad 1$$
$$1 \quad 5 \quad 10 \quad 10 \quad 5 \quad 1$$

Use loops to derive and print Pascal's triangle as shown.

Exercise 11.2

An n-digit number is an Armstrong number if the sum of the nth power of the digits is equal to the original number. For example, 153 is a three-digit number and

$$153 = 1^3 + 5^3 + 3^3$$

Write a program to find all three-digit Armstrong numbers.

Exercise 11.3

The *Kaprekar* numbers were introduced by Indian mathematician D. R. Kaprekar in 1980. These are nonnegative integers whose square can be split into two parts that add up to the original number again. Both parts of the sum must be positive (i.e., not 0). Consider the following example:

$$703^2 = 494209 \quad \text{and} \quad 494 + 209 = 703$$

X is a Kaprekar number for base b if there exist nonnegative integers n, A, and positive number B that satisfy the following conditions:

$0 < B < b^n$

$X^2 = Ab^n + B$

$X = A + B$

For the example given, $b = 10$ and $n = 3$. Write a program to calculate all the Kaprekar numbers between 1 and 10,000.

Exercise 11.4

Consider the "cubes" algorithm of Exercise 3.3. The algorithm derived using the analysis technique requires that the constituent digits be extracted. For a number, say 153, it is decomposed into its constituent digits, "1," "5," and "3," and each is cubed and the results summed. For example, the number n could be regarded as the digits "d1," "d2," and "d3," where

d1 = n / 100	(the hundreds digit)
d2 = (n - d1 * 100) / 10	(the tens digit)
d3 = n - (d1 * 100 + d2 * 10)	(the units digit)

Write a program using a loop to implement this algorithm.

Exercise 11.5

An alternative to the "cubes" algorithm can be derived by way of *synthesis*. This means the digits d1, d2, and d3 all have values 0 to 9. These individual values are then used to generate each number as

$$n = d1 * 100 + d2 * 10 + d3$$

The numbers and calculations can be performed using a set of nest loops. Write a program using a loop to implement this algorithm.

A Program = The Sum of Its Parts

Simplicity is prerequisite for reliability.

—Edsger W. Dijkstra

Introduction

Most programs are too big to be understood in a single chunk. When they design the program that makes the modern car run (all 35 million-odd LOC), they don't write all 35 million LOC in the same block under **main**. A better way to design a large program is to break it up into smaller pieces. There might be a piece to make the anti-lock breaking work, another piece to run the engine, and another to control the windows.

These pieces are called *functions*. Sometimes they are also called *procedures, subroutines,* or *modules*. A function is a self-contained program segment that carries out some specific, well-defined task. All the programs we have looked at so far contain at least one function: **main**. Separating code into distinct functions is an important aspect of programming. We can now tackle each of the parts of a problem in turn. This makes the program easier to maintain, easier to debug, and easier to extend. You can tune aspects of the program without affecting others. Most of the programs we have dealt with so far have honestly been too small to organize in modules. However, there is another reason to separate functionality in a program. Sometimes you may want to use a piece of code more than once. Putting the code in a function by itself allows the code to be accessed numerous times, at the expense (or not) of having to code it only once. Calculating a square root wouldn't be nearly as convenient if we had to write code to evaluate Newton's method every time, code that looks something like this:

```
double r, x, EPSILON = 1.0e-5;

x = r;
while ((x*x − r) > EPSILON)
        x = (x + r/x) / 2.0;
printf("The square root of %.2f is %.15f\n", r, x);
```

A lot less convenient? I would say so, and if you had to repeat the code every time you need to calculate a square root, it would be tedious. C has packaged this up in a function called **sqrt**, but you could do the same if you wanted.

```
double SQRT(double r)
{
    double x, EPSILON = 1.0e-5;;
    x = r;
    while ((x*x − r) > EPSILON)
        x = (x + r/x) / 2.0;
    return x;
}
```

Eventually, the programs you design will grow, both in complexity and length. Once programs start to contain subalgorithms, it is time to start thinking about modularizing your program. Every function should do one thing well.

Modularity

Modularizing means splitting up the functionality of your program. It is a form of program refinement that occurs at the design phase. We have already seen the use of modules by way of the functions found in the standard libraries such as **stdio.h**. Modularity is the basis for the notion of reusability. *Reusability* is where a segment of code is used again. A function is coded so that it can be executed, or "called," several times from several places within a program. It may also be called from other functions, or indeed from itself, a process called *recursion*. There are numerous benefits to using functions:

- To reduce redundancy in a program
- To enable the reuse of code throughout multiple programs
- To allow complex problems to be decomposed into simpler portions
- To improve readability of a program
- To make debugging easier
- To replicate beneficial mathematical and I/O functions
- To allow certain information to be hidden
- To improve the ability to extend a program

A good analogy to functions is a camera system. Digital cameras generally come in two formats: point-and-shoot (PS) and digital SLR. The former has all the capability built in, with no ability to modify the functionality of the camera. If it has a 28–52mm lens, then you can't change that. You can't use an 8mm fisheye lens because that functionality doesn't exist. Digital SLRs rarely come as a complete package, but rather as separate components: camera body, flashes, lenses, motor drive, storage media, filters, etc. All these components allow the camera system to be modified to fit a particular shooting environment. The same can be achieved with modular programming.

A Simple Function

The general syntax of a function is:

```
return_type function_name(parameter_list)
{
    function_body
    return expression;
}
```

Each function consists of a name, a return type, an argument list, and a function body. The first line in a function is known as the *function definition*. When a function is invoked, program control is transferred to the function. Once the function has carried out its intended action, control is returned to the point from which the function was accessed. The *return_type* is essentially the type of the function, representing the type of value it returns. It can be one of the standard types in C: **char, int, float,** or **double.** In addition it also allows for a special type known as **void.** The *function_name* follows the same naming conventions as those for variables in C. You cannot use names of functions that already exist, such as **scanf.** Make sure the name of a function is an appropriate length and is descriptive. The parentheses are used to enclose the *parameter_list.* This is where input is provided for the function. If we don't want to give the function any values, we can again use the word **void.** The *function_body* is the guts of the function, where things actually happen.

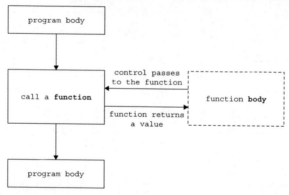

The simplest function, which follows, does nothing!

```
void do_nothing(void)
{ }
```

Both its return type and parameters are of type **void,** which indicates the absence of a type. A **void** does not require use of the **return** keyword. Now consider this function:

```
int add(int a, int b)
{
    int sum;
    sum = a + b;
    return sum;
}
```

This function, whose name is **add,** takes two arguments of type **int** as input and returns an **int.** It uses a temporary variable (so called because it only exists for the life of the function) named **sum** to hold the value of the summed variables **a** and **b.** The function could also be written as

```
int add(int a, int b)
{
    return a + b;
}
```

which essentially saves creating a temporary variable, yet achieves the same result. We can now *call* this function using the following code in **main:**

```
int result;
result = add(5,7);
```

In the context of an entire program, the function **add** looks like this:

```
# include <stdio.h>

int add(int a, int b)
{
        int sum;
        sum = a + b;
        return sum;
}

int main (void)
{
        int x=4, y=20, z;
        z = add(x,y);
        printf("%d\n", z);
}
```

The arrows indicate transfer of control. When add is called the values of x and y are passed to it, stored in a and b respectively. The value of sum is calculated as 4+20=24, and this value is returned and stored in z.

The Function Body

The body of a function is essentially enclosed by a compound statement, with left and right curly braces delimiting the code within a function. Sometimes when designing a function, it is useful to create an empty function. For example:

```
double calc_bacteriaGrowth()
{

}
```

This is known as a *stub.*

Naming Functions

As with variables, functions should have appropriate names that describe what the functions do. Here are some guidelines:

- Functions should have meaningful names. For example use **calc_bacteriaGrowth()** rather than **calc_bG()**. The exception is abbreviations or acronyms that are widely used, such as **gcd()** in mathematics.
- The prefixes **calc** and **comp** can be reserved for functions that perform some sort of computation.
- The prefix **find** can be reserved for functions that perform some sort of searching.
- The prefix **initialize** can be reserved for functions that perform some sort of variable initialization.
- The prefix **is** should be used for Boolean functions. For example: **is_odd.**
- Symmetric names should be used for functions that perform complementary operations. For example: **open/close, min/max, insert/delete.**
- Numbers or abbreviations can be used sometimes. For example: **deg2rad, plot3D**

For example, if we want to create a function to convert Fahrenheit to Celsius, we could use the following function names:

```
fahr2cels, fahr_to_cels, fahrenheit2celsius, celsius
```

The first three are fairly self-explanatory. The last one doesn't really indicate what happens with this function unless you work on the principle that it returns a Celsius, given a Fahrenheit. Of course, given that there is also a temperature scale of Kelvin, this may not be the best choice. The third choice is a bit too long. I would settle for the first because it is fairly concise and readable. You can then elaborate this to a whole group of functions:

```
fahr2cels, cels2fahr, cels2kelv, kelv2cels
```

Another example is defining a name for a function that calculates Fibonacci numbers by binary recursion:

```
Fibonacci_binaryR
Fib_binary_recursion
Fib_recursionB
binary_recursionFib
Fib_binaryRecursion
Fibonacci_by_binary_recusion
```

The possibilities are seemingly endless.

Functions Always Have Arguments!

One of the defining characteristics of functions is that they have a means of passing information to and from the function. There are two terms commonly used when referring to information passed to functions: parameters and arguments. The two terms are often used interchangeably, but *arguments* are more properly thought of as the *actual* values assigned to the *parameter* variables of the function. If we look again at the example from the previous section:

```
int add(int a, int b)
```

Here **a** and **b** are the *parameter* variables and when we call the function:

```
result = add(5,7);
```

the values 5 and 7 are the *arguments*. Alternatively, the equivalent terms *formal parameter* and *actual parameter* may be used. When a function is called, the arguments are mapped to the corresponding parameters in the function definition. It doesn't really matter that much what terms you want to use. The one thing you have to remember is that if we have *n* parameters in our function specification, then we have to pass *n* arguments to it when we call it. If we don't pass enough or pass too many, the compiler will probably complain. Now that we understand that functions need food, let's look at how we can give it to them and how they can give information back. In C there are two ways of passing information: *pass-by-value* and *pass-by-reference*.

Returning Values

The simplest way for functions to return values is to be defined using a *return_type*, in association with the **return** keyword. In effect the return statement causes execution to leave the current function and return to the point in the program that called the function. Let's go back to our simple example:

```
int add(int a, int b)
{
    int sum;
    sum = a + b;
    return sum;
}
```

Here the **return_type** is **int**, and the value returned is **sum**. The return statement could also have been written as:

```
return (sum);
```

It doesn't really matter as the parentheses are *optional*. Remember the if-else statement that determined whether a number was even or odd? Here's the same code encapsulated in a function:

```
int isEven(int a_number)
{
    if ((a_number % 2) == 0)
        return 1;
    else
        return 0;
}
```

This function again has **return_type** of **int,** and the value returned is either a 0 or a 1. But wait, there are two return statements here. How can this work? It works because the **if-else** statement only allows one path to be followed. So if **a_number** is even, **isEven** returns a value of 1; otherwise, it returns a value of 0. We can have *any* number of **return** statements in a function, only the first one encountered is executed. The value of the expression returned *must* match the value of the **return_type.** If it doesn't, the program will take care of it, but the result may not be what is expected. If we had the following function

```
int getPI(void)
{
    return 3.14159;
}
```

the value returned would be 3, because we tried to return a floating point number through an integer. Sometimes a function returns nothing. In this case use the **void** type. For example:

```
void askit()
{
    printf("Enter a number: ");
}
```

In general any nonvoid function can be used in any type of expression. When the function is called, the expression is evaluated and the value is returned. We have already done this numerous times using functions from the **math.h** library. For example:

```
area = pi * pow(radius, 2.0);
```

Here the value of **radius**^{2} is calculated, and the returned value is multiplied by **pi.**

Pass-by-Value

The easiest way of giving a function information is through pass-by-value. In *pass-by-value,* a copy of an argument is passed to the function. In the function **add,** there are two parameters, both of which as pass-by-value. This is a one-way transfer. No information is given back.

```
int add(int a, int b)
{
    int sum;
    sum = a + b;
    return sum;
}
```

We can call **add** in a number of ways:

```
int r1, r2, r3, x=4, y=20;
r1 = add(4,20);
r2 = add(x,y);
r3 = add(4,y);
```

In all cases the value returned is the same (24). It doesn't matter if you give the function a variable containing a value or a simple numeric value. All the function does is copy the value and leaves the variables, if used as arguments, alone.

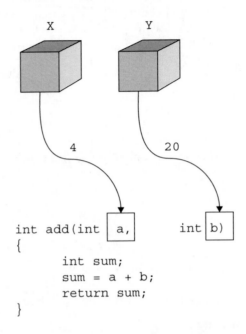

Note that not everything should be passed as a parameter. Do not pass something as a parameter if the same value is used in many different functions and is relatively stable. In these cases it may be appropriate to use a global variable: It is better to use one global variable than a dozen copies of the same variable. Remember that global variables *must* have a unique identifier. We cannot create a local variable with the same name.

Pass-by-Reference

There are times when writing a function that you may wish to return more than one value. This is not possible using the traditional return statement (or rather there is no *easy* way of doing this). Consider the following example, a function to swap two numeric values:

```
void swap(int x, int y)
{
    int temp;
    temp = x;
    x = y;
    y = temp;
}
```

The idea is to pass two integer variables and interchange their values using a temporary variable. The variable **temp** holds the value of **x** temporarily while **x** is assigned the value of **y**. The variable **y** then obtains the value of **x** stored in **temp.** By the end of the function, the values have been swapped, but there is one small problem. What is it?

Imagine we call the function in this manner:

```
int X=12, Y=4;
swap(X,Y);
```

When the function **swap** is entered, the values of **X** and **Y** are copied into **x** and **y** respectively. The values in **x** and **y** are then swapped with **x** obtaining the value 4, and **y** the value 12, and the function ends. All variables local to swap are destroyed, and the values of **X** and **Y** are 12 and 4, respectively. Nothing has changed, because **x** and **y** are pass-by-value parameters. To make this work, we have to use pass-by-reference.

What is *pass-by-reference?* It is a way of passing values using *pointers.* Yuk! Not pointers, you say. We first encountered pass-by-reference in **scanf**:

```
scanf("%d", &a_number);
```

If we just passed the variables instead of their address, there would be no way for **scanf** to assign a value to them.

For example, change the definition of the function **swap** to:

```
void swap(int *x, int *y)
{
    int temp;
    temp = *x;
    *x = *y;
    *y = temp;
}
```

We have now changed the parameters **x** and **y** to pointers → ***x, *y**. We could now call the function in this manner:

```
int X=12, Y=4;
swap(&X,&Y);
```

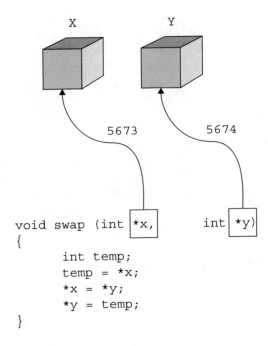

```
void swap (int *x,      int *y)
{
        int temp;
        temp = *x;
        *x = *y;
        *y = temp;
}
```

When the function is executed, the address of **X** is assigned to **x**, and the address of **Y** is assigned to **y**. The values of ***x** and ***y** are then interchanged. What happens in reality is that the values of **X** and **Y** are swapped. Executing the program yields, **X=4, Y=12**. Therefore if we look at this in diagram form, we get ***x** pointing to **X** and ***y** pointing to **Y**. This idea could also be extended to work with array elements:

```
int p[20];
swap(&p[i],&p[j]);
```

More on that later. Now let's look again at our function **add** and make the calculated value an integral part of the parameter list. This is now what our function **add** would look like:

```
void add(int a, int b, int *sum)
{
    *sum = a + b;
}
```

All we have to do is add the pass-by-reference parameter ***sum**. Now the whole function body becomes one line. We could call this in the following manner:

```
int sum;
add(4,7,&sum);
```

Scope in Functions

Consider again the concept of scope. If function **add** is declared as:

```
int add(int a, int b)
{
    int sum;
    sum = a + b;
    return sum;
}
```

we call the function using the following code fragment in the main program:

```
int result, a=4, b=20;
result = add(a,b);
```

It doesn't matter that the variables **a** and **b** are declared in two places. They both have different scope. **a** and **b**, used when the function is called, live in that portion of the program. **a** and **b**, used inside the function, only live as long as the function itself is alive. If we changed the code inside the function to:

```
int sum;
sum = a + b;
a = sum;
return sum;
```

the fact that we change the value of **a** makes no difference to the value of **a** outside the function. Its value is still 4. When the function **add** ends, **a**, **b**, and **sum** are destroyed.

Passing Functions to Functions

There is a possibility that we may want to write a function that takes another function as input. For example, consider the following code:

```
double calcM(double (*MathFun)(), double arg)
{
    return (*MathFun)(arg);
}
int main(void)
{
    printf("%.2f\n",calcM(sqrt,47.0));
}
```

This function actually passes the function **sqrt** as an input to the function **calcM**. We could substitute *any* function when calling **calcM**.

Converting Existing Code into a Function

Let's return again to the code that determines whether a number is odd or even and look at the process of converting this code to a function. Here's the code:

```
if ((a_number % 2) == 0)
```

```
        printf("%d is an even number\n", a_number);
    else
        printf("%d is an odd number\n", a_number);
```

what we want to do is create a function that returns the value 1 (true) if a number is even and 0 otherwise. All we need to do is wrap the code in a function and make some changes. First, we need a name for the function. Since it checks whether a number is even or not, an appropriate name might be **isEven**. It takes one value as input, and it already has a name: **a_number**. There is also one output, which, being 0 or 1, is also an **int**. Here's what the function looks like so far:

```
int isEven(int a_number)
{

}
```

Turning to the body of the function, which is essentially comprised of the previous **if-else** statement, we create a function that looks like:

```
int isEven(int a_number)
{
    if ((a_number % 2) == 0)
        printf("%d is an even number\n", a_number);
    else
        printf("%d is an odd number\n", a_number);
}
```

The only changes we have to make is replacing each of the **printf** statements with a **return** statement. If the expression in the **if** statement is true, then it returns a 1; otherwise, it returns a 0, so that:

```
int isEven(int a_number)
{
    if ((a_number % 2) == 0)
        return 1;
    else
        return 0;
}
```

Building Functions from Scratch

It is not hard to rewrite some of the built-in functions. In fact, it is a good task to familiarize yourself with how functions work. Take, for example, the function **round**, used to round a floating point number. Most C compilers provide the functions **floor** and **ceil**, but not all provide a function called **round**. Such a function is not that hard to create.

First, derive an algorithm for the function. The function **round** takes a floating point number as input and rounds the number depending on whether its quotient is less than 0.5 or greater than 0.5. Take the floating point number and subtract the whole number component. Now examine the fractional part. If this is less than 0.5, then the rounded number is the original whole number. However, if the fractional part is greater than or equal to 0.5, then add one to the original whole number, effectively rounding up. Here's the basic algorithm:

1. Obtain a floating point number.
2. Calculate the integer portion of the number.
3. Calculate the fractional part by subtracting the integer portion from the original number.
4. Identify if the fractional portion is less than 0.5 → round down.
5. Else identify if the fractional part is >= 0.5 → round up.

In pseudocode this might look like:

```
FUNCTION: round
BEGIN
      INPUT: F (a floating point number)
      Integer portion = CONVERT F to an integer
      Fractional portion = F — Integer portion
      IF (Fractional portion IS LESS THAN 0.5)
          RETURN Integer portion
      ELSE
          RETURN Integer portion + 1
      END
```

From this, we can effectively build the function:

```
1     int round(double f)
2     {
3          int whole;
4          double part;
5          whole = (int)f;
6          part = f — whole;
7          if (part < 0.5)
8               return whole;
9          else
10               return whole + 1;
11    }
```

The first line of the function denotes that (a) the function is called **round,** and (b) it has one input argument (pass-by-value) and returns a value of type **int.** Next we declare two variables to hold the integer and fractional portions of the divided image, named **whole** and **part** respectively. We derive the integer portion by casting the value stored in **f.** This could have been achieved in a similar fashion by just assigning **f** to **whole** (whole = f). We then subtract **whole** from **f,** leaving the fractional part. Finally we use an **if-else** statement to determine whether the fractional part is less than 0.5, or >= 0.5, and return an appropriately rounded value of the number. We would call this function in the following manner:

```
int xR;
xR = round(3.719);
```

It's not too difficult to create some functions from scratch. The elements are the same as would occur writing the algorithm as part of **main.** What differs is the input and output. We could also alter **round,** so that it returns the value of the rounded number in the parameter list. Let's look at the code for this:

```
1    void round(double f, int *whole)
2    {
3          double part;
4          *whole = (int)f;
5          part = f — *whole;
6          if (part >= 0.5)
7                *whole = *whole + 1;
8    }
```

Now notice the changes. First, the size of the function has actually *decreased.* The first changes have occurred in the function definition, where we have replaced the return value with a void and added a pass-by-reference (PbR) parameter called **whole.** Remember that pass-by-reference parameters are prefixed with a *. Now that **whole** has moved from within the function to the parameter list, we can remove its declaration within the function so that it won't be declared in two places. Now everywhere in the function we used **whole** before, we must use ***whole** now. The other part of the function body that has dramatically changed is the **if-else** statement. Since ***whole** already has the value of the truncated floating point number, we only have to determine if the fractional portion is greater than or equal to 0.5. If this is the case, add 1 to ***whole.** We would call this function in the following manner:

```
int xR;
round(3.719,&xR);
```

Now every time we make reference to **whole** inside the function, we are actually manipulating the memory location associated with **xR** in the place where the function is called.

Function Prototypes

A *function protoype* is a declaration of a function that is defined elsewhere. This is used in situations where you want to declare the functions before you implement them. For example:

```
#include <stdio.h>

int isEven(int a_number); // Function prototype

int main(void)
{
     // main code here
}
```

```
int isEven(int a_number)
{
    if ((a_number % 2) == 0)
        printf("%d is an even number\n", a_number);

    else
        printf("%d is an odd number\n", a_number);
}
```

Here the function prototype occurs *before* the main part of the program, but the actual implementation occurs *afterward*. In many ways it is a tidier way to program because it is easier to refer back to the **main** function. In general, function prototypes specify three things:

1. The return type of the function
2. The type of its parameters
3. The number of parameters

So we don't have to specify parameter names. The following function prototype would have worked just as well:

```
int isEven(int); // Function prototype
```

Just don't forget the semicolon at the end of the statement!

e.g. Humidex

Remember the humidex case study? We could now change that case study so that the actual calculation of the humidex is encapsulated in a function. Here's the solution again:

```
1    #include <stdio.h>
2    #include <math.h>
3
4    #define Kc 273.16
5
6    int main(void)
7    {
8        double dewpoint_T, air_T, vap_P, humidex;
9
10       // Input the dew-point and air temperatures
11       printf(Enter the dew point temperature");
12       scanf("%lf", &dewpoint_T);
13
14       printf(Enter the air temperature");
15       scanf("%lf", &air_T);
16
17       // Determine whether the input meets the calculation
18       // restrictions
```

```
19          if (dewpoint_T >= 15 && air_T >= 23)
20          {
21              // Convert the dew point temperature to deg Kelvin
22              dewpoint_T = dewpoint_T + Kc;
23
24              // Calculate the vapor pressure
25              vap_P = 6.11*exp(5417.753*((1.0/Kc)-(1.0/dewpoint_T)));
26
27              // Calculate the humidex
28              humidex = air_T + (0.5555 * (vap_P - 10.0));
29
30              // Output the humidex
31              printf("The humidex is: %.2f \n",humidex);
32          }
33
34              return 0;
35      }
```

Now if we look at the statements and comments from line 21 to line 29, these, basically make up our humidex calculations. To create a function from these, we first have to create a *wrapper*, the skeleton function that surrounds the code. The first part of the wrapper is the function header and describes the function's name **(Humidex)**, the name and type of variables passed to the function **(double dewpoint_T, double air_T)**, and the type of the return value, if any. In this case it is a **double**:

```
double Humidex(double dewpoint_T, double air_T)
```

We can now add a compound statement and a return statement to give:

```
double Humidex(double dewpoint_T, double air_T)
{
    return 0;
}
```

At this moment, we are returning 0, but that's fine. Now take lines 21 to 29 from the original program and transplant them into the body of the function:

```
double Humidex(double dewpoint_T, double air_T)
{
    // Convert the dew point temperature to deg Kelvin
    dewpoint_T = dewpoint_T + Kc;

    // Calculate the vapor pressure
    vap_P = 6.11*exp(5417.753*((1.0/Kc)-(1.0/dewpoint_T)));

    // Calculate the humidex
    humidex = air_T + (0.5555 * (vap_P - 10.0));
```

```
    return 0;
}
```

What's still missing? Because the vapor pressure is now calculated within the function, the variable **vap_P** moves inside the function, as does the variable humidex. We also have to return the value contained in humidex:

```
double Humidex(double dewpoint_T, double air_T)
{
    double vap_P, humidex;

    // Convert the dew point temperature to deg Kelvin

    dewpoint_T = dewpoint_T + Kc;

    // Calculate the vapor pressure

    vap_P = 6.11*exp(5417.753*((1.0/Kc)-(1.0/dewpoint_T)));

    // Calculate the humidex

    humidex = air_T + (0.5555 * (vap_P - 10.0));

    return humidex;
}
```

Once we have created a function, we also have to change what happens in the main program. We will now call the function and store the value in a variable **h**, which is local to the main program:

```
int main(void)
{
    double dewpoint_T, air_T, h;

    // Input the dew-point and air temperatures
    printf(Enter the dew point temperature");
    scanf("%lf", &dewpoint_T);

    printf(Enter the air temperature");
    scanf("%lf", &air_T);

    // Determine whether the input meets the calculation
    // restrictions
    if (dewpoint_T >= 15 && air_T >= 23)
    {
        h = Humidex(dewpoint_T, air_T);

        // Output the humidex
        printf("The humidex is: %.2f \n", h);
    }

    return 0;
}
```

If you are not totally comfortable with writing functions directly, write the code in the main function first. When you get it working correctly, *then* turn it into a function in its own right.

A Library of Functions

Just as a recipe is made up of many different ingredients, programs are made up of many small functions. Some we write ourselves; others we use from existing libraries.

Sometimes groups of like functions need to be stored in libraries. For example, **math.h** contains a bunch of mathematical functions. This allows us to write functions that we can use in multiple programs. It also allows us to hide the actual code if we prefer. There are a number of ways of achieving this.

Simple .c Files

The simplest approach to making a library is simply storing the relevant functions in a .c file, and use #**include** to include the file.

Header Files

Another approach is to use header files, similar to **stdio.h.** These files often contain information that a compiler needs, such as definitions and function prototypes. The header file is normally associated with a .c file. Header files contain the following types of information:

- Constants, such as **INT_MAX (math.h)**
- Macro functions, such as **isvowel() (ctype.h)**
- Function declarations, such as **pow() (math.h)**

For example if we create a library called **temp.h,** which holds functions related to temperature conversion, then the contents might look like:

```
double fahr2cels(double);
double fahr2kelv(double);
double cels2fahr(double);
double cels2kelv(double);
double kelv2fahr(double);
double kelv2cels(double);
```

The associated source code file, **temp.c,** will contain the actual implementations. For example:

```
double cels2fahr(double cels)
{
    return (cels * 9.0/5.0)  + 32.0;
}
```

We could then include the library in any program in the following manner:

```
#include "temp.h"
```

Creating Object Code

There are other ways of storing library files. They can be stored as *object code.* C source code can be compiled, even if the code doesn't contain a main function. This is quite easy to do at the command line. The function **cels2fahr.c** can be compiled using the **gcc** compiler in the following manner:

```
gcc cels2fahr.c -c
```

The **-c** option produces an object file called **cels2fahr.o** but prevents the compiler from trying to generate an executable file. This isn't possible because **cels2fahr.c** doesn't contain a **main** function. We can then call this function using the **extern** statement:

```
#include <stdio.h>

extern double cels2fahr(double cels);

int main(void)
{
    double cels, fahr;
    printf("Temperature in   Celsius? ");
    scanf("%lf", &cels);
    fahr = cels2fahr(cels);
    printf("Temperature in   Fahrenheit is %.2f\n", fahr);

    return 0;
}
```

The function prototype for **cels2fahr** includes the quantifier **extern**, which indicates that the function will be found externally. To create an executable file:

```
gcc temperature.c cels2fahr.o
```

Arguments to `main`

Due to the fact that **main** is itself a function, it too can pass arguments. Why? Primarily so you can create a program that takes arguments from the command line. The command line is how programs were compiled and executed in years past, and in Unix-based systems in the present. In fact **gcc** is a command-line based compiler. For example if we had a program called **search**, which looks through text files to find a particular word, it could be called in the following manner:

```
%>search manuscript.txt Tatooine
```

where **manuscript.txt** is the name of the file to search and **Tatooine** is the word to search for. We'll use this in the following example. The arguments of **main** are of the form:

```
int main(int argc, char *argc[])
```

The variable **argc** represents the number of items on the command line. The variable **argv** is an array of strings containing the actual items. For example, the following program prints out the arguments typed on the command line:

```
#include <stdio.h>

int main(int argc, char *argv[])
{
    int i;
    for (i=0; i<argc; i=i+1)
        printf("%d %s\n", i, argv[i]);
    return 0;
}
```

The output would look like this:

```
0    search
1    manuscript.txt
2    Tatooine
```

Notice that **argv[0]** is actually the name of the program itself. Not many people write programs that run from a command line anymore, but you never know when it might come in handy. In the example given, we could pass **argv[1]** to the function **fopen** to actually open the file and pass **argv[2]** to a function that actually performs the searching in the file. More on file I/O in Chapter 15.

Why Not Macros?

An alternative to very small functions is to create macros using **#define**. Macros are not the most optimal way of doing things, and there may be side effects, but there are also benefits. Macros are considered inline code, which means the program does not have to shift control to a function. Conversely, use the macro 100 times and you get 100 pieces of code inserted into the program, while functions only use one. Here's an example of two functions to calculate the maximum of two numbers and cube a number:

```
#define CUBE(x) (x * x * x)
#define MAX(x,y) ((x) > (y) ? (x) : (y))
```

Inline Functions

C99 provides the ability to define inline functions, which we have discussed briefly. These can be important because all function calls entail some type of overhead. This means it takes some time to call the function, pass the arguments to it, and return information. Creating inline functions primarily makes things go faster. To create an inline function, we use the function specifier **inline**. Usually these inline functions are defined before any functions in a program. For example:

```
#include <stdio.h>

inline void ask(void)
{
    printf("Enter a number:");
```

```
    }

int main(void)
{
    ask();
}
```

abort and **exit**

Two functions available in **stdlib.h** deal with *leaving* a program. The first of these is the **exit** function. **exit** *always* quits a program, regardless of where it is called, and returns control to the operating system. This is very different from a **return** statement, which just throws you out of a function. Using **exit** is the best way to terminate a program. For example, the following code will cause the program to terminate if a divide by zero error is encountered:

```
if (denom != 0.0)
    result = numer / denom;
else
    exit(0);
```

exit can take as an argument a value that represents the status of the program. The argument is normally set to zero to indicate success or something else to indicate failure. When we have to abnormally terminate a program, we can use a function called **abort**. This really means that we use **abort** where something has gone seriously wrong. If we rewrite the previous code using **abort**, which takes no arguments:

```
if (denom != 0.0)
    result = numer / denom;
else
    abort();
```

then the following message may be output:

```
Abort trap
```

That tells us things didn't go exactly as we had planned.

A Final Good Cleanup

If we use **exit** or **return**, there is a function we can call that does some cleanup. It's called **atexit**. It accepts as its argument the name of a function to call when the program quits. The functions passed to **atexit** may not take any arguments, but up to 32 functions may be called. Here's an example:

```c
#include <stdio.h>
#include <stdlib.h>

void clean_up(void)
{
    printf("Deleting temporary files\n");
    system("del *.tmp");
}

int main(int argc, char *argv[])
{
    atexit(clean_up);

    return 0;
}
```

This basic program registers **"clean_up"** to be called when the program exits. The function **clean_up** then proceeds to delete all temporary files used during the program. This leads us to the function **system**. All the functions that are registered must be **void-void**. That is, they have no parameters and do not return anything.

The `system` Function

In the last example we used the system function. Its general form is:

```
system(command);
```

The function sends *command* to the operating system's command shell. If we want to delete files on Windows, we could use **del *.tmp**, or on Unix **rm *.tmp**. This is a useful, but potentially dangerous command.

Epilog

How many is too many, you ask? The term Hrair is a number too large to count, from the fictional language Lapine used in Richard Adams's *Watership Down*. The term "hrair limit" is used by Ed Yourdon in his book *Modern Structured Analysis* to dictate the maximum number of functions that should be called from the main program, set between five and nine. It is based on the notion of short term memory capacity "7±2" proposed by cognitive scientist George A. Miller.[1] You can still call other functions from within the called function; just try not to "overload" the main program with 1,001 functions. Hence the use of libraries! I think this notion of "7±2" also works well with function parameters. Too many parameters may lead to rearrangement of parameters during a function call, a subtle error that may not manifest itself in any obvious manner.

---

[1]Miller, G., "The Magical Number Seven, Plus or Minus Two: Some Limits on Our Capacity for Processing Information," *The Psychological Review*, 1956, Vol. 63, 81–97.

Exercises

Exercise 12.1

In aircraft and rocket design, overall propulsive efficiency η is the efficiency, in a percentage, with which the energy contained in a vehicle's propellant is converted into useful energy to replace losses resulting from air drag or gravity or to accelerate the vehicle. It is represented as follows:

$$\eta = \eta_c \eta_p$$

where η_c is the cycle efficiency, or the proportion of heat energy in the fuel that is converted to mechanical energy by the engine. For jet engines, the *propulsive efficiency*, η_p, is highest when the engine emits an exhaust jet at a speed that is the same as the vehicle velocity. The formula for an air-breathing engine is

$$\eta_p = \frac{2}{1 + \frac{c}{v}}$$

where c is the exhaust speed, and v is the speed of the aircraft.

Design a function named **eta**, which takes two arguments, c and v, and returns the propulsive efficiency to the function **main**.

Exercise 12.2

Extend the Easter Sunday program of Exercise 10.2 to incorporate modularity. Use two functions, called **Julian_Easter** and **Gregorian_Easter**, which are called from the main program when the appropriate option is chosen by the user.

Exercise 12.3

Using the program for wind chill derived in Exercise 10.3, modularize the program by creating a function called **wind_chill** to perform the calculations and return the wind chill index.

Exercise 12.4

Using the programs of Exercises 11.4 and 11.5, turn the *analysis* and *synthesis* algorithms into functions named **cubed_analysis** and **cubed_synthesis** respectively.

Hooray for Arrays

Should array indices start at 0 or 1? My compromise of 0.5 was rejected without, I thought, proper consideration.

—Stan Kelly-Bootle

Introduction

Sometimes we want to use more than one object in a program. Imagine designing a program to calculate the average surface temperature for each year in the period 1856–2005 based on measurements taken from up to 3,000 stations. Such is the data provided by the Climate Research Unit at the University of East Anglia. One of the data sets these researchers provide is the Global Temperature Record, a time series that shows the combined global land and marine surface temperature record from 1856 to 2005. The British Met (Metrological Office) provides data for central England alone for each month, 1659 to 2006, which amounts to 347 times 12, or 4,164 pieces of data (excluding 2006).[1] Want to calculate the average for each year and maybe some other statistics? How would we get the data into a program? Where and how would we store it?

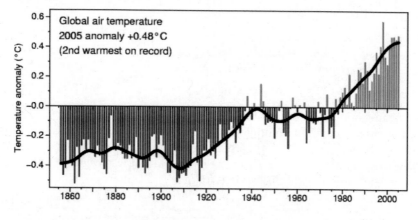

---

[1]http://www.met-office.gov.uk/research/hadleycentre/CR_data/Daily/HadCET_act.txt

Data from the Climate Research Unit, University of East Anglia (http://www.cru.uea.ac.uk/cru/info/warming/)

221

You'll get it the data from an existing file. But more on that later. What we're really concerned with here is storing and manipulating the data. To store 4,164 pieces of data, you could, of course, create one variable for *each* piece of data. That might look something like:

```
double jan_1659, feb_1659, mar_1659, apr_1659;
double may_1659, jun_1659, jul_1659, aug_1659;
double sep_1659, oct_1659, nov_1659, dec_1659;
```

Whew! Only 4,152 variables to go! You can see that this might be kind of a crazy methodology, especially when you figure out that there is no real easy way to input the data and store it. Lets try an example:

```
printf("Enter the temperatures for 1659: ");
scanf("%lf%lf%lf", &jan_1659, &feb_1659, &mar_1659);
scanf("%lf%lf%lf", &apr_1659, &may_1659, &jun_1659);
scanf("%lf%lf%lf", &jul_1659, &aug_1659, &sep_1659);
scanf("%lf%lf%lf", &oct_1659, &nov_1659, &dec_1659);
```

If your program crashes somewhere, it's back to square one! There must be an easier way—and there is. You can use arrays to store the information.

What Is an Array?

An *array* is one of the simplest forms of data structure, which is just a way of storing data in an efficient manner. In its simplest form, it is analogous to a vector (1D) or matrix (2D) in mathematics. Arrays hold a series of elements, usually of the same size and type. The concept of an array was first introduced in APL (short for A Programming Language) by Ken Iverson in 1964. An array can be declared using square brackets []. The basic format is:

```
type variable[size];
```

where **type** denotes the datatype associated with the array, **variable** denotes the name of the array, and **size** denotes its length. Getting back to the example, we could store each year separately, so an array for 1659 would look like:

```
double yr_1659[12];
```

This is an example of a **double** array. It tells the compiler that the variable being declared is an array containing multiple double precision values. This array is empty when it is created. This basically says that **yr_1659** is the name of an array that can store 12 **double** values. This is a neat little package. There is a more efficient way of storing ALL the data, but more on that later. This array is illustrated as follows:

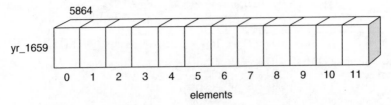

The first element equates to jan, the second to feb, and so on. To access an individual element of the array we use:

```
yr_1659[4] = 3.0;
```

Individual elements are accessed by their position in the array. This position is given by an *index*, which can also be called a *subscript*. The use of the number 4 within the square brackets denotes the fifth element of the array. Confused yet? Then read on!

Where Is Element 0?

One of the peculiarities of C is that the indices of an array start at zero. Yes, I know, it's confusing. The first element has an index of 0. The last element has an index of $n-1$, where n is the size of the array. C uses *zero*-based arrays. Other languages, such as MAT-LAB, are *one*-based, and some (e.g., Ada are n-based). An index n of an array is simply the address of the first element offset by n units. Consequently, index 0 points to the first element of the array. All descendants of C inherit this behavior. Forgetting that arrays begin with an index of zero is one of the most common sources of errors relating to arrays. The example array looks like this:

```
yr_1659[0] is the 1st element
yr_1659[1] is the 2nd element
yr_1659[2] is the 3rd element
yr_1659[3] is the 4th element
yr_1659[4] is the 5th element
yr_1659[5] is the 6th element
yr_1659[6] is the 7th element
yr_1659[7] is the 8th element
yr_1659[8] is the 9th element
yr_1659[9] is the 10th element
yr_1659[10] is the 11th element
yr_1659[11] is the 12th element
```

Subscripts

The *subscripts* used to access an element of an array need not be an integer constant. They can be any expression that evaluates to an integer. For example, if **i** and **j** are integer subscripts, then the following are all valid:

```
yr_1659[i+2]    yr_1659[i*2]    yr_1659[i+j]
```

For example, let's declare an array called **snow** to store the average snowfall for Toronto in the years 1996–2005:[2]

```
double snow[10] = {126.8,174.8,79.6,161.2,155.2,
                   99.0,100.7,143.8,121.3,146.8};
```

---

[2]http://www.climate.weatheroffice.ec.gc.ca/climateData/monthlydata_e.html

Now consider the following indices, where **i=5**:

```
snow[4]                    has the value 155.2
snow[i]                    has the value 99.0
snow[i+1]                  has the value 100.7
snow[i*2]                  Invalid! Attempt to access snow[10]
snow[(int)x[4]];           is the same as snow[155]
                           (which of course doesn't exist)
snow[i]=snow[i+1];         assigns 99.0 to snow[5]
y = snow[i++];             assigns y the value of snow[i], then
                           assigns 6 to i.
```

Arrays and scanf

We can also assign individual array elements values using the **scanf** function. For example:

```
scanf("%lf", &yr_1659[0]);
```

There is no way of reading a whole array using a single **scanf** statement. To read in the twelve values of **yr_1659** would require the use of a loop of the form:

```
for (i=0; i<12; i=i+1)
    scanf("%lf", &yr_1659[i]);
```

The one caveat is with strings, which *can* be read using a single **scanf**. (See Chapter 14).

Initializing Arrays

Once we have created an array, we want to store values in it. Like any variable, after it is created, all the elements are empty. If the data for 1659 is:

```
3.0  4.0  6.0  7.0  11.0  13.0  16.0  16.0  13.0  10.0  5.0  2.0
```

Then we could initialize the array **yr_1659** in a number of ways:

```
double yr_1659[12] =
{3.0,4.0,6.0,7.0,11.0,13.0,16.0,16.0,13.0,10.0,5.0,2.0};
```

OR

```
double yr_1659[] =
{3.0,4.0,6.0,7.0,11.0,13.0,16.0,16.0,13.0,10.0,5.0,2.0};
```

The only difference between these two is that the latter omits the size of the array. If we omit the size specification, the compiler automatically determines the size based on the number of initializers present. Or we could read it *directly* from the file, but we'll tackle that later. The general form of the direct array initialization is:

```
type variable[size] = {val1, val2, . . ., valn};
```

If the number of initialized values is less than the declared number of elements listed, the initializers are applied starting with the array element 0. All the other elements are initialized to zero. For example consider:

```
double yr_1659[12] = {0};
```

This is a neat way of initializing all the values of the array **yr_1659** to 0. With C99 we can also pick and choose the elements that are initialized. For example:

```
double yr_1659[] = {[9] = 10.0,5.0,2.0};
```

Here we use an index in brackets in the initialization list to specify a particular element. In this case it initializes **yr_1659[9]** to 10.0, **yr_1659[10]** to 5.0, and **yr_1659[11]** to 2.0. All others are initialized to zero.

Processing Arrays

Arrays can be processed very efficiently using loops. Instead of a statement such as

```
sum_1659 = yr_1659[0] + yr_1659[1]  + yr_1659[2] +
           yr_1659[3] + yr_1659[4]  + yr_1659[5] +
           yr_1659[6] + yr_1659[7]  + yr_1659[8] +
           yr_1659[9] + yr_1659[10] + yr_1659[11];
```

we can use a loop:

```
for (i=0; i<=11; i=i+1)
    sum = sum + yr_1659[i];
```

We can also use a loop to interactively initialize the array:

```
for (i=0; i<=11; i=i+1)
    scanf("%lf", &yr_1659[i]);
```

This is much nicer, especially if you are processing a huge array. We might also like to sequence through an array. Let's say we want to find the maximum temperature in **yr_1659**. The algorithm to locate the maximum value initially assumes that the first element is the largest number. As we sequence through the array, the maximum is compared to each element. When an element with a higher value is found, it becomes the new maximum. For example:

```
1    double max_temp;
2    max_temp = yr_1659[0];
3    for (i=1; i<12; i=i+1)
4        if (yr_1659[i] > max_temp)
5            max_temp = yr_1659[i];
```

The second line of code sets the maximum to the first element of **yr_1659**. Line 3 invokes a **for** loop to iterate through the remaining elements of the array, from element 1 to 11. The **if** statement within the **for** loop compares each element in turn against the value in **max_temp.** If a value is greater than **max_temp**, then **max_temp** is assigned its value. Some languages allow you to process portions of an array without having to use looping structures. However in C, you must use a loop to access the elements. For example, to sum the values of the summer months (June to August) you would use the following loop:

```
double sum=0.0;
for (i=5; i<=7; i=i+1)
      sum = sum + yr_1659[i];
```

Loops are an array's best friend.

 One caveat with arrays is that C *does not* check the value of the index being used. For example, try to access the 13th element of **yr_1659**, as in:

```
printf("%d", yr_1659[12]);
```

Sometimes the compiler won't report an error like this, just output some nonsense. Sometimes it will crash, other times it won't. *Be careful with subscripting.*

Two-Dimensional Arrays

It can be tedious to create 347 different arrays named: **yr_1659, yr_1660, . . . , yr_2005.** It's still a bit of a nightmare from a data storage point of view. An alternative is to create a *two-dimensional* (2D) array. This is just an *array of arrays*. For the temperatures this could be achieved by making the declaration:

```
double yr1659_2005[347][12];
```

This array now has 4,164 elements arranged into 347 rows and 12 columns. It's now a huge matrix, with one name: **yr1659_2005.** Each row will be used to store a year, and each of the columns a month in that year.

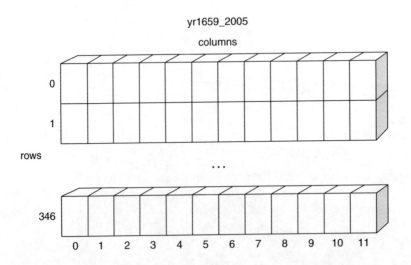

We can now use this array to calculate the means for each year, using just two loops. First we create an array to store the mean temperatures for each year. There are 347 years, so the array will have 347 elements:

```
double yr_Means[347];
```

We use the name **yr_Means**, because μ is commonly used to represent the arithmetic mean of a statistical population. So now, create two loops to handle passing through each of the elements. We want to pass though the months of each year (rows) and each year.

```
1   for (i=0; i<347; i=i+1)
2   {
3       sum = 0.0;
4       for (j=0; j<12; j=j+1)
5           sum = sum + yr1659_2005[i][j];
6       yr_Means[i] = sum / 12.0;
7   }
```

The statement on line 3 sets the values of sum to zero before each year (row) is processed. If we didn't do this, the sum would *compound* each year. The statement on line 6 assigns the summed value for a particular year divided by the number of months to the corresponding element in **yr_Means**. Note that the first **for** loop processes the indices of the rows (years), while the inner loop processes the indices of the columns (months). Remember also that both indices for the rows and columns start at zero. The rule of thumb is one loop for each dimension in an array. We could also have written lines 5 and 6 in another way:

```
5   yr_Means[i] = yr_Means[i] + yr1659_2005[i][j];
6   yr_Means[i] = yr_Means[i] / 12.0;
```

As long as the array **yr_Means** was initialized to zero first, maybe using:

```
double yr_Means[347] = {0.0};
```

Initializing 2D Arrays

As with 1D arrays, 2D arrays can be initialized at the time of declaration. Additional braces can be used to separate individual rows, for example:

```
double yr1659_2005 [347][12] =
{{3.0,4.0,6.0,7.0,11.0,13.0,16.0,16.0,13.0,10.0,5.0,2.0},
 {0.0,4.0,6.0,9.0,11.0,14.0,15.0,16.0,13.0,10.0,6.0,5.0},
 . . .
 {6.0,4.3,7.2,8.9,11.4,15.5,16.9,16.2,15.2,13.1,6.2,4.4}};
```

or:

```
double yr1659_2005 [347][12] =
{3.0,4.0,6.0,7.0,11.0,13.0,16.0,16.0,13.0,10.0,5.0,2.0,
 0.0,4.0,6.0,9.0,11.0,14.0,15.0,16.0,13.0,10.0,6.0,5.0,
 . . .
 6.0,4.3,7.2,8.9,11.4,15.5,16.9,16.2,15.2,13.1,6.2,4.4};
```

2D Arrays Are Really 1D Arrays

C doesn't actually treat multi-dimensional arrays as such. It actually turns every 1+ dimensional array into a 1D array. So **yr1659_2005** is represented by the compiler as a 1D array with 4,164 elements. But all this happens transparently, so don't worry about it.

Passing Arrays to Functions

Individual array elements can be passed to functions in a similar way to normal variables. For example, remember the function **swap** from the previous chapter? Here it is again:

```
void swap(int *x, int *y)
{
    int temp;
    temp = *x;
    *x = *y;
    *y = temp;
}
```

We could swap two elements of **yr_1659**. We do this by calling the function in the following manner:

```
swap(&yr_1659[4],&yr_1659[7]);
```

This will swap the fourth and seventh elements. If we pass individual elements of an array, they are treated in the same way as normal parameters with respect to pass-by-value and pass-by-reference. The great thing about arrays in that they provide a compact way of passing information to a function. Imagine if you had to pass the individual temperatures for each month? Too much overhead would be required. Now consider the following example function, which calculates the means for each year in a similar fashion to the code generated earlier.

```
void calc_means(double temp[347][12],
                int dx, int dy, double yr_Means[347])
{
    int i, j;
    double sum;

    for (i=0; i<dx; i=i+1)
    {
        sum = 0.0;
        for (j=0; j<dy; j=j+1)
            sum = sum + temp[i][j];
        yr_Means[i] = sum / 12.0;
    }
}
```

The function has four parameters, relating to the temperature array **(temp)**, its dimensions **(dx,dy)** and the array of means **(yr_Means)**. The outer **for** loop cycles through the years, while the inner **for** loop cycles through the months. In the main program, we could call this function is the following manner:

```
double muTemperature[347];
double yr1659_2005[347][12];
. . .
calc_means(yr1659_2005,347,12,muTemperature);
```

The difference with passing arrays lies in their behavior. In normal pass-by-value, a copy of a variable is passed to a function. If we did the same with arrays, a copy of the array would have to be made. That's fine for small arrays, but not so ideal for large arrays. If we passed **yr1659_2005**, we would have to use another 347×12 pieces of memory. To stop this from happening, whole arrays are passed as *pass-by-reference only*. However, do not use an ampersand (&) with an array name, because all arrays are passed by *address*, so they do not require one. If you use an & in front of an array name, you are essentially trying to pass *an address of an address*—and it won't work. Therefore, any changes made to the array by the function are made *directly* on the array itself. Be careful!

Multidimensional Arrays

1D or 2D arrays are the most commonly used, but C can declare arrays of any number of dimensions. For example we could create a 3D array to hold yearly temperature for 1659 to 2005 for 20 different locations in the world:

```
double global_yr1659_2005[20][347][12];
```

In this case we have swapped the dimensions around, so the first dimension represents the locations, the second represents the year, and the third represents the month. So an assignment like:

```
global_yr1659_2005[2][346][9] = 19;
```

would assign the value 19 to the third location, year 2005, and month October. This array effectively has 83,280 elements, or 20 rows, 347 columns, and 12 planes. As another example, consider storing words from a book. A book can be represented as a four-dimensional entity: the first dimension might represent the page number, the second dimension represents the line on a page, the third dimension represents the position of the word on the line, and the fourth dimension actually represents the word itself. So we could declare the following array:

```
char book[300][50][20][30];
```

This array **book**, represents a book with 300 pages, 50 lines per page, 20 words per lines, and a word length of 30 characters. That's 9 million elements! Therefore, a statement such as:

```
printf("%s", book[43][23][11]);
```

Would print the 11th word on the 23rd line of the 43rd page.

Using `sizeof`

Instead of having to pass the length of an array to a function, we can use the following macro to determine the size of an array within a function:

```
#define length(x) (sizeof(x) / sizeof((x)[0]))
```

A quick change in the macro

```
#define lengthT(x) (sizeof(x) / sizeof((x)[0][0]))
```

yields the total number of elements in a 2D array.

Variable Length Arrays

C99 allows us to use something called *variable length arrays* (VLA). This implies that a variable can be used when specifying the array dimensions. What it does *not* mean is that the length of the array can be modified after it is declared. That's why they work really well in functions, where storage is automatically created and destroyed when the function is called. For example:

```
int n=20;
double snow[n];
```

Declares an array **snow** with 20 elements. We can basically create the size of an array at runtime now, whereas before we were limited to specifying the size at compile time. Consider the following example:

```
1    int n;
2
3    printf("Enter the number of years: ");
4    scanf("%d", &n);
5
6    double snow[n];
```

We can now enter the length of the array *before* we actually declare it. This works well with arrays passed to functions. Consider the following function, which calculates the average snowfall for a number of years.

```
double mean_snowfall(int n, double a[n])
{
    int i;
    double sum=0.0;
    for (i=0; i<n; i=i+1)
        sum = sum + a[i];
    return sum/n;
}
```

When we create a function prototype for this function, we need to replace the dimensions with asterisks:

```
double mean_snowfall(int, double a[*]);
```

We can now call this function in the following manner:

```
double snow1970s[10];
double snow2000s[6];
double sum_1970s, sum_2000s;

sum_1970s = mean_snowfall(10,snow1970s);
sum_2000s = mean_snowfall(6,snow2000s);
```

The function **mean_snowfall** can now be called with different-sized arrays. Note the caveat here is that the size of the array occurs *before* the actual array on the parameter list. The caveat with VLA is that they can't be initialized in a declaration.

 Heat Index

Remember the humidex we calculated in the first case study? In the U.S.A., a similar measure called the heat index is used. It combines air temperature and relative humidity to determine an apparent temperature—how hot it actually feels. One way of calculating the heat index is by using matrices (for Fahrenheit):[3]

$$HI=\begin{bmatrix} 1 & T & T^2 & T^3 \end{bmatrix} \begin{bmatrix} 16.923 & 5.37941 & 7.28898e{-}3 & 2.91583e{-}5 \\ 1.85212e{-}1 & -1.00254e{-}1 & -8.14971e{-}4 & 1.97483e{-}7 \\ 9.41695e{-}3 & 3.45372e{-}4 & 1.02102e{-}5 & 8.43296e{-}10 \\ -3.8646e{-}5 & 1.42721e{-}6 & -2.18429e{-}8 & -4.81975e{-}11 \end{bmatrix} \begin{bmatrix} 1 \\ RH \\ RH^2 \\ RH^2 \end{bmatrix}$$

Now this problem can be easily solved using two-dimensional arrays. First we need to declare some arrays to hold the temperature and relative humidity calculations:

```
double temp[4][1], relH[4];
```

We can now store these values:

```
temp[0][0] = 1;
temp[1][0] = temperature;
temp[2][0] = temperature * temperature;
temp[3][0] = temperature * temperature * temperature;

relH[0] = 1;
relH[1] = rH;
relH[2] = rH * rH;
relH[3] = rH * rH * rH;
```

---

[3]Smith, Roland B., *Meteorology for Scientists and Engineers*, 2nd ed.

Now we have to declare the central matrix, which holds all the constant values used in the calculation:

```
double m[4][4] = {{16.923, 5.37941, 7.28898e-3, 2.91583e-5},
                  {1.85212e-1, -1.00254e-1, -8.14971e-4, 1.97483e-7},
                  {9.41695e-3, 3.45372e-4, 1.02102e-5, 8.43296e-10},
                  {-3.8646e-5, 1.42721e-6, -2.18429e-8, -4.81975e-11}};
```

Phew! That's a lot of typing. Double check the numbers to make sure they're right. Even a small error produces the wrong calculation.

Now we can use some loops to do the actual calculations. The first part of the calculation is a $[1 \times 4] \times [4 \times 4] = [1 \times 4]$, so we need a place to store the intermediary result:

```
double temp[4];

for (k=1; k<=4; k=k+1)
{
    sum = 0.0;
    for (i=1; i<=4; i=i+1)
        sum = sum + temp[i][0] * m[i][k];
    temp[k] = sum;
}
```

The second part of the calculation is a $[1 \times 4] \times [4 \times 1] = [1 \times 1]$, so we need a place to store the intermediary result:

```
double temp[4];
humidex = 0.0;
for (i=1; i<=4; i=i+1)
    humidex = humidex + (temp[i] * relH[i]);
```

Epilog

Arrays are the building blocks of data storage. You can store a digital picture in an array, or a text document, or even a song. Once you learn about pointers, arrays can be transformed into dynamic arrays . . . for the willing anyway. A dynamic array is one that can be resized, allowing elements to be added and removed. This means that the size of the array doesn't have to be fixed and can change, depending on the size of the data.

Exercises

Exercise 13.1

Write a program to derive and store Pascal's triangle (Exercise 11.1) in an array.

Exercise 13.2

Write a function to read a 4-by-4 matrix and output the sum of all its elements. Here is a sample run:

```
Enter a 4-by-4 matrix row by row:
1 2 3 4{Enter]
5 6 7 8[Enter]
10 11 12[Enter]
13 14 15 16[Enter]
Sum of the matrix is 136
```

Exercise 13.3

The interquartile mean (IQM) is a truncated mean and is similar to the scoring method used in sports that are evaluated by a panel of judges such as ice skating: discard the lowest and highest scores, and calculate the mean value of the remaining scores. In IQM, the lowest and highest 25 percent of scores are discarded:

$$x_{IQM} = \frac{2}{n} \sum_{i=\frac{n}{4}+1}^{\frac{3n}{4}} x_i$$

The series of numbers must be ordered for the process to work properly. Adapting the *bubblesort* algorithm from the case studies, write a program to calculate the interquartile mean of the following set of numbers:

5, 8, 4, 38, 8, 6, 9, 7, 7, 3, 1, 6

The program should contain a function **interquartile** that takes as input the array of numbers and calculates the interquartile mean.

Characters That String

Syntactic sugar causes cancer of the semicolon.
—Alan Perlis

Introduction

Until now we have dealt mostly with numbers. Programs also need to deal with individual characters and groups of characters known as *strings*.

What a Character!

As we learned earlier, characters are really just small integers. This just means that characters have an underlying integer-valued representation denoted by the ASCII table.

Character I/O

C provides two functions for dealing with character I/O: **getchar** and **putchar.** We use **getchar** to read in a single character. In reality the following two expressions are equivalent:

```
scanf("%c", &ch);
ch = getchar();
```

We use **putchar** to output a character. For example:

```
putchar(ch);
```

Here's a simple example that converts any input in lowercase to uppercase:

```
#include <stdio.h>
int main(void)
{
    char c;
```

```
        while ((c = getchar()) != EOF)
            if ('a' <= c && c <= 'z')
                putchar(c +'A' - 'a');
            else if (c == '\n')
                putchar('\n');
            else putchar(c);

        return 0;
}
```

Because the values of the letters in both the lower and uppercase characters occur in sequence, the expression 'a'+1 has the value 'b', and 'Z'–'A' has the value 25. If the variable **c** has the value of a lowercase letter, then the expression **c** +'A'–'a' has the value of the corresponding uppercase letter.

One of the problems with **getchar** is that it doesn't *really* read a single character from the input. It waits until you type the input and terminate it with something that signals the end of input, typically the pressing of the Enter key. It then returns a single character. However, it technically returns a single character from the *buffer*. For example, in the code

```
int num;
char ch;
scanf("%d", &num);
ch = getchar();
```

if we enter "67 g" when the program is running, 67 will be stored in **num**, and a space will be stored in **ch**. This is because the separating space is a character stored next in the buffer after the number 67. The **g** is ignored. If we instead enter "67g" with no spaces, **g** is stored in **ch**, because it is next in the buffer.

> The identifier **EOF** is mnemonic for "end-of-file," a symbolic marker that signifies the end of the stream of input. In Unix EOF is Ctrl-D, whereas in Windows it is Ctrl-Z followed by Enter. (See Chapter 15.)

Character Macros

The system provides a standard header file **ctype.h**, which contains a set of *macros* to analyze characters and functions that are used to convert characters. These macros all take an argument of type **int** and return an **int** value that is either nonzero (true) or zero (false).

MACRO	Return nonzero if:
isalpha(ch)	ch is a letter (a–z, A–Z)
isupper(ch)	ch is an uppercase letter (A–Z)
islower(ch)	ch is a lowercase letter (a–z)
isdigit(ch)	ch is a digit (0–9)
isalnum(ch)	ch is a letter or digit (a–z, A–Z, 0–9)
isxdigit(ch)	ch is a hexadecimal digit (0–9, a–z, A–Z)

`isspace(ch)`	ch is a white space character
`ispunct(ch)`	ch is a punctuation character
`isprint(ch)`	ch is a printable character
`isgraph(ch)`	ch is a printable character, but not a space
`iscntrl(ch)`	ch is a control character
`isascii(ch)`	ch is an ASCII character
`Isblank(ch)`	ch is a tab or space

These functions convert characters

MACRO	Effect
`toupper(ch)`	Changes **ch** from lowercase to uppercase
`tolower(ch)`	Changes **ch** from uppercase to lowercase
`toascii(ch)`	Changes **ch** to ASCII code

Looking now at the previous example, we can replace the cryptic character expressions with:

```
#include <stdio.h>
#include <ctype.h>

int main(void)
{
    char c;

    while ((c = getchar()) != EOF)
        if (islower(c))
            putchar(toupper(c));
        else if (c == '\n')
            putchar('\n');
        else putchar(c);

    return 0;
}
```

Basically we have replaced the expression **'a' <= c && c <= 'z'** with the macro **islower(c)**, and the character math **c +'A' – 'a'** with **toupper(c)**.

Strings

Arrays of characters are more commonly termed *strings*. Why do we deal with arrays of characters differently from arrays with numbers? Partially because characters work a little differently. A string is any sequence of characters enclosed in double quotes. In C a string is stored as an array of characters terminated by a special end-of-string marker called a *null character*. The null character is represented by the *escape sequence* \0 and denotes the end of string (EOS). The following string uses five storage locations, with the last character being the end-of-string marker.

J	e	d	i	\0							

This shows how the string "Jedi" would be stored in memory. Note the double quotes are not stored as part of the string. Because a string is stored as an array, the individual elements of the string can be manipulated in the same ways that elements in a numeric array are. The one difference is that C has functions that are specifically designed to handle strings. This is how we would declare this string:

```
char s[] = "Jedi";
```

This is because numbers and characters stored in arrays are quite different. If I have an **int** array containing the numbers 12, 7, 93, 41, and 78, the characteristic that binds these numbers together is the fact that they are all integers. They may all represent temperature measurements from a thermometer, but they are not connected together. If I put them together they become 127934178, which is a meaningless number. Strings on the other hand are essentially "words." Here "J", "e", "d", and "i" are bound together to form the word "Jedi." In strings, the characters taken individually are somewhat meaningless; collectively they form something.

Declaring Strings

Strings can be declared using the following format:

```
char str[20];
```

This declares **str** to be a character array of length 20. This means we can store 19 characters and the EOS character. Because strings are arrays, they operate in the same way, with indices in the range 0 . . . n–1. The following general format applies to strings:

```
char variable[size];
```

where **variable** denotes the name of the string, and **size** denotes its length. When we create a string, we have to be sure that the number of elements is at least one more than we need due to the EOS marker!

Initializing Strings

Just as numerical arrays can be initialized when they are declared, so too can strings. For example:

```
char dna[] = {'a','t','c','c','\0'};
```

There is a second equivalent syntax for initializing character arrays.

```
char dna[] = "atcc";
```

Note that for this syntax, we do not need the EOS marker.

String I/O

The first difference you will notice with strings occurs when you input and output them. There is a special way of reading them in, and C actually provides a separate I/O function especially for strings.

The first way is to simply use **scanf** with **%s** as the formatting character:

```
char str[20];
printf("Enter a string: ");
scanf("%s", str);
```

This code snippet reads a string in and stores it in the character array **str**. Notice that scanf reads in the whole string, not just an individual character. Also note that when scanf is used for inputting strings, the & is not used before the string name. Since the array name is a pointer constant (as in a normal array), it is equivalent to the address of the first storage location reserved for the string. Therefore **str** is equivalent to &str[0].

The caveat with this approach is that if we enter the text "**Jedi Knight,**" only the word *Jedi* is stored in **str**. The **scanf** function reads a set of characters up to either a blank space or a new line character. To properly enter the text "**Jedi Knight**" would require a **scanf** statement of the form:

```
char str1[10], str2[10];
printf("Enter a string: ");
scanf("%s %s", str1, str2);
```

Here the word **Jedi** would be assigned to the string **str1**, and **Knight** would be assigned to the string **str2**.

To read only *n* characters using scanf, we can use the following format:

```
scanf("%ns");
```

Therefore, scanf will read characters until the first whitespace character is encountered, or after n characters have been read. For output, we can use a **printf** statement of the following form:

```
printf("%s", str1);
```

A better way of reading in strings is using the **fgets** function. The **fgets** function reads an entire line, up to *n* characters or until the first newline character (Enter key) is encountered. Consider the following example:

```
char str[20];
printf("Enter a string: ");
fgets(str, 20, stdin);
```

This reads a maximum of 10 characters from the standard input (including the EOS character) and stores them in **str**. If we were to enter

```
I'm sorry, Dave. I'm afraid I can't do that.
```

then fgets would store "**I'm sorry, Dave. I'**", and the EOS character. If we entered only:

```
I'm sorry, Dave.
```

Then **fgets** would store the entire text, in addition to the newline character and the EOS character. The main differences between **scanf** and **fgets** are that (i) **fgets** is not limited by the occurrence of whitespaces in a string; (ii) **scanf** skips leading whitespace characters, whereas **fgets** doesn't; and (iii) **fgets** will read up to *n* characters including whitespaces.

For output, we can use the function **fputs**, which works in an analogous way to **fgets**:

```
fputs(str, stdout);
```

Here the string stored in **str** is output to the standard output (stdout).

 ## Assigning Strings

Strings *cannot* be assigned to one another. For example,

```
str1 = str2;
```

will *not* work. Nor can we compare two strings using == as in:

```
if (str1 == str2)
```

To achieve both these operations, we need to use predefined string functions.

String Library

There is an entire library of functions dedicated to working with strings: **string.h.** Here's a list of functions with a brief description.

> **strcat(s1,s2)**
> - Takes two strings as arguments and appends **s2** to **s1**. The string **s1** is returned.
>
> **strncat(s1,s2,n)**
> - Appends exactly **n** characters of **s2** to **s1**.
>
> **strcmp(s1,s2)**
> - Takes two strings as arguments. An integer is returned that is less than, equal to, or greater than zero, depending on whether **s1** is lexicographically less than, equal to, or greater than **s2**.
>
> **strncmp(s1,s2,n)**
> - Like **strcmp()**, but only compares the first **n** characters of the strings.
>
> **strcpy(s1,s2)**
> - The string **s2** is copied into **s1** until /0 is moved. Whatever exists in **s1** is overwritten. The value **s1** is returned.
>
> **strncpy(s1,s2,n)**
> - Like **strcpy()**, but only copies the first **n** characters of string **s1** into **s2**.
>
> **strlen(s)**
> - Counts the number of characters in the string **s** before \0 is returned.

To see how these functions work, let's start with the following strings:

```
char str1[20] = "Obi";
char str2[20] = "Wan";
int x;
```

First let's compare two strings to test whether they are equal:

```
x = strcmp(str1, str2);
```

In this case **x** has the value −1, because **Obi** is lexicographically less than **Wan**. If **str1** is equal to **str2**, then **strcmp** returns 0. If **str1** precedes **str2** alphabetically, **strcmp** returns a negative number, but if **str1** succeeds **str2**, **strcmp** returns a positive number. In actual fact **strcmp** compares characters using their numeric ASCII representations. In ASCII uppercase characters occur before lowercase characters, so **strcmp("K", "k")**; is negative. Most of the time we really only care if two strings match. Now let's look at joining strings together with **strcat**. The function name, short for *string concatenation*, basically involves appending the second string onto the end of the first.

```
strcat(str1, str2);
```

This means that **str1** now contains the string **ObiWan**. The second string **str2** is left unchanged. Now **strcat** doesn't bother to check to see whether the second string will fit into the first string. If there isn't enough space, there will be problems with accessing elements and some runtime problems.

We could use **strlen** to calculate the length of **str1**:

```
x = strlen(str1);
```

The value of **x** is 6. Now let's make a copy using the **strcpy** function. For example:

```
char str3[20];
strcpy(str3, str1);
```

This copies the string in **str1** to **str3**. This function is the string equivalent of the assignment operator. Some less commonly used string functions are:

strstr(s1,s2)

- Attempts to find the first occurrence of the substring **s2** inside the string **s1**. A pointer to the first occurrence of **s2** is returned, or NULL, if the string cannot be found.

strrchr(s,ch)

- Attempts to find the last occurrence of the character **ch** inside the string **s**. A pointer to the last occurrence of **ch** is returned, or NULL, if the character cannot be found.

strrstr(s,ch)

- Attempts to find the first occurrence of the character **ch** inside the string **s**. A pointer to the first occurrence of **ch** is returned, or NULL, if the character cannot be found.

 Hydroxide

In this example we will write and test a function **hydroxide** that returns a value of 1 if its input argument ends in the substring OH. We will test the function on the following data:

```
KOH   H2O2   NaCl   NaOH   C9H8O4   MgOH

#include <stdio.h>
#include <string.h>
```

```
int hydroxide(char s[])
{
    int sL;
    sL = strlen(s);
    if ((s[sL-2] == 'O') && (s[sL-1] == 'H'))
        return 1;
    else
        return 0;
}
```

The first line of the function

```
int hydroxide(char s[])
```

sets the name of the function as **hydroxide** and specifies the return type as **int** and the argument passed to the function as a character array, or string. The next two lines

```
int sL;
sL = strlen(s);
```

declare an integer variable **sL** and assign it the length of the string **s**, using the function **strlen** from the library **string.h**. Finally, an **if** statement is used to check whether the last two elements of the string consist of the letters "O" and "H" respectively.

```
if ((s[sL-2] == 'O') && (s[sL-1] == 'H'))
    return 1;
else
    return 0;
```

For example, consider the following rendition of **s**:

The length of the string is 4 (i.e., **sL=4**). So the algorithm checks position **sL-2** (element 2), and **sL-1** (element 3). In this case element 2 = "O" and element 3 = "H." Here's the main program:

```
void main(void)
{
    char S[12];
    printf("Enter a compound: ");
    scanf("%s",S);
    if (hydroxide(S))
        printf("%s is a hydroxide\n",S);
}
```

Strings as Pointers

There is another way to tackle strings. Instead of creating a string as an array, it is possible to create a string using a pointer. For example the definition

```
char *str2;
```

creates a pointer to a character. Once a pointer to a character is defined, assignment statements can be made such as:

```
str2 = "obi wan kenobi";
```

In this assignment, **str2** receives the address of the first position used to store the string. The main difference is in the way the pointer is created. If we declare a string in the traditional manner

```
char str1[20];
```

there is a fixed amount of storage for the array (in this case 20 characters). This causes the compiler to create a pointer constant. This precludes the use of an assignment statement, so the statement

```
str1 = "obi wan kenobi";
```

is not valid. We then have to use **strcpy** to assign values to the string. For example,

```
strcpy(str1,"obi wan kenobi");
```

explicitly creates a pointer variable first. The pointer is then used to hold the address of a string when the string is specified. Using a pointer to a character allows string assignments to be made. Both definitions allow initializations to be made during string assignment:

```
char str1[20] = "obi wan kenobi";
char *str2 = "obi wan kenobi";
```

From a storage perspective:

str1 reserves a series of 20 storage locations, and the first 15 are initialized.

str2 allows a variable length string to be stored.

Arrays of Strings

A simple extension to 1D strings is an *array of strings,* or 2D string:

```
char hydroxide[3][5];
```

The first element tells us how many strings, the second the maximum length of each string. This string can be initialized as follows:

```
char hydroxide[3][5] = {"NaOH","MgOH","KOH"};
```

This creates a 2D array of three rows and five columns of characters. Each row designates a different hydroxide. The rows are five columns in length to accommodate the element (maximum two characters), the hydroxide "OH," and a character for the NULL at the end of the string. 2D strings can also be created using pointers (more on this in the chapter on pointers). We don't have to specify the last number in square brackets when we reference the array. To print the hydroxides, we would use the code snippet:

```
for (i=0; i<3; i=i+1)
    printf("%s", hydroxide[i]);
```

In Chapter 13 we declared a multidimensional array called **book**

```
char book[300][50][20][30];
```

which is just a 4D array of strings with the last element [30] representing the maximum length of the words in the book. We can still use:

```
printf("%c", book[43][23][11][17]);
```

to print the 18th character of the 12th word, on the 24th line of the 44th page.

Getting Numbers from Strings

Sometimes we enter numbers as strings. For example if we enter an equation 5+27, we have a combination of both numbers (5,27) and symbols (+). How do we convert characters representing numbers to actual numbers we can use? The **stdlib.h** library includes three functions to perform this task: **atoi, atof,** and **atol. atoi** is concerned with converting an ASCII string to an integer and is pronounced "A to I." **atof** converts text to floating point numbers. **atol** converts text to **long.** Here's an example:

```
char input[20];
int temperature;
scanf("%s", input);
temperature = atoi(input);
printf("%d", temperature);
```

This snippet of code reads in a numeric temperature as a string and converts it to an integer using **atoi,** storing the resulting value in the variable **temperature.**

Assembling and Disassembling Strings

There are two functions for I/O related to strings: **sprintf** and **sscanf.** They are really like **printf** and **scanf** for strings. **sprintf** is used to "assemble" a string from smaller pieces, whereas **sscanf** may be used to disassemble a string into smaller pieces. For example:

```
char str1[20] = "obi wan kenobi";
char str3[40];
sprintf(str3, "%s", str1);
```

writes the string **str1** into **str3** rather than outputting to the standard output. In the same light, **sscanf** can be used to read from a string. For example, if we declare the following string

```
int day, month, year;
char date[12] = "06/11/2001";
```

then the statement

```
sscanf(date, "%d/%d/%d", &day,&month,&year);
```

extracts the data from the string **date** and converts it to integer form, storing it in the variables **day**, **month**, and **year**. This is an alternative to using the function **atoi**.

Exercises

Exercise 14.1

A social insurance number (SIN) is a number issued in Canada to administer various government programs. Social insurance numbers can be validated through a simple check digit process called the *Luhn Algorithm*. A SIN can be validated by multiplying each digit in the number by a corresponding 1 or 2. For example:

```
046 454 286
121 212 121
-----------
086 858 276
```

Notice that in the second-to-last column, the answer is 16. In this case, we simply add the two digits together and insert the result (1 + 6 =7). We then add all the numbers together:

```
0+4+6+4+5+4+2+8+6 = 50
```

If the SIN is valid, the sum will be divisible by 50.

Exercise 14.2

The international standard letter/number mapping found on telephones is

```
2 = ABC
3 = DEF
4 = GHI
5 = JKL
6 = MNO
7 = PQRS
8 = TUV
9 = WXYZ
```

For example **1-800-ADGJMPT** would become 1-800-2345678.

Write a program that prompts a user to enter a phone number as a string. The program should translate a letter in the phone number to a digit, and leave all other characters intact.

Exercise 14.3

A palindrome is a word, phrase, number, or other sequence of units that has the property of reading the same in either direction. For examples, "Madam, I'm Adam" is a palindrome because it is spelled the same reading it from front to back as from back to front. The number 12321 is a numerical palindrome. Palindromes date back at least to A.D. 79, as the palindromic Latin word square "Sator Arepo Tenet Opera Rotas" was found at the ruins of Herculaneum. Write a program containing one function (apart from **main**) named is_palindrome that checks to see if a word entered by the user is a palindrome. Test your program on (i) **tattarrattat** , the longest palindromic word found in the Oxford English Dictionary, coined by James Joyce in *Ulysses* (1922) for a knock on the door, and (ii) the Finnish word **saippuakivikauppias** (soap-stone vendor), claimed to be the world's longest palindromic word in everyday use.

Exercise 14.4

The Soundex Code, developed by Russell and Odell in the early 1900s, is a phonetic algorithm that provides a way of reducing similar-sounding words to a common code. The algorithm drops vowels and silent letters, removes double letters, and then assigns to the remaining letters the numbers from the following classes:

BFPV	1
CGJKQSXZ	2
DT	3
L	4
MN	5
R	6

If the Soundex codes of two words are the same, that means they are pronounced the same way. Words are first abbreviated using the following simple rules:

1. Leave the first letter of the word as is.
2. Delete all occurrences of A, E, I, O, U, W, H, and Y.
3. Replace double letters by a single letter.
4. Stop after 4 characters are produced.

Improvements to Soundex are the basis for many modern phonetic algorithms. For example:

HAWKSLEY → H~~AWK~~SL~~EY~~ → HKSL → H224

Write a function to compute the Soundex code of a word.

15

Input and Output

The system should treat all user input as sacred.
—Jef Raskin

Introduction

I/O, as we discussed earlier, is just shorthand for Input/Output. Computers are all about getting input, processing it, and providing output. That's what they do. These days there are a myriad of input devices. Examples include *USB* (Universal Serial Bus), and *FireWire* (also known as i.Link or IEEE 1394). If there is no input, then there is no output. When we talk about *standard I/O*, we mean the way the computer communicates with humans: keyboards for standard input, video screens for standard output. In C, these are called **stdin** and **stdout,** respectively. When we want to use standard I/O in C programs, we have to include the file **stdio.h,** the library file for standard I/O functions. With **stdio.h,** there is no I/O in C. The most basic I/O functions are **printf** and **scanf.** We have discussed them briefly, and you have no doubt figured out some of the more intricate formatting effects that can be achieved with them. This section describes them a little further.

Streams

Streams are preexisting input or output channels between a program and its environment. There are three basic streams:

- **stdin:** The standard input for reading (keyboard)
- **stdout:** The standard output for writing (monitor)
- **stderr:** The standard error for writing error messages

Printing with **printf**

The function **printf** has the following general format:

```
printf(format_string, arg1, arg2, . . ., argn);
```

Each **printf** has two basic parts in its parentheses. The first is the **format_string,** which refers to a character string containing certain required formatting information, and the second is **arg1, arg2,** etc., which are arguments that represent the individual input data items. Each of these arguments has its own *placeholder* or *type specification* in the **format_string.** In its simplest form, a type specification consists of a percent sign (%), followed by a set of *modifiers and characters* that indicate the type of the corresponding data item. A placeholder can be comprised of:

%[flags][width][.precision][length]type

where *type* is the type being specified, as described in Chapter 7. For example, f is the type for a **float,** therefore, **%f** with no conversions is the type specifier for outputting a **float.**

There are some tricky ways to format output from **printf,** mostly to make output from a program appear consistent and neat. Any other characters occurring in the **format_string** (i.e., normal characters) are printed directly to the output stream. The **format_string** is always delimited by double quotes.

Flags

The type specification identifies what the output will look like. The first set of modifiers are the *flag* characters. There are five flag characters: –, +, space, #, and 0. Zero or more of these can be present.

Flag	Meaning
–	left justification
+	displays signed values
space	displays signed values with a leading space if positive and a minus sign if negative
0	pads the field with zeros instead of spaces

Output Width

If we want to align our numbers at the decimal point, we set the output width of the number. To achieve this we use the **%wf** format where *w* represents the width of the field. For example:

```
printf("%10f", PI);   = xx3.141590
printf("%10f", PI*4); = x12.566360
```

The value 10 means that the number displayed is 10 characters wide, right justified, with some spaces *padded* on the left (represented by **x** here). If you use a format or the form **%-wf** format, the – sign indicates left justification.

Precision

If you print out floating point numbers using the default **%f**, you will notice most print out with a default precision of 6. Sometimes we don't want more than two places after the decimal point. To achieve this we use the **%.pf** format where *p* represents the precision beyond the decimal point. For example:

```
printf("%.2f", PI);
```

will print the value of the variable **PI** to 2 decimal places, so 3.14159 becomes 3.14. This can be used with **%e**, **%E**, and **%f**. If used with **%s** the *p* represents the maximum number of characters to be printed. Here are some examples:

```
double PI=3.14159265358979323846264;

printf("%.3f", PI); = 3.142
printf("%.10f", PI); = 3.1415926536

char str[] = "Obi-Wan Kenobi";

printf("%.6s\n", str); = Obi-Wa
```

Length Modifier

The optional length modifier specifies the size of the argument. For example:

```
printf("%lf", PI);              =          3.141590
```

The **l** specifies a long float, or double. Here's the comprehensive list of useful length modifiers of integers (**d**, **i**, and **u**):

Length Modifier	d,i	u
h	short	unsigned short
hh	signed char	unsigned char
l	long	unsigned long
ll	long long	unsigned long long

Together with the following for floating point numbers:

```
l   double (e, E, f, F)
L   long double (e, E, f, F)
```

Combining Precision and Width

It is also possible to combine these formatting criteria. For example:

```
printf("%10.2f", PI);           =          xxxxxx3.14
```

The value **10** means that the number displayed is 10 characters wide, right justified, with two places after the decimal point. This can be represented visually:

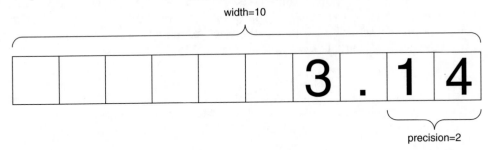

Here is an example with a string:

```
printf("%12.6s\n", str); = xxxxxxObi-Wa
```

Type Specifiers

The final component is a character that specifies the type of conversion to be applied.

```
i, d        integers
u           unsigned integers
f           floating point
e, E        floating point, scientific notation
c           character
s           string (array of characters)
%           a single % (as in %%)
```

Long Formatting Strings

Sometimes **printf** statements are too long to put on a single line. They can span more than one line as long as we don't break a quoted string in the middle. C will definitely complain about this. For example:

```
printf("The two real roots for the quadratic equation
are %.2f and %.2f\n", real_root1, real_root2);
```

This statement is *way* too long and, as a result, wraps around. It works, but it isn't very readable. There are a number of remedies. We could reduce the wording:

```
printf("The two real roots are %.2f and %.2f\n",
real_root1, real_root2);
```

but it still wraps around. We could now put it on two lines to tidy it up:

```
printf("The two real roots are %.2f and %.2f\n",
        real_root1, real_root2);
```

OR we could use two **printf** statements:

```
printf("The two real roots for the quadratic equation ");
printf("are %.2f and %.2f\n", real_root1, real_root2);
```

The output still occurs on one line.

`printf` Returning Values

The **printf** function also has a return value. It returns the number of characters printed. So printing:

```
int n;
n = printf("Serenity");
```

returns a value of 8 for **n.**

Scanning with `scanf`

The general form of a **scanf** statement is:

```
scanf(format_string, &arg1, &arg2, . . ., &argn)
```

Each **scanf** has two basic parts in its parentheses. The first, the **format_string,** refers to a character string containing certain required formatting information. The second is **arg1, arg2,** etc., which are arguments that represent the individual input data items. Each of these arguments has its own *placeholder* or *type specification* in the **format_string.** A placeholder consists of a percent sign **(%),** followed by a set of *modifiers,* which indicate the type of the corresponding data item. The two most useful conversion characters are those for integers and doubles:

```
%d    int
%lf   double
```

%lf stands for **long float,** which is synonymous with **double.**
The **format_string** is always delimited by double quotes.

Formatting Modifiers

Modifiers exist in **scanf** statements as well, although not to the extent as **printf.** For example, if we wanted to limit the amount of characters entered, we could use the following format string:

```
char str[20];
scanf("%5s", str);
```

Enter the word **tatooine,** and **scanf** actually only reads **tatoo.** Here input stops when the maximum field width is reached, or a white space is encountered. We can also use other characters within the formatting string, such as:

```
int day, month, year;
printf("Enter a date: ");
scanf("%d/%d/%d", &day, &month, &year);
```

This sequence read an **int**, expects to read a "/", reads another **int**, expects another "/", and finally reads the last **int**. Doing this we can specify an input format. Typing "06/11/2001" or "06/ 11/ 2001" might work, but "06 / 11 / 2001" probably won't.

Spaces in **scanf**

White space (such as blanks, tabs, or new lines) in the **format_string** match any amount of white space, including none, in the input. Everything else matches only itself. For example:

```
int a, b;
scanf("%d %d", &a, &b);
```

The space in the control string between the two conversion characters "**%d %d**" is strictly for readability. The following two formatting strings would work equally well:

```
scanf("%d%d", &a, &b);
scanf("%d %d", &a, &b);
```

However, when you enter a series of numbers, leave at least one space between the numbers, regardless of which formatting string is used. The space between the numbers clearly indicates where one number ends and the other one begins. Inserting more than one space has the same effect as inserting one space.

The only exception is when characters are input. For example:

```
scanf("%c%c", &a, &b);
```

causes **scanf** to store two characters in the variables **a** and **b** respectively. If you type "**X Y**," then **X** is stored in **a** and a space is stored in **b**. If the statement

```
scanf("%c %c", &a, &b);
```

is used, **scanf** looks for two characters separated by a space.

scanf and Buffered Input

One of the little niceties of C is character input using **scanf**. Except for %c, all other conversion characters skip over white spaces. We'll look at this later in this chapter.

scanf Returning Values

Like **printf, scanf** also returns a value. The return value has to do with the number of input items assigned, making this a useful feature in checking input. Consider as an example how this works in the following code:

```
int a_number, n;
n = scanf("%d", &a_number);
printf("Status? %d\n", n);
```

If we input a **12**, then the value of **n** returned is **1**, specifying that a valid integer was scanned. If we try to enter **s**, then **n** returns a value of 0. If we enter **23.7**, then **n** returns a value of 1. Why? Well since the **%d** truncates the **12.3** to 12, it still reads a valid integer.

Type Specifiers

Type specifiers are the same as for **printf**. The only notable exception is for **float** and **double**. Whereas **printf** will use **%f** to print both **float** and **double**, **scanf** requires a **%lf** to read a **double**.

Files and I/O

Chapter 13 discussed storing vast amounts of data in arrays. Now, most of the time that data is stored in a file, and it is much more useful to be able to read the data straight in from the file than to input it manually. The British Meteorological Office provides data for central England for each month 1659 to 2006.[1] The file is of the form:

	JAN	FEB	MAR	APR	MAY	JUN	JUL	AUG	SEP	OCT	NOV	DEC	YEAR
1659	3.0	4.0	6.0	7.0	11.0	13.0	16.0	16.0	13.0	10.0	5.0	2.0	8.83
1660	0.0	4.0	6.0	9.0	11.0	14.0	15.0	16.0	13.0	10.0	6.0	5.0	9.08
1661	5.0	5.0	6.0	8.0	11.0	14.0	15.0	15.0	13.0	11.0	8.0	6.0	9.75
1662	5.0	6.0	6.0	8.0	11.0	15.0	15.0	15.0	13.0	11.0	6.0	3.0	9.50
1663	1.0	1.0	5.0	7.0	10.0	14.0	15.0	15.0	13.0	10.0	7.0	5.0	8.58
1664	4.0	5.0	5.0	8.0	11.0	15.0	16.0	16.0	13.0	9.0	6.0	4.0	9.33
1665	1.0	1.0	5.0	7.0	10.0	14.0	16.0	15.0	13.0	9.0	6.0	2.0	8.25
. . .													
2005	6.0	4.3	7.2	8.9	11.4	15.5	16.9	16.2	15.2	13.1	6.2	4.4	10.44

MONTHLY MEAN CENTRAL ENGLAND TEMPERATURE (DEGREES C)
1659–1973 MANLEY (Q.J.R.METEOROL.SOC., 1974)
1974ON PARKER ET AL. (INT.J.CLIM., 1992)
PARKER AND HORTON (INT.J.CLIM., 2005)

Somehow, you have to find a way of reading the relevant information into the program. Let's first simplify the data file to one that only contains numbers. We will assume we know what year the file starts and what the rows and columns represent.

3.0	4.0	6.0	7.0	11.0	13.0	16.0	16.0	13.0	10.0	5.0	2.0
0.0	4.0	6.0	9.0	11.0	14.0	15.0	16.0	13.0	10.0	6.0	5.0
5.0	5.0	6.0	8.0	11.0	14.0	15.0	15.0	13.0	11.0	8.0	6.0
5.0	6.0	6.0	8.0	11.0	15.0	15.0	15.0	13.0	11.0	6.0	3.0
1.0	1.0	5.0	7.0	10.0	14.0	15.0	15.0	13.0	10.0	7.0	5.0
4.0	5.0	5.0	8.0	11.0	15.0	16.0	16.0	13.0	9.0	6.0	4.0
1.0	1.0	5.0	7.0	10.0	14.0	16.0	15.0	13.0	9.0	6.0	2.0
. . .											
6.0	4.3	7.2	8.9	11.4	15.5	16.9	16.2	15.2	13.1	6.2	4.0

---

[1]http://www.met-office.gov.uk/research/hadleycentre/CR_data/Daily/HadCET_act.txt

Binary versus Text

There are two basic types of files: text (or ASCII) and binary. A text file, like the temperature data, is written in ASCII text, so we can read it. A binary file is like the kind we create when we compile a program. It is inherently unreadable by humans. For example, digital photographs stored in formats like JPEG or TIFF are stored as binary files.

Opening a File

The first thing we want to do is tell the program what a file is and where it can be found. If it doesn't know this, it will just spit out a error. First we have to create a pointer to the file:

```
FILE *ifp;
```

The term **FILE** is a special type in C. It tells the compiler that the variable **ifp** (short for *input file pointer*, but you can call it anything you want) will point to a file. Now we have to associate this pointer with an actual file.

```
ifp = fopen("HadCET_act.txt", "r");
```

This tells the compiler that you wish to associate a file called **HadCET_act.txt** with the file pointer **ifp**, and you want to open it for reading. There are a number of different ways you can open a file. Have you ever tried to save a Word file, only to have Word tell you it is "read-only"? This means you can only read the file, not write anything to it. There are a number of different "modes," or ways you can open a file. For example:

r	Open a text file for reading
w	Truncate file to zero length or create text file for writing
a	Append: open or create text file for writing at end-of-file

You have to be careful when you use these, because if you open a data file using "**w**," for example:

```
ifp = fopen("HadCET_act.txt", "w");
```

you risk obliterating the contents of the file. All the data goes bye-bye, and there's no way of getting it back. However, if you want to open a file for writing, that works okay except that you may want to use **ofp,** for *output file pointer*. For example:

```
ofp = fopen("HadCET_act.txt", "w");
```

Reading from a File

Once the file is open, we have access to the data inside. We can read the data using a function similar to **scanf** called **fscanf**. This is **scanf** for files. It works the same way as normal **scanf**, except it has an additional parameter, telling you from where to read. For example, if we were to use the 2D array described earlier:

```
double yr1659_2005[347][12];
```

we could read the first element of the file into the first element of the array using the following statement:

```
fscanf(ifp, "%lf", &yr1659_2005[0][0]);
```

This basically reads a **double** from the file pointed to by **ifp** and stores it in element [0][0] of the array **yr1659_2005**. Nice, but it would be kind of cumbersome to have to read each element this way. Using two nested **for** loops, we can easily read the whole file into the array **yr1659_2005** really quickly.

```
for (i=0; i<347; i=i+1)
    for (j=0; j<12; j=j+1)
        fscanf(ifp, "%lf", &yr1659_2005[i][j]);
```

This works really well because we know that the file holds 4,164 pieces of data. Usually we have *some* idea about how much information is in a file.

Writing to a File

Once we have read in all the temperatures, we may wish to calculate the mean for each year and output the results to a file. Again we first have to create a pointer to the file:

```
FILE *ofp;
```

It tells the compiler that the variable **ofp** (short for *output file pointer*, but again you can call it anything you want) will point to a file. Now we have to associate this pointer with an actual file.

```
ofp = fopen("yearly_means.txt", "w");
```

Once the file is open, we can output data to it. In this case, the file **yearly_means.txt** does not have to exist. If it does exist, it is zeroed; if it doesn't exist, it is created.

We can write data using a function similar to **printf** called **fprintf**. It works the same way as normal **printf**, except it has an additional parameter, telling you *where* to read from. For example, if we were to use the array described earlier to store the mean temperatures for each year:

```
double yr_Means[347];
```

we could write them to the file associated with the handle **ofp**:

```
for (i=0; i<347; i=i+1)
    fprintf(ofp, "%.2lf ", yr_Means[i]);
```

This basically reads each element of **yr_Means** in turn and writes it into the file, followed by a space.

Closing a File

Once you have finished with a file, you have to close it. You can do this using the function **fclose**.

```
fclose(ifp);
fclose(ofp);
```

Checking That a File Actually Exists

If we want to check that a file exists before we access it properly, we can use the following piece of code:

```
if (ifp == NULL)
{
    puts("Sorry the file does not exist");
    return 1;
}
```

The Functions of I/O

In the example shown previously, we used a series of new functions: **fopen()**, **fclose()**, **fprintf()**, and **fscanf()**.

fopen

The function **fopen** is used to open a file. It has the following format:

```
handle = fopen(filename, mode);
```

filename is the name of the file you wish to open or create. **mode** is a tiny string that tells **fopen** how to open the file. Values for **mode** include:

mode	Opens a File for:	Is a File Created?	Existing File?
r	Reading	No	No file returns an error
w	Writing	Yes	Overwritten (truncated to zero)
a	Appending	Yes	Appended to
r+	Reading and writing	No	No file returns an error
w+	Reading and writing	Yes	Overwritten (truncated to zero)
a+	Reading and appending	Yes	Appended to

The **handle** represents the pointer to the physical file. If you are using binary files, then there are a separate series of modes available:

mode	Opens a File for:	Is a File Created?	Existing File?
rb	Reading binary	No	No file returns an error.
wb	Writing binary	Yes	Overwritten (truncated to zero)
ab	Appending binary	Yes	Appended to

fclose

The function **fclose** is used to close a file. It has the following format:

```
fclose(handle);
```

fscanf

The function **fscanf** is used to read from a file. It has the following format:

```
fscanf(handle, format_string, args);
```

fprintf

The function **fprintf** is used to write to a file. It has the following format:

```
fprintf(handle, format_string, args);
```

Getting and Putting

We covered **getchar/putchar** and **fgets/fputs** briefly in the previous chapter. The general form of **fgets** is

```
fgets(string, n, handle);
```

where *string* is the name of the character array, *n* is the number of characters to read and store in *string*, and *handle* is the pointer to the file. For the example in the chapter on strings, we used **stdin** to represent the file pointer *standard-input*; however, any file pointer can be used. For example:

```
FILE *ifp;
char dna[20];

ifp = fopen("gene.txt", "r");
fgets(dna, sizeof(dna), ifp);
```

reads a string from the file pointed to by **ifp** (gene.txt), up to **20** characters in length (including the EOS character), and stores it in the string **dna**. If the string entered is greater than 19, it will be truncated with the first 19 representing the string, and the 20th character representing the EOS, '\0', character. If the string entered is less than 19 characters, then the "Enter key" pressed will also be stored. For example:

```
Input:    GTCGGCTAGCAACCTGAGCTGAGATC
dna:      GTCGGCTAGCAACCTGAGC

Input:    AGCTGAGCGAACT
dna:      AGCTGAGCGAACT\n
```

The problem of having a string smaller than **sizeof(dna)** contain a newline character can be solved by overwriting it with a '\0' character:

```
str[strlen(str)-1] = '\0';
```

The function **fputs** can be similarly defined:

```
fputs(string, handle);
```

C also provides a **gets/puts** combination, but the reasons why **gets** should be avoided are outlined in the chapter on darker programming practices. C has file I/O versions of **getchar/putchar**, in the guise of **fgetc/fputc**. Consider **fgetc**:

```
char ch;
ch = fgetc(ifp);
```

Here the character will be read from the file pointed to by the file pointer, **ifp**, and stored in the variable **ch**. Similarly, for **fputc**:

```
char ch;
fputc(ch, ofp);
```

The character stored in **ch** is written to the file pointed to by **ofp**.

The Problem with Buffers

When you enter data, it is not immediately sent to the program. Until you press the Enter key, it is stored in a holding tank known as the *buffer*. The program then reads as much or as little as is required by the particular input function. Unread data remains in the buffer. Herein lies the problem with some input functions. For example, if we input two integers:

```
int a, b;
scanf("%d%d", &a, &b);
```

the buffer would look like:

11		23							

Then, **scanf** reads 11 into variable **a**, and 23 into variable **b**, effectively ignoring the whitespaces. When we're dealing with characters, however, whitespaces complicate input, partially because they are not ignored. If we change the input to add a character:

```
int a, b;
char ch;
scanf("%d%d%c", &a, &b, &ch);
```

and the buffer looks like this:

11		23		y					

then 11 is read into variable **a**, 23 into variable **b**, and a space is read into variable **ch**. To obtain the appropriate input would imply the buffer containing

11		23	y						

This may be counterintuitive, because when we type inputs we tend to want to put spaces in between to separate them. Similar problems can occur with other input functions. For example, consider two **fgets** functions that occur one after the other:

```
char street[15], suburb[15];

fgets(street,15,stdin);
fgets(suburb,15,stdin);
```

If the input is

```
Mount Pleasant Road, Toronto
```

then what will be stored is

> **street:** "Mount Pleasant"
> **suburb:** " Road, Toronto"

This happened because only the first 14 characters were stored in the string **street** (plus one EOS character), and because the buffer still contained the characters " **Road,**" they were read into the string **suburb**, before Toronto was read in.

Epilog

We have introduced the basics of I/O in C. There are, of course, more complex methods of accessing information stored in files. We may want to access the data in lumps called *blocks*. To do this we would have to specify the number of elements and the size of the elements. This is achieved using functions such as **fread()** and **fwrite()**. They are used to input/output "chunks" of data from a file, mostly in files containing different sized information.

There are also ways of accessing files in a nonsequential way using **fseek()** and **ftell()**. They use file pointers (not to be confused with memory pointers) that indicate a position in a file. **fseek()** is used to position a file pointer at a specific position in a file. **ftell()** returns the current position of the file position. Lastly, **rewind()** resets the file pointer back to position 0 in a file. I/O is also performed by other functions such as the time function, which communicates with the system clock to obtain a time.

Exercises

Exercise 15.1

Write a program that requests as input an angle expressed in degrees, minutes, and seconds in the format **dd:mm:ss** and converts it to whole and fractional degrees. There are 60 minutes in a degree, and 60 seconds in a minute. For example, 30:15:04 equals 30.25111 degrees. Make sure you check the validity of each of the components of the angle.

Exercise 15.2

Consider the file **metals.dat**, containing the name, chemical symbol, and density in gm/cm^3 of several metals:

```
aluminum Al 2.7
cobalt Co 8.9
copper Cu 8.94
gold Au 19.3
silver Ag 10.49
iron Fe 7.87
zinc Zn 7.14
nickel Ni 8.91
```

Write a program to read in the information and store the metal name and chemical symbol in 2D string arrays named **metal** and **symb** and the density in an array of doubles called **dens**. Print the information in formatted columns.

16

Random Numbers

The generation of random numbers is too important
to be left to chance.
—Robert R. Coveyou, Oak Ridge National Laboratory

Introduction

If something is random, it expresses an apparent lack of purpose, cause, or order. This means it shouldn't be predictable. Some might consider rain to be random. When it rains may be *somewhat* predictable, but exactly where, how hard, and for how long is certainly pretty random. Where a tornado lands and the direction it moves may also be random. So creating random numbers with a computer should be easy, right? Think again. There is nothing really chaotic about computers. They generally follow the straight and narrow.

Why would we be interested in random numbers? When we design programs such as games, cryptography, or forest growth simulations, we would prefer that the program is driven by a lack of predictability. Take, for example, the humble maple tree. Maple trees propagate through dispersal of seeds known as auto-rotating *helicopters*. The seeds are aerodynamic, and are picked up by the wind and travel to the ground like little propellers. When they leave the tree and where they land is entirely random. When you create a simulation to model tree seed dispersal, you might have some underlying conditions, such as wind direction and speed, but to make the simulation completely believable, you would have to add an element of randomness in the seed dispersion. Indeed, maybe the characteristics of the wind itself could be determined using randomness.

Computers are great at generating something called *pseudo-random numbers*, or numbers that appear to be random but are actually generated based on previous random numbers. They are not as adept at creating truly random numbers. Truly random numbers are unpredictable, nonrepeating, and nondeterministic. One of the most important applications of random numbers is *cryptography*, the process of encrypting and decrypting information to keep it safe. There is no security without randomness and unpredictability. Things must seem random, for if they were predictable, it would be easier to hack into secure transactions.

Random numbers are useful in fields from bioinformatics to the design of music players. Mutations occur in DNA in cells all the time. Mutations in DNA can arise from radiation, chemical agents, replication errors, or a whole bunch of other sources. Mutations in DNA sequences are best triggered in a random fashion, using a random-number generator. Or consider the "shuffle" command on your iPod. It uses random numbers to choose which songs it will play.

Random Numbers

In an ideal scenario, genuine random numbers could be created using some physical source of randomness, such as thermal noise or radioactive decay (it is impossible to predict the decay of individual atoms). Devices exist to generate random numbers by using a nuclear decay radiation source, such as some kinds of commercial smoke detectors, which is detected by a Geiger counter attached to a PC. There has been work on the use of digital cameras, such as webcams, to photograph chaotic macroscopic phenomena. A group at Silicon Graphics imaged Lava lamps to generate random numbers.[1] Of course, not many computers are hooked up to a device that measures radioactive decay, so we have to find another way. There are a series of random inputs available to computers, including:

- System date and time
- Time since system boot
- Contents of the stack
- Memory status (bytes allocated, free)
- Network packet data (sent, received)

The current *system time* is an excellent source of randomness, because the time will never be exactly the same.

Pseudo-Random Numbers

Pseudo-random numbers are generated by *pseudo-random number generators* (PRNG). An early computer-based PRNG was suggested by John von Neumann in 1946, sometimes called the *middle-square method*. It is very simple: Take any number, square it, remove the middle digits of the resulting number as your "random number," then use that number as the seed for the next iteration. For example, squaring the number 1,111 yields 1,234,321, which can be written as 01234321, an 8-digit number being the square of a 4-digit number. This gives 2,343 as the random number. Repeating this procedure gives 4896 as the next result, and so on. One of the first algorithms to derive pseudo-random numbers is the *linear congruential method* (LCM), introduced by Lehmer in 1951. It basically generates a new random number r_{n+1} by calculating:

$$r_{n+1} = (ar_n + c) \bmod m$$

---

[1]U.S. Patent 5732138: "Method for seeding a pseudo-random number generator with a cryptographic hash of a digitization of a chaotic system."

where a, m, and c determine the randomness of the sequence. The maximum repetition period is denoted by m. Statistical research by Park and Miller[2] identified a set of "best" parameters. It turns out that a and m can take on few values, with m nearly always prime. Park and Miller identified the parameter values $a = 16807$, $m = 2147483647$, $c = 0$ as producing the most statistically random values for 32-bit signed integers. This is termed the *Minimal Standard Generator*. For producing 16-bit values, a good set of parameters is $a = 171$, $m = 30269$, $c = 0$. There if we use the values for 32-bit numbers and start with $r_0 = 1$, we get the following sequence:

$$16807 r_0 \bmod 2147483647 = 16807$$
$$16807 r_1 \bmod 2147483647 = 282475249$$
$$16807 r_2 \bmod 2147483647 = 1622650073$$
$$16807 r_3 \bmod 2147483647 = 984943658$$

In C, the library **stdlib.h** contains functions to deal with random numbers. The most basic of these is **rand()**. For example:

```
int randomNum;
randomNum = rand();
```

This will generate a nice number, say 330177771. Run the program a million times and you will *always* get this number. Other programmers using the same compiler may get the same number. Why? Because computers are deterministic machines; that is, they don't exhibit random behavior. In general, **rand()** will generate a random number between 0 and **RAND_MAX,** which is also defined in **stdlib**. In Xcode, on an Intel Duo processor, this is 2147483647 (the 8th Mersenne prime). You can obtain successive random numbers in a sequence by successive calls to **rand()**. Here's an example that generates a sequence of 100 random numbers:

```
int i, randomNum;
for (i=1; i<=100; i=i+1)
{
    randomNum = rand();
    printf("%d ", randomNum);
}
```

The problem is, if you run this program 20 times, and you will get the *same* sequence of numbers every time. This is a good example of pseudo-randomness.

A sequence of pseudo-random numbers eventually repeats itself and can *always* be reproduced precisely given the same seed. A *seed* is a value used to calculate the first number. This would lead to some problems in both game development and growth simulation. In game development, after playing the same game a number of times, the way the game behaves could be entirely predictable. Actually there isn't much to the **rand** algorithm.

```
static unsigned long next = 1;

int rand(void)
{
```

[2]Park, S. K., and Miller, K. W., "Random number generators: Good ones are hard to find," *Communications of the ACM*, 1988, Vol. 31, No. 10, 1192–1201.

```
        next = next * 1103515245 + 12345;
        return ((unsigned int) (next / 65536UL) % 32767UL);
}
```

That algorithm is an insignificant embellishment on the basic LCM, in that it uses a **long** (32-bit signed integer) for the seed, but returns only a positive **int** (16-bit signed integer). As you can see, the simplistic nature of the algorithm means that if you know the seed you can predict the sequence of numbers being generated.

Seeding Random Numbers

Just like the maple tree, C can use a special function to create seeds, to propagate random numbers. We can achieve this by using the **srand()** function. To really make this work the number used as a seed has to be different every time. One way of doing this is using a function such as **time** (found in the **time.h** library). For example, the random number generator could be seeded using a number based on the current system time:

```
int randomNum;
srand(time(0));
randomNum = rand();
```

This will generate a new number every time it is run. The function **time(0)** is used as an argument when calling **srand()**. In the function call **time(0)**, the parameter 0 is passed. A call to **time(0)** returns a number based on the current time (which always changes), which is passed to **srand()**, which seeds the random number generator. Note that the same initial value of a seed will *always* return the same sequence of numbers. Again the actual algorithm for **srand()** is relatively simple:

```
void srand(unsigned int seed)
{
        next = seed;
}
```

However, the granularity[3] of system clocks may leave something to be desired; for example, many languages only report the time in seconds. A fast application might request two seeds in less than a second, producing two identical random sequences. Thankfully, in most C compilers, the function **time** obtains the number of seconds elapsed since 00:00 hours, January 1, 1970 UTC from the system clock.

Calculating a Number within a Range

In the context of generating random numbers, an algorithm should distribute numbers evenly across a range of n numbers such that the probability of generating a number is

---

[3]Granularity relates to the level of detail. Fine granularity implies many small components.

$1/n$. This is called a *uniform distribution*. Now this is fine, but there may be times when we want to generate a number within a certain specified range, say between 0 and p. For example, to get a number between 0 and 9, we could use the following code:

```
int d;
d = (randomNum % 10);
```

Or to make it within the range 1 and 10:

```
int d;
d = (randomNum % 10) + 1;
```

Any positive number divided by 10 will give a remainder of between 0 and 9, adding 1 gives a range of between 1 and 10. If you want a range [p..q], try:

```
int d;
d = p + randomNum % (q - p);
```

This will seem to work, but only if **p** divides evenly into **RAND_MAX**. Otherwise, you are eliminating the uniform distribution. The solution is to divide by **RAND_MAX** for numbers in the range [p...q]:

```
int d;
d = p + randomNum / (RAND_MAX / ((q - p) + 1));
```

If we generated 10,000 pseudo-random numbers in the range 1 to 10 using this method (**p=1, q=10**), we would get the following distribution of numbers:

1	962
2	1,040
3	1,026
4	976
5	959
6	1,008
7	997
8	1,007
9	993
10	1,031

For most purposes, that distribution is pretty uniform. Another way to get numbers in a range is to call **rand()** until you get a number that fits within your range. This is called the *rejection* method:

```
int p, randomNum;
p = RAND_MAX / q;

do
    randomNum = rand() / p;
while (randomNum >= q );
```

What about Random Floating Point Numbers?

Another challenge is producing random floating point numbers. I'm sure there isn't just one solution to this problem. You could derive floating point numbers between 0 and 1 using the following method:

```
int randomNum;
double drand;
srand(time(0));
randomNum = rand();
drand = randomNum / (double) RAND_MAX;
```

Here the value **drand** stores a floating point random number calculated by dividing the random integer generated by the maximum random number, represented by **RAND_MAX**, which is cast to a **double**.

Other Random Number Generators

One of the problems with the LCM algorithm is that if r is too large, multiplying by another large value may cause arithmetic overflow. To prevent this, we can use an approximate factorization of m, based on the formula known as Schrage's Method:

$$q = m/a$$
$$p = m \bmod a$$
$$k = r_i/q$$

$$r_{i+1} = a(r_i - kq) - pk$$

To eliminate the problem of overflow, Schrage's Method precalculates the constant ratio of m/a, and uses that factor to reduce the size of both the seed and the constants.

Epilog

A really good pseudo-random number generator known as the *Mersenne Twister* was developed by Makoto Matsumoto and Takuji Nishimura in 1997.[4] Essentially, the Mersenne Twister is a very large linear-feedback shift register. The algorithm operates on a 19,937 bit seed, stored in an 624-element array of 32-bit unsigned integers. The value 219937-1 is a Mersenne prime; the technique for manipulating the seed is based on an older "twisting" algorithm—hence the name Mersenne Twister. One of the interesting aspects of this program is that it uses binary operations, as opposed to time-consuming multiplication, for generating numbers.

---

[4]Matsumoto, M., and Nishimura, T., "Mersenne twister: A 623-dimensionally equidistributed uniform pseudo-random number generator," *ACM Transactions on Modeling and Computer Simulation*, 1998, Vol. 8, No. 1, 3–30.

Does the Shuffle feature on your iPod really randomly select songs? Apple seems to think so, but it uses a modified form of random numbers based on "no replacement." Basically once a song is played, it is removed from the list. This can be achieved by keeping track of tracks played. When a new track is randomly selected, the algorithm checks whether it has been played before. If it has, then a new random track is selected. This continues until all tracks have been played. Sometimes when using this feature, it seems as though the songs aren't random at all, but is it just a case of our minds finding patterns where there really aren't any? This usually occurs when a track from the same album or artist is played and we begin to believe the algorithm isn't random. Out of the 730 songs on my iPod, 61 are from R.E.M., meaning that roughly 1 in 12 songs will be from R.E.M. But remember, the algorithm can only be as good as pseudo-random number generator it uses. Maybe Apple has really good seeds, such as duration of the last scroll-wheel touch, time, or decimal date?

Exercises

Exercise 16.1

The infinite monkey theorem states that a monkey hitting keys at random on a keyboard for an infinite amount of time will almost surely type or create a particular chosen text, such as the complete works of Shakespeare. Now, suppose a keyboard has only alphabetical characters, 26 keys, and the word to be typed in is "bacon." Typing at random, the chance that the first letter typed is b is 1/26, as is the chance that the second letter typed is a, and so on. The events are independent, so the chance of the first five letters matching *bacon* is $(1/26)^5$, or 0.00000219. Using a random number generator, design a program to simulate the typing monkeys. Use the program to count how many characters have to be generated until the word "vox" appears. Does this agree with $(1/26)^3$ for a three-letter word? Your program should continuously create letters, for example:

```
asfgfldgueibwcnsuwtsfdgvhdtdhefivivokgrwopajauqwegdvox
```

Every time a letter is added, a three-letter word should be checked. The three-letter word is composed of the current letter and the two previous letters. In the above example, the word "asf" is checked first, then "sfg," then "fgf," and so on.

17

To Iterate Is Human, to Recurse Divine

In order to understand recursion one must first understand recursion.

—Anonymous

Introduction

Sometimes you want a function to solve its own problems. By this I mean you give it the overall problem and let the function break it into constituent parts until it gets to the point where it can pose a solution. In programming it is possible to solve the looping problem by not actually using an explicit loop construct. This idea is known simply as *recursion.* Let's consider an example. The Droste effect is a Dutch term for a specific kind of recursive picture. A picture exhibiting the Droste effect depicts a smaller version of itself in a place where a similar picture would realistically be expected to appear. This smaller version then depicts an even smaller version of itself in the same place, and so on.

What Is Recursion?

Recursion is a process an algorithm goes through when one of the steps in the algorithm involves rerunning the same algorithm. An algorithm that goes through recursion is said to be *recursive.* Fractals are generated using a form of recursive algorithm. A fractal is a shape that is recursively constructed or *self-similar*—that is, a shape that appears similar at all scales of magnification. The Romanesco broccoli is a good example of very fine natural fractals. Trees and ferns are also fractal in nature and can be modeled on a computer by using a recursive algorithm.

In its simplest form, recursion asks the following questions:

1. Are we done yet? If so, return the results. (Without a termination condition like this, recursion would go on forever).

2. If not, simplify the problem, solve those simpler problem(s), and assemble the results into a solution for the original problem. Then return that solution.

Imagine you have a chocolate bar with almonds. Eating the squares with just nuts in them can be a recursive process. Here's a rough algorithm:

```
Eat_Chocolate_Bar(b)
if b is a single square
      if b contains an almond
            Eat the chocolate square
      endif
else
      Break_Chocolate_Bar(piece1, piece2)
      Eat_Chocolate_Bar(piece1)
      Eat_Chocolate_Bar(piece2)
endif
```

Eventually the entire bar will be processed.

Programming with Recursion

Recursion occurs in a program when a function calls itself. This self-referential process, called *direct recursion*, sometimes implements the divide-and-conquer paradigm.

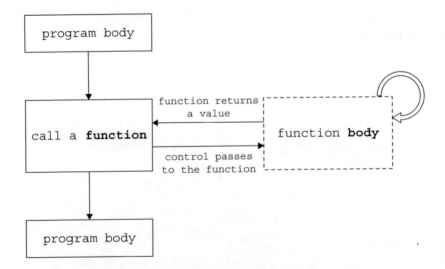

In many cases the core of a recursive function is a simple if statement of the form:

```
if (this is a simple case)
    solve it
else
    simplify the problem using recursion
```

A simple example is the case of calculating the sum of the first n positive numbers. Here is a function to perform the task iteratively using a loop:

```
int sum(int n)
{
    int i, sum=0;
    for (i=1; i<=n; i=i+1)
        x = x + i;
    return x;
}
```

Here is the same task performed using recursion:

```
int sum(int n)
{
    if (n <= 1)
        return n;
    else
        return (n + sum(n–1));
}
```

The recursive version seems a lot more eloquent, doesn't it? Let's look at what happens if we try to execute the recursive function with $n = 3$.

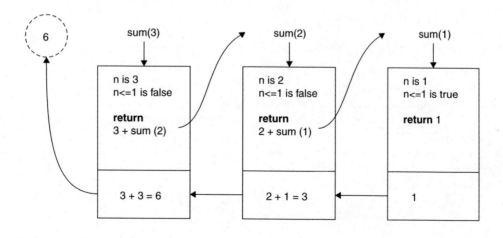

When an integer **n** is passed to **sum()**, the recursion activates **n** nested copies of the function before returning, level by level, to the original call. Or, looking at it another way:

What **sum()** Returns

Function Call	Value Returned
sum(1)	1
sum(2)	2 + sum(1) = 2 + 1
sum(3)	3 + sum(2) = 3 + 2 + 1

The most basic recursion follows a simple pattern. There is typically a *base case* tested on entry to the function. Then there is a *general recursive case* in which one of the variables, often an integer, is passed as an argument in such a way as to ultimately lead to the base case. In **sum()**, the variable **n** was reduced by one each time until the base case with **n** equal to 1 was reached.

Making Tails of Recursion

There are a myriad of different types of recursion. *Tail recursion* is a form of linear recursion where the recursive call is the last event processed by the function. A good example is calculating the greatest common divisor (GCD):

```
int gcd(int m, int n)
{
    int r;
    if (m < n)
        return gcd(n,m);
    r = m % n;
    if (r == 0)
        return (n);
    else
        return (gcd(n,r));
}
```

Some recursive functions, like Fibonacci, have more than one call to themselves. Functions with two recursive calls are referred to as *binary recursive* functions (e.g., Towers of Hanoi). In *nested recursion,* one of the arguments to the recursive function is the recursive function itself!

Sometimes a recursive function doesn't even need to call itself. Some functions work in pairs. For example, function F_1 calls function F_2, which in turn calls function F_1. Such a process is called *mutual* or *indirect recursion.*

Recursion != Fibonacci

Open any textbook on introductory programming or algorithms, and you will invariably find some form of the Fibonacci series, used to illustrate the notion of recursion. The Fibonacci series has a naturally recursive definition, and as such it is easy to implement. Consider the following implementation in C using binary recursion:

```c
long fibonacci(long n)
{
    if (n == 1 || n == 2)
        return 1;
    else
        return fibonacci(n-1) + fibonacci(n-2);
}
```

In principle there is nothing wrong with this example, but when recursion is introduced to solve a problem that is more efficiently solved in an iterative manner, we begin to question the merits of using recursion. We'll look at this more in the case study on Fibonacci.

Classical Recursion Algorithms

Factorial

The factorial of a natural number n is the product of all positive integers less than or equal to n. This is written as $n!$ and pronounced "n factorial." The notation $n!$ was introduced by Christian Kramp in 1808. For example:

```
5! = 1 * 2 * 3 * 4 * 5
```

n	n!
1	1
2	2
3	6
4	24
5	120
6	720
7	5040
8	40320
9	362880
10	3628800
20	2432902008176640000

The factorial is a good candidate for recursion, because its behavior is recursive. For example:

```
1! = 1
2! = 1 * 2             = 1! * 2
3! = 1 * 2 * 3         = 2! * 3
4! = 1 * 2 * 3 * 4 = 3! * 4
```

The algorithm for this is relatively simple:

$$1! = 1$$
$$n! = n * (n - 1)! \quad \text{for } n > 1$$

From this we can derive a simple recursive function:

```
long factorial(long n)
{
    if (n == 1)
        return 1;
    else
        return n * factorial(n—1);
}
```

Examine the process of calculating **factorial(4)**.

	What **factorial()** Returns
Function Call	Value Returned
factorial(1)	1
factorial(2)	2 * factorial(1) = 2 * 1
factorial(3)	3 * factorial(2) = 3 * 2 * 1
factorial(4)	4 * factorial(3) = 4 * 3 * 2 * 1

Towers of Hanoi

The Towers of Hanoi is a mathematical game or puzzle. It was invented by the French mathematician Edouard Lucas in 1883. He was inspired by a legend that tells of a Hindu temple where the pyramid puzzle might have been used for the mental discipline of young priests. Legend says that at the beginning of time the priests in the temple were given a stack of 64 gold disks, each one a little smaller than the one beneath it. Their assignment was to transfer the 64 disks from one of the three poles to another, with one important stipulation: A large disk could never be placed on top of a smaller one. The priests worked very efficiently, day and night. When they finished their work, the myth said, the temple would crumble into dust and the world would vanish. The number of separate transfers of single disks that would have to be made to transfer the tower is 264-1, or 18,446,744,073,709,551,615 moves. If the priests worked day and night, making one move every second, it would take slightly more than 580 billion years to accomplish the task! The puzzle consists of three pegs, and a number of discs of different sizes that can slide onto any peg. The puzzle starts with the discs neatly stacked in order of size on one peg, smallest at the top, thus making a conical shape.

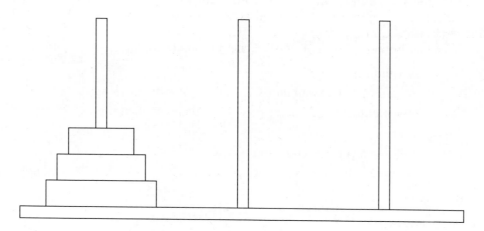

The objective of the game is to move the entire stack to another peg, obeying the following rules:

- only one disc may be moved at a time
- no disc may be placed on top of a smaller disc

Here's a basic algorithm for solving the problems:

1. Use the (N–1) disk solution to get the first N–1 disks to the right order on peg B.
2. Move the Nth disk to peg C.
3. Use the (N–1) disk solution to move the N–1 disks from peg B to peg C.

Here is the code for the function:

```
void move(int N, int from, int to, int using)
{
    if (N > 0)
    {
        move(N—1, from, using, to);
        printf ("move %d —> %d\n", from, to);
        move(N—1, using, to, from);
    }
}
```

To call the function from main we write:

```
move(N, 1, 3, 2);
```

This is a quite complex algorithm. Its innate simplicity is marred by a difficulty in understanding (or trying to explain) the recursion.

Greatest Common Divisor

We visited the algorithm for the greatest common divisor (GCD) in Chapter 3. Here's a refresher. Given two integers, x and y, and assuming x is greater than or equal to y, determine if y is zero. If it is, then x is the GCD. If it isn't, repeat the process using r, and the remainder after integer division of x by y. Here's the algorithm for identifying the GCD:

1. Acquire two numbers, x and y.
2. Is x greater than y? If not, swap the two numbers, making x the larger.
3. Calculate the modulus, r, of x and y (i.e., the remainder when x is divided by y).
4. Test if y is zero.

    a. If y is zero, the algorithm ends, and the GCD is x.

    b. If y is not zero, set x to the value of y, and assign y the value of r. Repeat step 3.

This algorithm lends itself very easily to recursion.

```
int gcd(int x, int y)
{
    if (y == 0)
        return x;
    else
        return gcd(y, x%y);
}
```

Note that small errors can be ignored by the compiler. Consider the following rendition of **gcd**:

```
int gcd(int x, int y)
{
    if (y == 0)
        return x;
    else
        gcd(y, x%y);
}
```

Almost exactly the same, right? Run it and we will *always* get an answer of zero. The compiler thinks it's okay because syntactically it is. Logically there is a **return** statement missing. The program will recurse fine, but in the last instance it will return **x**, which is zero. It has to do with register allocations, which we won't delve into here. Needless to say, we could spend hours trying to find a bug like this!

Epilog

There are *many* more complex problems that can be solved using recursion. Some are specifically geared toward recursion, such as the quicksort, or searching through a maze. However, sometimes the elegance and simplicity of a recursive algorithm is marred by the inability to quickly understand what is happening in the algorithm. Furthermore, algorithms such as Fibonacci are adept at using oodles of processor time and resources. If a problem can be expressed in an iterative or recursive manner with equal ease, it is preferable to use the iterative solution because it is generally faster and consumes less memory.

Think carefully before using a recursive solution.

Exercises

Exercise 17.1

Write a recursive version of the palindrome checking function of Exercise 14.3.

Exercise 17.2

Ackermann's function can be defined recursively for nonnegative integers m and n as follows:

$$A(m,\ n) = \begin{cases} n+1 & \text{if } m = 0 \\ A(m-1,1) & \text{if } m > 0 \text{ and } n = 0 \\ A(m-1, A(m,\ n-1)) & \text{if } m > 0 \text{ and } n > 0 \end{cases}$$

Write a recursive function to calculate Ackermann's function.

Exercise 17.3

Write a non-recursive version of the Towers of Hanoi algorithm.

Exercise 17.4

Find the square of a positive integer using only adds, subtracts, multiply by 2 (left shift), and recursion. Use the following equation:

$$x^2 = (x-1)^2 + 2x - 1$$

in which x^2 can be calculated if $(x-1)^2$ is known.

Code Tricks

The competent programmer is fully aware of the strictly limited size of his own skull; therefore he approaches the programming task in full humility, and among other things he avoids clever tricks like the plague.
—Edsger Dijkstra

Introduction

This chapter offers some neat tricks associated with programming and the concept of code optimization.

A Bit of This and a Bit of That

Let's examine briefly the more advanced topic of working with bits. Bitwise operations work on one or two binary numbers—that is, 0 and 1. There are six basic bit operators in C:

<<	Shifts bits to the left
>>	Shifts bits to the right
&	Bitwise AND operator
|	Bitwise OR operator
^	Bitwise Exclusive OR operator (XOR)
~	Bitwise one's complement

The values on which these operate *must* be integers.

Shifting Bits Left and Right

The first two operators << and >> shift bits. Consider the following code:

```
int a, b;
a = 24;
b = a >> 1;
printf("%d -> %d\n", a, b);
```

The output from this is 24 -> 12. Notice that the bitwise shift of 1 to the right has decreased the calculated value by half. A shift by 2 bits will result in a value of 6, and so on. Using the << (left-shift) operator will result in an increase by a factor of 2. In binary, the value 24 is 11000. Shifting this right results in:

11000 → 01100

All the bits move left a position, and the empty slot created on the left is filled with a 0. The bits that move past the end disappear! Shifting left adds zeros to the end. For example:

11000 → 110000

Therefore, 24 becomes 48, which is represented by 110000.

Printing Out Binary Numbers

In its infinite wisdom, **printf** lets you print out decimal, octal, and hexadecimal numbers, but NO binary! Why? Who really knows?

```
void print_binary(int n)
{
    char bin[17];
    int i;

    for (i=0; i<16; i=i+1)
    {
        if (n & 0x8000)
            bin[i] = '1';
        else
            bin[i] = '0';
        n = n << 1;
    }
    bin[16] = '\0';
    printf("%s", bin);
}
```

Now 0x8000 in hexadecimal represents the number 32768, which when converted to binary gives:

1000000000000000

That's why the character array holds 17 elements: 16 for the converted bits, and one for the end-of-string character. The code **n & 0x8000** checks to see if the bit in **n** is a 1, using the bitwise AND operator. So, first time around for **n=24**:

```
1000000000000000    0x8000
0000000000011000    24
0                   24 & 0x8000
```

Then the left-shift operator moves everything left one bit:

```
0000000000110000    24
```

This continues until we get **0000000000011000** stored in the array **bin**.

The interesting thing here is that we actually use hexadecimal numbers to perform bitwise operations.

Bitwise AND and OR

The next two operators, & and | work in a way similar to their logical counterparts. So:

```
    00010100100  AND          00010100100  OR
    10000101100               10000101100
=   00000100100           =   10010101100
```

Flotsam and Jetsam

The last two operators, ^ (XOR) and ~ (complement) work like this:

```
    00010100100  ^           00010100100  ~
    10000101100
=   10010001000           =   11101011011
```

Swapping Things Around

When we looked at swapping the contents of two variables earlier, we used the following code:

```
int a, b, temp;
temp = a;
a = b;
b = temp;
```

There are other simple ways to swap two numbers in C *without* a temporary variable. Let's look briefly at three different ways.

Method 1: The Arithmetic Way

The first method is done simply using addition and subtraction:

```
a = a + b;
b = a - b;
a = a - b;
```

For example: a=10, b=8;

```
a = (10+8) = 18
b = (18-8) = 10
a = (18-10) = 8
```

Method 2: More Arithmetic

The second method is done using more convoluted arithmetic:

```
b = (a * a) / a + (a = b) - a;
```

Method 3: It's a Bit Swap

Both the previous methods only work on numbers. The third method uses a method known as the *XOR swap*. It uses a XOR bitwise operation to perform the swap:

```
a ^= b;
b ^= a;
a ^= b;
```

For example if a = 2 (010), and b = 4 (100)

```
a = a ^ b;    =    010
              =    100
              =    110

b = b ^ a     =    100
              =    110
              =    010

a = a ^ b     =    110
              =    010
              =    100
```

The algorithm is not uncommon in embedded code, where there is often limited space available for temporary swap space.

Neat Tricks with Strings

Printing Weird Characters

Sometimes in output we might want to use something like the Greek character π. Printing the extended characters can be quite challenging in C. Although many systems don't support the extended character set, it can be achieved using the UTF-8 character encoding. It is able to represent any character in the Unicode standard, yet it is backwards compatible with ASCII. UTF-8 encodes each character (code point) in 1 to 4 octets (8-bit bytes), with the single octet encoding used only for the 128 US-ASCII characters.

For instance in Xcode, we can print characters to the Terminal using:

```
printf("%c%c\n", 0xcf, 0x80);
```

This prints the character equivalent to the UTF-8 code **cf80**, which is π. The second example prints the phrase πr^2:

```
printf("%c%cr%c%c\n", 0xcf, 0x80, 0xc2, 0xb2);
```

Here are some useful codes:

c2 b0	degrees	°
c2 b2	squared	2
c2 c3	cubed	3
c2 bd	half	½
88 9e	infinity	∞
89 a4	less than or equal	≤
89 a5	greater than or equal	≥

The * Modifier

The * character can be used within the format strings of both **printf** and **scanf**. Instead of using a number for the field width in a specifier in a **printf** statement, you can use *. The value still has to be supplied, but this way it is supplied with a value passed to **printf**. For example:

```
printf("%*d", width, num);
```

This uses the value supplied by the variable **width** to specify the field width. The * in **scanf** serves another purpose. When placed between the % and the type specifier, it causes **scanf** to skip over the corresponding input. For example:

```
int num;
char c;
scanf("%d%*c%c", &num, &c);
```

This causes a number to be stored in the variable **num**, the next character (a space) is discarded, and a character to be stored in the variable **c**. This deals nicely with the problem of %c reading the next character in the buffer, which in this case is always a space.

String of Words

One of the caveats of **scanf** and strings is that they only read characters up until the next space encountered. To read a full sentence of characters, you often have to use **fgets**. However, there is another way of reading strings with blank characters: the %[..] specifier, which reads a string of words. The use of %[c] means that only the characters specified within the brackets (c) are permissible in the input string. If the input string contains any other characters, the string is terminated at the first instance of the character. The specifier %[^c] does the reverse. For example:

```
char sentence[80];
scanf("%[^\n]", sentence);
```

This will read all the characters in a sentence until a newline is encountered, effectively storing a whole sentence including spaces and storing it in the string **sentence**.

What Is Lint?

Most people think of lint as the stuff you find in the lint filter in the dryer.

Lint was also the original name given to a particular tool that flagged suspicious and nonportable constructs (i.e., likely to be bugs) in C language source code. The term is now applied generically to tools that flag suspicious usage in software written in any computer language. The term *lint-like behavior* is sometimes applied to the process of flagging suspicious language usage. Lint-like tools generally perform static analysis of source code. *Static Code Analysis (SCA)* is a term applied to the analysis of software that is performed without actually executing programs built from that software (analysis performed on executing programs is known as *dynamic analysis*). In most cases the analysis is performed on some version of the source code. It is kind of like the lint filter in a dryer, trapping the little bits of lint off clothes.

Structures

Another optimization technique is using *data aggregates*. In many respects, arrays are the simplest form of data aggregate, dealing with groups of identically typed variables. Sometimes, however, there is a need for structures composed of varying variables. For example, if we look at the GPS case study, for each position there is a latitude and longitude that are themselves composed of fields for storing degrees, minutes, seconds, and decimal degrees. For example:

```
int degLat_P1, minLat_P1, secLat_P1;
char dirLat_P1;
double decLat_P1;
```

It would be nice to encapsulate this data into one entity. Then instead of passing five pieces of information to and fro, you would only need to pass one. C enables us to achieve this with a data aggregate known as a **struct**. One of the main reasons to use a structure is to encapsulate information and reduce parameter passing overhead.

Creating Structures

A **struct** is sort of like an array except that each element can have a different type. The elements of a **struct**, commonly called *fields* or *members*, have names instead of subscript values. Our GPS data could be incorporated into a **struct** in the following manner:

```
struct position {
    int deg, min, sec;
    char dir;
    double decD;
};
```

This declares a structure template called **position** (its *tag name*). To use this, we have to declare an actual variable:

```
struct position Lat_p1;
```

This declares **Lat_p1** as a variable with the form of **position**. We could then create similar declarations for the remaining GPS parameters:

```
struct position Lat_p1, Long_p1, Lat_p2, Long_p2;
```

Alternatively we could use the following declaration:

```
struct position p1[2], p2[2];
```

Assigning Values to Structures

Declaring **p1** and **p2** as arrays with two elements, each element is itself a structure. Now that we have declared the structures, we somehow have to access the fields. One way of doing this is through the dot "." operator. For example, to assign the positional information of Toronto, you could use the following assignments:

```
Lat_p1.deg = 43;
Lat_p1.min = 39;
Lat_p1.sec = 0;
Lat_p1.dir = 'N';
```

or in the context of the array of structures **p1**:

```
p1[0].deg = 43;
p1[0].min = 39;
p1[0].sec = 0;
p1[0].dir = 'N';
p1[1].deg = 79;
p1[1].min = 23;
p1[1].sec = 0;
p1[1].dir = 'W';
```

Another way of doing this is to declare a pointer to a structure:

```
struct position *Lat_p1;
```

Then to access a field, we would use the right-arrow operator –>, as in:

```
Lat_p1->deg = 43;
Lat_p1->min = 39;
Lat_p1->sec = 0;
Lat_p1->dir = 'N';
```

Passing Structures to Functions

Like anything else, structures can be passed to functions, either as pass-by-value or pass-by-reference. In most cases you will want to use the latter, because passing the address is faster and doesn't require the entire structure to be copied. There are two exceptions to this rule: (1) the structure is really small, or (2) the structure is not to be altered within the function. Let's look at the function **convert_DD** from GPS, converted to use the **struct position:**

```
void convert_DD(struct position *p)
{
    double ms, d;
    ms = p->min + (p->sec/60.0);
    d = ms/60.0;
    p->decD = p->deg + d;
}
```

Returning Structures

It is possible to return a structure or a pointer to a structure. For example, rewriting **read_pos** from GPS gives us:

```
struct position read_pos(void)
{
    struct position p;
    printf("Degrees: ");
    scanf("%d", &p.deg);
    printf("Minutes: ");
    scanf("%d", &p.min);
    printf("Seconds: ");
    scanf("%d", &p.sec);
    scanf("%c", &p.dir);
    printf("Direction: ");
    scanf("%c", &p.dir);
    return p;
}
```

Types

The keyword **typedef** is used to tell the compiler that something is really something else. What **typedef** is *not* is a way to create a new type. For example:

```
typedef int integer;
```

Here **typedef** creates an alias for the **int** type. Or maybe:

```
typedef long long extreme;
```

Echo Base

Humans tend to use base 10, the decimal system, while computers use base 2, or binary. Twelve in decimal is 1100 in binary. There is also hexadecimal (hex), or base 16, which represents 12 as C. These are really just different representations of numbers. We probably use base 10 because we have 10 toes and 10 fingers and thumbs. In fact the word *digit* is also the anatomical term referring to fingers and toes. The Babylonians used sexagesimal, or base 60. Why does this matter? There are situations where you might want to print out a hexadecimal version of a character rather than the decimal version. Hexadecimal numbers are, for example, commonly used in HTML.

Base two (binary) only uses digits from $\{0,1\}$. For example:

$$1100_2 = 1 \times 2^3 + 1 \times 2^2 + 0 \times 2^1 + 0 \times 2^0$$
$$= 12_{10}$$

Unfortunately, there are no binary constants in C.

Base 16 (hexadecimal) needs to use non-Arabic digits $\{0, 1, 2, 3, 4, 5, 6, 7, 8, 9, A, B, C, D, E, F\}$

$$10F_{16} = 1 \times 16^2 + 0 \times 16^1 + F \times 16^0$$
$$= 271_{10}$$

To create a hex constant in C, use a leading **0x**:

```
int x = 0xAB; // 10*16 + 11 = 171
```

Base 8 (octal) needs uses the digits $\{0, 1, 2, 3, 4, 5, 6, 7\}$

$$127_8 = 1 \times 8^2 + 2 \times 8^1 + 7 \times 8^0$$
$$= 87_{10}$$

To create a octal constant in C, use a leading **0**:

```
int o = 017; // 1*8 + 7 = 15
```

Printing Different Bases

You can use **%x** or **%X** formats to format any **int** as a hex. For example,

```
int value=167;
printf("%x %X", value);
```

would result in the following being printed:

```
a7 A7
```

You can use **%o** format to format any **int** as an octal. For example,

```
int value=167;
printf("%o", value);
```

would result in the following being printed:

```
247
```

You can also print out hex strings using **%c:** For example:

```
printf("%c",0x9C);
```

prints out the £ symbol.

Complex Array Pointers

How do pointers relate to arrays? Consider the following declaration:

```
int v[42];
```

The array name is essentially the address of the first element in an array. A one-dimensional array can be accessed using a pointer representation:

```
v[i] = *(v + i)
```

This provides another way of accessing elements in multidimensional arrays in C. For example, a two-dimensional array in C can be accessed in the same way as a 1D array. Consider the following two-dimensional array:

```
int m[24][24];
```

If we were to print out the following addresses:

```
printf("address of m:        %p\n", m);
printf("address of m[0][0]:  %p\n", &m[0][0]);
printf("address of m[0]:     %p\n", m[0]);
```

we find the following:

```
address of m:        0xbffff9ec
address of m[0][0]:  0xbffff9ec
address of m[0]:     0xbffff9ec
```

What does this output tell us? When we declare a one-dimensional array, placing **[m]** after the name tells the compiler that it is an array with **m** elements. For a two-dimensional array, placing **[n]** for the second dimension has the compiler create an array of size **m**, in which each element is an array of size **n**. So **m**, **m[0]**, and **&m[0][0]** all have the same value, but they aren't the same thing. To obtain the first element for each of the above requires the following:

```
m:              **m
m[0][0]:    m[0][0]
m[0]:        *m[0]
```

To access the element **m[i][j]**, C actually finds the memory associated with **m[i]+j**. The expression m[i] points to the ith row of the array. Therefore m[i]+j point to the jth element in the ith row of the array. The subscript **j** actually acts as an offset to the base address of the ith row. This is because arrays are not stored as a two-dimensional structure. The following is one method of accessing array elements in a two-dimensional array:

```
m[i][j] = *(*(m+i)+j)
```

The following also works:

```
m[i][j] = **m+i*Ncols+j
m[i][j] = *(m[i]+j)
m[i][j] = *matrix[i]+j
```

Confused yet? This is just to show you that there are *many* ways to access array elements using pointers.

19

Program Testing

Testing can only prove the presence of bugs, not their absence.
—Edsger Dijkstra

Introduction

Software is ubiquitous. In a Boeing 777, the pilots control its engines via a piece of software known as the full authority digital engine control (FADEC). There is no mechanical link from cockpit to the engines; if the software fails, the engines cannot be controlled (although aircraft have multiple redundant systems). The first perceivable effect of software failure may have occurred during the loss of NASA's Mariner 1 mission to Venus in 1962, although it is now considered something of an urban myth. In the years that followed, there have been numerous aerospace incidents; however, a recent event punctuates the seriousness of algorithm failure. In February 2007, 12 USAF F-22 Raptor jets were being deployed from Hawaii to Japan. En route, a software glitch crashed the onboard navigations system as they crossed the international date line, forcing the jets to turn back. The problem seemed to be associated with the change from 179 59′59.99″ W to 180, and then to 179 59′59.99″ E which occurs at the international date line. Most of this code (approximately 2.2 million LOC) was written in Ada, which has extraordinary exception handling capabilities. The question was whether out-of-bounds values for longitudinal information had been considered. Apparently, the navigational system (Global Positioning Inertial Navigation Systems [GINS]) had never been physically tested crossing the date line, but only on simulated real-world inputs. When it crossed the date line for the first time, it crashed, as did the backup, bringing down with it all navigational systems and much of the aircraft's instrumentation.

The process of testing is paramount to the success of software. Testing can be an art, a disjointed approach performed in a laissez-faire manner, or more of a science with test data and cases carefully selected. If a laissez-faire approach is used, there is no way to control testing, to know how thorough it is, or to know when it is complete. Testing is probably the most critical component of the software development process. It is a distinct process from debugging. Once the syntax errors and obvious runtime errors have been removed, then the process of testing can get underway. Never assume that simply because a compiler accepts a program, produces an executable, and yields correct numerical results that the program is correct. Many programs contain logic errors that are concealed in a maelstrom of code, causing the program to become unstable when they manifest themselves. Complex, ill-tested code is often *brittle*, meaning that the software may appear reliable but will fail badly when presented with unusual data. Brittleness in software can be caused by algorithms that do not work for the full range of input data.

Good Testing = Lower Failure Rate

The rationale for testing can be best illustrated in a real-time data-processing environment. One such environment exists in railway technologies aimed at traffic supervision and regulation. One such system is the SACEM system, which controls the train movements on RER A, one of the five lines in the RER rapid transit system in Paris. To increase transport capacity, the headway was reduced from 2.5 minutes to 2 minutes, leading to a shorter distance between trains. Two of the objectives of SACEM were (i) a catastrophic failure rate lower than 10^{-9} per train per hour of operation and (ii) the frequency of inadvertent stops lower than 2.10^{-3} per train per hour. How does it work? At each processing cycle (312 ms), the train-borne computer (i) identifies the most constraining obstacle immediately ahead of the train; (ii) determines the distance between the train's position and the abscissa of this obstacle; (iii) compares this distance with the deceleration distance necessary to compensate the speed function and potential energy, taking into account the braking characteristics of the train; and (iv) generates an order. The software was written in Modula-2: 14,000 lines for the train-borne portion, and 7,000 lines for the fixed portion. Testing was in the form of (i) manufacturer's unit tests and application of formal proofs and (ii) RATP (Paris Public Transportation Authority) static and dynamic analysis, real-time functional tests. The onboard system is not duplicated due to its high reliability and the fact that it affects only one train. If the wayside system fails, all trains revert to the 2.5-minute headway. The ground-based systems are duplicated, with automatic switch-over in case of failure. No incidents have *ever* been reported. Good testing reduces failure and leads to a lower failure rate.

Why Failure Is (Sometimes) Good

In 1940, the Tacoma Narrows Bridge, a mile-long suspension bridge in Washington State collapsed due to a lack of structural integrity. Shortly after its construction in July 1940, it was discovered that the bridge would sway and buckle dangerously in windy conditions. This resonance was longitudinal, meaning that the bridge buckled along its length, with the roadbed alternately raised and depressed in certain locations, imparting the nickname "Galloping Gertie." The failure of the bridge occurred when a never-before-seen twisting "torsional" motion occurred. In 2004, the roof of Terminal 2E at Charles De Gaulle Airport in Paris collapsed. The terminal roof was weakened by temperature changes that caused the building's outer shell to shift by 1–2 cm daily. This, in turn, wore down the concrete roof, causing the structure to be overstressed.

Both of these were destructive failures, and yet engineering uses such incidents to its advantage by examining what went wrong and improving on future designs. Engineering structures have bounds placed upon them by the constraints of the materials used in their construction. Software, it seems, has no bounds. Structures sometimes have a related "wear-out" phase, in which software failures can occur without warning. Is failure bad? The idea of failure has been cited as central to the comprehension of fields such as engineering. Henry Petroski once said: *"Engineering has as its first and foremost objective the obviation of failure ... but lessons learned from disasters can do more to advance engineering knowledge than all the successful machines and structures in the world"*.[1] Software failure ultimately leads to algorithm refinement and redesign. If each step in the evolutionary path of algorithms were entirely successful, there would be little incentive for improvements. The study of failure is valuable, since each failure provides information that can be used to prevent similar failures.

What Is Testing?

There are essentially three things to test in a program: (i) correctness, (ii) implementation efficiency, and (iii) computational complexity. Tests for implementation efficiency attempt to find ways to make a correct program faster. It is essentially a process of redefining existing code. Tests for computational complexity look at the inherent complexity of an algorithm. Finally, tests for correctness deal with verifying that the program actually does what it was designed to do. Even though software may be well designed, this does not guarantee that its translation into code will be correct, neither does merely assuming that zero compiler errors and convincing output imply correctness. Testing is one of the core elements of programming. To design a successful program, you have to evaluate it using test cases. Let's go back to the license plate algorithm from Chapter 3. This is a fairly simple algorithm when a car is stationary, but in most cases the processing must be performed on an image taken of an object moving at upwards of 60 km/h. The software designed to perform this task may seem simple, but there are numerous situations that compromise performance:

- Poor image resolution, usually because the plate is too far away but sometimes resulting from the use of a low-quality camera.
- Blurry images, particularly motion blur.
- Poor lighting due to changing weather conditions or passing objects (clouds), and low contrast due to overexposure, reflection, or shadows.
- An object obscuring part of the plate, quite often a tow bar, dirt on the plate, or a damaged plate.
- A different font used for the text on the plate.
- Character misclassification due to similar characters: 1, I, and l, 0 and O, 2 and Z, 5 and S, 8 and B.

So the task is not as easy as one may think. Glenford Myers in his classic book *The Art of Software Testing* defines *testing* as *"the process of executing a program with the intent of finding errors."*[2] Software testing may be construed as partly a destructive process, but there

---

[1]H. Petroski, *To Engineer Is Human* (New York: Vintage Books, 1992).

[2]Myers, G. J., *The Art of Software Testing*, John Wiley & Sons, 1979.

is no easy way of finding out if a program really works. The art of testing is often described as *the process of demonstrating that errors are not present*. However, with the right input, this isn't a difficult task. More taxing is working with the assumption that a program contains defects and testing the program to find as many of these as possible. Psychologically, this process seems to have a negative undertone. It is akin to materials testing in engineering. To test the constraints of a material, you subject it to stress testing—that is, you identify the material's limitations by breaking it. A *defect* is present if the program does not do what it is intended to do. Is it possible to find *all* the defects in a program? In a simple program, such as deciding whether a number is even or odd, it may be possible to find all the errors. Finding all the errors becomes more difficult as the complexity of the program increases.

What Are We Trying to Find?

So what kind of defects are we trying to identify through testing? The first are defects that originate in the requirements phase: incorrect external constants, conflicting requirements, or requirements incorrectly interpreted. Next are design defects: incorrect analysis of computational error, incompatible data representations, inadequate error traps, failure to handle exceptions, logic problems, or weak modularity. Finally there are code defects. These can be subdivided into problems with logic/control and data computations. The former includes unreachable code, improper structure nesting, improper sequencing, and infinite loops. The latter includes missing validity tests, incorrect access of array elements, mismatched parameters, faulty initializations, and misuse of variables. The list is seemingly endless.

Reliability and Robustness

Testing is intrinsically linked to the notion of *reliability*: the characteristic of a component, or a system made up of many individual components, expressed by the probability that it will perform its particular function within a specific environment for a given period of time.[3] Reliability is usually concerned with some form of statistical analysis and behavior prediction based on testing. However, reliability in engineering is easier to discern than reliability in software. Materials fail for a number of reasons: misuse, inherent weakness, degradation, wearing out, catastrophic. Software doesn't wear out, so it's hard to affix a means of failure. It is possible to misuse software, say by trying to load more data than it is capable of dealing with. Some failures may be gradual, such as compound numerical inaccuracies, but most are sudden or catastrophic. One of the goals of program testing is to ensure that the program solves the problem that it was supposed to solve, giving the correct answer. Yielding the correct answer under all conditions is a requirement commonly known as *robustness*. A program that fails to provide the correct result is not considered robust. Robustness is a characteristic that tends to increase over time as failures are discovered and corrected.

---

[3]R. Lewis, *An Introduction to Reliability Engineering* (New York: McGraw-Hill, 1970).

How Much to Test?

How do we know when a program has been tested enough? To properly test a program, every instruction in the program should be executed at least once. In simple programs, this is not difficult; but as the complexity grows, through the use of loops and decision structures, the task of checking every path becomes more challenging. In simple programs, often the component of the program that requires the most testing is the part that interacts with a human, as incorrect input is often the cause of program failure. The problem with programs is that it is seldom possible to test all contingencies. The sheer number of tests applied is often of little significance in itself. Unlike destructive testing of materials that literally causes material to wear out, programs do not wear out. If a program can properly add three integers, then it goes without saying that it will probably be able to add three similar integers correctly. Sheer testing also does not guarantee that all eventualities will have been tested.

When to Test?

A program should be tested in a stepwise manner. Start with testing the input to the program, then progressively increase the complexity. It should be a process that starts when you begin designing the algorithm and continues throughout the implementation process. What sort of data does the program require? What are its constraints? Once the input modules have been implemented, test them: Is the input properly received? What happens if an extreme value is input? Next test the computations: Are the values calculated correct?

Black and White Boxes

There are essentially two forms of basic testing: black box and white box. *Black-box testing,* sometimes termed *input-output testing,* literally treats the entire program as a black box. The testing is not at all concerned with the internal behavior of the program. It doesn't care the least bit whether or not the algorithm is efficient or what type of data structures were used. All it cares about is running the program with certain input and validating the output generated, that is, *functional* testing. Black-box testing resembles *stress testing.* It might involve functional testing, which ensures that the functionality specified in the requirements works; usability testing; or performance testing. On the flip side is *white-box testing,* also known as *clear-box* or *glass-box testing,* in which the internal behavior of a program is examined, that is, *structural* testing. Test cases are used to test all possible paths through the program. White-box testing includes methods such as unit testing and integration testing. *Unit testing* can be used to examine individual software units (e.g., functions) to determine whether they function correctly. *Integration testing* examines the interfaces between various units (e.g., passing information between functions). One methodology for unit testing might be the following:

1. Trace through the code, identifying all loops and decisions.
2. List all possible conditions for the decisions, and three cases for each loop: execute 0, 1, and >1 times.

3. Devise a test case to execute each item in step 2.

4. Determine the expected results.

5. Run the tests.

What white-box testing doesn't test, however, is if something has been left out—for example, a program to calculate means that uses integer versus floating-point division, or a compound interest program that rounds the values instead of using the fractional component. *Grey-box testing*, which is, as one might imagine, a combination of the two methods, is a compromise of the two extremes.

Test Cases

To test a program, we need test cases. A *test case* is a detailed process for testing a particular aspect of a program. For example, certain inputs may have specific data requirements (e.g., dates), which should be tested to ensure data is entered correctly. For numeric fields, one should test lower and upper bounds; for ASCII input, whether or not the input is valid. When deriving test cases, you must think diabolically about the kinds of things users might do with your program. Look at all inputs. What happens when a user enters a value that is out of range? Look at every calculation. Is there a chance for an overflow somewhere? A divide-by-zero? A simple test case consists of the function being tested, an input, and an expected output. There are several types of test cases:

- Basic test cases check simple functionality.
- Boundary test cases check the limits of functionality.
- Failure test cases check failure conditions and error handling.

Consider the following simple program to identify whether a number is odd or even:

```
 1  #include <stdio.h>
 2
 3  int main(void)
 4  {
 5      int a_number;
 6      printf("Enter a number: ");
 7      scanf("%d", &a_number);
 8      if (a_number % 2 == 1)
 9          printf("odd\n");
10      else
11          printf("even\n");
12      return 0;
13 }
```

There is only one **if-else** statement in this code, and no loops, for a total of two paths through the program. Consider the following test cases (black-box testing) for the even/odd program:

1. A test case with valid even numbers (e.g., 12, 4, 78, -22).
2. A test case with valid odd numbers (e.g., 17, 91, -37).
3. A test case with 0. (Zero is normally considered even.)

For each, there is an input and an expected outcome. Now consider the white-box test table for the program. The branches for the program are shown in the accompanying table, together with possible outcomes. Columns have been included for cross-checking which conditions are satisfied by the test cases generated.

Decision or loop	Possible outcomes	Test cases			
		1	2	3	4
a_number % 2 == 1	TRUE		X		X
	FALSE	X		X	

The four test cases for the white-box testing:

Test case	Input	Expected outcome	Actual outcome
1	12	even	?
2	91	odd	?
3	0	even	?
4	-37	odd	?

In the case of an odd/even programs, one can test the values 0, 1, and 2 and extrapolate the fact that if the program works for the value 1, it is unlikely to fail for the value 3. If a sorting algorithm works for 100 numbers, it is likely that it will work equally well for 1000, or 1,000,000 numbers. For basic testing, use the following criteria for test cases:

1. Test the *normal* cases, that is, the most general cases for which the program was designed.

2. Test the *extremes*. These include the fringes of the input range that would be accepted as valid data. Examples include very large and very small numbers. This is sometimes known as *boundary* value testing. There is also the case of volume data versus one or two pieces. What happens to empty strings? Remember that input extremes may not produce output extremes. There are also areas of the program in which extremes may occur, for example, divide by zero.

3. Test the *exceptions*. Test data that falls outside the acceptable range. If a program is not designed to handle zero or negative numbers, what happens when such data is input? What happens when text entered is larger than the corresponding string that should store it? Or the amount of data elements exceeds the capacity of an array? The worst-case scenario occurs when the program *accepts* this sort of data. Erroneous data can easily be input through typing errors or misunderstanding of input instructions.

Test Data

Paramount to the success of testing is the selection of test data. Test cases should be well designed, for their purpose is to see if the program works correctly, not to see how fast it works, or how many tests can be carried out. Sometimes testing involves "miniaturization" of data. Some data sets can be large with the resulting output from the program easy to decipher. Take, for instance, the case of sorting a list of numbers. If we sort 1,000,000 integers, it is easy to determine if the results are accurate by passing through the list. If we are processing an image of size 1000 × 1000, containing 1,000,000 elements, it is difficult to view the processed results. So, instead, we may use a test matrix of 10 × 10 to test the algorithm. There are three main types of test data:

- constructed data
- modified real data
- real data

Constructed data refers to data specifically created to test a program. Constructed data can be separated into controlled and random data. *Controlled* data is used to see if the program works at all. It can create situations that may rarely occur. *Random* data is used to indicate errors that might not be apparent otherwise. Random data may be harder to verify but may lead to catastrophic failure. *Modified real data* allows for certain circumstances to be tested. It also allows deliberate errors to be introduced to ensure that error-checking modules work. For testing whether an ISBN check digit is valid, we could first use the formula and a fake ISBN to generate a check digit, which can be subsequently used to test the algorithm. We could then take a real ISBN and modify it to make it invalid and see if the program flags it as an invalid ISBN. Next we could try a series of real ISBNs with various values of the check digit. If we were using a 10-digit ISBN, we might also try X as the check digit.

Extreme and Boundary Testing

Programs should be tested for special cases and extreme values. Programs tend to fail far more often because of the use of extreme values, and programmers tend to forget about them. Most programs produce valid results for input that conforms to certain constraints. Input that violates these constraints may generate invalid results. Most times, the program itself is not at fault. A value will be calculated, but it will not be correct. This is often the case in expressions that use a range of values. If a specification for a program uses input that is constrained, this should be checked for. In some cases, this is defensive programming. For example, consider a program to calculate the orbital velocity of a satellite, that is, the speed needed by a satellite to orbit the earth. The calculation can be represented by the following formula:

$$V_c = \sqrt{\frac{GM}{r}}$$

where V_c is the velocity for a circular orbit (metres per second), M is the mass of the planet, G is the universal gravitational constant, and r is the distance from the satellite to the centre of the planet. The value r can be calculated as follows:

$$r = R_c + h$$

where R_e is the mean earth radius, and h is the height of the orbit in kilometers. One of the requirements of the program is that at heights (h) less than 320 km, the drag produced by the atmosphere will slow the satellite down, causing it to descend into the denser portion of the atmosphere where it will burn up like a meteor. The height of the orbit is the only input, but the following test cases should be included, assuming no defensive programming has yet been incorporated. Here are a series of extreme and normal test cases used in the context of black-box testing:

Test case	Input (h)	Expected outcome	Actual outcome
1	0	error < 320	7.91
2	100	error < 320	7.85
3	-100	error < 320	7.97
4	320	7.72	7.72
5	35600	3.08	3.08

Obviously the first three extreme test cases failed, even though they returned values that appear correct. The first input puts the satellite on the earth's surface, traveling across the ground at 7.91 km/s, which is obviously incorrect. The next value could be more plausible, but it too is below the threshold of a successful orbit. The third value is actually below the earth's surface. The last two normal test cases produce valid results. However, testing with only these two will give a false sense of robustness. The program can now be modified to check for values less than 320 and act accordingly.

Exhaustive Testing

To find all errors in the program, we would have to resort to exhaustive testing in which every possible input condition is used as a test case. But as programs' complexity grows, so too does exhaustive testing. If we write a C compiler, then we would have to create tests representing all valid C programs (which is close to an infinite number of programs) and all invalid C programs to ensure that the compiler actually detects all syntax errors. As you can imagine, this is quite impossible. In most programs, testing every possible case may not be achievable. If we have a small program that calculates the area of a rectangle and takes two pieces of data as input (A, B), then if we could test the program for all possible values of A and B, then we could determine its correctness. However for 32-bit integers, there are 2^{32} possible values for A and B, resulting in 2^{64} combinations of the pair A $\times$ B. The program will fail at some point because the greatest value that can be stored as an integer is 2^{32}, so A $\times$ B > 2^{32} will cause failure. Is it possible to check all possible paths through a program? Consider the following piece of code:

```
int num;
parity = num % 2;
if (parity == 0)
    printf("The number is even\n");
else
    printf("The number is odd\n");
```

Here the program can follow only one of two paths through the code. Now consider the **if-else** skeleton from the quadratic equation program of Chapter 6:

```
if (expr1)
    if (expr2)
        A;
    else
        B;
else {
    if (expr3)
        C;
    else if (expr4)
        D;
    else
        E;
}
```

Now there are five possible paths through the **if-else** sequence:

```
expr1(true)   → expr2(true)   → A
expr1(true)   → expr2(false)  → B
expr1(false) → expr3(true)   → C
expr1(false) → expr3(false)/expr4(true)  → D
expr1(false) → expr3(false)/expr4(false) → E
```

If we execute similar code to this within a loop that is executed five times, there are now 5^5 (3125) possible sequences. It is almost impossible to exhaustively test such a program. To exhaustively test a postal address system that uses handwriting recognition to decipher the address on envelopes, it would be necessary to obtain a piece of handwriting from every living person to see if the system could decipher the writing.

Coincidental Correctness

Coincidental correctness occurs when defective code produces correct results for some test cases. Consider the following code embedded in a program somewhere:

```
num = a + a;
```

The + is incorrect and should be a *; however, if the value of **a** is 2.0, the value calculated will always be correct. The code effectively hides the defect.

Testing Outside the Box

Tsutomu Matsumoto, a Japanese cryptographer, recently decided to look at testing existing commercial biometric fingerprint devices.[4] These security systems attempt to identify people based on their fingerprints. It has been alleged for years that these devices are extremely secure, and using an imitation finger will by no means fool the system. Matsumoto and his students at the Yokohama National University begged to differ. They showed that existing systems could be reliably fooled with a little ingenuity and some simple household supplies. His idea was to use gelatin, the stuff used to make Gummi Bears. First, he made a plastic mold from a live finger. Then, he poured liquid gelatin into the mold and let it set. This gelatin fake finger fooled fingerprint detectors about 80 percent of the time. His more remarkable experiment involved *latent* fingerprints or accidental impressions. He took a fingerprint left on a piece of glass, enhanced it with fumes from superglue, and then photographed it with a digital camera. Using Photoshop®, he improved the contrast and printed the fingerprint onto a transparency sheet. Then, he took a photosensitive printed-circuit board (PCB) and used the fingerprint transparency to etch the fingerprint into the copper, making it three dimensional. Finally, he made a gelatin finger using the print on the PCB. This also apparently fooled fingerprint detectors about 80 percent of the time. Matsumoto tried these attacks against 11 commercially available fingerprint biometric systems and was able to reliably fool all of them. The results are enough to scrap the systems completely and to send the various fingerprint biometric companies packing. What is more interesting is that Matsumoto was thinking outside the box when he came up with the idea of gelatin. Obviously biometric scanner manufacturers didn't think it necessary to try this approach. In a similar way, Prof. Stephanie Schuckers from Clarkson University used Play-Doh to create fake fingers that fooled the scanners 90 percent of the time. However, she has also worked on an algorithm that detects the spread of perspiration from the pores out to the ridges of a live person's finger, so the Play-Doh fingers fooled the system only 10 percent of the time.

Epilog

Sometimes testing a program requires creative thinking. Testing can lead to an algorithm failing. Failure leads to algorithm refinement. If each step in the evolutionary path of

---

[4]T. Matsumoto et al., "Impact of Artificial Gummy Fingers on Fingerprint Systems." Optical Security and Counterfeit Deterrence Techniques IV, 2002.

algorithms were entirely successful, there would be little incentive for improvements. The term *undebuggability* was coined by Cherniak[5] in 1988. Debuggability implies that when designing a test, there should be some expectation that some day, the test may fail. When software is undebuggable, it implies that it may never fail. Undebuggability is the Achilles heel of software.

Exercises

Exercise 19.1

Write a program that reads three edges of a triangle and computes the perimeter if the input is valid. Otherwise, display that the input is invalid. The input is valid if the sum of any two edges is greater than the third edge.

Exercise 19.2

In an iPod, there are N tracks played in a "random" order when *shuffle* is selected. If there are three tracks on the iPod, then there are six ways of arranging how they are played:

$$[1,2,3], [1,3,2], [2,1,3], [2,3,1], [3,1,2], [3,2,1]$$

The iPod must pick one of these six arrangements, called *permutations*, at random. A permutation is an ordered list without repetitions. The number of permutations of a sequence can be calculated using

$$P^n_r = \frac{n!}{(n-r)!}$$

where

   r is the size of each permutation

   n is the size of the sequence from which elements are permuted

   ! is the factorial operator

For example, if $n = 10$, and $r = 3$, then $P^{10}_3 = 720$. Using the factorial function from the chapter on recursion, implement the algorithm above. Test the program using the example given above and two other test cases: $n = 10$ and $r = 4$, and $n = 40$ and $r = 4$. Does the program work? If not, find out why.

Exercise 19.3

Write a series of test cases for the wind-chill program of Exercise 10.3.

---

[5]C. Cherniak, "Undebuggability and Cognitive Science," *Communications of the ACM*, 31, no.4 (1988): 402–12.

Exercise 19.4

Test the program of Exercise 14.4 using the following surnames that sound the same but are spelled differently:

BENNETT, BENNET, BENETT, BENNITT = B530

STEVENS, STEPHENS, STIEVENS = S315

It is also possible to test the algorithm using homonyms. For example:

elusion, elution

bow, bough

hair, hare, herr

hoard, horde, hoared

medal, meddle, metal, mettle

paw, poor, pore, pour

raze, rays, raise

Is it possible to find a series of words that sound the same but make the algorithm fail?

I Point, Therefore I Am

Pointers have been lumped with the goto statement as a marvelous way to create impossible to understand programs. —Kernighan and Ritchie

Introduction

Every C program containing pointers should contain a disclaimer of the form:

> Warning: This section may contain explicit information about the use of pointers. Discretion is advised for novice programmers and those wary of pointers.

The reason? Pointers are arguably one of the most confusing constructs in C programming. Part of the reason for this is the continued use of obscure symbols in C terminology. This section briefly outlines some of the core pointer concepts.

What is a Pointer?

A *pointer* is a variable whose value just happens to be a memory address. We encountered pointers the first time we used **scanf**. In essence we have been using them since the start. Then we encountered more when we used pass-by-reference in functions. Fundamentally we have to remember that pointers have to do with memory, or more specifically, positions in memory called *addresses*. Using pointers we can manipulate the values stored at specific memory addresses. As such, they are among the most powerful of programming structures.

Memories of C

C has three different *pools* of memory:

Static: global variable storage, permanent for the entire run of the program

Stack: local variable storage (continuous memory)

Heap: dynamic storage (large pool of memory, not allocated in contiguous order)

For example:

```
int theforce;
```

On an Intel Core Duo, the variable uses 4 bytes of memory. This memory can come from one of two places. If a variable is declared outside of a function, it is considered global, meaning it is accessible anywhere in the program. Global variables are *static*, and there is only one copy for the entire program. The *heap* is a bunch of memory that can be used dynamically. The heap is generally used by dynamic allocator functions such as malloc. If you want 4kb of memory for an object, the dynamic allocator will obtain it from the heap. The *stack* is used to store variables used on the *inside* of a function. Once a function finishes running, all the memory it uses is freed up. The stack is a special region of memory. Stack memory is divided into successive frames in which each time a function is called, it allocates itself a fresh stack frame. Consider the following example with associated comments:

```
#include <stdio.h>
#include <stdlib.h>

int x=7;

int main(void)
{
    int y;
    char *str;

    str = malloc(100);
    free(str);

    return 0;
}
```

The variable **x** is *static* storage, because of its global nature. Both **y** and **str** are dynamic *stack* storage that is deallocated when the program ends. The function **malloc** is used to allocate 100 bytes of dynamic *heap* storage to **str**. Conversely, the function **free** deallocates the memory associated with **str**.

* Operator

Pointer variables are prefixed by an asterisk when they are declared. If **p** is used to denote a pointer variable, then ***p** defines the object currently pointed to by **p**. We experienced this in pass-by-reference parameters when we looked at functions. Therefore;

```
int *x;
```

implies the variable **x** is a pointer to an *int*. We can create any type of pointer variable. We can use **printf** with the %p specifier to output the address value of the variable in hexadecimal. if we use

```
printf("%p\n", x);
```

we would get:

```
0xbffffb14
```

To assign a value to **x**, we would use the format:

```
*x = 12;
```

Pointers and I/O

There are a couple of tricks when dealing with pointers and I/O. The first is obtaining a value to store at an address using **scanf**. When we read a normal **int** using **scanf**, we normally need an ampersand operator to represent the address of the variable in question. However, if we tried doing this under Pelles C:

```
int *x;
scanf("%d", &x);
```

We would get an error of the form: "**Bus error.**" Some compilers such as gcc will trigger a warning. This will work with the following expressions:

```
scanf("%d", &*x);
scanf("%d", x);
```

The first **scanf** has the effect of overkill. It is best to realize that **scanf** knows x is a pointer, in a similar way that it knows a string is a pointer. When we want to print out the value stored in **x**, we use:

```
printf("%d", *x);
```

& Operator

You have already experienced this operator in the **scanf** function. When you execute a **scanf** function of the form

```
scanf("%d", &x);
```

the program will read an integer from standard input and store it in the variable **x**. Essentially this says: "Take the value read from the keyboard and store its value at the address in memory pointed to by x."

The ampersand is the *address-of* operator. This operator is most commonly used in returning values from functions, but more about that later. For example, say we declare a normal integer and want to assign its value to **x**. We could use as expression of the form:

```
int *x, y=24;

x = &y;
```

Here **x** is assigned the location of the variable **y** in memory. The ampersand is used to extract the address of **y**, *not* the value contained in **y**. We can now access the content of **y** via the pointer variable *x. Note that the asterisk is not used when a pointer variable is initialized.

 The following expression DOES NOT WORK:

```
*x = &y;
```

But some compilers, such as gcc, will throw back a warning of the form:

```
warning: assignment makes integer from pointer without a
cast
```

Pointers and Strings

Pointers work a little differently with arrays, as we have already seen with strings. For example, we can happily use a **scanf** statement without an & to read in a string:

```
char word[20];
scanf("%s", word);
```

This is because arrays are really pointers in disguise. This is often a source of confusion. We can create a pointer to a character, and assign the string to it:

```
char *s;
s = word;
```

Now we don't need to use an &. Strings are the exception to the rule in C. The compiler knows any string identifier is already a pointer. Pointers can be used to initialize strings:

```
char *jedi = "Mara Jade";
```

The problem here is that once we have created a string in this manner, it cannot be altered. Any attempt to change something in the string **jedi** will result in some sort of segmentation fault, such as an "Access Violation" in Pelles C.

2D Strings as Pointers

As we saw in Chapter 14, 2D character arrays can be used to store words. The example we used was:

```
char hydroxide[3][5] = {"NaOH","MgOH","KOH"};
```

which works well because there isn't much waste. Now image we need to create a 2D character array to words from a book. Say the smallest word contained in the book is the article "a" and the largest is "meteorological." To create a 2D string to store all the words, say 100,000, it would need to be declared as:

```
char words[100000][14];
```

which you can imagine consumes a whole bunch of unnecessary memory if there are only 1,000 words with a length greater than 10. There is another way to do this. A simple extension to single string pointer declarations is the use of an *array of pointers*. For example, the following declaration:

```
char *hydroxide[3];
```

Creates an array of five elements, where each element is a pointer to a character. Being individual pointers, each pointer can be assigned to point to a string using string assignment statements. For example:

```
hyroxide[0] = "NaOH";
hyroxide[1] = "MgOH";
hyroxide[2] = "KOH";
```

The initializations of the hydroxides can also be incorporated within the array definition:

```
char *hydroxide[] = {"NaOH", "MgOH", "KOH"};
```

This is what it looks like visually:

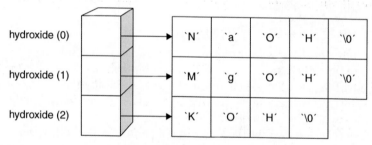

You cannot change the values once they have been created.

What is the difference between an array of pointers and an array of strings? The array of strings is a rectangular array, where all rows are the same length. The array of pointers is a *ragged* array, where the length of each row is determined by the length of the string it holds. The ragged array always saves on storage space.

Returning Strings from Functions

If we use pointers, we can now return strings from functions using the **return** statement. In the following example, we can return a character string by declaring the return value as a pointer to a character.

```
char* pH(double pHlevel)
{
    if (pHlevel < 7.0)
        return "base";
    else if (pHlevel > 7.0)
        return "acid";
```

```
        else
            return "neutral";
    }
```

which could be called in the following manner:

```
    char *s;
    s=pH(3.8);
```

Pointers and Arrays

Like many things in C, there is another way of using arrays. Let's return to an example from Chapter 13:

```
    double yr_1659[12];
```

To assign a value to the fifth element of **yr_1659**, we would traditionally use:

```
    yr_1659[4] = 3.0;
```

which refers to the same memory contents as:

```
    *(yr_1659+4) = 3.0;
```

This basically adds 4 to the initial pointer to access the fifth element of the array. Every element of an array can be accessed in a similar fashion. Basically when a compiler sees an array identifier, it translates it to a pointer to the initial element of the array. The compiler then interprets the array subscript as an offset from the root address position. This is partially why the first subscript in an array is 0.

What pointers *cannot* do is initialize a numeric array. So the following will not work:

```
    double *yr_1659 =
    {3.0,4.0,6.0,7.0,11.0,13.0,16.0,16.0,13.0,10.0,5.0,2.0};
```

Allocating Memory with `malloc`

The function **malloc**, which is pronounced **MAL-lock,** is short for *memory allocation* and is used for exactly that purpose. Here's a 5-second introduction for those who are really interested. To use **malloc** we need to include **stdlib.h.** For example:

```
    1    int *yr_1659;
    2    yr_1659 = (int *)malloc(12);
    3    *(yr_1659+1) = 4;
```

The first line creates a pointer to an integer. The second line allocates 12 pieces of storage to **yr_1959** of type **int.** The third line sets the second element of the "array" to the value 4.

malloc has relatives. **realloc** is used to resize memory originally defined using **malloc**, and **free** is used to release memory allocated by **malloc**. In the previous example, at the end of the program, we would use free like this:

```
free(yr_1659);
```

If we want to create a 2D strings array and be able to change elements within it, we have to use **malloc** as well.

```
char *hydroxide[3], comp[5]; int i, j;

for (i=0; i<3; i=i+1)
    hydroxide[i] = (char *)malloc(5);

for (i=0; i<3; i=i+1){
    scanf("%s", comp);
    strcpy(hydroxide[i],comp);
}
```

Here we are creating an array of pointers with three elements in it. Each element in the array has five pieces of **char** storage associated with it. See all the fun you could have playing with memory! Well, maybe not.

Pointers and Comments

When you become proficient in C, you will probably use a lot more pointers. Watch what you are doing, though. Suppose we have a pointer **ptr**, and want to use ***ptr** to get the contents of the address being pointed at.

```
double *ptr, a;
*ptr = 2.76;
a = 1.0/*ptr + 7.9;
```

Do you see any problem here? The **1.0/*ptr + 7.9** looks a lot like the start of a comment. This is one of the few places in C where a space is significant. We need to change the line to:

```
a = 1.0 / *ptr + 7.9;
a = 1.0/(*ptr) + 7.9;
```

Weird and Wonderful Memory Problems!

The Unix operating system defines a number of different incidents relating to memory access.[1] A *buffer overflow* occurs when a program writes to a memory address on the program's call stack outside of the intended data structure. Here's an example of a buffer overflow:

---

[1] N. P. Smith, "Stack Smashing Vulnerabilities in the UNIX Operating System," 1997. http://www.comms.scitech .sussex.ac.uk/fft/security/Stack_Smashing_Vulnerabilities_in_the_UNIX_Operating_System.pdf

```
void buffer_overflow(char *str)
{
    char buffer[10];
    strcpy(buffer, str);
}

int main (void)
{
    char *str = "Do or do not, there is no try";
    // length of str = 30 bytes
    buffer_overflow(str);
    return 0;
}
```

This will cause unexpected behavior, usually in the form of a *segmentation fault*, because a string (**str**) of 30 bytes has been copied to a location (**buffer**) that has been allocated only 10 bytes. The extra bytes run past the buffer and overwrite space. A *fandango on core* is a generic term for all bugs involving a wild pointer that has run out of bounds, causing core dumps or corruption of dynamic memory allocation space. A variety of fandango on core, an *overrun screw* is a generic term for C programming bugs that scribble past the end of an array. A lack of bounds checking makes this a fairly common occurrence in the C programming language. A variety of overrun screw, *smashing, trashing,* and *scribbling* the stack are reserved for a C programming case in which the execution stack is corrupted by writing past the end of a data structure, such as a local array. Smashing, trashing, or scribbling the stack is said to happen when a C function or routine jumps to a random address and overruns a fixed-size buffer with excessively large input data.

Epilog

This is where we leave the world of pointers. You can use pointers for infinitely many things, but they are best suited for creating and manipulating data structures such as linked lists and trees.

Interacting with Programs

A common mistake people make when trying to design something completely foolproof is to underestimate the ingenuity of complete fools.

—Douglas Adams

Introduction

In the early days of computing, humans interacted with computers through media such as punch cards. In the 1970s came a slow progression to screens and keyboards, and in the 1980s came the mouse. The progress in how humans interact with machines is becoming more transparent, more natural with the advent of technologies such as Apple's gesture language and multi-touch screens; yet, at the same time, we are evolving away from computers in the traditional sense. Today computers abound in many devices, from kitchen appliances to home thermostats, kiosks, cell phones, and electronic readers. Paramount to many of these devices is a sense of usability—how usable is the device/program controlling the device? Many programs suffer from a lack of usability, from the insipid error messages of compilers to lack of ease in programming a thermostat or washing machine. In the early days of the Macintosh operating system, error messages were often of the form shown here:

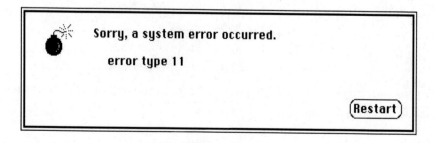

Sorry, a system error occurred.

error type 11

(Restart)

This dialog box suffers from three aspects of acutely bad design: a bewildering error message, an inappropriate visual icon, and a failure to allow the user to exit from the program. The error message supplied to the user ("error type 11") was meaningless, unless the user had access to the list of appropriate error codes. The error actually means "miscellaneous hardware exception error," which, in itself, is cryptic. This is actually a processor-generated error, which is not covered and identified by error codes 01 to 10. This is akin to saying, "Sorry an error has occurred in the program, probably because you typed something. I know what the error is, but I don't really want you to know. Just click on the Restart button and I will reboot the system." It may have been more meaningful for the message to have read, "Sorry, a hardware error that I can't identify has occurred," but not by much. They may just as well have auto-restarted the system with no dialog. Humans interact with computers through input devices such as keyboards, mice, and touch-tablets. Programs, conversely, interact by means of messages and prompts visualized on the screen or through the control of some electronic device.

Limitations of Humans

People are not computers, despite that fact that we try and model computers after how the human mind works. Humans get tired, bored, and irritable, besides which they have two important limitations related to data: (i) they have short-term memory capacity and (ii) they have limited information input rate. Humans have three basic types of memory: sensory, short-term, and long-term. Sensory memory retains impressions of sensory information for approximately 200 to 500 milliseconds after something is perceived. Short-term memory (STM) is the information buffer between a person's long-term memory (LTM) and his or her environment. Information enters this buffer either from long-term memory through thinking or from the senses (e.g., auditory, visual) by means of reception. STM is capable of retaining approximately seven items of information at any one time, for about 2 seconds.[1] The limitations of human memory ultimately impact how users interact with a program. Human aren't very good at remembering obscure codes or transferring information from one screen to another. A well-designed user interface will help users achieve their goals.

Usability

Usability denotes the ease with which people can employ a particular tool or other human-made object in order to achieve a particular goal. In programming, it implies the elegance and clarity with which the interaction with a computer program or a web site is designed. Usability is just as important a part of programming as coding itself. The trick is that programs are written by humans and, as such, should provide an understandable medium. Failure to incorporate good usability principles has a number of consequences:

1. *Learnability*: the amount of time required to learn the system may be lengthened.
2. *Efficiency*: it may take longer to perform tasks.

---

[1]G. A. Miller, "The Magical Number Seven, Plus or Minus Two: Some Limits on Our Capacity for Processing Information," *Psychological Review* 63 no. 2 (1956): 81–97.

3. *Memorability*: a user may not remember how to use the system.

4. *Errors*: a user should be able to recover from errors.

Many of the problems associated with usability have to do with how errors and other inadequacies are communicated to users.

Good Examples of Bad Messages

The examples described in this chapter relate predominantly to error messages; in the programs we are writing, usability is in the form of the messages used to communicate with the user. Error messages are the linch-pins of usability. Consider the following example of bad error messages:

```
Error: Keyboard not found. Press F1 to continue.
Unexpected error, quitting.
Error 0000: No errors found, restarting computer.
The iPod cannot be updated. An unknown error occurred (1418).
```

Even the most user-focused company can produce error messages that are less than usable. A good example of a bad error message is the feared 404 error message found on the Internet. A 404 error message means that the server was successfully contacted but could not retrieve the file requested by the client (browser). This can happen because of an outdated or expired link, a linking error on the site itself, or a user typo. A bad error message is of the following form:

```
Error 404—Not found
```

A better way of dealing with this error might be any of the following:

Oops . . . I don't have that page.

The page you are looking for appears to have been moved, deleted, or does not exist.

We're sorry; we can't find what you're looking for.

Good Error Messages

Users **never** want error messages. Why do we have so many bad error messages? Because since the early days, it has been accepted that the proper way for software to interact with humans was to demand input, and to complain when the human failed to achieve perfection! An example is

```
Action aborted due to file specification error.
```

This example aptly illustrates the internal workings of a program percolating up to the user level. The term *file specification error* is well understood by programmers and is synonymous with the fact that the file **does not exist**. The message would be better if it was reworded to

```
Sorry, the file XYZ does not exist in this location.
```

This message is explicit, written in English, and polite and precisely describes the problem. It doesn't provide advice on how to fix the problem per se, but it does say, "does not exist in this location," requiring the user to locate the file first. Another good example is

```
System error &H80004005 (-2147467259) Unspecified error
```

The programmer has allowed programming details to "leak out" into the user interface. This "unspecified error" is accompanied by a very large negative number "-2147467259." An experienced programmer will recognize this as a potential overflow error, but who really knows? Here are some guidelines on what good error messages should embrace:[2]

- An *explicit* indication that something has gone wrong. The worst error messages are the ones that just don't exist.
- The use of *human-readable* language, instead of anything that resembles programming "speak."
- *Polite* phrasing that doesn't blame users or imply that they did something wrong.
- A *precise* description of the problem.
- *Constructive* advice on how to fix the problem.

Wording

The use of messages when prompting for input or outputting results should follow principles of legibility, brevity, clarity, and consistency. Try and minimize the use of jargon: words that are unfamiliar to the user should not be used. This jargon is often called a *programmerism* and can make the user feel as if the interface has been written in a foreign language. Use words that are unambiguous; avoid words or phrases that can be interpreted in more than one way.

- Use short simple sentences, simple descriptive words, and minimal punctuation.
- Use positive statements as they are more easily understood than negative statements. Avoid words that imply blame, failure, or tragic consequences. Examples of words to be avoided include *invalid*, *illegal*, and *fatal*.
- Use active voice messages, which are easier to understand than passive voice ones.
- Use neutral wording.
- Make error messages specific, informative, and brief.

Consider the leap-years program found in the case studies. The error message used to check for years input that were earlier than 1582 was

```
Sorry, invalid year.
```

The problem with this error message is that it is not very informative. We could also have written

```
Sorry, the year entered cannot be used.
```

---

[2]http://www.useit.com/alertbox/20010624.html.

But this is equally as uninformative. The user is missing one piece of information critical to his or her continued use of the program—*why* the year was invalid. A more expressive message might be the following:

```
Sorry, the year entered cannot be used. Leap years
can be calculated only ßfor the Gregorian calendar (>1582).
```

User Input Messages

For command-line–based programs, requesting data from the user is the most critical aspect of the human-computer interface. Poorly designed input can result in reduced usability. Errors made by users are inevitable; however, careful design of input processes can reduce the frequency and consequences of errors. When asking for input, we sometimes design messages that incorporate aspects of self-identification; that is, we presume too much about how the user will interpret the message. For example:

```
Enter the mortgage rate (%):
```

Some users may interpret this as entering a number between 0 and 100; others may interpret it as a number between 0 and 1—for example, 5.63 percent or 0.0563 percent. It may be easier to use this message:

```
Enter the mortgage rate (0.0-100.0):
```

The user will then enter a percentage that can be divided by 100.0 within the program. Another example is phone numbers. If we prompt for a phone number using the prompt

```
Phone number:
```

Do we enter 519-824-4120, or (519)824-4120, 5198244120, or 824-4120? Each has its own context. The use of parentheses usually denotes some sort of optional information, which, given that most phones use 10-digit dialing, is somewhat superfluous. A good example of a data element that has wide variation in format is the date:

2001	A four-digit year
6/11/01	Three sets of digits separated by slashes, although there is an ambiguity in the order of day-month-year, with many variations.
6.11.01	Decimal points used as field separators.
6.XI.01	European railway date system
11/2001	Sometimes only month-year are given.

Use of international standard dates:

year-month-day-hour-minute-second

For example:

011106.085906

These are unambiguous, compact, and simple to compare time relationships—for computers. Humans may face challenges, however. Here are some examples of guidelines to follow:

1. Make input prompts clear and understandable.

   ```
   Enter the wind temperature (Celsius):
   ```

2. Use a single entry field for each prompt.

   ```
   Enter the dam width (m):
   Enter the dam height (m):
   ```

3. Show the correct input format.

   ```
   Enter the starting date (DD/MM/YYYY):
   ```

4. If appropriate, show default values.

   ```
   Enter the percentage (0-100):
   ```

5. Display unit designators. Use units that are most familiar to the user (km/hr versus metres/second).

   ```
   Enter the tree circumference (inches):
   ```

6. Use a standard character, such as a colon, to denote a prompt for input.

   ```
   Enter the number of series :
   ```

Humanization of Input

Programs invariably rely on input to run. The way data is represented or gathered is extremely important to the context of how an algorithm operates. One of the challenges with designing a program is relating to the *humanization* of input, and that relates to how the data is stored in the program. A license plate in Quebec typically is made up of seven characters: the first three are digits; the last three are alphabetic characters—for example: 000 ABC. In its most common form, the license plate is represented as two pieces of data separated by a space. To use this data requires knowledge of how a user will input this information. If it were keyed in as

   ```
   0 0 0 ABC
   ```

then we could ask that the input be read as three distinct digits, followed by three distinct characters:

   ```
   scanf("%d %d %d %c%c%c", &n1,&n2,&n3,&c1,&c2,&c3);
   ```

This is not the most natural approach, as it relates well to how the data is read in by **scanf**. Extra key presses are required, which is contrary to natural inclination. The three digits must be separated; otherwise, they will be read in as a single number. We could read the numeric data in as one number, as in

```
scanf("%d %c%c%c", &n1,&c1,&c2,&c3);
```

The input could then be input as

```
000 ABC
```

However, leading zeros will be ignored, so 007 will become 7 when stored in the variable **n1**. This is the most natural form of input for the user, as the license is entered exactly as it appears on the plate. Is it the best input format? Probably, but not the best way of storing the license. Now take into account the fact that Quebec passenger vehicle plates[3] can be any one of three formats:

000 ABC   **ABC 000**   **000H000**

The most natural way of storing the information is in the form if a string, which takes into consideration all three formats:

```
char s[8];
fgets(s,8,stdin);
```

Epilog

The goal of usability is to design systems that minimize the barriers between the human's cognitive model of what he or she wants to accomplish and the computer's understanding of the user's task. When it comes to design, simplicity is key. Einstein put it aptly when he said, "Everything should be made as simple as possible, but no simpler." Even more apt is da Vinci's "Simplicity is the ultimate sophistication." Do not attempt to create overcomplicated user interfaces to control simple programs.

Exercises

Exercise 21.1

Snow water equivalent (SWE) is a measurement of snowpack that relates to the amount of water it contains. It is equivalent to the depth of water that would theoretically result if the entire snowpack melted simultaneously. Snow water equivalent can be presented in units of kg/m^2 or meters of depth of liquid water that would result from melting the snow. SWE is the product of depth and density:

SWE = depth (m) $\times$ density (kg/m^3) (units: kg/m^2)

SWE = depth (m) $\times$ density (kg/m^3) / density of water (kg/m^3) (units: m)

To determine the SWE, you need to know the density of the snow and the density of water $(1000kg/m^3)$. The density of new snow ranges from 5 percent when the temperature is -10°C to about 20 percent when the temperature is 0°C. After snow falls, its density

---

[3] http://www.saaq.gouv.qc.ca/en/vehicle_registration/categories/passenger.php.

increases because of gravitational settling, wind packing, melting, and recrystallization. Snowpack densities are approximately 20 to 30 percent in the winter and 30 to 50 percent in the spring. Consider the following program to calculate SWE:

```c
#include <stdio.h>
#define H20den 1000

int main(void)
{
    double snowDep, snowDen, snowH20equiv;

    printf("depth: ");
    scanf("%lf", &snowDep);
    printf("density: ");
    scanf("%lf", &snowDen);

    snowH20equiv = snowDep * snowDen / H20den;

    printf("The SWE is: %.2f\n", snowH20equiv);

    return 0;
}
```

Compile and run the program. What is missing from this program? Fix the program to make it more usable.

Exercise 21.2

Using the program from Exercise 9.3, create a usable interface to deal with both metric and imperial measurements.

22

Making Things Go Faster

Premature optimization is the root of all evil in programming.

—C.A.R. Hoare

Introduction

When you design a program, the primary concern is how accurately and reliably it runs. Programs exist to perform some task, not to run in the shortest possible period of time. If the task cannot be completed, or completed accurately, then having it run fast is a waste of time. In addition, efficiency is a feature that can be added; accuracy is not. An accurate yet inefficient program can be optimized and made more efficient; the same is not true for an unreliable fast program. Inaccurate programs are useless, no matter how fast they run. Forget about how efficient a program is—unless there is cause to be efficient. Program *efficiency*, however, is vital in real-world applications, particularly in the context of speed and space.

In the case of *space*, there are environments in which the amount of processing power and storage is constrained. Consider the Mars Exploration Rovers, Spirit and Opportunity. These six-wheeled robots have been exploring Mars since their arrival in 2003 as part of the Mars Exploration Rover (MER) mission. At the heart of each of the Mars rovers is a computer system on a single board in the form of a RAD6000 with 128 MB of DRAM. Its circuits are hardened to absorb radiation that would otherwise ruin the sensitive hardware. In comparison to earth-bound PCs, this processor is somewhat of an underperformer. Its simple 1.1-million transistor processor runs at a top speed of 25 MHz, compared to an Intel Core 2 Duo processor found in the MacBook Pro, which has 291 million transistors. The Space Shuttle is a pretty sophisticated piece of hardware, so it must be packed with pretty fast computers, right? Not so. The current general-use laptop aboard the space shuttle is an IBM ThinkPad 760XD specially modified for use in space. The 760XD uses a 166 MHz Pentium MMX microprocessor. Compare that to an Intel multicore processor, or the IBM BlueGene/L with 131,072 processors, 32,768 GB of memory and a speed of 280,600 gigaflops. So creating software for "low-tech" systems is much more challenging than it is for a fast system. Programs written for the rovers must be compact and efficient, sparingly using the 128 MB of available memory.

In the case of speed, certain applications are required to perform within time constraints. Good examples include address recognition software within mail-sorting systems, and certain types of product quality inspection systems in manufacturing. Postal sorting machines typically process in excess of 60,000 items per hour. These systems typically scan the entire piece of mail and then perform online video coding to decipher the address. In manufacturing, especially of food products, speed is needed on manufacturing lines to identify items deemed of lower quality. A good example is a system that performs quality inspection of pizzas.

The best approach is to design a program without any concern for efficiency. Then if the program runs accurately but is costly to run or needs to run on a platform with limited resources, optimization should be considered. In the recent past, efficiencies of various programming structures were important due to the low processor speeds. Now with an abundance of processing power, efficiencies are discernibly more difficult to implement. A typical program spends most of its time executing a small portion of code, and as such increasing the efficiency of small pockets of code that are executed one to two times is a squandering of resources. Some may consider the process of making a program more efficient somewhat antiquated in the face of the computing resources available. For small programs performing small tasks on fast machines, this is certainly true. For large software systems, it may be a necessary process defined in the design phase.

Code Optimization

To make code more efficient, you can *optimize* it. Optimization may imply improvements in code speed or storage capacity. To optimize code, you have to find a bottleneck. Indeed, improving about 20 percent of code is often responsible for 80 percent of the results. This stems from the *Pareto* principle (80-20 rule), which states that for many phenomena, 80 percent of the consequences stem from 20 percent of the causes. Optimization may involve many different approaches. It may involve changing how a programming structure executes or choosing a different algorithm. Regardless of the approach, the first task in optimizing code is determining what should be optimized. This is easily achieved by segmenting the program into regions. Then we can estimate the total time each region takes to execute and use this information to determine which region of the program should receive the greatest effort toward optimization. Every program will contain one region that consumes more runtime than any other. In some compilers, a *profiler* can be used to determine the timing of the segments. Once a segment to optimize has been identified, the potential improvement must also be estimated. If a segment takes 40 percent of the total program time, but only a 5 percent efficiency can be achieved, this would result in a 0.4 * 0.05 = 0.02 = 2 percent increase in efficiency. Most of the techniques used to make a program more efficient do not affect the program's readability. However, some qualities of programming languages such as C's shortcut operators actually decrease the readability of a program. Consider these basic rules:

1. Optimize ONLY if necessary.
2. Locate the region to be optimized.
3. Find a way of optimizing the code.

Measuring Time

Determining the efficiency of a program requires some means of measuring the time the code takes to run. When a program executes, its runtime is the sum of three parts:

1. Compute time: the time needed to execute the instructions
2. Voluntary wait time: the time the program must wait for the completion of an event that it initiated
3. Involuntary wait time: the time the program must wait due to other programs

In some applications, it is desirable to increase the speed of the algorithm, which can usually be achieved through reducing parts 1 and 2. However, there is sometimes a downside to increasing the speed of a program, from an increase in storage requirements to an increase in the programming effort. Ultimately, the effort devoted to increasing the speed of a program has to take a number of factors into account. It may not be reasonable to expend a great deal of effort for a relatively limited reduction in compute time, say for a program that is run only once. Conversely, a function that is frequently run could benefit from extensive computation reduction. If we really want to calculate how long it takes to perform a long division, we can create some code to do this. The execution of a single division is too fast; so it's best to perform the calculation a series of times, say 1 billion.

```
int main(void)
{
    long a, b=255, c=255, i;

    for (i=1; i<=1000000000; i=i+1)
        a = b / c;

    return 0;
}
```

On a 2.16 Gz Intel Core 2 Duo, this takes about 6.0 seconds. Now, we can subtract out all the time not associated with the divide. This is achieved by removing the divide from the program. Now running it we get 3.09 seconds of user time. This implies 6.0 − 3.09 = 2.91 seconds for the division operations, and dividing by 1,000,000,00 we get an estimate for each divide instruction of 2.91e-9 seconds per division. You can time this on the command line using the following command once the program has been compiled (the executable program is **a.out**):

```
> time ./a.out
```

which gives the following output:

```
real    0m6.067s
user    0m6.032s
sys     0m0.008s
```

The real time is the time elapsed from the beginning to end of the program, the user time is the time used by the program itself, and the system time is the time used by the system calls invoked by the program. Timing can also be achieved using the **time.h** library. This library gives access to information and functions necessary to measure the running time of any portion of a program. In the following examples, the **clock** function is used, which approximates the amount of time the program has been running. Also used is the constant **CLOCKS_PER_SEC** to convert the result to real-time units. Here's a neat bit of code:

```c
#include <stdio.h>
#include <time.h>
int main(void)
{
    clock_t start, end;
    double cpu_time_used;
    start = clock();

    // Code to time here

    end = clock();
    cpu_time_used = ((double)(end - start))/CLOCKS_PER_SEC;
    printf("%.2f\n", cpu_time_used);
}
```

For example, we could run a loop 1 billion times, performing various operations. Here's the code:

```c
long i;
double sum=0.0;
for (i=0; i<1000000000; i=i+1)
    sum = sum + i;
```

Here are some statistics for Xcode running on an Intel Core 2 Duo processor:

```
1 billion additions = 4.17 seconds
1 billion multiplications = 5.10 seconds
1 billion divisions = 7.06 seconds
```

Let's compare different ways of calculating i^2 and summing the results through 1 billion iterations:

```
sum = sum + i * i;           = 4.44 seconds
sum = sum + pow(i,2.0);      = 6.49 seconds
```

This implies that **pow** is indeed slower. This may not always be true. It really depends on how the compiler generates the code, but in general i*i is more efficient than **pow(i,2.0)**.

Arithmetic Operations

Arithmetic operations are all done at different speeds, so it is helpful to know which ones are faster. Addition and subtraction are generally faster to perform than multiplication and division, which are in turn faster than mathematical functions such as **pow**. Meek and colleagues[1] outline the following relative times for arithmetic operations (although this table was first cited in 1980, the underlying concepts should hold):

integer assignment = 1

integer addition/subtraction = 1.5

real assignment = 2

real addition/subtraction = 3

real multiplication = 5

integer to real conversion = 6

integer multiplication = 8

division = 9

exponentiation to integral power = 35

exponentiation to real power = 115

arithmetic functions (log, sqrt etc.) = 150+

Therefore, from a speed point of view, a $\times$ 0.5 is more efficient than a/2.0. Consider the case of two algorithms for summing the first 1..N numbers:

```
int i, sum=0;

A      for (i=1; i<=N; i=i+1)
            sum = sum + i;


B      sum = N * (N+1)/2
```

If $N = 10$ and a value of 1 is assigned for a comparison, then the loop structure of algorithm A will have 1 + 10 + 10*(1+1.5) = 36, and the summation statement will be 10*(1+1.5) = 25. So the sum for algorithm A will be 61. Algorithm B (assuming integer math) involves an integer assignment (1), an integer multiplication (8) and division (9), and an integer addition (1.5), for a grand total of 19.5, which implies it is three times as fast. In the case of exponentiation, x^2 is better represented by x*x than it is by pow(x,2.0), x+x is faster than 2.0*x, and x*0.1 is faster than x/10.0. Now, it is interesting that as N increases, the relative time of algorithm B remains static, whereas that of algorithm A always increases. For $N = 100$, algorithm A becomes 351 + 250 = 601.

Sometimes arithmetic operations can be made more efficient by rearranging an equation:

```
X = 2 * Y + (A - 1) / P + 2 * T;
```

can be changed to

```
X = 2 * (Y + T) + (A - 1) / P;
```

eliminating one multiplication. Consider the following rules when optimizing arithmetic expressions:

---

[1]B. L. Meek and P. M. Heath, *Guide to Good Programming Practice* (Chichester, England: Ellis Horwood, 1980).

- Integer arithmetic is faster than floating-point arithmetic.
- Addition and subtraction are faster than multiplication.
- Multiplication is faster than division, instead of dividing by 2, multiply by 0.5.

The multiplication of integer variables by powers of two can be replaced by left shifts. For example:

```
x = y * 4;
```

could be rewritten as:

```
x = y << 2;
```

In a similar fashion, division of integer variables by powers of two can be replaced by a right shift. But after testing these calculations 1 billion times, there was a difference between the two operations. One can go overboard making such optimizations, and, therefore, it is important to keep a sense of balance. Don't make drastic changes to equations at the expense of clarity.

Eliminating Redundancy

Computational inefficiency is often caused by the calculation of unnecessary expressions. Consider as an example the familiar quadratic equation. The two roots of the equation can be computed using the following two expressions:

```
r1 = (-b + sqrt(b*b - 4.0 * a * c)) / (2.0 * a);
r2 = (-b - sqrt(b*b - 4.0 * a * c)) / (2.0 * a);
```

On an average compiler, these statements require calls to two functions, 10 multiplications and divisions, and four additions and subtractions for evaluation. However, if we look more closely, we notice that the expressions contain redundant subexpressions, namely the discriminant b^2-4ac, and the denominator 2 * a. As both these expressions are not used elsewhere, they need to be calculated only once. Similarly, the two calls to function **sqrt** can be reduced to one.

```
denom = 2.0 * a;
discr = sqrt(b*b - 4.0 * a * c);
r1 = (-b + discr) / denom;
r2 = (-b - discr) / denom;
```

We can make some further changes, notably replacing the multiplication in **denom** by a faster addition:

```
denom = a + a;
```

The final computation then requires one function call, five multiplications and divisions, and four additions and subtractions, making it considerably more efficient. Ironically, this is an example in which the effort involved is probably overzealous, as the calculation itself does not require much computation time. Eliminating subexpressions can be summarized using the following rule:

Redundant functions are treated in the same way as redundant expressions. For example, Cartesian coordinates can be converted from spherical coordinates using the following equations:

```
x = r * sin(theta) * cos(phi);
y = r * sin(theta) * sin(phi);
z = r * cos(theta);
```

which can be reduced to

```
sinT = sin(theta);
x = r * sinT * cos(phi);
y = r * sinT * sin(phi);
z = r * cos(theta);
```

If the value of an expression does not change between multiple occurrences of that expression, then it should be evaluated only once, and its value assigned to a new variable that replaces all occurrences of the original expression. Certain mathematical expressions such as polynomials can be factored to reduce the amount of computation. For example, $y = 7 x^3 + 4x^2 + 6x + 11$ could be expressed as:

```
y = 7*x*x*x + 4*x*x + 6*x + 11;
```

This requires six multiplications and three additions. Factored, the polynomial is expressed as

```
y = ((7*x + 4)*x + 6)*x + 11;
```

requiring three multiplications and three additions. On the other hand, there are some cases in which functions cannot be reduced. For example:

```
x = rand(x) + rand(x);
```

may not be reduced to

```
x = 2.0 * rand(x);
```

The calls to **rand** do not return identical results even though the parameters are the same, so the function is not really reducible.

Loop Peeling

Loop *peeling* (or loop *splitting*) attempts to simplify a loop or eliminate dependencies by breaking a loop into multiple loops that have the same bodies but iterate over different contiguous portions of the index range. A useful special case is simplifying a loop with a problematic first (or first few) iteration by performing that iteration separately before entering the loop. Here is an example of loop peeling. Suppose the original code looks like this:

```
int vector[100], r[100], i;
for (i=0; i<1000; i=i+1){
    r[i] = vector[i-1] * vector[i];
}
```

The problem here is the fact that the loop cannot safely handle the case of **vector[i-1]** when i = 0, for the index becomes -1, which is illegal. A better solution would be to peel the first iteration off:

```
int vector[100], r[100], i;
r[0] = vector[0];
for (i=1; i<1000; i=i+1){
    r[i] = vector[i-1] * vector[i];
}
```

Removing Loop-Independent Expressions

Expressions in loops that perform a calculation independent of the loop should be evaluated outside the loop. This is sometimes known as loop *streamlining*:

```
for (i=1; i<=1000; i=i+1)
    sum = sum + pow(x,4.0);
```

should be replaced by

```
powX = pow(x,4.0);
for (i=1; i<=1000; i=i+1)
    sum = sum + powX;
```

We remove the expression **pow(x,4.0)** because its calculation is independent of the loop and would otherwise be calculated 1000 times. Consider the following nested loop:

```
for (i=1; i<=100; i=i+1)
    for (j=1; j<=100; j=j+1)
        for (k=1; k<=100; k=k+1)
```

The nested structure loops $100 \times 100 \times 100 = 1,000,000$ times, meaning that a statement such as **pow(x,4.0)** would be executed 1 million times. For a nested loop structure, the deeper a loop is nested, the higher the dividend with respect to efficiency. Always optimize inner loops first.

The same principle can be applied to nested loops, by moving independent expressions from an inner loop outward. For example, some repeated calculations make use of the subscript as part of the calculation:

```
for (i=1; i<=100; i=i+1)
    for (j=1; j<=100; j=j+1)
        A[i][j] = B[i][j] + c/i;
```

The calculation **c/i** is a repeat calculation and should be removed from the inner loop. A better way to code this is

```
for (i=1; i<=100; i=i+1){
    ci = c / i;
    for (j=1; j<=100; j=j+1)
        A[i][j] = B[i][j] + ci;
}
```

Now the value c/i is calculated 100 times instead of 10,000 times.

Loop Fusion

One of the greatest bottlenecks in improving efficiency is eliminating loops. The best way of cutting down the amount of time spent in loops is to decrease the number of loops, hence decreasing overhead associated with incrementing indexes and testing. This is termed loop *fusion, jamming,* or *merging.* For example, consider the following two loops, each of which initializes an array:

```
int a[1000], b[1000], i, j;

for (i=0; i<1000; i=i+1)
    a[i] = 0;
for (j=0; j<1000; j=j+1)
    b[j] = 0;
```

These loops involve 2000 index increases and tests. This can be reduced by half by merging the loops:

```
int i, a[1000], b[1000];

for (i=0; i<1000; i=i+1)
{
    a[i] = 0;
    b[i] = 0;
}
```

Loop Unrolling

Every iteration of a loop requires modification and testing of the loop variable. This overhead can be reduced if the number of iterations of the loop is small, say less than five. This is called *unrolling* the loop. The previous example could be unrolled, further reducing overhead:

```
int i, a[1000], b[1000];

for (i=0; i<1000; i=i+2)
{
    a[i] = 0;
    b[i] = 0;
```

```
        a[i+1] = 0;
        b[i+1] = 0;
}
```

The most extreme case is to eliminate the loop completely and work as sequential line code. For example:

```
for (i=1; i<=3; i=i+1)
{
    x = x + sqrt(i);
}
```

would arguably be better expressed as:

```
x = x + sqrt(1) + sqrt(2) + sqrt(3);
```

Dead Code Elimination

Code that doesn't actually do anything useful or permanent is known as *dead code*. Dead code elimination just removes such code. A similar concept is *unreachable code*, which is code that is impossible to reach. For example:

```
if (x == 100)
    . . .
else {
    . . .
    if (x == 100)
        . . .
}
```

The nested test for whether x is equal to 100 can be eliminated because it can never be reached. That case would have been caught by the first expression in the opening **if** statement.

Array Subscripts

Calculating subscripts for arrays can be quite time consuming; however, if an expression contains more than one reference to an array item, it may be more beneficial to assign the element to a variable. For example:

```
p = (vector[i] * sqrt(vector[i])) - vector[i];
```

which uses three subscript evaluations could be changed to

```
v = vector[i]
p = (v * sqrt(v)) - v;
```

which uses only one subscript evaluation.

Don't Be Too Clever

What does the following code do?

```
for (i=1; i<=N; i=i+1)
    for (j=1; j<=N; j=j+1)
        m[i-1][j-1] = (i/j) * (j/i);
```

Here, **i** and **j** are both integers, and integer division is performed. This means that the left-hand side of the equation equals 1 if and only if **i** equals **j**. This code puts ones in the diagonal of **m**, and zeros elsewhere.

The code is clever, but also rather perplexing to the uninitiated. The code is definitely not clear enough. A better rendition is

```
for (i=0; i<N; i=i+1) {
    for (j=0; j<N; j=j+1)
        m[i][j] = 0.0;
    m[i][i] = 1.0;
}
```

This code is now reasonably clear. It even executes faster because of the lack of division operations. If **N = 500**, then the first rendition runs in 0.015 seconds, the second in 0.0 seconds. It may seem trivial, but in large systems, 0.015 seconds can make all the difference.

There is another way, which is again clever, but also fast:

```
int m[10][10] = {0};

for (i=0; i<N; i=i+1)
    m[i][i] = 1.0;
```

The declaration of **m** actually sets all the elements to zero, leaving only the diagonal elements to be set to 1.

Space

Space was once considered the final frontier, but in reality, most systems have ample memory such that it is not as big an issue as it used to be. Not that that gives carte blanche to write the sort of memory hogging code that some programmers do. There are still situations, such as legacy systems and space-constrained environments (e.g., the space shuttle), in which saving on space is all important. Strings are a good example of storage. In C, strings can be statically or dynamically allocated. Statically allocated arrays are of the form

```
char sentence[100][15];
```

The character array could be used to store 100 words, each of length 14 (remember the end-of-string character). One disadvantage of this approach is that you must specify the array size ahead of time—the maximum number of characters that will ever be needed. If someone enters a word longer than 14 characters in length, it will not be stored properly. If someone enters only

```
We seem to be made to suffer. It's our lot in life.
```

it will only use 12 "words" in the 2D array, for a total of 40 characters (the spaces aren't stored), and 12 end-of-string terminators, wasting 1448 char storage spaces. A second way of representing the string might be

```
char *sentence[N];
```

Once stored, this dynamic array takes up only 40 + 12 = 52 storage spaces. Both these methods assume the string is first read into a character buffer, divided into words, and then stored into the 2D arrays. The difference is that the dynamic array can be created after the sentence has been read into the buffer and processed to determine the number of words in the sentence, N.

Compiler Optimization

The easiest way of optimizing code is having your compiler do the optimization for you. Compilers normally have a set of optimizing options. First, a decision has to be made on whether to optimize for size or speed. One optimization may be to eliminate redundant code, looking for operations that produce no useful result when performed. Examples of redundant code include

```
x = x + 0;
```

where no code is generated. When the compiler examines such a statement, it removes it from the compiled code. Another compiler optimization replaces operations with equivalent but faster ones. For example, replacing costly multiplication and division operators with left-shift and right-shift operators:

```
        x = y * 16              ->              x = y << 4
```

The compiler can also "unroll" loops.

Enabling optimization on a compiler such as gcc entails specifying the appropriate optimization level on the command line. For example, the following command line instructs the optimizer to focus on reducing the size of the resulting executable:

```
$ gcc -Os test.c -o test
```

Consider some of the following optimization levels for **gcc**:

  -O0   no optimization
  -O1   Compile as quickly as possible and reduce the resulting code size and execution time.
  -O2   More optimizations, but none that would trade speed for space, or vice versa.
  -Os   Optimize for size. Enables all -O2 optimizations that do not typically increase code size.

EPILOG

How important is algorithm efficiency? Historically, optimizing programs was a core skill, since machines had limited resources and ran slowly. There are still areas of programming that benefit greatly from running more efficiently. Examples include game programming, digital-signal processing, and resource-constrained environments such as embedded systems and real-time systems. Computers are at least as great a threat to climate change as the global aviation industry. The computing industry contributes roughly 2 percent of global carbon emissions, comparable to the global aviation industry. Improving algorithm efficiency helps reduce the load on computers and hence reduces carbon emissions.

Exercises

Exercise 22.1

Consider the following equation:

$$Y = Ax^3 + Bx^2 + Cx + D$$

The most straightforward way of writing this equation is

```
Y = A*pow(x,3.0) + B*pow(x,2.0) + C*x + D;
```

Using the **pow** function is extremely inefficient. There are more efficient ways of coding this equation. What are they?

Exercise 22.2

Using the following sample solution from Exercises 11.5/12.4:

```
void cubed_synthesis(void)
{
    int d1, d2, d3, n;

    for (d1=0; d1<=9; d1=d1+1)
        for (d2=0; d2<=9; d2=d2+1)
            for (d3=0; d3<=9; d3=d3+1)
            {
                n = d1 * 100 + d2 * 10 + d3;
                if (d1*d1*d1+d2*d2*d2+d3*d3*d3 == n)
                    printf("%d ", n);
            }
}
```

This is not the most efficient implementation. Identify the ways this function could be made more efficient.

23

The Dark Side of Programming

Luke Skywalker: Is the dark side stronger?

Yoda: No . . . no . . . no. Quicker, easier, more seductive.

Introduction

Now we come to the "dark" side of programming; concepts and structures that exist but in all likelihood shouldn't really be used for one reason or another.

Shortcut Operators

Two of the most controversial operators in C are the shortcut operators ++ and −−. In C you might write an expression of the form x+++++y. Niklaus Wirth sums up the problems associated with these operators in a recent paper entitled "Good Ideas, through the Looking Glass."[1] He poses two examples:

```
x+++++y+1
++x+++y
x+++y++
```

Let's say we give x and y each the value 1. The first two expressions don't compile using gcc (thankfully), while the third produces a result of 2 (x++ + y++ implies use of the values of x and y before incrementing them). The only reason the first two don't work is because of a lack of white space and the particular compiler's inability to parse the expression. If we add white spaces, we get:

```
x++ + ++y+1     = 1+(2+1) = 4
++x + ++y       = 2+2 = 4
```

---

[1]Wirth, N., "Good ideas, through the looking glass," *IEEE Computer*, 2006, Vol. 39, No 1, 28–39.

Some C compilers may be able to compile this jumbled mess, and that's where the problem lies. Wirth's statement sums it all up: "I find absolutely surprising the equanimity with which the programmer community worldwide has accepted this notational monster." Enough said.

= Versus ==

Wirth also talks about the use of = as an assignment operator. Apparently this goes back to the development of Fortran in 1957, when the tradition of using = for equality was set aside, and instead = was used for assignment. ALGOL corrected this problem by using :=, as did Pascal, but C and its descendants have continued the Fortran tradition. Just be careful!

I'll Have a Side Effect to Go

A *side effect* is an operation performed in addition to the main operation executed by the statement. It is likely something you don't want to happen. Consider this example:

```
radius = 5;
result = ++radius;
```

The first statement assigns to **radius** the value 5. The second statement assigns to **result** the value of **radius** after it has been incremented (side effect). Here's another more potent example. Imagine you perform the following calculation:

```
i = 2;
s = square(i++);
```

This looks innocent enough. But say **square** is a macro designed to square a number:

```
#define square(x) ((x) * (x))
```

If you expand the macro, you get this:

```
i = 2;
s = ((i++) * (i++));
```

Suddenly the value returned is 6 because **i** is not incremented once as expected, but twice. And **s** can be assigned the wrong value. This statement is ambiguous. Basically the expression is evaluated in the following manner:

1. Take the value of **i** (2), store it temporarily, then increase the value stored in **i** by 1.
2. Take the new value of **i** (3) and multiply it by the stored value (2). Increment the value of **i** by 1.
3. Assign the calculated value to **s** (6).

The Goto of Spaghetti

The nastiest of programming constructs, the **goto** statement, persists. When first designed, it mirrored the effect of the jump statement in instruction sets and could be used to construct conditional and repetitive statements. The **goto** statement existed before structured programming using **if** and loops came into being. It was used to construct loop-like entities of the form:

```
        int i = 0;

loop:
    sum = sum + i;
    i = i + 1;
    if (i <= 100)
        goto loop;
```

Enough was said in the early 1970s on this subject, but it deserves a small review, as there are those who still tout its usefulness. Many early languages had **goto** statements; indeed, many current languages still have them. Jensen and Wirth summed up the **goto** statement best of all in their *PASCAL: User Manual and Report* of 1975:

> A goto statement should be reserved for unusual or uncommon situations where the natural structure of an algorithm has to be broken.[2]

Kernighan and Plauger put it another way:

> Jumping around unnecessarily in a computer program has proved to be a fruitful source of errors, and usually indicates that the programmer is not entirely in control of the code.[3]

Every now and then someone asks if it is okay to use **goto** statements in their programs. After all, why would any programming language provide such a construct unless it were useful? Unfortunately languages often contain constructs that seem useful, but in reality only exist because they haven't been removed. Using statements like **goto** leads to spaghetti code. *Spaghetti code* is an uncomplimentary term for source code that has a complex and tangled control structure, especially one using many **goto** statements or other "unstructured" branching constructs. Kernighan and Ritchie included a **goto** statement in C, but they referred to it as "infinitely abusable" and suggested that it "be used sparingly, if at all". Here is an example of using **goto** in C:

```
go_back:
printf("Enter a numerator and demoninator: ");
scanf("%f %f",&num,&denom);
```

---

[2]Jensen, L., and Wirth, N., *PASCAL: User Manual and Report*, Springer Verlag, 1975, 226.

[3]Kernighan, B.W., and Plauger, P.J., *The Elements of Programming Style*, McGraw-Hill, 1978.

```
if (denom == 0)
    goto go_back;
else
    goto divide;
divide:
```

When the program sees the **goto** in the true portion of the **if** statement, it immediately jumps to the **go_back** label, which in this case happens to be at the start of the block of code. Labels are single words terminated with a colon, :. Observe the unpredictable way the flow of execution jumps from one area to another. It may seem as though the program flows nicely, but remember that this is a simple piece of code. More complex code would result in a mess. This could have been written using a **while** loop:

```
while (1)
{
    printf("Enter a numerator and demoninator: ");
    scanf("%f %f",&num,&denom);

    if (denom == 0)
        continue;
    else
        break;
}
```

The fall from grace of **goto** statements was orchestrated in the early 1970s when a group of eminant computer scientists concluded that programs should use structured programming incorporating control structures such as loops and if-then-else statements instead of goto. The most famous criticism of goto came from Edsger Dijkstra in a 1968 letter titled "Go To Statement Considered Harmful."[4] There may be *some* acceptable uses for the goto statement, such as fatal exceptions, a term equivalent to the *alarm exits* of Dijkstra. For languages that lack exception handling mechanisms, goto statements may be the only option.

Code Obfuscation

We saw an example of obfuscated code in Chapter 4, in guise of the "12 Days of Christmas." What is code obfuscation, you ask? The word *obfuscation* means making something less clear and harder to understand. In programming, obfuscation is used to transform the code into a form that is functionally identical to the original code but is much more difficult to understand and reverse-engineer. The "12 Days of Christmas" code achieves this using three elements:[5]

1. Elimination of all white space

---

[4]Dijkstra, E. W., "Go to statement considered harmful," *Communications of the ACM*, 1968, Vol. 11, No. 3, 147–148.

[5]Ball, T., "Reverse Engineering the Twelve Days of Christmas," Microsoft Corp., 1998, http://research.microsoft.com/~tball/papers/XmasGift/

2. Use of conditional and list expression instead of the more familiar **if-else** statement and statement blocks

3. A simple encoding of the poem's strings

Another good example of obfuscated code generates mazes of arbitrary length:

```
#include <stdio.h>

char M[2],A,Z,E=40,J[40],T[40];main(C){for(*J=A=scanf("%d",&C);
--                E;         J[              E]              =T
[E    ]= E)   printf("._");  for(;(A-=Z=!Z)  ||    (printf("\n|"
)     ,   A    =              39                ,C              --
)     ;   Z   ||    printf   (M    ))M[Z]=Z[A-(E      =A[J-Z])&&!C
&     A   ==              T[                                     A]
|6<<27<rand()|||!C&!Z?J[T[E]=T[A]]=E,J[T[A]=A-Z]=A,"_.":"|"];}
```

Just like:

4

```
 --  --  --  --  --  --  --  --  --      --  -- --  --  --  --  -- --  --   -- --  --  --  --  --  --    -- --  --  --  --  --  -- --  -- --  --     --  --
|  |  |  |  |  |  |  |  |   | ._. ._|  |  |  |  | ._| |  |  .  |  |  |  | . |  |  |  | . |  |  |  | . |  |  | . |_.|
|  ._|  |  |  |  |  |  |  |  | ._. |  | ._| L. . .  |  |  | ._. |_| |  |  |  |  | ._| |_| |  |_|
| |_._. |  | . |  |  |  |  | |_|  |  | ._| . |  | L_L. ._| . . |  |  |  |  |  |  |  |  |  |  |  |
L_L._L ._._L ._._L ._._._L ._._._L ._._._._L_L_L ._._._L_L_L ._._._._L ._._._._L
```

Three words of advice: **DON'T DO IT.**

The Conditional Operator

The conditional operator, sometimes called the *ternary* operator, is essentially a shorthand form of the **if-else** expression. An expression of the form

```
if (a_number % 2 == 0)
    result = 1;
else
    result = 0;
```

can be rewritten as

```
result = ((a_number%2) ? 1 : 0);
```

The general form of the operator is:

```
expr1 ? expr2 : expr3
```

The first operand, **expr1**, is the test condition. The second and third operands represent the final value of the expression. Only one of them is selected. If **expr1** is nonzero, the value of the expression is **expr2**; otherwise, it is **expr3**. This is kind of neat, but it is a shorthand, so be careful how and where you use it.

C Can Be a Dangerous Language

True. Using C you can do things that other languages can't. We can delve down into the depths of a system and change things that probably shouldn't be changed. Want to run a system command, which would normally be run from the command line? You can by using the function **system**. On Windows we could use

```
system("dir");
```

to get a listing of the files in a folder (or directory in old-speak!). Or we could write something much more dangerous, which might move files or wipe them clean away. Unless you know what you are doing, don't use these functions!

Why Strings Can Be Tricky

One of the problems with C is that it is quite easy to overflow buffers, especially when dealing with strings. This is partially because C does not manage the length of strings. One of the functions that is susceptible to buffer problems is the C **gets** function, which is called with the following syntax:

```
char str[20];
gets(str);
```

This function reads data from the standard input into the memory pointed to by the string **str**, until there is a newline, or EOF is encountered. It then returns a pointer to the buffer. The problem is that no matter how large the buffer is, it can always be overloaded with more data than it is designed to hold. If the buffer lives on the program stack, then it is possible to overwrite important data, leading to *stack smashing*.

If the input text is

```
the quick brown fox jumped
```

then **str** will contain the entire string even though there are 26 characters. If the input string is

```
the quick brown fox jumped over the lazy dog
```

then a segmentation fault will likely occur. One way of avoiding such problems is using the **fgets** function; fgets takes three parameters: the buffer to fill, the maximum number of characters to get, and the file to get the data from (**stdin** for standard input).

```
char str[20];
fgets(str,sizeof(str),stdin);
```

Note that **fgets** stores a '\n' character when a newline is entered, whereas **gets** does not. When the same text is input, it is truncated to "the quick brown fox." Another problematic function is **strcpy**.

```
char s1[20], s2[40];
strcpy(s1,s2);
```

Here, no attempt is made to ensure that **s1** is big enough to hold the contents of **s2**.

Epilog

There are features in any language that just shouldn't be used. There is nothing good about obfuscated code, yet many programmers' code ends up looking like this because they haven't taken the time to (a) use proper style or (b) **document their code.** Write readable code that's well commented, and you will be rewarded with code that is *maintainable.*

The Final Frontier

Computers in the future may weigh no more than 1.5 tons.
—Popular Mechanics (1949)

It's All Just Science Fiction

Sometime in the future, computers may write code for us. Maybe, given a series of constraints, they too will solve problems using some form of biologically inspired computability. Computers will evolve, probably at a rate far more notable than the languages and systems they run. Maybe by the 24th century or sooner, we will be using the bioneural circuitry of *Star Trek*. These "gel-packs" are composed of synthetic cerebral neurons suspended in a gel matrix. The neural fibers in the gel pack are created artificially and resemble humanoid neurons, while the bioneural systems mimic the working of the humanoid brain and are significantly faster and more efficient than optical circuitry.

What about applications of the future? What sort of algorithms will we be considering? Consider how data affects devices such as the fictitious transporter from *Star Trek*. In his book *The Physics of Star Trek*,[1] Lawrence Krauss suggests the average human body has 10^{28} atoms of matter (i.e., beyond yottabytes into the realm of xonabytes). This would equate to 1.e+16 one terabytes drives (assuming SI units). Even at $400 for one terabyte, that would cost you roughly 4.e+9 trillion dollars to set up the disk farm to store the data. Even assuming you actually have the storage capacity, the ability to "energize" the body and the power to process it (yeah, a *lot* of assumptions), you still have to get the information where you want it. With a current 10-gigabit network, assuming 10 gigabits per second, or Gbps (SI), would take 2.54e+11 years. Now if the age of the universe is approximately 13.7 billion years old,[2] then it would take approximately 19 times longer. This sort of stuff is a little out of our league, but it illustrates where computing is going. If we want to transport a human in 8 seconds, we would need a 10 xonabit network. Oh, and did I mention it would have to be wireless?

---

[1] *The Physics of Star Trek*, Lawrence M. Krauss, Harper Collins, 1996.
[2] NASA's Wilkinson Microwave Anisotropy Probe (WMAP) project

Now move slightly onto DNA computing and you will quickly understand why it is becoming a contender to eventually outdo silicon-based computing. Assuming a standard concentration of 0.06 g DNA/liter, one could store theoretically 10^{20} "words" in 1,000 liters. Nice. Maybe not a practical desktop system, but they said the same about computers 50 years ago.

Actually the algorithms may not be as challenging as the hardware to make them work.

A Good Read

The number of computing books that grace the shelves of most programmers' bookshelves is utterly astounding. Some are truly excellent, while others are extremely difficult to read, with hundreds upon hundreds of pages of syntax and snippets of code. There is something to be said for more of the "classic" computing books. Let's face it, C programming hasn't changed all that much in the last 35 years. It will probably evolve, but no one is going to decide that the **do-while** loop should be more aptly termed **repeat-until** or that pointers are no longer useful. Other languages will no doubt evolve, whether descendants of C, or hybrids. Some of the computing books listed in this chapter are older and may be hard to get these days, but all provide an interesting look at various aspects of computing.

What Books on C Are Good?

This book is not meant to be an exhaustive guide to C. Interested readers should track down the following resources:

Harbison III, S. P., and Steele Jr., G. L. *C A Reference Manual*, 5th ed., Prentice Hall, 2002.

Kernighan, B. W., and Ritchie, D. M. *The C Programming Language*, 2nd ed., Prentice Hall, 1988.

Kernighan, B. W., and Plauger, P. J. *The Elements of Programming Style*, 2nd ed., McGraw-Hill, 1978.

Prata, S. *C Primer Plus*, 4th ed., SAMS, 2002.

Van der Linden, P. *Expert C Programming: Deep C Secrets*, Prentice Hall, 1994.

What about Programming?

Böszörményi, L., Gutknecht, J., and Pomberger, G. *The School of Niklaus Wirth: The Art of Simplicity*, Morgan Kaufmann, 2000.

Dijkstra, E. W. *A Discipline of Programming*, Prentice Hall, 1976. (Math warning!)

Sherman, P. M. *Techniques in Computer Programming*, Prentice Hall, 1970.

Wirth, N. *Algorithms + Data Structures = Programs*, Prentice Hall, 1976.

Historically Speaking

Some books on the history of computing include:

Broy, M., and Denert, E. *Software Pioneers: Contributions to Software Engineering*, Springer, 2002.

Campbell-Kelly, M. *From Airline Reservations to Sonic the Hedgehog: A History of the Software Industry*, The MIT Press, 2004.

Ceruzzi, P. E. *A History of Computing*, 2nd ed., The MIT Press, 2003.

Laing, G. *Digital Retro: The Evolution and Design of the Personal Computer*, Sybex, 2004.

Rojas, R., and Hashagen, U. *The First Computers—History and Architecture*, The MIT Press, 2002.

Williams, M. R. *A History of Computing Technology*, 2nd ed., John Wiley & Sons, 1997.

Break the Code!

Some books on the codes and ciphers are:

Curtin, M. *Brute Force: How DES Got Broken*, Copernicus Books, 2005.

Ferguson, N., and Schneier, B. *Practical Cryptography*, Wiley, 2003.

Haufler, H. *Codebreakers' Victory: How the Allied Cryptographers Won World War II*, NAL Trade, 2003.

Pincock, S. *Codebreaker: The History of Codes and Ciphers*, Walker and Company, 2006.

Schneier, B. *Applied Cryptography: Protocols, Algorithms, and Source Code in C*, 2nd ed., Wiley, 1995.

I Can See!

Some books on image processing and vision include:

Davies, E. R. *Machine Vision: Theory, Algorithms, Practicalities*, 3rd ed., Morgan Kaufmann, 2004.

Gonzalez, R. C., Woods, R. E., and Eddins, S. L. *Digital Image Processing Using MATLAB*, Prentice Hall, 2003.

Gonzalez, R. C., and Woods, R. E. *Digital Image Processing*, 2nd ed., Prentice Hall, 2002.

Nixon, M., and Aguado, A. S. *Feature Extraction & Image Processing*, Newnes, 2002.

Parker, J. R. *Algorithms for Image Processing and Computer Vision*, Wiley, 1996.

Some Books on Biometrics and Stuff

Li, S. Z., and Jain, A. K. *Handbook of Face Recognition*, Springer, 2005.

Maltoni, D., Maio, D., Jain, A. K., and Prabhakar, S. *Handbook of Fingerprint Recognition*, Springer, 2005.

Thulborn, T. *Dinosaur Tracks*, Chapman and Hall, 1990.

Wayman, J., Jain, A., Maltoni, D., and Maio, D. *Biometric Systems: Technology, Design and Performance Evaluation*, Springer, 2004.

I Know C, Therefore I Am?

What about C? In reality it doesn't really matter what language you learn first. Remember it's not about the language you learn, it's about the concepts of programming. MATLAB[3] is extensively used in the aerospace, biomedical, and pharmaceutical industries. A good example is NASA's use of MATLAB to generate fault-protection code for Deep Space 1, whose primary mission was to test high-risk technologies. In this instance MATLAB was used to *automatically generate* C code. So C is still about. In fact, in many cases C is used in combination with languages such as MATLAB. In many industries a combination of languages helps bring a project together. There were apparently 35 different languages used on the development of the Boeing 777. In many mission-critical systems (aerospace, rail, naval), Ada is still the language of choice.

What Does the Future Hold?

It is hard to predict how programming as we know it today will evolve. Programmers still use older languages. C might be around for another couple of hundred years, or some descendant of it, anyway. In the 1968 movie *2001: A Space Odyssey*, the computer HAL (short for Heuristically programmed ALgorithmic computer) is depicted as being capable not only of speech recognition, facial recognition, and natural language processing, but also lip reading, art appreciation, interpreting emotions, expressing emotions, and reasoning. By 2001 many of these ideas were still too far-fetched. Even nearing the latter part of the decade, there haven't really been great strides in areas such as expressing emotions and reasoning, though algorithms for speech and facial recognition have progressed in leaps and bounds. Facial recognition really involves isolating a face in an image and extracting features from the image that could be compared to faces already in a database. All these processes require software, and software requires well-designed, innovative algorithms, coded in a readable, efficient, well-documented manner.

> *Interviewer:* HAL, you have an enormous responsibility on this mission, in many ways perhaps the greatest responsibility of any single mission element. You're the brain, and central nervous system of the ship, and your responsibilities include watching over the men in hibernation. Does this ever cause you any lack of confidence?
>
> *HAL:* Let me put it this way, Mr. Amor. The 9000 series is the most reliable computer ever made. No 9000 computer has ever made a mistake or distorted information. We are all, by any practical definition of the words, foolproof and incapable of error.[4]

---

[3]Mathworks. http://www.mathworks.com

[4]*2001: A Space Odyssey* (1968)

Home Energy Footprint

Everybody talks about the weather, but nobody does anything about it.

—Mark Twain

The Problem Description

All electricity-generating systems have a carbon footprint; that is, at some point during their construction and/or operation, carbon dioxide is emitted. Energy produced by what are classically known as the fossil fuels (coal, oil, gas) has the largest footprint because these fuels are burned during operation. Non–fossil fuel energies such as wind, solar, hydro, biomass, wave/tidal, and nuclear are low carbon or carbon neutral because they do not emit CO_2 during operation. However, in most cases, they are not carbon free because CO_2 is emitted during some phase of their life cycle, be it construction or maintenance.

Program Requirements

The carbon footprint for energy is usually expressed as kilograms of CO_2 equivalent per kilowatt-hour of generation ($kgCO_2eq/kWh$). Consider the following energy sources of electricity generation on the basis of $kgCO_2eq/kWh$:

Conventional coal:	>1.0
Coal gasification:	<0.8
Oil	0.65
Gas	0.5
Solar	0.058
Hydro	0.020
Wind	0.00464
Nuclear	0.005

In Ontario, on average, 0.242kg of CO_2 emissions are produced per kWh (2008). This is computed based on the contribution of every type of energy used to generate electricity. Ontario's electricity-generation mix is 32 percent nuclear, 22 percent hydro, 18 percent coal, 24 percent gas, 3 percent wind, and 0.2 percent other.[1] The total CO_2 released can be calculated as the number of kWh used multiplied by the $kgCO_2$ released per kWh.

Program Specification

Input(s):   Electrical consumption (kWh>0)

Output(s): CO_2 emissions in kg

To calculate the CO_2 emissions resulting from the use of electricity, we multiply the number of kilowatt-hours of electricity consumed in a year by the electricity emissions intensity.

Algorithm Design

1. Identify the number of kg of CO_2 emitted per kWh.
2. Obtain input for the electrical consumption, in kWh.
3. Calculate the CO_2 emissions.
4. Output the CO_2 emissions.

This algorithm can be represented as pseudo-code in the following manner:

```
SET the number of kg of CO2 emitted per kWh
PROMPT for the number of kilowatt hours
CALCULATE the total kg of CO2 emitted
OUTPUT the kg of CO2 emitted
```

Quite a simple algorithm. The third step could be elaborated further, by forming an equation of the form

```
total CO2 = number kWh × CO2 emitted per kWh
```

The Program

Here is the corresponding C code for the algorithm.

```
1   #include <stdio.h>
2   #define CO2rel 0.242
3
4   int main(void)
5   {
```

---

[1]Estimated 2009 electricity generation mix, Independent Electricity System Operator, IESO, www.ieso.ca.

```
6        double n_kWh;
7        double CO2_energy;
8        printf("Emissions for Home Electricity\n");
9        printf("Enter the number of kWh: ");
10       scanf("%lf", &n_kWh);
11
12       CO2_energy = n_kWh * CO2rel;
13
14       printf("  CO2 emissions = %.2fkg\n", CO2_energy);
15
16       return 0;
17  }
```

Code Walkthrough

The first thing you will notice is that the body of the code is indented and certain groupings are separated by blank lines. This is indicative of programming style. The numbers to the left offer a way of indicating line numbers and do not exist in a normal program.

Now let's examine the code. The first line of the program (1) includes the standard input/output library, **stdio.h**. This line is needed in nearly every C program we write; otherwise, there is no way to communicate with the user. If we look a little further on to lines 4, 5, 16, and 17, we find the skeleton of the program. The skeleton essentially "contains" the program:

```
4    int main(void)
5    {
     ...
16       return 0;
17  }
```

Now this program is fairly simple. It prompts for an input, reads in a value, performs a calculation, and outputs the calculated value. There aren't any fancy decisions to be made, nor any repetition—that comes in a more complicated algorithm. For now, looking back at the algorithm, we notice three pieces of information that are needed within the program:

```
number of kWh used
CO2 released per kWh
total CO2 released
```

Knowing that the program needs these three pieces of information means that we have to create three variables to store the values. Think of some identifiers (names) that could be used to create variables (the ones we have chosen are in bold):

```
number_kWh_used, numberkWh, n_kWh
CO2_released_kWh, CO2_released, CO2_emitted, CO2rel
CO2_total, CO2_energy, CO2_electricity
```

Why have we chosen these particular identifiers? Large identifiers such as **number_kWh_used** are certainly very descriptive; however, at 15 characters, they are slightly too long. On the other hand, **n_kWh** uses the prefix **n** to equate to "number of." Similarly, for CO_2 released per kWh, we chose **CO2rel**. Sometimes when we create a program we have to look beyond the current "interpretation" of the program. For the final variable to store the calculated value of total CO_2 released, we could naturally have chosen **CO2_total**; however, we might want to augment the program later by including CO_2 released from heating or airplane travel, so implying that we are calculating the total may not be absolutely true. In this case, we chose to use **CO2_energy**, as it describes the CO_2 released by electrical power. Now the work we are dealing with uses real numbers, as implied by the value 0.236 (CO_2 emissions per kWh), so we will declare all our variables as type double (fractional types).

```
6   double n_kWh;
7   double CO2_energy;
```

Note that we have chosen to describe CO2rel as a "constant." This is helpful as it allows us to easily change the value in future renditions of the program.

```
2   #define CO2rel 0.236
```

Line 8 contains information statements that will print out on the screen. The **printf** statement on line 9, however, prompts the user for some input, in this case the number of kilowatt-hours.

```
9   printf("Enter the number of kWh: ");
10  scanf("%lf", &n_kWh);
```

This is followed by a **scanf** statement that reads in the value input by the user and stores it in the variable **n_kwh**. Line 12 does all the work:

```
12  CO2_energy = n_kWh * CO2rel;
```

It basically multiplies the value stored in **n_kWh** by the **CO2rel** and stores the resulting number in the variable **CO2_power**. The final statement on line 14 deals with printing out the result stored in **CO2_power**.

```
14  printf("   CO2 emissions = %.2fkg\n", CO2_energy);
```

Testing the Program

Now that the program has been designed and the code written, we can build (compile) and test it. Testing the program relies on the creation of a series of test cases and checking the results manually. Testing in this case is fairly straightforward because there is only one input. If we run the program with an input of 500.0, we get

```
Emissions for Home Electricity
Enter the number of kWh: 500.0
CO2 emissions = 118.00kg
```

Now everything works quite fine. What happens when we accidentally input -500? We get an answer of -118.00kg. You might think this is an error, but if we had a renewable energy system and were transmitting excess power to the grid, this might actually be the right answer. To fix this, there are a number of options:

- Leave the program as is.
- Change the program to deal with negative numbers.
- Change all numbers to absolute (positive) numbers.

Dam Forces

You could not step twice into the same river; for other waters are ever flowing on to you.

—Heraclitus

The Problem Description

The force of water is important when designing a dam. The pressure of water stored behind it produces a horizontal force. The location of this force is also important. If it is near the top of the dam, then the dam may fail by overturning; near the base, then it may fail by sliding. At the water surface, the pressure is zero. The force on the dam does not depend on the amount of water stored—only its depth.

Program Requirements

The pressure on the dam wall is not constant, but rather it varies down the face of the dam. A simple method is to use a formula that is derived from combining all the small forces into a large force called the resultant *force*.[1] The force on a dam,[2] F (Newtons), is calculated from the water pressure and the area of the dam face:

$$F = \rho g A Y \tag{1}$$

where ρ is the density of water (1000 kg/m^3), g is gravity constant[3] (9.81 m/s^2), A is area of the face of the dam (m^2), and Y is the depth from the water surface to the centre of the area of the dam (m). $A = b * h$ where b is the width of the dam, and h the depth of the water. When the width of the dam is not given, assume $b = 1$, and the force is then the force per metre length of the dam.

The depth from the water surface to the centre of the dam is

$$Y = h/2 \tag{2}$$

---

[1]This formula works for simple, vertical dams.

[2]M. Kay, *Practical Hydraulics* (London: Spon Press, 1998).

[3]ρ and g together define the specific weight of water, which equals $9810 \ N/m^3$

For example, the Verzasca Dam in Switzerland is 380 m in length with a water depth of 220 m. So the force can be calculated as

$$F = 1000 \times 9.81 \times (220 \times 380) \times (220 / 2)$$

$$= 90212760000\text{N}$$

$$= 90212760 \text{ kN per metre of the dam}$$

The position of this force is also important. The point at which the resultant force is applied is called the *centre of pressure*. To calculate *D*, the depth from the water surface to the centre of pressure, the following formula can be used:

$$D = \frac{h^2}{12Y} + Y \tag{3}$$

For example:

$$D = (220^2) / (12 \times 110) + 110$$

$$D = 146.67\text{m below the water surface}$$

Program Specification

Input(s):   Height and width of the dam.

Output(s):   Force in kN per metre of the dam, and centre of pressure.

To calculate the area of the dam face (*A*) requires a fourth equation, which takes the height (*hD*) and width (*wD*) of the dam as input:

$$A = hD \times wD \tag{4}$$

The output from Eq. 1 is in Newtons, and a conversion to Kilonewtons requires dividing the result by 1000.

Algorithm Design

The design involves a series of sequential calculations:

1. Input the height and width of the dam (in metres).
2. Calculate the area of the dam (Eq. 4).
3. Calculate the depth from the water surface to the centre of the dam (Eq. 2).
4. Calculate the force on the dam (Eq. 1).
5. Calculate the centre of pressure (Eq. 3).
6. Output the results of steps 4 and 5.

This algorithm can be represented as pseudo-code in the following manner:

```
SET the density of water
SET the gravity constant
PROMPT for the height and width of the dam face
CALCULATE the area of the dam face
```

```
CALCULATE the depth from the water surface to the
          centre of the dam
CALCULATE the force on the dam
CALCULATE the centre of pressure
OUTPUT the force and centre of pressure
```

Implementing the Program

The first part of the program ensures that the code written has access to the standard input/output library:

```
#include <stdio.h>
```

Without this library, there is no way to communicate with the user. Now we can formulate the rest of the program skeleton:

```
#include <stdio.h>

int main(void)
{
    return 0;
}
```

With that out of the way, we can deal with the variables needed to store the various inputs and values from calculations performed. The descriptions that follow include some alternatives variable names (identifiers chosen are in bold). There are two input values:

> Width of the dam face: wD, damW, **damWidth**, dam_width
> Height of the dam face: hD, damH, **damHeight**, dam_height

In addition there are four calculated values:

Centre of depth:	cD, cntDep, **ctrDepth**, centre_depth
Area of the dam face:	aD, areaD, **damArea**, area_of_dam
Force on the dam:	**force**, forceD, force_dam, fD
Centre of pressure:	cP, cntPres, **ctrPres**, centre_pres

The choice of identifiers is a compromise between their length and level of self-description. There are probably dozens of identifiers for the force applied to the dam; however, **fD** is probably too short and not descriptive enough, whereas **force_on_the_dam** is too long, although very descriptive. We can declare them as type **double** due to the need for floating-point calculations:

```
double damWidth, damHeight;
double ctrDepth, damArea, force, ctrPres;
```

The next step in the algorithm requires prompting for and obtaining the input values:

```
printf("Height of the dam (metres>0): ");
scanf("%lf", &damHeight);
```

```
printf("Width of the dam (metres>0): ");
scanf("%lf", &damWidth);
```

Both the prompt messages suggest that the input should be in metres, with values greater than zero. This is a proactive way of reducing errors in the program, but it does not guarantee that values less than or equal to zero won't be entered. A series of defined values are used within the program, namely the density of water and a gravity constant, which can be defined as symbolic constants in the following manner:

```
#define h2O_dens 1000.0
#define gravC 9.81
```

Now that we have all the information, we can proceed to applying the equations. The first to be calculated is the area of the dam face (Eq. 4):

```
damArea = damHeight * damWidth;
```

Next we calculate the depth from the water surface to the dam centre, using Eq. 2:

```
ctrDepth = damHeight / 2.0;
```

Note that the 2 in Eq. 2 converts to 2.0 to ensure floating-point arithmetic is performed. The third calculation involves finding the actual force on the dam, using Eq. 1, so

$$F = \rho g A Y$$

becomes

```
force = h2O_dens * gravC * damArea * ctrDepth;
```

which produces a force value in Newtons. To convert to Kilonewtons, we alter the equation, so that the value produced is divided by 1000.

```
force = (h2O_dens * gravC * damArea * ctrDepth) / 1000.0;
```

The final calculation involves the position of the force on the dam, using Eq. 3. The equation is a fractional computation, so we will do each part of the fraction separately. The numerator h^2 can be calculated using simple multiplication:

```
ctrPres = (damHeight * damHeight);
```

We could have also used the **pow** function, **pow(damHeight,2.0)**, but this is not the most efficient way of performing this calculation. Now we can add the denominator $(12Y) + Y$:

```
ctrPres = (damHeight * damHeight)/
          (12.0 * ctrDepth) + ctrDepth;
```

The final part of the program requires us to output the relevant information:

```
printf("The force on the dam wall is "
       "%.2f kN per metre\n", force);
printf("The centre of pressure is "
       "%.2fm below the water surface\n", ctrPres);
```

The first **printf** statement outputs the force on the dam wall, whereas the second **printf** statement outputs the centre of pressure. Always remember to include units; otherwise, the calculations are less meaningful. Notice the strings in the **printf** statements are spread over two lines. This is a feature known as *string joining*.

The Program

```c
#include <stdio.h>
#define h2O_dens 1000.0
#define gravC 9.81

int main(void)
{
    double damWidth, damHeight;
    double ctrDepth, damArea, force, ctrPres;

    // Input the dam measurements
    printf("Calculation of dam forces.\n");

    // Input with data validation for height of water
    printf("Height of the dam (metres>0): ");
    scanf("%lf", &damHeight);

    // Input with data validation for dam width
    printf("Width of the dam (metres>0): ");
    scanf("%lf", &damWidth);

    // Calculate the area of the face of the dam
    damArea = damHeight * damWidth;

    // Calculate the depth from the water surface to
    // the dam centre
    ctrDepth = damHeight / 2.0;

    // Calculate the force on the dam (in kilonewtons)
    force = (h2O_dens * gravC * damArea * ctrDepth) / 1000.0;

    // Calculate the position of the force on the dam
    ctrPres = (damHeight * damHeight)/
              (12.0 * ctrDepth) + ctrDepth;

    // Output the information
    printf("The force on the dam wall is "
           "%.2f kN per metre\n", force);
```

```
        printf("The centre of pressure is "
                "%.2fm below the water surface\n", ctrPres);

        return 0;
}
```

Testing the Program

Now that the program has been designed and the code written, we can build (compile) and test it. Testing the program relies on the creation of a series of test cases, and checking the results manually. Testing in this case is fairly straightforward because there are only two inputs. If we run the program with a dam height of 220 m and a width of 380 m, we get the following:

```
Calculation of dam forces.
Height of the dam (>0): 220
Width of the dam (>0): 380
The force on the dam wall is 90212760.00 kN per metre
The centre of pressure is 146.67m below the water surface
```

Being Defensive

It might seem that because there are only two inputs that defensive programming is not necessary; however, nothing could be further from the truth. If a user enters a negative number for either, the program will run; however, the answers it produces will not be correct. So to protect against this, we use a simple **do-while** loop to encapsulate each of the printf/scanf combinations. Basically, this code will loop around until such time that the input is greater than zero. Consider the defensive code for the dam height:

```
do {
    printf("Depth of the water in the dam (>0): ");
    scanf("%lf", &damHeight);
} while (damHeight <= 0.0);
```

Estimating Dinosaur Speed and Gait

Dinosaurs are nature's special effects.

—Robert T. Bakker

The Problem Description

In Michael Crichton's book *Jurassic Park*, scientists use blood from fossilized mosquitoes that have been suspended in tree sap since the Mesozoic Era to reconstruct the DNA of dinosaurs, filling chromosomal gaps with modern frog genes. Nice idea, but it probably wouldn't work. However, the visual effects used in the movie rendition of the book were pretty spectacular. How are effects such as reproducing dinosaurs as computer generated imagery (CGI) and integrating them into films performed so seemlessly? Part of the work is done through animation, the art of bringing objects to life. If you want to try your hand at animation, you could try using free open-source software such as Blender. This software contains hundreds of algorithms that deal with modeling and rendering objects and physics-based motion algorithms to give an object "life." However, animating a dinosaur requires knowledge of how a dinosaur moves.

Now imagine that you want to analyze dinosaur behavior by performing a computer simulation of their biomechanics. Similar techniques were used in the BBC series *Walking with Dinosaurs*. How do you go about making it as realistic as possible? Part of the magic of making dinosaurs come alive is movement. Objects that sit still aren't very interesting! To simulate their motions you have to speculate somewhat on how their legs and bodies moved. You can do some investigations by calculating their speed and gait.

Program Requirements

Dinosaurs footprints actually tell you a lot about the animal that made them. The study of tracks left by dinosaurs can tell you about the skin structure and padding of dinosaur feet and whether a particular dinosaur traveled in herds. Primarily footprints can give you information on how the foot is structured, how the animal walked (two legs or four?), and how fast it moved. Now you can speculate on the dinosaurs' speed. Huge dinosaurs with short legs probably moved very slowly; small dinosaurs with spindly legs were probably quite agile. In 1976, British zoologist R. McNeill Alexander used living animals such as elephants to formulate an equation relating an animal's speed *(S)*, hip height *(h)*, and stride length *(SL)*. The stride length measures the distance of one footprint from another, while leg length is the measurement from hip to ankle. The equation formulated for speed (m/sec) is:[1]

$$v = 0.25g^{0.5}SL^{1.67}h^{-1.17} \tag{1}$$

where *g* is a gravitational constant, 9.8 m/sec². Leg length is estimated using Alexander's equations relating hip height to the length of the part of the foot that hits the ground. Thulborn suggested that for running dinosaurs, a better estimate of speed is given by the formula:[2]

$$v = \left[gh(SL/1.8h)^{2.56} \right]^{0.5} \tag{2}$$

Thulborn also suggested that for trotting gaits, the mean of both formulas could be used. Gait describes the pattern and synchrony of footfalls made by an animal. Alexander showed that for relative stride length the ratio SL/h is an indicator of gait. It can be used to determine whether an animal is:

walking: SL/h is less than 2.0
trotting: SL/h is between 2.0 and 2.9
running: SL/h is greater than 2.9

To calculate hip-height conversion factors, Thulborn suggests the following approximations for dinosaurs (Eq. 3), based on foot length (FL):

FL < 0.25m		FL > 0.25m	
Small theropods	h=4.5FL	large theropods	h=4.9FL
Small ornithopods	h=4.8FL	large ornithopods	h=5.9FL
Small bipedal	h=4.6FL	large bipedal	h=5.7FL

Quadrupedal dinosaurs are more challenging because the hind foot has a larger padded area. For sauropods (e.g., Apatosaurus), Thulborn suggests h=5.9FL, but other suggestions include:

Ceratopsians (e.g., Triceratops) *h=5.4FW* (FW=foot width)

Ankylosaurs h=3.7FW

Stegosaurs h=6.0FW or *h=5.0FL*

---

[1]Alexander, R. M., "Estimates of speeds of dinosaurs," *Nature*, 1976, Vol. 261, 129–130.

[2]Thulborn, T., *Dinosaur Tracks*, Chapman and Hall, 1990.

Program Specification

Input(s):   foot length, conversion factor, stride length

Output(s): Values representing the gait and speed of a dinosaur

Algorithm Design

1. Input SL, FL, and an appropriate conversion factor.
2. Calculate the hip height.
3. Calculate the relative stride (gait).
4. Calculate the speed based on the gait.
5. Output the gait and speed.

The fourth point can be further elaborated upon: If the gait is walking, use the formula of Alexander; if the gait is running, use the formula of Thulborn. Otherwise (if trotting), use the mean of the two formulas.

Deriving the Program

How do we go about designing a solution? The basics of the problem dictate that decisions have to be made based on the type of gait calculated.

The first part of the program deals with inputting information. This requires us to use some **printf** and **scanf** statements to formulate the "user interface" portion of the program. To achieve this, we must create some variables to store the various pieces of information:

Stride length	`SL, stride_length, strideL`
Hip height	`HH, hip_height, hipH`
Speed	`V, speed`
Conversion factor	`conversion_factor, Cfactor`
Foot length	`FL, foot_length, footL`
Gait	`G, gait`

The trick with choosing a name for a variable is to name it in such a manner that it is self-commenting (i.e., it doesn't need to be described further). Some of the names listed previously parallel those used in the original equations (e.g., **SL** to represent stride length). These are good in the context of an equation, to keep the equation short and easy to understand, but in a program we need something a little more descriptive. The next choice, **stride_length** is certainly descriptive, but suffers from being too long. A nice medium in the last choice **strideL**. The **L** in stride length is used to represent length and is a good choice, because other variables, notably foot length, can also use it. The word **stride** is then used to describe the type of length being stored. The same goes for height, which uses **H** as a suffix. Variables chosen are shown in bold. First we do some I/O to input the foot length:

```
printf("Enter the foot length: ");
scanf("%lf", &footL);
```

Now is a good time to perform the first of the calculations, to derive the hip height. We need to provide a mechanism for the user to choose the conversion factors. The best way is to translate Eq. 3 into an **if-else** sequence using the value of **footL,** in association with an I/O pairing to input the actual conversion factor:

```
printf("Conversion factors: \n");
if (footL < 0.25) {
    printf("theropods: 4.5\n");
    printf("ornithopods: 4.8\n");
    printf("bipedal: 4.6\n");
}
else if (footL >= 0.25) {
    printf("theropods: 4.9\n");
    printf("ornithopods: 5.9\n");
    printf("bipedal: 5.7\n");
}

printf("Enter the conversion factor: ");
scanf("%lf", &Cfactor);
```

The formulas of Thulborn shown in Eq. 3 can be translated as follows:

```
hipH = Cfactor * footL;
printf("The hip height = %.2f\n", hipH);
```

Now we can defer to reading in the stride length:

```
printf("Enter the stride length: ");
scanf("%lf", &strideL);
```

Next, we can calculate and output the gait:

```
gait = strideL / hipH;
printf("The gait is %.2f ", gait);
```

We could expand this to output the form of the gait:

```
if (gait <= 2.0)
    printf("(walking)\n");
else if (gait > 2.0 && gait < 2.9)
    printf("(trotting)\n");
else
    printf("(running)\n");
```

Now it is time to calculate the speed, which involves both the formulas of Thulborn (Eq. 2) and Alexander (Eq. 1).

```
if (gait <= 2.0)
    speed = 0.25 * pow(9.8,0.5) * pow(strideL,1.67) *
                              pow(hipH,-1.17);
else if (gait > 2.0 && gait < 2.9)
    v1 = 0.25 * pow(9.8,0.5) * pow(strideL,1.67) *
                              pow(hipH,-1.17);
    v2 = pow((9.8 * hipH * pow((strideL/1.8*hipH),2.56)),0.5);
    speed = (v1+v2) / 2.0;
else
    speed = pow((9.8 * hipH * pow((strideL/1.8*hipH),2.56)),0.5);
```

The first part of the if statement deals with the situation where gait is walking, the second part where the gait is trotting, and the final part where the gait is running.

```
printf("The speed of the dinosaur is %.2lf m/s\n");
```

The Program

```
#include <stdio.h>
#include <math.h>

int main(void)
{
    double footL, Cfactor, strideL, hipH;
    double gait, v1, v2, speed;

    printf("Estimating Dinosaur Speed and Gait\n\n");
    printf("Enter the foot length (m): ");
    scanf("%lf", &footL);

    printf("Conversion factors: \n");
    if (footL < 0.25) {
        printf(" theropods: 4.5\n");
        printf(" ornithopods: 4.8\n");
        printf(" bipedal: 4.6\n");
    }
    else if (footL >= 0.25) {
        printf(" theropods: 4.9\n");
        printf(" ornithopods: 5.9\n");
        printf(" bipedal: 5.7\n");
    }
    printf("Enter the conversion factor: ");
    scanf("%lf", &Cfactor);
```

```
// Calculate the hip height
hipH = Cfactor * footL;
printf("The hip height = %.2f m\n", hipH);

printf("Enter the stride length (m): ");
scanf("%lf", &strideL);

// Calculate the gait
gait = strideL / hipH;
printf("The gait is %.2f ", gait);

if (gait <= 2.0)
    printf("(walking)\n");
else if (gait > 2.0 && gait <= 2.9)
    printf("(trotting)\n");
else
    printf("(running)\n");

if (gait <= 2.0)
    speed = 0.25 * pow(9.8,0.5) * pow(strideL,1.67)
                        * pow(hipH,-1.17);

else if (gait > 2.0 && gait < 2.9){
    v1 = 0.25 * pow(9.8,0.5) * pow(strideL,1.67)
                        * pow(hipH,-1.17);
    v2 = pow((9.8*hipH*pow((strideL/1.8*hipH),2.56)),0.5);
    speed = (v1 + v2) / 2.0;
}
else
    speed = pow((9.8*hipH*pow((strideL/1.8*hipH),2.56)),0.5);

printf("The speed of the dinosaur is %.2f m/s \n", speed);

return 0;
}
```

Testing the Program

The program can be tested using the following data from Alexander:[3]

Track-maker	FL(cm)	h(m)	SL(m)	SL/h	V(m/s)
bipedal	53	2.1	3.0	1.4	2.0
bipedal	24	1.0	2.4	2.5	3.6
bipedal	27	1.1	1.3	1.2	1.2

[3]Alexander, R. M., "Estimates of speeds of dinosaurs," *Nature*, 1976, Vol. 261, 129–130.

For these values hip height was calculated using *4FL* and only Eq.1. We can use this to verify that our program is working. Using the actual hip-height conversion factors we get:

Track-maker	FL(cm)	h (m)	SL (m)	SL/h	V (m/s)
bipedal	53	3.02	3.0	0.99	1.34
bipedal	24	1.1	2.4	2.17	4.2
bipedal	27	1.54	1.3	0.84	0.73

The output looks like:

```
Estimating Dinosaur Speed and Gait
Enter the foot length (m): 0.27
Conversion factors:
   theropods: 4.9
   ornithopods: 5.9
   bipedal: 5.7
Enter the conversion factor: 5.7
The hip height = 1.54 m
Enter the stride length (m): 1.3
The gait is 0.84 (walking)
The speed of the dinosaur is 0.73 m/s
```

Epilog

The calculations are more complicated than this, of course. In reality there were many types of dinosaurs: some were running, some were walking, and some were hopping. Some were bipedal, some were quadrupedal, some were small, and some were gigantic. If you're interested in more on this topic I urge you to refer to the book by Thulborn, which is one of the best references on the topic of dinosaur tracks.

Humidex

Rain! whose soft architectural hands have power to cut stones, and chisel to shapes of grandeur the very mountains.

—Henry Ward Beecher

The Problem Description

The *humidex* or *heat index* (HI) is an index (a computed value as opposed to something measured) devised to describe how hot or humid weather feels. It is based on the work of J. M. Masterton, and F. A. Richardson[1] at the Atmospheric Environment Service of Environment Canada in 1979. The humidex combines the temperature and humidity into one number to reflect the perceived temperature. A humidex of 40 with, for example, a temperature of 30° C means that the sensation of heat when it is 30° C and the air is humid is more or less the same as when it is 40° C and the air is dry. However, this interpretation is a mere indication of physiological reactions, not an absolute measure. The humidex is only significant when it is greater than 30. Therefore, we only calculate and display its value when the dew point temperature is 15° C or greater and the air temperature is 23° C or greater. At lower temperatures, the humidex is too close to the temperature to make a significant difference. The humidex is broadly used in Canada, where extremely high readings are rare except in the southern regions of Ontario, Manitoba, and Quebec. Generally, the humidex decreases as latitude increases. Of all Canadian cities, Carman, Manitoba has had the highest recorded humidex measurement: 53 on July 25, 2007.

---

[1]Masterton, J. M., and Richardson, F. A., "Humidex, a method of quantifying human discomfort due to excessive heat and humidity." Atmospheric Environment Service, CLI 1-79, Canada, 1979.

The formula for calculating the humidex is:

$$humidex = air\_temperature + h \qquad (1)$$

where

$$h = (5.0/9.0)*(e - 10.0) \qquad (2)$$

and *air_temperature* is the temperature of the air in °C, and *e* is the vapor pressure in hPa (mbar) given by:

$$e = 6.11 * \exp\left[5417.7530 * \left(\left(\frac{1}{273.16}\right) - \left(\frac{1}{dewpoint}\right)\right)\right] \qquad (3)$$

Program Requirements

The dew point (temperature) is a measure of the humidity content in the air. It indicates the amount of moisture in the air. The dew point temperature should be given in Kelvins (temperature in K = temperature in °C + 273.16) for the formula to work. The magic number 5417.7530 is a rounded constant based on the molecular weight of water, latent heat of evaporation, and universal gas constant.

Program Spepcification

Calculate the humidex given a dew point temperature and air temperature in degrees Celsius.

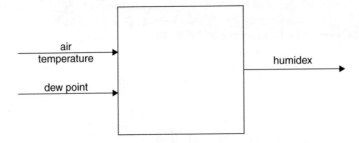

Input(s):   The temperature of the air in °C, and the dew point temperature
Output(s):   A "temperature" representing the humidex

The relationship between the inputs and the humidex is derived using Eqs. 1–3. In addition to these equations, we need an equation to convert the dew point temperature to Kelvin.

$$dew\_point_k = \text{dew point in °C} + 273.16 \qquad (4)$$

Algorithm Design

1. Obtain the dew point temperature and the air temperature.
2. Convert the dew point temperature from Celsius to degrees Kelvin (Eq. 4).
3. Calculate the vapour pressure using Eq. 3.
4. Calculate the humidex using Eqs. 1 and 2.
5. Output the humidex.

Deriving the Program

For this case study, we will look at deriving a solution step by step. The first step in creating a program from the algorithm involves using a simple C program skeleton:

```c
#include <stdio.h>
int main(void)
{
    return 0;
}
```

The next part of the solution involves creating a series of variables to hold the information. There are two inputs: (1) the temperature of the air, and (2) the dew point temperature and two intermediary variables to hold the vapor pressure and humidex calculations. Now let's identify some possibilities for variable names:

Air temperature:	airtemp, Air_temp, airT, air_T
Dew point temperature:	dew_point, dewpoint_T, dewP_T
Vapor pressure:	vapor_pressure, vap_P, vapPres
Humidex:	humi, humidex, Humidex

From these we have chosen the following series of variables:

```c
double dewpoint_T, air_T, vap_P, humidex;
```

These variables are all self-documenting, so they don't really need any comments. They are all declared as **double** as it is not certain temperature values will be whole numbers and the nature of the equations suggests floating point calculations.

The value **Kelvin** denotes the absolute Kelvin temperature constant:

```c
#define Kelvin 273.16
```

Now our skeleton program should look like:

```c
#include <stdio.h>
#define Kelvin 273.16
int main(void)
{
    double dewpoint_T, air_T, vap_P, humidex;
    return 0;
}
```

The next part involves prompting for the dew point temperature and air temperature, storing them in **dewpoint_T** and **air_T** respectively.

```
printf("Enter the dew point temperature: ");
scanf("%lf", &dewpoint_T);

printf("Enter the air temperature: ");
scanf("%lf", &air_T);
```

The **printf** statements affect the prompting for the user, whereas the corresponding **scanf** statements facilitate storage of the inputs. We have now satisfied the first portion of the algorithm and can attempt the next part, which involves converting the dew point temperature from Celsius to degrees Kelvin using:

```
dewpoint_T = dewpoint_T + Kelvin;
```

So now our program should look like:

```
#include <stdio.h>

#define Kelvin 273.16

int main(void)
{
    double dewpoint_T, air_T, vap_P, humidex;

    printf("Enter the dew point temperature: ");
    scanf("%lf", &dewpoint_T);

    printf("Enter the air temperature: ");
    scanf("%lf", &air_T);

    dewpoint_T = dewpoint_T + Kelvin;

    return 0;
}
```

Next we use Eq. 3 to calculate the vapor pressure.

```
vap_P = 6.11*exp(5417.753*((1.0/Kelvin)-(1.0/dewpoint_T)));
```

Since we are using the **exp** function, we should also include the **math.h** library at the top of the program.

```
#include <stdio.h>
#include <math.h>
```

The final step involves calculating the humidex using a combination of Eqs. 1 and 2:

```
humidex = air_T + ((5.0/9.0) * (vap_P — 10.0));
```

Then we can print out the value for the calculated humidex:

```
printf("The humidex is: %.2f \n", humidex);
```

Now that the program is essentially finished, it is time to add finishing touches, like comments, although for long programs, comments should be added as you code.

```c
#include <stdio.h>
#include <math.h>

#define Kelvin 273.16

int main(void)
{
    double dewpoint_T, air_T, vap_P, humidex;

    // Input the dew point and air temperatures
    printf("Enter the dew point temperature: ");
    scanf("%lf", &dewpoint_T);

    printf("Enter the air temperature: ");
    scanf("%lf", &air_T);

    // Convert the dew point temperature to deg Kelvin
    dewpoint_T = dewpoint_T + Kelvin;

    // Calculate the vapor pressure
    vap_P = 6.11 * exp(5417.753*((1.0/Kelvin) -
            (1.0/dewpoint_T)));

    // Calculate the humidex
    humidex = air_T + (0.5555 * (vap_P - 10.0));

    // Output the humidex
    printf("The humidex is: %.2f \n", humidex);

    return 0;
}
```

Being Defensive

Keep in mind that your program should check the incoming temperatures to determine whether the temperatures fall within the constraints for calculating the humidex. This is a good opportunity to use some defensive programming techniques to "trap" these problems before they manifest themselves in the program.

In the problem scope there was a statement to the effect: "Therefore we only calculate and display its value when the dew point temperature is 15° C or greater, and the air temperature is 23° C or greater." Consider the modified code:

```c
#include <stdio.h>
#include <math.h>

#define Kelvin 273.16
```

```
int main(void)
{
    double dewpoint_T, air_T, vap_P, humidex;

    // Input the dew point and air temperatures
    printf("Enter the dew point temperature");
    scanf("%lf", &dewpoint_T);

    printf("Enter the air temperature");
    scanf("%lf", &air_T);

    // Determine whether the input meets the calculation
    // restrictions

    if (dewpoint_T >= 15 && air_T >= 23)
    {
        // Convert the dew point temperature to deg Kelvin
        dewpoint_T = dewpoint_T + Kelvin;

        // Calculate the vapor pressure
        vap_P = 6.11*exp(5417.753*((1.0/Kelvin)-
                                  (1.0/dewpoint_T)));

        // Calculate the humidex
        humidex = air_T + (0.5555 * (vap_P - 10.0));

        // Output the humidex
        printf("The humidex is: %.2f \n",humidex);
    }

    return 0;
}
```

The program now only performs the calculation if the constraints are met, otherwise it exits.

Testing the Program

We can test the program using a dewpoint temperature of 15, and an air temperature of 30. The resulting humidex is 33.98.

Digging a Little Deeper

The dew point tells us the absolute humidity. The dew point is the temperature the air must be cooled to in order for condensation to occur. The higher the humidity, the closer the dew point is to the air temperature. When the humidity is 100 percent, the dew point and the temperature are the same. The dew point can never be higher than the temperature of the air at any given time. Humidity can be measured in several different ways, but most commonly humidity is reported as the relative humidity. *Relative humidity* (RH) is the ratio of the amount of moisture in the air compared to the amount the air is capable of holding at a given temperature, expressed as a percentage. So a relative humidity of 50 percent indicates the air, at the current temperature, holds 50 percent of the moisture it is capable of holding. In very dry climates, the RH is low, while in moist climates, it is high. Humans tend to react with discomfort to high dew points. Those accustomed to continental climates often begin to feel discomfort when the dew point reaches between 15 and 20° C (59 to 68° F).

Why are there two formulas? Well, there is more than one way to calculate the humidex. What about if we have the air temperature and the relative humidity? Then you can change your program so that the input is air temperature and relative humidity, and use a formula for calculating the dew point.

Here is a formula to calculate the dew point in degrees Celsius to within ±0.4° C. It is valid for

$$0° C < T < 60° C$$
$$0.01 < RH < 1.0$$
$$0° C < Td < 50° C$$

where

T = temperature in degrees Celsius

RH = the relative humidity as a fraction (not percent)

Td = the dew point temperature to be calculated

$$Td = \frac{b \cdot \gamma(T, RH)}{a - \gamma(T, RH)}$$

where

$$\gamma(T, RH) = \left(\frac{aT}{b + T} \right) + \ln(RH)$$
$$a = 17.27$$
$$b = 237.7C$$
ln is the natural logarithm.

This really only causes a change in the program before the vapor pressure is calculated:

```
double rel_H, air_T, gamma;

// Input the dew point and air temperatures
printf("Enter the relative humidity in %%: ");
scanf("%lf", &rel_H);

printf("Enter the air temperature: ");
scanf("%lf", &air_T);

// Calculate the dew point temperature
gamma = ((a*air_T)/(b+air_T)) + log(rel_H/100.0);
dewpoint_T = (b * gamma) / (a - gamma);
```

Testing the Program

To test the program you will have to find some values that reflect the true humidex.[2] You could use the following table.

T (C°)	RH (%)							
	100	95	90	85	80	75	70	65
23	33	32	32	31	30	29	28	27
24	35	34	33	33	32	31	30	29
25	37	36	35	34	33	33	32	31
26	39	38	37	36	35	34	33	32
27	41	40	39	38	37	36	35	34
28	43	42	41	41	39	38	37	36
29	46	45	44	43	42	41	39	38
30	48	47	46	44	43	42	41	40
31	50	49	48	46	45	44	43	41
32	52	51	50	49	47	46	45	43
33	55	54	52	51	50	48	47	46
34	58	57	55	53	52	51	49	48

Epilog

The Canadian humidex differs slightly from the heat index used in places like the US, or Australia. It combines air temperature and relative humidity to determine an apparent temperature. Windsor, Ontario is actually one of the most humid cities in Canada. It actually holds the title for city with the most humidex days 35 degrees or above (28 days). If you want to go to the other end of the spectrum, Yellowknife hold the record for extreme wind chill (–64C), and the most high wind chill days (–30 or below), at 101 days.

---

[2]Available from Environment Canada (http://www.msc-smc.ec.gc.ca/cd/brochures/humidex_table_e.cfm)

Power of a Wind Turbine

Kites rise highest against the wind, not with it.
—Winston Churchill

The Problem Description

Renewable energy is energy that can be replenished at the same rate as it is used. Renewable energy sources contributed approximately 18 percent of global electricity generation in 2006. Wind power is renewable and contributes to greenhouse gas mitigation because it removes energy directly from the atmosphere without producing net emissions of greenhouse gases such as CO_2. A wind turbine is a device for converting the kinetic energy in the wind into the mechanical energy of a rotating shaft. This mechanical energy is then converted into electrical energy by a generator. In 2008, worldwide capacity of wind-powered generators was about 121 gigawatts (GW), representing 1.5 percent of worldwide electricity usage. In 2009 in Germany, there were approximately 19,460 wind turbines representing a capacity of 25 GW. Globally, wind power generation more than doubled between 2005 and 2008.

Now the question is how much energy is in the wind? An estimated 1 to 3 percent of energy from the sun that hits the earth is converted into wind energy. This is about 50 to 100 times more energy than is converted into biomass by all the plants on the planet through photosynthesis.

Program Requirements

The world's largest wind turbine generator is the Enercon E-126 (manufactured by the German companies *Enercon* and *REpower* and rated at approximately 7 MW. It has a rotor blade diameter of 126 metres, and the rotors sweep an area of $\pi \times (\text{diameter}/2)^2 = 12470$ m^2! This is an offshore wind turbine situated at sea level with a known air density. To calculate the power in watts, we calculate the power (w) in the area swept by the wind turbine rotor.

$$w = 0.5 \cdot \rho \cdot A \cdot V^3 \tag{1}$$

where

> w = power in watts (1,000 watts = 1 kilowatt)
> ρ = air density (about 1.225 kg/m³ at sea level, less higher up)
> A = rotor swept area, exposed to the wind (m²), also called the *capture area*
> V = wind speed in metres/second (20 mph = 9 m/s)

The E-126 is rated at 6 MW in 30 mph (14 m/s) winds, and so putting in the known values we get

> $w = 0.5 \times 1.225 \times 12470 \times (14)^3$
> $w = 0.6125 \times 12470 \times 2744$
> $w = 20,958,329$ watts

This gives a wind power of around 21 megawatts (mW). Why is the power of the wind so much larger than the rated power of the turbine generator? The answer is *Betz' Law* and inefficiencies in the system. Betz' Law says that you can only convert less than 16/27 (or 59.3 percent) of the kinetic energy in the wind to mechanical energy using a wind turbine.

Therefore, to calculate wind turbine power, we extend the equation

$$P = w \cdot Cp \cdot Ng \cdot Nb \tag{2}$$

where

> Cp = coefficient of performance (0.59 Betz' limit, 0.35 for an average system)
> Ng = generator efficiency (80 percent for a permanent magnetic generator)
> Nb = gearbox/bearing efficiency (normally approximately 95 percent)

For the E-126, the calculation becomes

> $P = 20958329 \times 0.45 \times 0.8 \times 0.95$
> $P = 7,167,749$ watts

By multiplying the rated power output (kW) by the rough capacity factor (*CF*) by the number of hours in a year (8760), a crude estimate of annual energy production (AEP) in kWh can be calculated:

$$AEP = (P/1000) \cdot CF \cdot 8760 \tag{3}$$

For the E-126 and CF = 0.3 (capacity factors for wind are typically 20 to 40 percent), *AEP* can be calculated as

> $AEP = (7167749/1000) \times 0.3 \times 8760$
> $AEP = 18,836,844$ kWh

Program Specification

The program has six inputs with varying units and ranges of acceptable values, and one output.

Inputs:

Rotor blade diameter	(metres)
Wind speed	(metres per second)
Air density	(kg/m³)
Coefficient of performance	(0.0–0.59)
Generator efficiency	(0.0–1.0)
Gearbox/bearing efficiency	(0.0–1.0)

Output:

Power	(watts)

These are the six core inputs, although the rotor sweep area used by the formula can be determined by calculating the area of the circle created using the diameter of the rotor blade. This first requires a formula, in the form of the area of a circle:

$$area = \pi r^2 \tag{4}$$

As the input for the rotor blade is given as a diameter, this has to be divided by 2 to obtain the radius (r). The output is converted from watts to kilowatts by dividing by 1000.

Algorithm Design

The basic algorithm calls for a series of steps performed in a sequential manner.

1. Obtain inputs.
2. Calculate the radius of the rotor blade.
3. Calculate the rotor sweep area (Eq. 4).
4. Calculate the power of the wind turbine (Eqs. 1, 2).
5. Output the power in kilowatts.

Implementing the Program

The first part of designing a solution involves creating variables to hold the data input, and also the information calculated. These are given here:

Rotor blade diameter	(metres)
Wind speed	(metres per second)
Air density	(kg/m³)
Coefficient of performance	(0.0–0.59)
Generator efficiency	(0.0–1.0)
Gearbox/bearing efficiency	(0.0–1.0)
Rotor sweep area	calculated
Wind turbine power	calculated
Power in the area swept by rotor	calculated

As much of the data includes real numbers, it seems appropriate that the variables be of type **double**. The challenge here is to create identifiers to associate with each of the variables:

Rotor blade diameter	**rotorDiam**, rotor_bladeD, rotorblade
Wind speed	**windSpd**, wind_speed
Air density	**airDen**, air_density, airdensity_m3
Coefficient of performance	**coeffPer**, coefficient_perf
Generator efficiency	**genEff**, generator_efficiency
Gearbox/bearing efficiency	**gearEff**, gearbox_efficiency
Rotor sweep area	**sweepArea**, rotor_area
Wind turbine power	**turbine_power**
Sweep area power	**sweepPower**

We can then declare the variables:

```
double rotorDiam, windSpd, airDen, coeffPer, genEff;
double gearEff, sweepArea, turbine_power, sweepPower;
```

Next we deal with the user inputs. This is where we start to look at the process of usability, even though there may be no graphical user interface in this program. The user input is controlled via a text-driven user interface, and it is important to get this correct. For example, for rotor blade diameter, the following message could be used:

```
Enter the rotor blade diameter:
```

The problem here is that the designer has neglected to inform the user what units are required. Without knowledge of the fact that the diameter should be expressed in metres, the user may enter the data in feet, which will have an effect on the remaining calculations, resulting in the wrong output. Also, we know what is meant by "rotor blade diameter," but some users may interpret this as the diameter of the shaft of one of the blades, so we may have to find a better way of stating what data we would like to obtain from the user. It may be better to phrase it in the following form:

```
Enter the diameter of the turbine rotor:
```

Now add units:

```
Enter the diameter of the turbine rotor (metres):
```

or even

```
Diameter of the turbine rotor (metres)?
```

Now let's construct input dialogues for the remaining inputs:

```
Wind speed (metres/sec)?
Air density (kg/m3)?
Coefficient of performance (0.0-0.59)?
Generator efficiency (0.0-1.0)?
Gearbox efficiency (0.0-1.0)?
```

The last two may have default values of 0.8 and 0.95, reflecting 80 percent and 95 percent efficiency, respectively. Setting default values is easier in the context of a GUI, not as easy here. We could change the dialogs to

```
Generator efficiency (0.0-1.0: avg=0.8)?
Gearbox efficiency (0.0-1.0: avg=0.95)?
```

Now that we have designed the dialogs, we can translate them into C statements:

```
printf("Diameter of the turbine rotor (metres)? ");
printf("Wind speed (metres/sec)? ");
printf("Air density (kg/m3)? ");
printf("Coefficient of performance (0.0-0.59)? ");
printf("Generator efficiency (0.0-1.0)? ");
printf("Gearbox efficiency (0.0-1.0)? ");
```

Each of these statements should be followed by an accompanying **scanf** statement to store the data entered in the appropriate variable:

```
printf("Diameter of the turbine rotor (metres)? ");
scanf("%lf", &rotorDiam);
printf("Wind speed (metres/sec)? ");
scanf("%lf", &windSpd);
printf("Air density (kg/m3)? ");
scanf("%lf", &airDen);
printf("Coefficient of performance (0.0-0.59)? ");
scanf("%lf", &coeffPer);
printf("Generator efficiency (0.0-1.0)? ");
scanf("%lf", &genEff);
printf("Gearbox efficiency (0.0-1.0)? ");
scanf("%lf", &gearEff);
```

At this point, we have input all the relevant data but have not dealt with any data range constraints. We will deal with this later. The next portion of the design deals with calculations. The first equation deals with calculating the rotor sweep area:

Rotor Sweep Area = $\pi \times (\text{diameter}/2.0)^2$

which translated gives

```
sweepArea = pi * pow(rotorDiam/2.0,2.0);
```

Here the constant π is replaced by a variable storing the value of 3.14159.

```
#define pi 3.14159
```

It also uses the **pow** function, found in the library **math.h**, to calculate the radius squared. As the diameter is input, we will first have to convert it into the radius equivalent by dividing the diameter by 2.0. Now that we have the **rotorArea** calculated, we can calculate the wind turbine power using the following equation:

$w = 0.5 \cdot \rho \cdot A \cdot V^3$

Now we can substitute the appropriate variables:

```
sweepPower = 0.5 * airDen * sweepArea * pow(windSpd,3.0);
```

The second equation can now be used to calculate the turbine power:

$$P = w \cdot Cp \cdot Ng \cdot Nb$$

Now we can substitute the appropriate variables:

```
turbine_power = sweepPower * coeffPer * genEff * gearEff;
```

The final step involves outputting the result, as a function of kilowatts. First, we will consider a dialogue to output to the user:

```
The power of the wind turbine is XYZ kilowatts.
```

Next we can convert this into a **printf** statement:

```
printf("The power of the wind turbine is "
       "%.2f kilowatts\n", turbine_power/1000.0);
```

The Complete Program

```c
#include <stdio.h>
#include <math.h>
#define pi 3.14159

int main(void)
{
    double rotorDiam, windSpd, airDen, coeffPer, genEff;
    double gearEff, sweepArea, turbine_power, sweepPower;

    printf("Diameter of the turbine rotor (metres)? ");
    scanf("%lf", &rotorDiam);
    printf("Wind speed (metres/sec)? ");
    scanf("%lf", &windSpd);
    printf("Air density (kg/m3)? ");
    scanf("%lf", &airDen);
    printf("Coefficient of performance (0.0-0.59)? ");
    scanf("%lf", &coeffPer);
    printf("Generator efficiency (0.0-1.0)? ");
    scanf("%lf", &genEff);
    printf("Gearbox efficiency (0.0-1.0)? ");
    scanf("%lf", &gearEff);

    sweepArea = pi * pow(rotorDiam/2.0,2.0);

    sweepPower = 0.5 * airDen * sweepArea * pow(windSpd,3.0);
```

```
turbine_power = sweepPower * coeffPer * genEff * gearEff;

printf("The power of the wind turbine is ");
        "%.2f kilowatts\n", turbine_power/1000.0);

return 0;
}
```

Input Validation

The problem with the program as it stands is that there is no input validation. This means that if the wrong data is input, the program may fail. The last three inputs have range constraints built into the input dialogs; however, the first three do not. Each of these has a series of constraints placed upon it:

Rotor blade diameter	> 0
Wind speed	> 0
Air density	0–1.225

We could encapsulate each input in a loop to verify input:

```
do
{
    printf("Diameter of the turbine rotor (metres)? ");
    scanf("%lf", &rotorDiam);

}while(rotorDiam <= 0)
```

The **do-while** loop provides for infinite looping, until such time as the value stored in **rotorDiam** is greater than zero. If it is less than or equal to zero, then the input prompt will recur. The same concept can be applied to each of the inputs.

Testing the Program

To make sure the program works, let's try it out on the information for E-126:

```
Diameter of the turbine rotor (metres)? 126
Wind speed (metres/sec)? 14
Air density (kg/m3)? 1.225
Coefficient of performance (0.0-0.59)? 0.45
Generator efficiency (0.0-1.0)? 0.8
Gearbox efficiency (0.0-1.0)? 0.95
The power of the wind turbine is 7167.16 kilowatts
```

Epilog

Writing a program like this isn't all that difficult. As long as we can get the logic right, it flows easily from top to bottom. There is a lot of number crunching involved in predicting the efficiency of power-generating devices.

Radiometric Dating

The hair on the Chekurovka mammoth was found to have a carbon-14 age of 26,000 years but the peaty soil in which it was preserved was found to have a carbon-14 dating of only 5,600 years.

—*Radiocarbon Journal*, Vol. 8, 1966

The Problem Description

Radiometric dating is a technique used to date materials based on a knowledge of the decay rates of naturally occurring isotopes and the current abundances. It is our principal source of information about the age of the Earth and a significant source of information about rates of evolutionary change. While the moment in time at which a particular nucleus decays is random, a collection of atoms of a radioactive nuclide decays exponentially at a rate described by a parameter known as the *half-life*, usually given in units of years when discussing dating techniques. After one half-life has elapsed, one half of the atoms of the substance in question will have decayed. Many of these radioactive substances eventually decay to a final, stable decay product. For example, Uranium-235 decays to Lead-207.

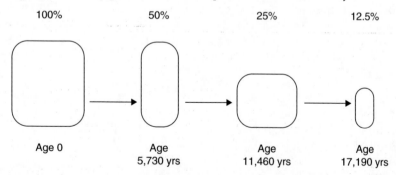

Let's consider *carbon dating*. An organism acquires carbon from carbon dioxide throughout its lifetime. Plants acquire it through photosynthesis, while animals acquire it through the eating of other animals and plants. Carbon—we're all full of it! When an organism dies, it stops acquiring C^{14} and the existing isotope decays. Carbon decays with a half-life of 5,730 years. The proportion of C^{14} left in an organism provides an indication of the time it perished. The process of carbon dating was discovered by Willard Frank Libby and his colleagues in 1949. In 1960, Libby was awarded the Nobel Prize in chemistry for his method to use C^{14} for age determination.

Program Requirements

A radioactive isotope of an element is an unstable form of the element. It spontaneously decays into another element over a period of time. Radioactive decay is an exponential process. If Q_0 is the initial quantity of a radioactive substance at time $t = 0$, then the amount of that substance that will be present at any time t in the future is given by:

$$Q(t) = Q_0 e^{-\lambda t} \tag{1}$$

where λ is the radioactive decay constant. Because radioactive decay occurs at a known rate, it can be used as a clock to measure the time since the decay started. If we know the initial amount of the radioactive material Q_0 present in a sample, and the amount of the material Q left at the current time, we can solve for t in Eq. 1 to determine how long the decay has been going on. The resulting equation is:

$$t_{decay} = -\frac{1}{\lambda} \ln\left(\frac{Q}{Q_0}\right) \tag{2}$$

In point of fact, Q_0 represents the number of atoms at time 0, and Q the number of atoms remaining after radioactive decay. We can treat $\dfrac{Q}{Q_0}$ as a ratio, where $Q_0 = 100$.

Eq. 2 has practical applications in many areas of science. Archeologists use a radioactive clock based on carbon-14 (C^{14}) to determine the time that has passed since a once-living thing died. Carbon-14 is continually taken into the body while a plant or animal is living, so the amount of it present in the body at the time of death is assumed to be known. The decay constant of carbon-14 is known to be 0.00012097/year, so if the amount of carbon-14 remaining now can be accurately measured, then Eq. 2 can be used to determine how long ago the living thing died. Consider the following four elements and their respective decay constants:

Carbon, C^{14} ($\lambda = 0.00012097$)
Rubidium, Rb^{87} ($\lambda = 1.42 \times 10^{-11}$)
Uranium, U^{235} ($\lambda = 9.72 \times 10^{-10}$)
Potassium, K^{40} ($\lambda = 5.34 \times 10^{-10}$)

Program Specifications

Input(s):	The type and amount (%) of the element remaining
Output(s):	Age of the specimen in years
Formula:	The relationship between the inputs and the age of the specimen is derived using Eq. 2.
Modularity:	The program will incorporate a function to accomplish the task of calculating the date of the artifact.

Algorithm Design

1. Select an element to date an object.
2. Obtain input for percentage of the element remaining (0–100).
3. Calculate the number of years using Eq. 2.
4. Output the age of the specimen.
5. Return to Step 1.

Deriving the Program

As usual we begin the program with the program skeleton:

```
#include <stdio.h>

int main(void)
{
    return 0;
}
```

Due to the fact that we are calculating a logarithm in Eq. 2, we should also incorporate the math library:

```
#include <math.h>
```

Decay constants for four elements are used in this program, so it is best to express these using **define** statements:

```
#define C14 0.00012097
#define Rb87 1.42e-11
#define U235 9.72e-10
#define K40 5.34e-10
```

We have to choose variables to store the input and calculations. There are two basic inputs, one representing the element selected, the other the percentage of the element remaining in the sample. The output consists of the age of the sample:

```
double percRem, age;
int opt;
```

We have chosen **percRem** to represent the percentage of the element remaining, a decimal value from 0 to 100, and **age** to represent the calculated age of the sample. The variable **opt** will hold the element chosen from the menu. We could have used other identifiers:

```
double percent_Remaining, age_of_sample;
int element_option;
```

The problem with these identifiers is that although they are descriptive, they are somewhat long, which makes their use restrictive in equations. Now we must deal with the "menu" of elements. First, we include a descriptive message:

```
printf("RADIOMETRIC DATING\n");
```

Then the menu looks like:

```
printf("(1) Carbon 14\n");
printf("(2) Rubidium 87\n");
printf("(3) Uranium 235\n");
printf("(4) Potassium 40\n");
printf("Please select an isotope, or 0 to quit: ");
```

This allows the user to select the number associated with a particular isotope, or zero to quit the program. This is followed by a way of entering the selection and storing it in the variable named **opt**:

```
scanf("%d", &opt);
```

Next we prompt for the percentage of the element remaining, storing the value in **percRem**:

```
printf("\nEnter the percentage of the element remaining: ");
scanf("%lf", %percRem);
```

Now that we have dealt with the program input, we will digress to work on the function that calculates the age of the object. We have decided to call this function **radiometric_dating**. It takes two inputs, one the decay constant **(decayC)** and the other representing the percentage of the chosen element remaining **(remaining)**. We also use one variable local to the function, **age**, as an intermediary value to store the calculated age. The benefit of using a function is the ability to calculate the age using *any* element instead of writing the same equation multiple times. The function looks like this:

```
double radiometric_dating(double decayC, double remaining)
{
    double age;

    age = (-1.0/decayC) * log(remaining/100.0);

    return age;
}
```

In the equation for **age** we use the function **log** from the **math.h** library, which is synonymous with the natural logarithm. Both the function parameters and local variables are of type **double.** Back to the main program, we can use a **switch** statement to calculate the age using the appropriate element:

```
switch (opt)
{
    case 1: age = radiometric_dating(C14,percRem);
            break;
    case 2: age = radiometric_dating(Rb87,percRem);
            break;
    case 3: age = radiometric_dating(U235,percRem);
            break;
    case 4: age = radiometric_dating(K40,percRem);
            break;
}
```

Here we use the value of **opt** to select the appropriate action. In each case the decay constant associated with the particular element chosen is passed to the function **radiometric_dating,** as well as the value of **percRem.** The result is returned from the function and assigned to the variable **age.** The body of each **case** statement contains a **break,** to ensure follow-through does not occur. The final portion of the program involves printing out the age using the statement:

```
printf("\nThe age of the sample is %.2f years\n\n", age);
```

As it stands, this program will work once and then exit. What we wanted in the requirements is a program that will loop continuously. This can be achieved using an infinite loop, in this case provided by a **while** loop. We can then encapsulate the code we just wrote inside the infinite loop. For instance:

```
while(1)
{

    // Menu prompt
    // Input percentage of element remaining
    // Switch statement to calculate age

}
```

Now we just have to add a couple more statements *after* the menu option has been prompted:

```
if (opt == 0)
    break;
else if (opt < 0 || opt > 4){
    printf("Sorry that option does not exist.\n\n");
    continue;
}
```

This basically says that if zero is chosen, the program should exit, so the break statement transfers control of the program outside the infinite **while** loop and the program terminates. Otherwise, it checks if the option chosen is outside the allowable options and prints an appropriate message. The complete program follows.

The Program

```c
#include <stdio.h>
#include <math.h>

#define C14 0.00012097
#define Rb87 1.42e-11
#define U235 9.72e-10
#define K40 5.34e-10
double radiometric_dating(double decayC, double remaining)
{
    double age;

    age = (-1.0/decayC) * log(remaining/100.0);

    return age;
}

int main(void)
{
    double percRem, age;
    int opt;

    while(1)
    {
        printf("RADIOMETRIC DATING\n");
        printf("(1) Carbon 14\n");
        printf("(2) Rubidium 87\n");
        printf("(3) Uranium 235\n");
        printf("(4) Potassium 40\n");
        printf("Please select an isotope, or 0 to quit: ");
        scanf("%d", &opt);

        if (opt == 0)
            break;
        else if (opt < 0 || opt > 4){
            printf("Sorry that option does not exist.\n\n");
            continue;
        }

        printf("\nEnter the percentage of the element remaining: ");
        scanf("%lf", &percRem);
```

```
switch (opt)
{
        case 1: age = radiometric_dating(C14,percRem);
                    break;
        case 2: age = radiometric_dating(Rb87,percRem);
                    break;
        case 3: age = radiometric_dating(U235,percRem);
                    break;
        case 4: age = radiometric_dating(K40,percRem);
                    break;
}

        printf("\nThe age of the sample is %.2f years\n\n", age);
}
    return 0;
}
```

Testing the Program

We can test the program with a known entity, the half-life of carbon-14:

```
RADIOMETRIC DATING
(1) Carbon 14
(2) Rubidium 87
(3) Uranium 235
(4) Potassium 40
Please select an isotope, or 0 to quit: 1

Enter the percentage of the element remaining: 50

The age of the sample is 5729.91 years
```

Your answer should be approximately 5,730, which is the half-life of C-14, as stated in the *CRC Handbook of Chemistry and Physics.*

Now if you try the program with a percentage of zero, it will most likely work, although the answer might be something like:

```
The age of the sample is inf years
```

Maybe we should do some defensive work!

Being Defensive

The problem with zero is that if you don't have any percent of an element, then likely the object being dated has already disappeared! When we try to calculate **log(0)**, we get an answer that is undefined. The other problem lies with entering 100, which presumes that 100 percent of the element is remaining. If none has decayed, there's no point in calculating the age of the sample! If you enter 100 into the program, you might get an answer like:

```
The age of the sample is −0.00 years
```

which I suppose is technically true, apart from the minus sign, anyway. To forestall these problems, we could encapsulate the statements that prompt for the percentage remaining into a **do-while** loop, as follows:

```
do {
    printf("\nEnter the percentage of the element remaining: ");
    scanf("%lf", &percRem);
} while (percRem <= 0 || percRem >= 100);
```

Here the loop iterates while the value of **percRem** input is less than or equal to 0 or greater than or equal to 100. If we enter 100, it iterates and prompts for the input again. If we enter 99.9, it exits the loop and proceeds with the program.

Epilog

How accurate is radiometric dating? The accuracy is dependent in part on the half-life of the radioisotope involved. For example, C^{14} has a half-life of 5,730 years, so an organism that has been dead for 50,000-odd years will have very little C^{14} left, making it difficult to date. Uranium-235 and Uranium-238 have half-lives of 700 million and 4.5 billion years, respectively, and Rb^{87} has a half-life of 50 billion years. Errors here are reputed to be 30–50 million years for a 3 billion year sample.

Ariane 5

I do not fear computers. I fear the lack of them.
—Isaac Asimov

The Problem Description

This is not so much a problem, but an example relating to debugging.

On June 4, 1996, an unmanned Ariane 5 rocket was launched by the European Space Agency in Kourou, French Guiana. After initiation of the flight sequence, at an altitude of about 3,700m, the rocket veered off its path and disintegrated. The failure of the Ariane rocket was caused by the complete loss of guidance and altitude information 37 seconds after the start of the main engine ignition sequence.[1] This loss of information was due to a software error in the Inertial Reference System (using the French acronym, SRI). The SRI has its own internal computer that measures the speed of the rocket at short fixed intervals, using a strap-down inertial platform with laser gyros and accelerometers, and calculates the distance traveled. It does this by multiplying the speed by the duration of the interval. Once computed, the position is passed to the on-board computer (OBC), which calculates the steering commands to control the nozzles of the solid boosters and main Vulcain cryogenic engine, via servovalves and hydraulic actuators. To improve reliability, two SRIs operate in parallel and feature identical software and hardware. One SRI is active; the other is in "hot" standby, whereby the outputs are ignored. If the OBC detects a failure of the active SRI, it switches to the standby unit.

---

[1]Le Lann, G., "An analysis of the Ariane 5 flight 501 failure—A system engineering perspective," *Workshop on Engineering of Computer-Based Systems*, IEEE, 1997, 339–346; Nuseibeh, B., "Ariane 5: Who Dunnit?" *IEEE Software*, 1997, Vol. 14, 15–16; Jezequel, J-M., and Meyer, B., "Design by contract: The Lessons of Ariane," *IEEE Computer*, 1997, Vol. 30, 129–130.

What Happened?

At 36.7 seconds the computer within the backup inertial reference system, which was working on standby for guidance and altitude control, became inoperative. This was caused by an internal variable related to the horizontal velocity of the launcher *exceeding a limit* in the software of this computer. Approximately 0.05 seconds later the *active* inertial reference system, identical to the backup system in hardware and software, failed for the same reason. Since the backup inertial system was already inoperative, correct guidance and altitude information could no longer be obtained. As a result of its failure, the active inertial reference system transmitted essentially diagnostic information to the launcher's primary computer, where it was interpreted as flight data and used for flight control calculations. The flight control calculations resulted in a command being issued to the booster nozzles, and the main engine nozzle to compensate for an altitude deviation that had never occurred. A rapid change of altitude occurred, which caused the launcher to disintegrate at 39 seconds due to aerodynamic forces.

Why Did It Happen?

Before lift-off certain calculations are performed to align the inertial reference system. This software was designed for the Ariane 4 and really served no purpose on Ariane 5. On Ariane 4 this process was allowed to operate for approximately 40 seconds after lift-off. On Ariane 4 flights using the same type of inertial reference system, there has been no such failure because the trajectory during the first 40 seconds of flight is such that the particular variable related to horizontal velocity cannot reach, with an adequate operational margin, a value beyond the limit present in the software. Ariane 5 has a high initial acceleration and a trajectory that leads to a build-up of horizontal velocity five times more rapid than for Ariane 4. The higher horizontal velocity of Ariane 5 generated, within the 40-second time frame, the excessive value that caused the inertial system computers to cease operation.

A *software exception* was raised during the execution of a numeric conversion. An attempt was made to convert a 64-bit floating point number representing to the horizontal velocity (Horizontal Bias) of the rocket with respect to the platform to a 16-bit signed integer. This conversion resulted in an overflow error because the largest value that can be stored in a 16-bit signed integer is typically 32,768. A number of factors ultimately contributed to this scenario:[2]

- Omission of precondition checking
- Error handling by execution termination
- No validation of input
- No extensive testing

---

[2]Ben-Ari, M., "The bug that destroyed a rocket," *SIGCSE Bulletin*, 2001, Vol. 33, 58–59.

The Algorithm

1. Acquire guidance information from SRI.
   a. Get information from laser gyros and accelerometers.
   b. Calculate distance traveled.
2. Calculate position of rocket.
3. Calculate steering commands.
4. Control boosters and main engine.

The Program

Extremely long!

How Could It Have Been Avoided?

The problem could ultimately have been avoided by following the specifications that stated the Horizontal Bias should correspond to 16 bits. Defensive programming would also have helped checking the precondition, perhaps using an assertion or exception handling.

```
assert(hor_vel > MAX_BIAS)
```

Epilog

This problem involves both a discussion on overflow errors and on how such small errors lead to a cascading effect that can affect other systems. While a software exception was the root cause of the system failure, other factors played contributory roles, including the interaction between hardware and software systems. The first of these existed in the actual software design process: Ariane 4 trajectory data was used in the specifications and simulations of Ariane 5, when the Ariane 5 trajectory was known to be different. The second relates to the notion of redundancy. Redundancy is often used to reduce component failures and increase system reliability. Ariane 5 contained both a primary and backup IRS, both with the same software, resulting in exactly the same behavior: They shut themselves down exactly as they were designed to do.

Heron's Formula

To the extent math refers to reality, we are not certain; to the extent we are certain, math does not refer to reality.
—Albert Einstein

The Problem Description

Heron of Alexandria (10–70) was a Greek engineer and geometer who lived in Alexandria, Hellenistic Egypt. His most famous invention was the first documented steam engine, the *aeolipile*. He is credited with deriving a formula to calculate the area of a triangle whose sides have lengths *a*, *b*, and *c*. A proof of the formula can be found in Heron's book *Metrica*. More recently, writings of the Arab scholar Abu'l Raihan Muhammed al-Biruni have credited the formula to Heron's predecessor Archimedes.

Program Requirements

The formula is extremely basic:

$$area = \sqrt{s(s-a)(s-b)(s-c)} \tag{1}$$

where *s* is the *semiperimeter* of the triangle:

$$s = \frac{a+b+c}{2} \tag{2}$$

Program Specification

Input(s):   The length of the sides of the three triangles

Output(s): A number representing the area of the triangle

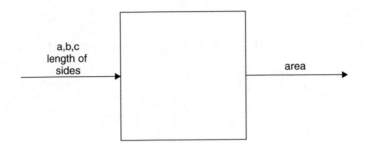

The relationship between the inputs and the area of the triangle is derived using Eq. 1.

Algorithm Design

1. Obtain the three sides of the triangle.
2. Calculate the semiperimeter of the triangle using Eq. 2.
3. Calculate the area of the triangle using Eq. 1.
4. Output the area.

Deriving the Program

For this first case study, we will look at deriving a solution step by step. The first step in creating a program from the algorithm involves using a simple C program skeleton:

```
#include <stdio.h>

int main(void)
{
    return 0;
}
```

The next part of the solution involves creating a series of variables to hold the information. There are three inputs. Each holds one side of the triangle and two intermediary variables to hold the semiperimeter and the area calculations. Identify some possibilities for variable names:

Triangle sides: `sideA, A, sideA_of_triangle`

Area: `triangle_area, area, A`

Semiperimeter: `semiperimeter, S, semiP`

From these we have chosen the following series of variables:

```
double sideA, sideB, sideC, area, semiP;
```

These variables are all self-documenting, so they don't really need any comments. They are all declared as **double** as it is not certain temperature values will be whole numbers and the nature of the equations suggests floating point calculations.

So now our skeleton program should look like:

```
#include <stdio.h>

int main(void)
{
    double sideA, sideB, sideC, area, semiP;
    return 0;
}
```

The next part involves prompting for the three sides of the triangle, storing them in **sideA**, **sideB**, and **sideC**, respectively.

```
printf("Enter the three sides of the triangle: ");
scanf("%lf%lf%lf", &sideA, &sideB, &sideC);
```

We have now satisfied the first portion of the algorithm and can attempt the next part, which involves calculating the semiperimeter of the triangle:

```
semiP = (sideA + sideB + sideC) / 2.0;
```

So now our program should look like:

```
#include <stdio.h>

int main(void)
{
    double sideA, sideB, sideC, area, semiP;

    printf("Enter the three sides of the triangle: ");
    scanf("%lf%lf%lf", &sideA, &sideB, &sideC);

    semiP = (sideA + sideB + sideC) / 2.0;

    return 0;
}
```

The final step involves using Eq. 2 to calculate the area:

```
area = sqrt(semiP * (semiP-sideA) *
                     (semiP-sideB) * (semiP-sideC));
```

Since we are using the **sqrt** function, we should also include the **math.h** library at the top of the program.

```
#include <stdio.h>
#include <math.h>
```

Then we can print out the value for the calculated area:

```
printf("The area of the triangle is: %.2f \n", area);
```

Now that the program is essentially finished, it is time to add finishing touches, like comments, although for long programs, comments should be added as you code.

```
#include <stdio.h>
#include <math.h>

int main(void)
{
    double sideA, sideB, sideC, area, semiP;

    printf("Enter the three sides of the triangle: ");
    scanf("%lf%lf%lf", &sideA, &sideB, &sideC);

    semiP = (sideA + sideB + sideC) / 2.0;
    area = sqrt(semiP * (semiP-sideA) *
                        (semiP-sideB) * (semiP-sideC));

    printf("The area of the triangle is: %.2f \n", area);

    return 0;
}
```

Being Defensive

What we obviously missed is checking to see whether the three sides of the triangle we input are actually valid. If someone enters 30, 30, 100, this is obviously not going to work! You will likely get an answer that looks like:

```
The triangle area is nan
```

We can perform two types of test. The first checks to see that all the side measurements are greater than zero, because we can't have negative measurements. So we could use a test of the form:

```
test1 = (sideA > 0) && (sideB > 0) && (sideC > 0);
```

Secondly, the sum of any two side lengths must be greater than the third side length:

```
test2 = (sideA + sideB > sideC) &&
        (sideA + sideC > sideB) &&
        (sideB + sideC > sideA);
```

therefore

```
if (test1 && test2){
    semiP = (sideA + sideB + sideC) / 2.0;
    area = sqrt(semiP *(semiP-sideA) * (semiP-sideB)
                            * (semiP-sideC));
    printf("The triangle area is %.2f \n", area);
}
else
    printf("This is not a triangle\n");
```

Testing the Program

The following is the output from this program for input 3.0, 5.0, and 7.0.

```
The triangle area is 6.5
```

Leap Years

Some months have 30 days, some months have 31 days; how many have 28?

The Problem Description

The algorithm for the Julian calendar was introduced in 46 BC by Julius Caesar and is comprised of 365 days divided into 12 months and a leap day is added to February every four years. Hence, the Julian year is on average 365.25 days long. The algorithm for the Gregorian calendar, a modification of the Julian algorithm, was first proposed by the Calabrian doctor Aloysius Lilius and was decreed by Pope Gregory XIII, for whom it was named, on February 24, 1582. The Gregorian Calendar was devised both because the mean year in the Julian Calendar was slightly too long, causing the vernal equinox to slowly drift backwards in the calendar year, and because the lunar calendar used to compute the date of Easter had grown conspicuously in error as well. The Gregorian calendar system dealt with these problems by dropping a certain number of days to bring the calendar back into synchronization with the seasons. It also slightly shortened the average number of days in a calendar year by omitting three Julian leap-days every 400 years.

Program Requirements

A *leap year* is a year containing an extra day. The Gregorian Calendar is based on a mean solar year of 362.25 days (365d 5h 48m 46s), which is why we have a leap year every four years to add a day for the previous three quarter days we missed. Unfortunately, the Earth's orbital period is still not exactly 365.25 days long, so corrections have been added like "years divisible by 100 are not leap years unless they are divisible by 400, in which case they are." Therefore, 1600, 2000, and 2400 are leap years, but 1700, 1800, 1900, and 2100 are not.

Program Specifications

Input(s):   A numeric value consistent with a (4 digit) year
Output(s):   A phrase remitting whether the year is a leap year or not

Algorithm Design

1. Input the year.
2. Decide whether the year is a leap year or not.

The following cumulative rules decide which years are leap years:

1. A year divisible by 4 is a leap year.
2. A year that is divisible by 100 is not a leap year.
3. A year that is also divisible by 400 is a leap year.

Ahhh, a set of rules. So here's the fun part: We have to create a set of relational expressions that satisfy the three rules. This is the hardest part of deriving the algorithm. The mechanics of the program are somewhat simple. Let's look at each rule in turn.

A year divisible by 4 is a leap year.

This rule could be expressed in pseudocode as:

```
IF the year is divisible by 4
THEN it is a leap year
```

A year that is divisible by 100 is not a leap year.

This rule could be expressed in pseudocode as:

```
IF the year is not divisible by 100
THEN it is a leap year
```

A year that is also divisible by 400 is a leap year.

This final rule could be expressed in pseudocode as:

```
IF the year is divisible by 400
THEN it is a leap year
```

Now we must combine these rules;

```
IF ((the year is divisible by 4) AND
    (the year is not divisible by 100)) OR
    (the year is divisible by 400)
THEN it is a leap year
ELSE it is not a leap year
```

The only thing left now is the expression controlling the **if** statement. If we draw a flow diagram of what could happen, we get something like:

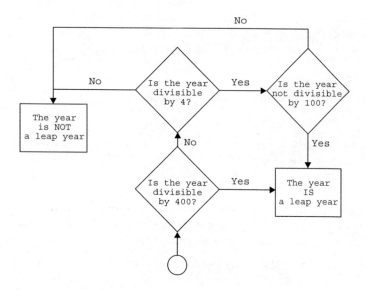

Deriving the Program

The rest of the program is somewhat trivial (or so it will seem after you wade through the expressions). Let's do the easy part first, setting up the skeleton of the program, which looks like this:

```
#include <stdio.h>

int main(void)
{
    return 0;
}
```

The first part of the program ensures the program has access to the Standard Input/Output library:

```
#include <stdio.h>
```

Now we can start the main program:

```
int main(void)
{
```

We include a **return** statement to indicate all went well when the program ends:

```
return 0;
```

Now we end the main program:

```
}
```

Next we have to deal with the stuffing: What does the program actually do? We know it takes a four-digit number as input, so we should declare a variable to store the year in (we use an integer because years are normally expressed as whole numbers):

```
int aYear;
```

We can include a **printf** statement to ask the user to input the year:

```
printf("Enter a year: ");
```

It probably would be quite nice to include a **scanf** statement to read the value input and store it in the variable **aYear**:

```
scanf("%d", &aYear);
```

Now the tricky part: If the program basically has to output whether or not a year is a leap year, then we have to incorporate a decision structure in our program. The most appropriate one, of course, is an **if-else** statement. In pseudocode we could write this as:

```
If the year is a leap-year
Then output "???? is a leap year"
Else output "???? is not a leap year"
```

So our program now looks something like:

```
#include <stdio.h>

int main(void)
{
    int aYear;
    printf("Enter a year: ");
    scanf("%d", &aYear);

    if ( )
        printf("The year %d is a leap year", aYear);
    else
        printf("The year %d is not a leap year", aYear);
    return 0;
}
```

Is the year divisible by 4 AND not divisible by 100?

```
aYear % 4 == 0 && aYear % 100 != 0
```

Or is the year divisible by 400?

```
aYear % 400 == 0
```

Is the year divisible by 400 OR is the year divisible by 4 AND NOT divisible by 100?

```
aYear % 400 == 0 || aYear % 4 == 0 && aYear % 100 != 0
```

The trick here is that the && operator has precedence over the || operator. So you may like to add some parentheses and swap the expressions around a little so it makes more logical sense:

```
(aYear % 4 == 0 && aYear % 100 != 0) || (aYear % 400 == 0)
```

which gives:

```
if ((aYear % 4 == 0 && aYear % 100 != 0) || (aYear % 400 == 0))
    printf("The year %d is a leap year", aYear);
else
    printf("The year %d is not a leap year", aYear);
```

The Program

The program itself isn't long at all, just basically an **if-else** statement. Now we'll embellish it with some comments.

```c
#include <stdio.h>

int main(void)
{
    int aYear;

    // Input the year
    printf("Enter a year: ");
    scanf("%d", &aYear);

    if ((aYear % 4 == 0 && aYear % 100 != 0) || (aYear % 400 == 0))
        printf("The year %d is a leap year\n", aYear);
    else
        printf("The year %d is not a leap year\n", aYear);

    return 0;
}
```

Testing the Program

This is indeed a tricky program, not because it's hard, but because it's hard to get the logic right the first time. Testing the program requires us to make up a series of test cases:

Years that are leap years: 2000, 1896, 2004

Years that are not leap years: 1900, 1700, 1879

Being Defensive

What happens if you enter a year of 800? It will stipulate that it is a leap year, when really it isn't! We may want to check that the year being queried is 1582 or beyond; otherwise, other circumstances may hold.

```
if (aYear < 1582)
    printf("Sorry, invalid year");
```

Epilog

The caveat is that the *tropical* year is currently about 365.242199 days long, and the Gregorian leap year rule gives an average year length of 365.2425 days. This provides for an error of 0.000301 days per year. So in 3,322 years the calendar will be out one day. But hey, probably by this time the equinox will have changed a bit too. Of course, the Gregorian Calendar itself provides for a bit of a mess. For example:

- The Gregorian calendar was first adopted in Italy, Poland, Portugal, and Spain in 1582. This was done by dropping 10 days in October (Ottobre).

- In Great Britain (and colonies), the Gregorian calendar was adopted much later— 11 days were dropped in September 1752.

- Russia did not adopt the Gregorian calendar until Lenin took power. So the October Revolution actually took place in November in the Julian calendar. Therefore, historical work written before October 1917 might be a little hazy when it comes to dates! The Eastern Orthodox Church, however, still uses the Julian calendar, so it celebrates Christmas on January 7.

Population Ecology

The power of population is indefinitely greater than the power in the earth to produce subsistence for man.

—Thomas Malthus

The Problem Description

A number of laws relate to population ecology. The *exponential model* for population growth is associated with Thomas Robert Malthus (1766–1834), an English demographer and political economist who first realized that any species can potentially increase in numbers according to a geometric series. The exponential model, often called the Malthusian Law, is widely regarded in the field of population ecology as the first principle of population dynamics. This law says that when birth and death rates are constant, a population will grow (or decline) at an exponential rate.[1] There are many applications of the exponential model: microbiology (growth of bacteria), conservation biology (restoration of disturbed populations), insect rearing (prediction of yield), plant or insect quarantine (population growth of introduced species), and fishery (prediction of fish dynamics).

Program Requirements

If a species has nonoverlapping populations (e.g., annual plants), and each organism produces R offspring, then population numbers N in generations $t=0,1,2, \ldots$ is equal to:

$$N_1 = N_0 \cdot R$$

$$N_t = N_0 \cdot R^t$$

When t is large, then this equation can be approximated by an exponential function:

$$N_t = N_0 e^{rt} \tag{1}$$

---

[1]Malthus, T. R., *An Essay on the Principle of Population*, J Johnson, London, 1798.

where N_t is the population density at time t (hours, days, years), N_0 is the initial population density, e is the base of the natural logarithm, and t is the amount of time of population increase. Parameter r is known as the *Malthusian parameter, intrinsic rate of increase, instantaneous rate of natural increase,* or *instantaneous growth rate*. In the simplest population, all individuals in the population are considered equivalent, so it can be interpreted as a difference between the birth (reproduction) rate and the death rate:

$$\frac{dN}{dt} = (b - m)N = rN \tag{2}$$

where b is the birth rate and m is the death rate. Birth rate is the number of offspring organisms produced per one existing organism in the population per unit time. Death rate is the probability of dying per one organism. When $r > 0$, there is exponential growth, when $r < 0$ there is exponential decay, and when $r = 0$, there is equilibrium.

Assumptions of the exponential model include:

1. Continuous reproduction (e.g., no seasonality)
2. All organisms are identical (e.g., no age structure)
3. Environment is constant in space and time (i.e., resources are unlimited)

The exponential model is robust, giving reasonable precision even if these conditions are not met. Organisms may differ in their age, survival, and mortality. But the population consists of a large number of organisms, and thus their birth and death rates are averaged. However, for populations in the real world, exponential growth is not possible. Populations can't continue to grow larger forever because resources are limited and as density increases, so do competition and mortality while *natality* (fecundity) decreases. Thus, population growth decreases, eventually leveling off at zero population growth. The *carrying capacity* (symbolized by K) for a given population is the level at which population growth ceases, or levels off. At this point, the population is theoretically in equilibrium with its environment, and the equation to predict population size must be modified to include this limit. Thus, the equation for *logistic growth* is

$$N_t = \frac{N_0 K}{N_0(K - N_0)e^{-rt}} \tag{3}$$

developed by Belgian mathematician Pierre Verhulst in 1838. Sometimes because of time lags as populations respond to food or other environmental conditions, population numbers may fluctuate/oscillate instead of maintaining a steady level. Classic examples include lynx and snowshoe hare populations, lemmings, and the relationship between mole and songbird populations and periodical cicadas. Lynx prey on snowshoe hares, so as the hare population gradually increases, the supply of twigs upon which the hares feed decreases and the lynx population gradually increases, out of sync by several years. As the lynx population increases, the snowshoe hare population decreases due to increased predation (and less twigs per hare). As the hare population decreases, there is less food for the lynx, so their population gradually decreases. Thus levels of these two populations fluctuate in about a nine- to ten-year cycle. Lemming populations typically fluctuate in three- to four-year cycles. Usually, a year or two before periodical cicadas emerge, while larger larvae are present underground, the mole population increases in response to the increased food supply, and then after the cicadas emerge, drastically decreases due to starvation. However, in the year the cicadas emerge, insectivorous songbirds use this ready food supply to feed their young. Thus, in that year, increased numbers of songbirds successfully fledge, resulting in greater competition for food the following year, when the cicadas are not present. Thus, to a certain degree, mole and songbird populations fluctuate in 17-year cycles, influenced by availability of periodical cicadas as food.

Program Specification

Input(s):   The initial size of the population, the growth rate, and the time period

Output(s): A number representing the anticipated population size

Algorithm Design

1. Obtain values for the initial population and growth rate.
2. Obtain a value for the time period (number of generations).
3. Calculate the new population using Eq. 1.
4. Print out the size of the population.

The Program

```
#include <stdio.h>
#include <math.h>

int main(void)
{
    int numG, initPop; finalPop;
    double growthRate          ;

    printf("Enter the initial population: ");
    scanf("%d", &initPop);
    printf("Enter the number of generations: ");
    scanf("%d", &numG);
    printf("Enter the population growth rate: ");
    scanf("%lf", &growthRate);

    finalPop = initPop * exp(growthRate * numG);

    printf("The population in %d generations is
            %.2f\n", numG, finalPop);

    return 0;
}
```

Deriving the Program

This is a relatively easy program to construct. First we will use the program skeleton:

```
#include <stdio.h>

int main(void)
{
    return 0;
}
```

Next we have to deal with the types and names for the variables we will use in the program. From Eq. 1 it is apparent that four pieces of information need variables: population growth rate, number of generations, initial population, final population.

We could identify some possibilities for variable names:

r	=	growthRate
t	=	numG
N_0	=	initPop
N_t	=	finalPop

We have decided to declare the last three variables as integers. Why, you may ask? The equation itself deals with real numbers, but when calculating populations of living entities, it's best to deal with whole numbers. You can't really have 0.3 of a beetle. Population generations are generally whole numbers as well. The only outlier is the growth rate, which over an entire population may be a fractional number. This gives:

```
int numG, initPop, finalPop;
double growthRate;
```

Next we deal with the input:

```
printf("Enter the initial population: ");
scanf("%d", &initPop);
printf("Enter the number of generations: ");
scanf("%d", &numG);
printf("Enter the population growth rate: ");
scanf("%lf", &growthRate);
```

Next we get to the crux of the problem, dealing with Eq. 1.

```
finalPop = initPop * exp(growthRate * numG);
```

Remember the factor e in the equation relates to calculating the exponential as provided by the C function **exp** found in the **math.h** library, which incidentally should also be included:

```
#include <math.h>
```

The final statement prints out the result:

```
printf("The population in %d generations is
        %.2f\n", numG, finalPop);
```

Testing the Program

Try some examples. If a grain beetle population starts at 100 individuals, has no growth restraints, and has an *r* value of 0.75 individuals/week, how many beetles will there be after *x* weeks?

$$N_3 = 100e^{(0.75*3)} = 948$$

$$N_{82} = 100e^{(0.75*82)} = 5.1 \times 10^{28}$$

If each beetle weighs 10mg, than after 82 weeks the population of beetles will weigh approximately the same as the earth (5.972×10^{21}).

Extending the Program

So far our program calculates the exponential growth. To extend it to deal with logistic growth as well isn't too difficult. First, there is a fourth input representing the carrying capacity:

```
int carryK;
```

Next we have to deal with actually inputting the carrying capacity:

```
printf("Enter the carrying capacity: ");
scanf("%lf", &carryK);
```

Finally we change the equation to reflect Eq. 3:

```
finalPop = (initPop * carryK) /
           (initPop * (carryK - initPop) * exp(-growthRate * numG));
```

Now the program for logistic growth looks like:

```
#include <stdio.h>
#include <math.h>

int main(void)
{
    int numG, initPop, finalPop, carryK;
    double growthRate, finalPop;

    // Input parameters
    printf("Enter the initial population: ");
    scanf("%d", &initPop);
```

```c
    printf("Enter the number of generations: ");
    scanf("%d", &numG);
    printf("Enter the population growth rate: ");
    scanf("%lf", &growthRate);
    printf("Enter the carrying capacity: ");
    scanf("%d", &carryK);

    // Calculate Logistic Growth
    finalPop = (initPop * carryK) /
               (initPop * (carryK - initPop) *
                exp(-growthRate * numG));

    printf("The population in %d generations is %.2f\n",
           numG, finalPop);

    return 0;
}
```

CS11

Fibonacci

The good, of course, is always beautiful, and the beautiful
never lacks proportion.
—Plato

The Problem Description

The Fibonacci numbers were conceived by European mathematician Leonardo of Pisa
(1175–1250), who called himself Fibonacci (fib-on-arch-ee), short for Filius Bonacci, "the
son of Bonaccio," since his father's name was Guglielmo Bonacci. Fibonacci introduced
the decimal Hindu-Arabic number system to Europe in 1202 (Roman numerals were used
until then) and was responsible for writing *Liber Abbaci* (1202, revised 1228), *The Book of
the Abacus*. Among the many problems in *Liber Abbaci* is the famous *paria coniculorum*, or
rabbit problem: Suppose a newly born pair of rabbits, one male, one female, are put in a
field. Rabbits can mate at the age of one month so that at the end of its second month a
female can produce another pair of rabbits. Suppose that our rabbits never die and that
the female always produces one new pair (one male, one female) every month from the
second month on. The puzzle that Fibonacci posed was: "How many pairs will there be in
one year?" The answer involves a series of numbers:

    1, 1, 2, 3, 5, 8, 13, 21, 34, 55, 89 . . .

The rabbits problem is not very realistic. It seems to imply that brother and sisters
mate, which leads to genetic problems. We can get round this by saying that the female of
each pair mates with any male and produces another pair. Another problem, which again
is not true to life, is that each birth is of exactly two rabbits, one male and one female.
However, regardless of the impetus for finding the series, the numbers themselves are sci-
entifically interesting. In the latter half of the nineteenth century, a French mathematician
named Edouard Lucas went on to study the same recurrence with starting values 2 and 1
(2,1,3,4,7,11,18,29, . . .). This version of the numbers became known as *Lucas* numbers.
Lucas was the person who made the term *Fibonacci numbers* popular and was also an
architect of the Towers of Hanoi puzzle. Still too abstract you say? This is often the extent
of knowledge given on this problem.

The Fibonacci numbers appear in numerous mathematical problems. The surprising thing about the Fibonacci sequence is that it turns out to occur in many different places in nature. The way in which the spiral patterns of sunflower seeds and pine cones grow is described by the sequence, and it is common for the number of petals on a flower to be a Fibonacci number. Four-leaved clovers are less common than five-leaved ones because five is in Fibonacci's sequence and four isn't! The Fibonacci series has been used in diverse applications, from the generation of musical compositions,[1] to color selection in planning a painting.[2] The role of the Fibonacci numbers in botany is sometimes called *Ludwig's law*. Around the turn of the 18th century the well-known astronomer Johanne Kepler observed that the Fibonacci numbers are common in plants. The arrangement of structures such as leaves around a stem, scales on a pine cone or pineapple, florets in the head of a daisy, and seeds in a sunflower is an aspect of plant form known as *phyllotaxis*.

Fibonacci numbers also appear in flowers, by counting the number of petals, or pairs of petals. An iris has 3 petals, buttercups have 5, some delphiniums have 8, corn marigolds have 13, asters have 21, and daises have 34, 55, or 89 petals. This pattern is not followed by every plant of a species but seems to characteristic of a species as a whole. The pattern of leaves as they spiral up a stem, quite often occurs in a Fibonacci sequence. If the leaves of any plant grew in straight lines—directly above and below each other—then any leaf or branch that was not at the top would have its sunlight obscured by the leaves or branches above it. Leaves more often than not occur as Fibonacci ratios. For example, in phyllotaxis ratio revolutions/(leafs:buds), apple, apricot, and cherry trees have a 2/5 ratio, a pear has 3/8, and an almond 5/13. A phyllotaxis of 2/5 implies five leaves are produced in two complete rotations. Fibonacci phyllotaxis affords optimal illumination to the photosynthetic surface of plants, since it allows for the least amount of overlap. Davis explains the presence of leaf spirals in different species of palms, citing two for the sugar palm, five for the coconut palm, and eight for the wild date palm.[3] One other place that plant life reflects the Fibonacci sequence is in the seed heads of numerous plants. The seeds are often distributed in the head in two distinct sets of spirals that radiate from the center of the head to the outermost edge in clockwise and counterclockwise directions. The spirals are logarithmic in character. The number set exhibited by the double set of spirals is intimately bound up with Fibonacci numbers. It appears that the reason for this formation is to allow the seedheads to pack the maximum number of seed in the given area. The most perfect example of phyllotaxis are afforded by the common sunflower *(Helianthus annuus,L.)*. A smaller sunflower head, which is approximately 3–5 inches across the disk, will have exactly 34 long and 55 short curves. A larger head 5–6 inches in diameter will show 55 long curves crossing 89 shorter ones. Consider the following image of a sunflower head.[4] The shallower spiral of this sunflower repeats 34 times, while the steeper spiral repeats 55 times.

---

[1]Norden, H., "Proportions and the composer," *The Fibonacci Quarterly*, 1972, Vol. 10, No. 3, 319–322.

[2]Bicknell Johnson, M.," Fibonacci chromotology or how to paint your rabbit," *The Fibonacci Quarterly*, 1978, Vol. 16, 426–428.

[3]Davis, T. A., "Why Fibonacci sequence for palm leaf spirals?" *The Fibonacci Quarterly*, 1971, Vol. 9, 237–244.

[4]Church, A. H., *On the Relation of Phyllotaxis to Mechanical Laws*. 1904, London: Williams and Norgate. (Plate VII)

Fir cones[5] and pineapples have modified leaves crowded together on relatively short stems. In the fir cone, as in the sunflower, two sets of spirals are obvious. Scales are arranged in helical whorls called *parastichies* (e.g., eight rows winding in one direction, with five in the other). In pineapples[6] there are three forms of parastichies, 5 rows winding slowly up the pineapple, 8 rows ascending more steeply in the opposite direction, and 13 rows winding very steeply in the first direction. Bananas, on the other hand, have either three or five flat sides.

The characteristic of this sequence is that each number is the sum of its two immediate predecessors. In other words, the Fibonacci numbers F_n are generated by the simple recurrence:

$$F_n = \begin{cases} F_{n-1} + F_{n-2} & \text{if } n > 2 \\ 1 & \text{if } n = 2 \\ 1 & \text{if } n = 1 \end{cases}$$

---

[5]Brousseau, A., Brother, "Fibonacci statistics in conifers," *The Fibonacci Quarterly*, 1969, Vol. 7, pp. 525–532.

[6]Onderdonk, P. B., "Pineapples and Fibonacci numbers," *The Fibonacci Quarterly*, 1970, Vol. 8, pp. 507–508.

Program Specification and Design

Input(s): A number representing the number of Fibonacci numbers to calculate

Output(s): A series of Fibonacci numbers

This can be described algorithmically as:

1. Assign the first two Fibonacci numbers, 1 and 2, to f1 (F_{n-2}) and f2 (F_{n-1}).
2. Add f1 to f2 and store the value in fibonacci, the new Fibonacci number (F_n).
3. Store the value of f2 in f1 so that f1 will contain the F_{n-2} Fibonacci number.
4. Store the value of fibonacci in f2 so that f2 will contain the F_{n-1} Fibonacci number.
5. Output, then repeat this process.

The Program(s)

The neat thing about the Fibonacci series is that there are a number of ways of converting the basic algorithm into its code representation.

The Naive Recursive Algorithm

The original formula lends itself to a natural example of binary recursion:

```
int fib_BinaryR(int n)
{
    if (n <= 2)
        return 1;
    else
        return fib_BinaryR(n-1) + fib_BinaryR(n-2);
}
```

This algorithm certainly generates the correct answer, but what is its computational cost—that is, how long does it take? If **n** is less than 2, the function halts almost immediately. However, for larger values of **n**, there are two recursive calls of **fib**. This implies that the running time of the algorithm grows at exponential time. Here is the Fibonacci call tree for calculating the fifth Fibonacci number, which just happens to be 5.

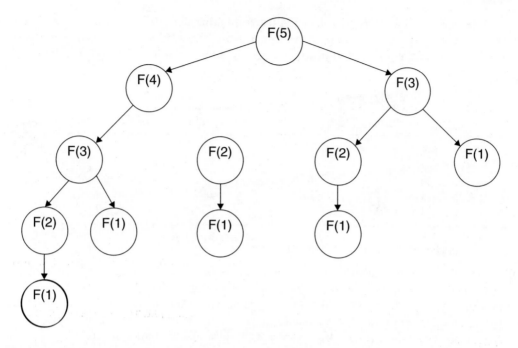

The biggest problem with using recursion to calculate the Fibonacci numbers is the time spent recalculating already calculated Fibonacci numbers. For example, when calculating F(40) using recursion, F(39) is calculated once, F(35) is calculated 8 times, and F(0) is calculated 165,580,141 times, for a total of 331,160,281 function calls. This is interesting considering that such an analysis is rarely made in textbooks, where Fibonacci numbers are often used as the first example of branched recursive functions. Very few textbooks discuss alternatives to binary recursion for Fibonacci. Indeed, the use of Fibonacci numbers to illustrate binary recursion is a good example of when *not* to use recursion. This is the simplest algorithm—and the most computationally expensive.

The Simple Recursive Algorithm

An alternative is to use simple linear recursion. Here the two previous Fibonacci numbers are stored as parameters to a recursive function.

```
int fib_LinearR(int a, int b, int n)
{
    if (n <= 2)
        return b;
    else
        return fib_LinearR(b,a+b,n-1);
}
```

The Fibonacci numbers are calculated using the function call: **fib(1,1,n)**. Note the two parameters **a** and **b**, which hold two successive Fibonacci numbers. This recursive version takes linear time. We tested each of these algorithms on a 2.8Mhz dual-core Pentium with 1GB of RAM.

	Binary Recursion		Linear Recursion	
	Function Calls	Time (sec)	Function Calls	Time (sec)
n = 3	3	0	2	0
n = 10	109	0	9	0
n = 20	13529	0.265	19	0
n = 25	150049	3.203	24	0
n = 30	1664079	36.909	29	0

Space Complexity: An Iterative Algorithm

The next most common algorithm makes allowances for the fact that efficiency isn't always the major protagonist in algorithm design. If an algorithm is slower, you can always run it longer and wait for the result. However, there is usually finite memory in which programs can run, so space becomes an issue in algorithm design. Consider the recursive process outlined previously. The space used by a recursive algorithm is the total space used by all recursive calls at a particular time. This includes space for variables, function arguments, and overhead space for each call.

An iterative algorithm incorporates some form of looping structure. Given the values of the first two Fibonacci numbers, a loop is used to calculate the (n-2) remaining numbers. Each step through the loop uses only the previous two values of F(n), which requires some swapping around of values so that everything stays in the appropriate places:

```
int fib_Iterative(int n)
{
    int i, f1=1, f2=1, f;
    for (i=3; i<=n; i=i+1){
        f = f1 + f2;
        f1 = f2;
        f2 = f;
    }
    return f;
}
```

The loop involves three actions. First, the first two Fibonacci numbers are added to form the next Fibonacci number in the sequence. Now the values are shifted forward one unit, so **f1** gets the value of **f2**, and **f2** gets the value of the newly calculated Fibonacci number. The one caveat with this approach is that there is no way of storing all the numbers.

An Algorithm Using Dynamic Programming

This approach uses an array to register previous results, rather than recomputing them. The added benefit here is that *all* Fibonacci numbers up until *n* are stored.

```c
int fib_Dynamic(int n)
{
    int i, f[n];
    f[0] = f[1] = 1;
    for (i=2; i<n; i=i+1)
        f[i] = f[i-1] + f[i-2];
    return f[n-1];
}
```

An Algorithm Using Matrices

This approach is somewhat of a mathematical trick with matrices:

$$\begin{bmatrix} 1 & 1 \\ 1 & 0 \end{bmatrix}^n = \begin{bmatrix} F(n+1) & F(n) \\ F(n) & F(n-1) \end{bmatrix}$$

This is what the code (which isn't that efficient) looks like:

```c
int fib_Matrix(int n)
{
    int i;
    int m[2][2] = {{1,1},{1,0}};
    int t[2][2];

    for (i=3; i<=n; i=i+1){
        t[0][0] = m[0][0];
        t[0][1] = m[0][1];
        t[1][0] = m[1][0];
        t[1][1] = m[1][1];
        m[0][0] = t[0][0] + t[0][1];
        m[0][1] = t[0][0];
        m[1][0] = t[1][0] + t[1][1];
        m[1][1] = t[1][0];
    }
    return m[0][0];
}
```

C isn't really geared to deal with matrix operations, so sometimes the code doesn't look that pretty.

An Algorithm Using Binet's Formula

There are, of course, certain algorithmic limitations to this conventional approach to calculating Fibonacci numbers. The nth Fibonacci number must be defined in terms of the two before it, so to calculate the 100th, you have to calculate the 99 numbers before it. Is there a formula that solves only the nth and does not need previous values? Yes, the formula is Binet's formula, which uses the golden section number:

$$Fib(n) = \frac{Phi^n - (1 - Phi)^n}{\sqrt{5}}$$

Here's the actual code:

```
double fib_Binet(int n)
{
    double phi;
    if (n<2)
        return 1;
    phi = (1.0+sqrt(5.0))/2.0;
    return (pow(phi,n)-pow(1-phi,n))/sqrt(5.0);
}
```

What About Large Fibonacci Numbers?

The one little problem with large Fibonacci numbers has to do with machine precision. Remember how we talked about really large numbers? On a Pentium D, using Pelles C, the maximum value of a **long long** is defined as:

9223372036854775807

If we try to calculate F_{100}, we get to F_{91} and F_{92} and we get:

4660046610375530309
7540113804746346429

which is fine, but if we now try to calculate F_{93}, we get:

−6246583658587674878

which means the numbers have wrapped around. Adding F_{91} and F_{92}, we get:

12200160415121876738

which is 2976788378267100931 larger than the largest integer it can hold. Now it wraps this around starting at the minimum integer which is −9223372036854775808, so now we get −6246583658587674878.

How do we calculate numbers larger than this F_{92}? We could use **double** or **unsigned long long,** but we will get have problems with the accuracy of calculations. Actually everything works fine until we hit F_{40} whose result is:

102334154.999999991559

Instead of 102334155. Subsequently, the errors just compound. But there is another, trickier way. We could store each of the Fibonacci numbers in a row of an integer array and process the rows. Read on.

Using Arrays to Calculate Large Fibonacci Numbers

Herein lies a good example of thinking outside the box. How do we solve this problem of calculating large Fibonacci numbers? Surely there is no point calculating them if the answers are incorrect. The answer may lie in the means of calculating them. Sure, one solution is finding a machine with 64-bit architecture and running the code there. But that doesn't solve the underlying problem. Then we start to realize that to calculate these large numbers, we have to remove the dependency on number representation. How do we do this? One way is to treat the numbers as a series of digits next to one another. We can store each of these digits as an element in an array. Once we have broken the large numbers into single-digit numbers, we can apply simple addition. For example, if we add the numbers 473 and 139, the first thing we would do is write the numbers one above the other as in the following figure.

First, we add the 3 and 9 = 12, which implies write the 2, carry the 1. Next we add 7+3 = 10, and add the carry, 10+1=11. Finally, 4+1 plus the carry 1 = 6. This approach produces efficient solutions that are easy to output.

Let's create a two-dimensional array, where rows are used to store successive Fibonacci numbers and the columns of each row are used to store the digits in each Fibonacci number. Let's say we want to calculate the first 30 Fibonacci numbers, and we allow 6 digits for the maximum number. So now we have a 20 array of size 30 × 6 elements. For example, the number 233, would be stored as:

0	0	0	2	3	3

The number is stored as the digits 2, 3, and 3, right-justified. The remaining elements of the number are set to zero. By seeding the array with the first two Fibonacci numbers, 1 and 1, we start an iterative process by which we calculate the next Fibonacci number by performing addition using the digits of the previous two Fibonacci numbers, similar to how you would do it on paper. So after eight iterations, our array looks like:

0	0	0	0	0	1
0	0	0	0	0	1
0	0	0	0	0	2
0	0	0	0	0	3
0	0	0	0	0	5
0	0	0	0	0	8
0	0	0	0	1	3
0	0	0	0	2	1

To calculate the ninth Fibonacci number works as follows. We add the digits in the last column of the array, in this case 3 + 1. Because this number is less than 10, we don't have to carry, so we can place the 3 in position [8,5]. Moving onto the previous column we now add 1 + 2, which again is less than 10, so we place it in position [8,4].

	c0	c1	c2	c3	c4	c5
r6	0	0	0	0	1	3
r7	0	0	0	0	2	1
r8	0	0	0	0	3	4

Now let's do a case where there is a carryover, calculating the 15th Fibonacci number. In the last column we get 3 + 7 = 10, so we place a 0 in element [14,5] and carry a 1. We move back a column and add 3 + 7 = 10 and 1 for the carryover, which equals 11. We now place a 1 in element [14,4] and carry a 1 again. Now we move back a column again to the last two digits and add 2 + 3 + 1(carry) = 6, which is placed in element [14,3].

r12	0	0	0	2	3	3
r13	0	0	0	3	7	7
r14	0	0	0	6	1	0

The same idea could be used to generate large factorials. Here's the code for the function:

```
void Fibonacci_P(int n)
{
    int fib[200][50];
    int i,j,k,r,s1,carry=0,sum,temp=0,t;

    // Initialise the 2D array to zero
    for (i=0; i<200; i=i+1)
        for (j=0; j<50; j=j+1)
            fib[i][j] = 0;

    // Set the first two Fibonacci numbers
    fib[0][49] = 1;
    fib[1][49] = 1;

    // Caculate the remaining Fibonacci numbers
    for (k=2; k<n; k=k+1){
        // Find the start of the last Fibonacci in the array
        r = 0;
        while (fib[k-1][r] == 0)
            r = r + 1;
        // Reset the carry variable
        carry = 0;
        // Starting from the left of the array,
        // sum the corresponding column elements
        // for two consecutive rows.
        for (s1=49; s1>=r; s1=s1-1){
            sum = (fib[k-1][s1] + fib[k-2][s1]) + carry;
            // If the sum is greater than or equal
            // to 10, calculate the carry and leftover.
            // For example 3+7=10, carry=1, sum=0 (leftover)
            if (sum >= 10){
                temp = sum % 10;
                carry = (sum - temp)/10;
                sum = temp;
                if (s1 == r)
                    r = r - 1;
            }
            else
                carry = 0;
            // Assign the sum to the appropriate
            // position in the array
            fib[k][s1] = sum;
        }
```

```
// Print the Fibonacci numbers
t = 0;
while (fib[k][t] == 0)
    t = t + 1;
// Print the Fibonacci sequence number
// (column width=4, left justified)
printf("%-4d", k+1);

// Print each of the elements in the row to
// create the Fibonacci number
for (j=t; j<50; j=j+1)
    printf("%d",fib[k][j]);
printf("\n");
    }
}
```

Testing the Program

We could test the program by checking the numbers produced against some sequence of Fibonacci numbers somewhere. However, there is another way to check if a number is a Fibonacci, using a simple test derived by Gessel in 1972.

> N is a Fibonacci number if and only if 5 N2 + 4 or 5 N2 −4 is a square number.

For example:

- 5 is a Fibonacci number since $5 \times 5^2 - 4$ is 121, which is 11^2
- 4 is not a Fibonacci number since neither $5 \times 4^2 + 4 = 84$ nor $5 \times 4^2 - 4 = 76$ are perfect squares.

Epilog

The Fibonacci numbers are directly related to another mathematical entity: the golden ratio, which is approximately 1.6180339887. It is usually denoted by the mathematical constant phi. Since the Renaissance, many artists and architects have proportioned their works to approximate the golden ratio—especially in the form of the golden rectangle, in which the ratio of the longer side to the shorter is the golden ratio—believing this proportion to be aesthetically pleasing. They are related in that if a Fibonacci number is divided by its immediate predecessor in the sequence, the quotient approximates phi, for example 987/610 = 1.6180327868852.

CS12

Sieve of Eratosthenes

Give me a lever long enough and a fulcrum on which to place it, and I shall move the world.

—Archimedes

The Problem Description

A prime number (or *prime*) is a natural number that has exactly two (distinct) natural number divisors, which are 1 and the prime number itself. Why are prime numbers important? Primarily because they are used as the basis for creating *public key cryptography* algorithms such as RSA (an encryption algorithm named after its three authors: Ron Rivest, Adi Shamir, and Leonard Adleman). One method of determining prime numbers is called the *Sieve of Eratosthenes,* named after the Greek mathematician, geographer, and astronomer Eratosthenes (276–196 BC). Eratosthenes lived in Alexandria and is noted for devising a system of latitude and longitude, and for being the first known to have computed the circumference of the Earth. The Sieve of Eratosthenes was first described in the work of Nichomachus of Gerasa (first century AD), entitled *Introductio Arithmeticae.* His method of finding primes is called a *sieve* because it is like taking all of the numbers (up to some maximum) and running them through a sieve to separate out all of the primes.

Program Requirements

A prime number (such as 2, 3, or 5) is a natural number (positive whole number) that is only divisible by itself and 1. The other natural numbers greater than 1, called *composite numbers,* are the products of prime numbers. The number one is neither prime nor composite.

To determine if a number is prime or composite and list its prime factors, we often have to experiment by dividing by primes from a list of primes. We divide by 2, 3, 5, etc. And if none of these divisions comes out even, then our number is a prime. Let's try 91, which looks like it might be a prime. We try 2, 3, 5, and those don't come out even. But, when we divide by 7, we get 13. So, $91 = 7 \times 13$ and is composite.

There is a fairly simple method for making a list of primes. We will start with a list of all of the numbers from 2 to 100:

```
 2  3  4  5  6  7  8  9 10
11 12 13 14 15 16 17 18 19 20
21 22 23 24 25 26 27 28 29 30
31 32 33 34 35 36 37 38 39 40
41 42 43 44 45 46 47 48 49 50
51 52 53 54 55 56 57 58 59 60
61 62 63 64 65 66 67 68 69 70
71 72 73 74 75 76 77 78 79 80
81 82 83 84 85 86 87 88 89 90
91 92 93 94 95 96 97 98 99 100
```

We now make 2 bold (you can circle it), identifying it as prime (it is not divisible by lesser primes), and set to zero every second number after 2:

```
 2  3  0  5  0  7  0  9  0
11  0 13  0 15  0 17  0 19  0
21  0 23  0 25  0 27  0 29  0
31  0 33  0 35  0 37  0 39  0
41  0 43  0 45  0 47  0 49  0
51  0 53  0 55  0 57  0 59  0
61  0 63  0 65  0 67  0 69  0
71  0 73  0 75  0 77  0 79  0
81  0 83  0 85  0 87  0 89  0
91  0 93  0 95  0 97  0 99  0
```

We have now identified 3 as a prime. It is not divisible by lesser primes. And we set to zero every third number after 3. Some of these are already set to zero. We will just skip over those:

```
 2  3  0  5  0  7  0  0  0
11  0 13  0  0  0 17  0 19  0
 0  0 23  0 25  0  0  0 29  0
31  0  0  0 35  0 37  0  0  0
41  0 43  0  0  0 47  0 49  0
 0  0 53  0 55  0  0  0 59  0
61  0  0  0 65  0 67  0  0  0
71  0 73  0  0  0 77  0 79  0
 0  0 83  0 85  0  0  0 89  0
91  0  0  0 95  0 97  0  0  0
```

We do the same thing with 5, and then 7:

```
 2   3  0  5  0   7  0   0  0
11  0 13  0  0  0 17  0 19  0
 0  0 23  0  0  0  0  0 29  0
31  0  0  0  0  0 37  0  0  0
41  0 43  0  0  0 47  0  0  0
 0  0 53  0  0  0  0  0 59  0
61  0  0  0  0  0 67  0  0  0
71  0 73  0  0  0  0  0 79  0
 0  0 83  0  0  0  0  0 89  0
 0  0  0  0  0  0 97  0  0  0
```

And now, we can stop! We may want to go on and try 11. But that is unnecessary. No more numbers will be crossed out, between 2 and 100. Do you see why?

We can stop at the square root of 100, which is 10. The reason for this is that any number less than 100 (91, for example), which is divisible by a number greater than the square root of 100 (13, in this example), is also divisible by a number less than the square root of 100 (7, in this example). So, we have already crossed out all such numbers.

Removing the zeros, we have this list of primes:

2 3 5 7 11 13 17 19 23 29 31 37 41 43 47 53 59 61 67 71 73
79 83 89 97

Program Specifications and Algorithm Design

Input(s): A number n, greater than 0

Output(s): A series of numbers representing all the primes from 2 to n

The algorithm is not exceedingly complex and can be solved using arrays. There are three preliminary steps:

1. Determine the highest factor to check for. This is the square root of the last number in the list, rounded down.
2. Create a list of primes, which starts empty.
3. Create a list of numbers that remain to be checked. It starts filled with all integers from 2 to the last number in your list.

This algorithm will produce all primes up to $n > 2$

1. List all integers 2, . . . , n
2. Let $a = 2$
3. Cross out all multiples of a except for a itself.
4. If all integers between a and n are crossed out, then stop. Otherwise, replace a with the next largest integer which has not been crossed out. If this new a is greater than `sqrt(n)` then stop.
5. Go to step 3.

The Program

```c
#include <stdio.h>
#include <math.h>

//    The Sieve of Eratosthenes
//    A program to calculate the prime numbers from 1 to N

void sieve(int N, int p[N])
{
    int i,j,k;

    // Set the upper limit to check for factors
    k = sqrt(N);

    // Mark all multiples of i by setting them to zero
    for (i = 2; i <= k; i++)
    {
        for (j = 0; j < N; j++)
            if (((p[j] % i) == 0) && (p[j] != i))
                p[j] = 0;
    }
}

void main(void)
{

    int i,N; // array counters

    printf("Enter the boundary to check for primes: ");
    scanf("%d", &N);

    // Array of integers, primes[0], . . . primes[N-1]
    int primes[N];

    // Initialize the array to the values 1->N
    for (i = 0; i < N; i++)
        primes[i] = i + 1;

    sieve(N, primes);

    // Print the unmarked entries of prime
    printf("Prime numbers from 1 to %d =\n", N);
    for (i = 1; i < N; i++)
        if (primes[i] != 0)
            printf("%d ", primes[i]);
}
```

Dissecting the Program

The first part of the solution actually involves setting up the main part of the program.

```
void main(void)
{
    int i, N; // array counters

    printf("Enter the boundary to check for primes: ");
    scanf("%d", &N);

    // Array of integers, primes[0], . . . primes[N–1]
    int primes[N];

    // Initialize the array to the values 1–>N
    for (i = 0; i < N; i++)
        primes[i] = i + 1;

    sieve(N, primes);

    // Print the unmarked entries of prime
    printf("Prime numbers from 1 to %d =\n", N);
    for (i = 1; i < N; i++)
        if (primes[i] != 0)
            printf("%d ", primes[i]);
}
```

Here we identify four variables local to the main program:

```
int i, N;
```

The first value is an index variable for the loop, the second stores the value of the upper limit of number to check for primes. Next we ask the user for the value of this latter variable.

```
printf("Enter the boundary to check for primes: ");
scanf("%d", &N);
```

Now we can actually create a variable-length array named **primes** of length N (a C99 construct):

```
int primes[N];
```

The next statement is a **for** loop that initializes the values in the array. We chose to set the array elements 0 to N–1 to the values 1 to N respectively.

```
for (i = 0; i < N; i++)
    primes[i] = i + 1;
```

We can now write the expression that will call our function:

```
sieve(N, primes);
```

Finally, we output the appropriate primes using a series of **printf** statements:

```
printf("Prime numbers from 1 to %d =\n", N);
for (i = 1; i < N; i++)
    if (primes[i] != 0)
        printf("%d ", primes[i]);
```

The loop cycles from 1 to N, ignoring the 0th element, 1 , which is not a prime number. It then checks every element of the array. If the element is not zero, then it represents a prime number and it is printed out.

Now that we have the main program complete, we can work on the function, using the prototype given:

```
void sieve(int N, int p[N])
{
    int i,j,k;

    // set the upper limit to check for factors
    k = sqrt(N);

    // mark all multiples of i by setting them to zero
    for (i = 2; i <= k; i++)
        for (j = 0; j < N; j++)
            if (((p[j] % i) == 0) && (p[j] != i))
                p[j] = 0;
}
```

Testing The Program

Testing the program is somewhat trivial because it only takes on input, N. So try testing it by using a small value of N, say 20. You should obtain the following results:

```
2  3  5  7  11  13  17  19
```

Now you could aim high, and try for 1,000:

```
2   3 5 7 11 13 17 19 23 29 31 37 41 43 47 53 59 61 67 71 73
79 83 89 97 101 103 107 109 113 127 131 137 139 149 151 157
163 167 173 179 181 191 193 197 199 211 223 227 229 233 239
241 251 257 263 269 271 277 281 283 293 307 311 313 317 331
337 347 349 353 359 367 373 379 383 389 397 401 409 419 421
431 433 439 443 449 457 461 463 467 479 487 491 499 503 509
521 523 541 547 557 563 569 571 577 587 593 599 601 607 613
617 619 631 641 643 647 653 659 661 673 677 683 691 701 709
719 727 733 739 743 751 757 761 769 773 787 797 809 811 821
823 827 829 839 853 857 859 863 877 881 883 887 907 911 919
929 937 941 947 953 967 971 977 983 991 997
```

Of course, you could also try some spurious input, say −100.

In Pelles C, this would probably result in the following error message:

```
Exception: Stack overflow
```

Not something you really want to happen. It's best to do a bit of defensive programming and add some code to the effect of:

```
if (N < 1){
    printf("Bounds less than 1 not allowed\n");
    exit(1);
}
```

Epilog

The successor to the Sieve of Eratosthenes is the *Sieve of Atkin,* a fast, modern algorithm for finding all prime numbers up to a specified integer. It is really just an optimized version of the Sieve of Eratosthenes.

Roman Numerals

Programming graphics in X is like finding the square root of Pi using Roman numerals.

—Henry Spencer

The Problem Description

The system of Roman numerals originated in ancient Rome, probably adapted from Etruscan numerals. They remained in common use until about the 14th century, when they were replaced by Arabic numerals It is based on seven basic symbols:

I or i = 1
V or v = 5
X or x = 10
L or l = 50
C or c = 100 (centum)
D or d =   500
M or m =   1,000 (mille)

One of the caveats of Roman notation is *subtractive notation*. Originally 4 was represented as IIII but in more modern times is represented as IV. Subtractive notation arose from regular Latin usage: The number 18 was *duodeviginti,* or "two [deducted] from twenty"; the number 19 was *undeviginti,* or "one [deducted] from twenty."

Program Requirements

In general, Roman numerals can be converted mathematically by simply assigning a numerical value to each letter, according to the following chart, and calculating the total:

Roman	M	D	C	L	X	V	I
Arabic	1,000	500	100	50	10	5	1

Although the historical practice has varied, the modern convention has been to arrange the letters from left to right in order of decreasing value; the total is then calculated by adding the numerical values of all the letters in the sequence. For example:

$$MDCLXVI = 1{,}000 + 500 + 100 + 50 + 10 + 5 + 1 = 1666$$

A well-known, but still often confusing feature of modern Roman numerals is the subtraction principle, which requires that a lower numeral appearing before a higher one be subtracted from the higher value, not added to the total. For example, IX is the Roman numeral for 9 (i.e., 10 – 1). For example:

$$MCMLXLVIII = 1{,}000\ 100\ 1{,}000\ 50\ 10\ 50\ 5\ 1\ 1\ 1$$
$$= 1{,}000 + (1{,}000 - 100) + 50 + (50 - 10) + 5 + 1 + 1 + 1$$
$$= 1{,}998$$

In the same way XIX represents the number 19 (X + IX, or 10 + 9) rather than 21, which is written as XXI (10 + 10 + 1). Likewise, the Roman numeral for the year 1995 is usually written as:

$$MCMXCV = M + CM + XC + V$$
$$= 1000 + 900 + 90 + 5$$
$$= 1995$$

Program Specification and Algorithm Design

Input(s): A number in Roman numeral format

Output(s): The Arabic numeral equivalent of the Roman numeral

Algorithm:

1. Use a variable, sum, to store the accumulated sum of the Roman numeral.
2. Compare the first two letters of the Roman numeral. Is the first letter less than the second letter, e.g. I < V?
   a. True:
      Subtract the value of the lesser letter from the value of the superior letter.
      Add the difference to the variable Sum.
      Delete the letters from the Roman numeral.
   b. False:
      Add the value of the first letter to Sum.
      Delete the first letter from the Roman numeral.
3. Are there letters left in the Roman numeral? If Yes, Repeat 2.
4. The final value of the variable Sum is the Arabic equivalent.

For example, let's convert R = XXXIV.

```
Sum = 0;
Loop 1:    X is equivalent to X
                Sum = Sum + 10 = 10
                R = XXIV
Loop 2:    X is equivalent to X
                Sum = Sum + 10 = 20
                R = XIV
Loop 3:    X is greater than I
                Sum = Sum + 10 = 30
                R = IV
Loop 4:    I is less than V
                Diff = V – I = 5 – 1 = 4
                Sum = Sum + 4 = 34
                R = empty
Arabic Numeral = 34
```

The Program

```c
#include <stdio.h>
#include <string.h>
#define N 50

int main(void)
{
    char Roman[N];
    int num[N], Arabic;
    int i, size;

    printf("Enter a Roman numeral: ");
    scanf("%s", Roman);

    size = strlen(Roman);

    for (i=0; i<size; i++)
        switch (Roman[i]){
            case 'i': ;
            case 'I': num[i] = 1;
                    break;
            case 'v': ;
            case 'V': num[i] = 5;
                    break;
            case 'x': ;
            case 'X': num[i] = 10;
                    break;
```

```
                  case 'l': ;
                  case 'L': num[i] = 50;
                            break;
                  case 'c': ;
                  case 'C': num[i] = 100;
                            break;
                  case 'd': ;
                  case 'D': num[i] = 500;
                            break;
                  case 'm': ;
                  case 'M': num[i] = 1000;
          }

      // Deal with Roman numeral subtraction
      // If x[i] < x[i+1], then subtract x[i] from
      // x[i+1] and set x[i] to 0

      for (i=0; i<size-1; i++)
      {
          if (num[i] < num[i+1])
          {
              num[i+1] = num[i+1]-num[i];
              num[i] = 0;
          }
      }

      Arabic = 0;
      // Add up all the numbers
      for (i=0; i<size; i++)
          Arabic = Arabic + num[i];

      printf("The Arabic equivalent of %s is %d\n", Roman, Arabic);

      return 0;

}
```

Dissecting the Program

The first part of the solution involves creating a string (character array) to hold the value of the roman numeral, as it is composed of the characters: i, v, x, l, c, d, m.

```
char Roman[N];
```

Also needed are an integer array to hold the integers corresponding to each Roman numeral, and a variable to hold the result.

```
int num[N], Arabic;
```

The value **N** denotes the size of the array and is defined as:

```
#define N 50
```

We also need a variable to store the size of the string and a loop index variable.

```
int i, size;
```

The next part involves prompting for the roman numeral and reading the correspon-ding string into the character array **Roman**.

```
printf("Enter a Roman numeral: ");
scanf("%s", Roman);
```

For traversing the character string, we will need to calculate the length of the Roman numeral.

```
size = strlen(roman);
```

The next step involves storing the integer equivalent of each Roman numeral in the array **num**. This is achieved using a **for** loop and a **switch** statement. The **for** loop cycles through each character in the string **Roman**, checks to see if it is a lowercase or uppercase Roman numeral, and stores the corresponding value from Table 1 in the array **num**.

```
for (i=0; i<size; i++)
    switch (Roman[i]){
        case 'i': ;
        case 'I': num[i] = 1;
                  break;
        case 'v': ;
        case 'V': num[i] = 5;
                  break;
        case 'x': ;
        case 'X': num[i] = 10;
                  break;
        case 'l': ;
        case 'L': num[i] = 50;
                  break;
        case 'c': ;
        case 'C': num[i] = 100;
                  break;
        case 'd': ;
        case 'D': num[i] = 500;
                  break;
        case 'm': ;
        case 'M': num[i] = 1000;
    }
```

Consider the following code segment:

```
switch (Roman[i]){
    case 'i': ;
    case 'I': num[i] = 1;
              break;
```

This basically says:

> If **Roman[i]** is an 'i' or an 'I', then set **num[i]** to the value 1.

The next step involves dealing with the subtraction principle. We solve this by iterating through the array **num** and searching for situations where **num[i] < num[i+1]**. When this occurs, we set **num[i+1] = num[i+1]−num[i]** and set **num[i] = 0**.

```
for (i=0; i<size-1; i++)
{
    if (num[i] < num[i+1])
    {
        num[i+1] = num[i+1]−num[i];
        num[i] = 0;

    }
}
```

The final step involves summing the values of **num** and storing the cumulative values in the variable **Arabic.**

```
Arabic = 0;

for (i=0; i<size; i++)
    Arabic = Arabic + num[i];

printf("The Arabic equivalent of %s is %d\n", Roman, Arabic);
```

Testing the Program

The program can be tested by trying a series of examples:

1,944	MCMXLIV
1,812	MDCCCXII
2,000	MM
39	XXXIX
3,547	MMMDXLVII

Being Defensive

This program works fine if the input is valid; however, if the string **xxg** is input, it produces the following output:

```
The decimal equivalent of xxg is 2012712965
```

This occurs because **g** is undefined as a Roman numeral, so when the conversion occurs in the array **num** we get the following values stored:

i	Roman[i]	num[i]	Arabic
0	x	10	0 + 10 = 10
1	x	10	10 + 10 = 20
2	g	?	20 + ? = 2012712965

The value of **num[2]** is a garbage number, which, when added to the 20 calculated previously, produces an incorrect output. This dilemma could be solved by including a function validates the Roman numeral as containing the correct characters.

```c
int isValid(char Roman[N])
{

    int i, size, Valid=1;
    size = strlen(Roman);

    for (i=0; i<size; i++)
        switch (Roman[i]){
            case 'i': ;
            case 'I': ;
            case 'v': ;
            case 'V': ;
            case 'x': ;
            case 'X': ;
            case 'l': ;
            case 'L': ;
            case 'c': ;
            case 'C': ;
            case 'd': ;
            case 'D': ;
            case 'm': ;
            case 'M': ;
                        break;
            default : Valid = 0;
        }
    return Valid;

}
```

The **for** loop iterates through each character in the string **Roman,** and if any of them is not a valid lowercase or uppercase Roman numeral, it sets the variable **Valid** to 0. This is called from the main program by including the following:

```
if (isValid(Roman))
{

    for (i=0; i<size; i++)
        switch (Roman[i]){
            case 'i': ;
            case 'I': num[i] = 1;
                      break;

    . . .

    printf("The decimal equivalent of %s is %d\n", Roman, Arabic);
}
else
    printf("Sorry, the Roman numeral is not valid\n");
```

Another way of writing the code in the **switch** statement is to use the string function **strstr.** By storing the valid characters in a string, we can use **strstr** to search the string to see if each element in the Roman numeral exists. If an element does not exist, then **strstr** returns NULL. The function would change to look like:

```
int isValid(char Roman[N])
{
    int i, size, Valid=1;
    char validRch[] = {"iIvVxXlLcCdDmM"};
    char *valptr, *Re=malloc(1);

    size = strlen(Roman);

    for (i=0; i<size; i++)
    {
        *Re = Roman[i];
        valptr = strstr(validRch, Re);
        if (valptr == NULL)
            Valid = 0;
    }

    return Valid;
}
```

The code *Re=malloc(1) actually creates a pointer to a char of size 1, to store the individual characters of the Roman numeral, using the expression *Re=Roman[i]. The function strstr returns the memory address where the character is found in the string validRch, or NULL if it does not exist. If any of the characters in the Roman numeral are not valid, the flag Valid is set to zero, otherwise it retains its entry value of 1.

Epilog

The notation of Roman numerals has varied over the past two millennia. Originally it was common to use IIII to represent 4 instead of IV. But in more modern times the subtractive notation has become the norm. What is more difficult is creating a system that performs Roman arithmetic.

Caesar Cipher

Two can keep a secret if one is dead.

—Anonymous

The Problem Description

Cryptography, derived from the Greek word κρυπτοσ meaning hidden, is the science of creating and decoding secret messages whose meaning cannot be understood by others who might intercept the message. In the language of cryptography, the message you are trying to send is called the *plaintext;* the message you actually send is called the *ciphertext.*

Program Requirements

Around 50 BC, Julius Caesar sent secret messages to Cicero using a scheme that is now known as a Caesar cipher. The Roman historian *Suetonius* described Caesar's encryption system in his work *De Vita Caesarum* (Life of Julius Caesar 56):

> "If he had anything confidential to say, he wrote it in cipher, that is, by so changing the order of the letters of the alphabet, that not a word could be made out. If anyone wishes to decipher these, and get at their meaning, he must substitute the fourth letter of the alphabet, namely D, for A, and so with the others.[1]

While Caesar's was the first recorded use of this scheme, other substitution ciphers are known to have been used earlier. Julius Caesar's nephew Augustus also used a cipher, but with a shift of one (Suetonius, *Life of Augustus 88*):

> "Whenever he wrote in cipher, he wrote B for A, C for B, and the rest of the letters on the same principle, using AA for X."

---

[1]Suetonius (C. AD 69–after 122), *De Vita Caesarum, Divus Iulius (The Lives of the Caesars, The Deified Julius)*, written C. AD 110.

Caesar used it with a shift of three to protect messages of military significance. Each letter is replaced by the letter k positions ahead of it in the alphabet (and you wrap around if needed). The table below gives the Caesar cipher when $k = 3$.

Original: A B C D E F G H I J K L M N O P Q R S T U V W X Y Z

Caesar: D E F G H I J K L M N O P Q R S T U V W X Y Z A B C

For example, Caesar's famous quote "Veni, vidi, vici," written in a report to Rome 47 BC after conquering Farnakes at Zela in Asia Minor in just five days ("I came, I saw, I conquered") would be converted to "yhql, ylgl, ylfl". The name of HAL, the computer in Arthur C. Clarke's *2001* is a one-step Caesar cipher of IBM.

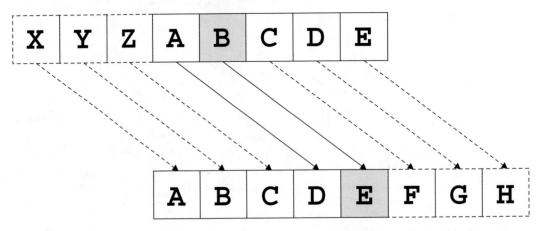

We can design a program that takes as input the offset parameter k and applies a Caesar cipher with shift $= k$ to a sequence of letters read from standard input. The encryption can be represented using *modular arithmetic* by first transforming the letters into numbers, according to the scheme, A = 0, B = 1, . . . , Z = 25. Encryption of a letter n by a shift k can be described mathematically as:

$$E(n) = (n + k) \bmod 26 \tag{1}$$

To decipher the text simply involves using the reverse equation:

$$D(n) = (n - k + 26) \bmod 26 \tag{2}$$

Program Specification

Input(s):   A character string, a choice of encoding/decoding, and an offset

Output(s): The encoded/decoded string

Modularity:1. Define a function **char2int** that converts a lowercase letter in the range a to z into a corresponding integer in the range 0 to 25.

2. Define a function that performs the inverse function to **char2int**, called **int2char**.

3. Define a function **encode** that encodes a string using a given shift factor. The shift factor in the range 0 to 25 to a lowercase letter in the range a to z. Characters such as white spaces, punctuation, and numbers should be returned unshifted.

4. Define a function **decode** that performs the inverse function to **encode**.

5. Define a function that converts any uppercase characters in a string to lowercase.

Algorithm Design

This program is composed of five separate functions in addition to the main program. The core algorithm is as follows:

1. Choose whether to (1) encode or (2) decode a string.

2. Input string representing the (1) plaintext or (2) ciphertext.

3. Convert the string completely to lowercase.

4. If the choice is encode, branch to the function **encode**.

5. If the choice is decode, branch to the function **decode**.

6. Output the string representing the (1) ciphertext or (2) plaintext.

Function: **string2lower**

1. Input a string.

2. Check each character of the string. If the character is in uppercase, convert it to lowercase.

3. Return the lowercase string.

Function: **char2int**

1. Input a character.

2. Calculate the integer equivalent in the range 0 to 25. The ASCII value of a is 97, so subtract 97 from the character.

3. Return the integer equivalent.

Function: **int2char**

1. Input an integer.

2. Calculate the character equivalent in the range a to z. The ASCII value of a is 97, so add 97 from the integer value of 0 to 25.

3. Return the character equivalent.

Function: encode

1. Input a plaintext string.
2. Calculate the length of the string.
3. For every element in the string:
   a. Calculate the index for the element using the function **char2int**.
   b. Calculate the shift using Eq. 1.
   c. Place the new character in the ciphertext string using the function **int2char**.
4. Output the ciphertext string.

Function: decode

1. Input a ciphertext string.
2. Calculate the length of the string.
3. For every element in the string:
   a. Calculate the index for the element using the function **char2int**.
   b. Calculate the shift using Eq. 2.
   c. Place the new character in the plaintext string using the function **int2char**.
4. Output the plaintext string.

The Program

```c
#include <stdio.h>
#include <ctype.h>
#include <string.h>

int char2int(char c)
{
    return (c - 97);
}

char int2char(int d)
{
    return (d + 97);
}

void encode(char *plainT, char *cipherT, int offset)
{
    int i, L, shift, n;

    L = strlen(plainT);
    for (i=0; i<L; i=i+1)
        if (!isspace(plainT[i]))
        {
```

```c
            n = char2int(plainT[i]);
            shift = (n + offset) % 26;
            cipherT[i] = int2char(shift);
        }
        else
            cipherT[i] = plainT[i];
    cipherT[L] = '\0';

}

void decode(char *cipherT, char *plainT, int offset)
{
    int i, L, shift, n;

    L = strlen(cipherT);
    for (i=0; i<L; i=i+1)
        if (!isspace(cipherT[i]))
        {
            n = char2int(cipherT[i]);
            shift = (n - offset + 26) % 26;
            plainT[i] = int2char(shift);
        }
        else
            plainT[i] = cipherT[i];
    plainT[L] = '\0';
}

void string2lower(char *s)
{

    int i, L;

    L = strlen(s);

    for (i=0; i<L; i=i+1)
        if (isupper(s[i]))
            s[i] = tolower(s[i]);

}

int main(void)
{

    char plainT[40], cipherT[40], trash;
    int offset, code;

    printf("Caesar Cipher\n\n");
    printf("(1) encode or (2) decode? ");
    scanf("%d", &code);
    scanf("%c", &trash);
```

```
    if (code == 1)
    {
        printf("Enter a plaintext string: ");
        fgets(plainT,40,stdin);
        string2lower(plainT);
    }
    else if (code == 2)
    {
        printf("Enter a ciphertext string: ");
        fgets(cipherT,40,stdin);
        string2lower(cipherT);
    }
    printf("Enter an offset: ");
    scanf("%d", &offset);

    if (code == 1)
    {
        encode(plainT,cipherT,offset);
        printf("The ciphertext is: %s\n", cipherT);
    }
    else if (code == 2)
    {
        decode(cipherT,plainT,offset);
        printf("The plaintext is: %s\n", plainT);
    }

    return 0;
}
```

Dissecting the Program

This is a long program compared to some we have developed, just shy of 100 LOC. It's probably best to look at the **main** part first and then deal with each of the functions. The first portion of code declares each of the variables used. In this case we have two strings to hold each of the plaintext and ciphertext. We also use a variable **trash** to deal with buffered characters when using **scanf**, and an integer variable, **offset**, to hold the numerical offset of the cipher:

```
char plainT[40], cipherT[40], trash;
int offset, code;
```

Now we can prompt users for some input regarding their choice of encoding or decoding. Note here that the code is read, and then the return character is read into **trash**, clearing all buffered input.

```
printf("Ceasar Cipher\n\n");
printf("(1) encode or (2) decode? ");
scanf("%d", &code);
scanf("%c", &trash);
```

The next portion of code reads in the string and stores it in the appropriate variable depending on whether the user selected encoding or decoding. In each case it prompts the user for a string, reads in the string using **fgets,** and converts the string to lowercase using the function **string2lower.**

```
if (code == 1)
{

    printf("Enter a plaintext string: ");
    fgets(plainT,40,stdin);
    string2lower(plainT);

}
else if (code == 2)
{

    printf("Enter a ciphertext string: ");
    fgets(cipherT,40,stdin);
    string2lower(cipherT);

}
```

The function **string2lower** just passes through the string using a **for** loop and checks each element of the string. If it is an uppercase character, it converts it to lowercase. Now we prompt the user for the offset value:

```
printf("Enter an offset: ");
scanf("%d", &offset);
```

Next we process the string, based again on the user-selected option:

```
if (code == 1)
{

    encode(plainT,cipherT,offset);
    printf("The ciphertext is: %s\n", cipherT);

}
else if (code == 2)
{

    decode(cipherT,plainT,offset);
    printf("The plaintext is: %s\n", plainT);

}
```

The first function, **encode**, deals with encoding a string. It has three parameters: the plaintext string, an empty string to store the ciphertext string, and the offset value.

```
void encode(char *plainT, char *cipherT, int offset)
{

}
```

Aside from the variable declarations, the first line of the function body deals with calculating the length of the string.

```
L = strlen(plainT);
```

We then use this value to cycle through the string using a **for** loop:

```
for (i=0; i<L; i=i+1)
```

The body of the loop consists of an **if-else** statement of the form:

```
if (!isspace(plainT[i]))
{
    n = char2int(plainT[i]);
    shift = (n + offset) % 26;
    cipherT[i] = int2char(shift);
}
else
    cipherT[i] = plainT[i];
```

It first checks to see if the element of the string is not a space. If it isn't a space, then it passes the character to the function **char2int**, which associates a value in the range 0 to 25 with the character by finding its ASCII code and subtracting 97. We then calculate the proper shift value using Eq. 1, use the function **int2char** to convert back to an ASCII value, and store it in the ciphertext string **cipherT**. It achieves this by adding 97 to the value between 0 and 25. If the string element is a space, it just copies the space into **cipherT**. At the end of the string, it terminates **cipherT** in the proper manner:

```
cipherT[L] = '\0';
```

The function **decode** works in an analogous manner, converting the ciphertext into plaintext.

```
void decode(char *cipherT, char *plainT, int offset)
```

The only real difference is that the equation changes to decode the ciphertext using the given offset and Eq. 2:

```
shift = (n - offset + 26) % 26;
```

Testing the Program

We can easily test the program by encoding a plaintext message and then decoding the ciphertext produced. We can check manually if the offset has been performed correctly. We may also want to test a series of inputs:

- A plaintext string with both upper and lowercase characters
- A plaintext string with white spaces and punctuation
- A plaintext string with numeric characters

Here's a sample run of the program:

```
Ceasar Cipher

(1) encode or (2) decode? 1
Enter a plaintext string: code monkey
Enter an offset: 7
The ciphertext is: jvkl tvurlf
```

Enhancing the Program

There are many ways in which this program might be enhanced. For example, we might like to encode numeric digits found in the program as uppercase characters. So using the following shift (digit + 16):

0	1	2	3	4	5	6	7	8	9
A	B	C	D	E	F	G	H	I	J

We could make the ciphertext even more cryptic by stripping out all white spaces and punctuation. "The quick brown fox jumped over the lazy dog" would become:

```
thequickbrownfoxjumpedoverthelazydog
```

which is then encoded. This can be achieved by using the following function:

```
void strip_string(char *s, char *r)
{
    int i, j, L;
    j = 0;
    L = strlen(s);

    for (i=0; i<L; i=i+1)
        if (isalpha(s[i]))
        {
            r[j] = s[i];
            j = j + 1;
        }
    r[j] = '\0';

}
```

This function has two parameters: an input string, **s**, containing the string with spaces, and an output string, **r**, containing the string with spaces stripped. The code uses a **for** loop to pass through the array. It only copies alphanumeric characters to the output string, thereby bypassing any spaces. The full program for this variant can be found in Appendix F.

Epilog

Although this cipher system seems simple, the code was never broken by Caesar's enemies and served as a very secure form of communication. Today the science of cryptography is highly sophisticated, and simple codes such as the Caesar Cipher can be broken quickly and easily. The Caesar Cipher has a major weakness. Once you determine the codes for one letter, the codes for every other letter are also known. To top that off, deciphering a message is somewhat straightforward: just try each of the 26 possible shifts of the alphabet and see which makes the most sense. The other weakness is that every letter in the text is encoded each time by the same letter in the cipher alphabet. A Caesar shift of 13 is performed in the *ROT13* algorithm, a simple method of obfuscating text used in some Internet forums to obscure text, but it is not used as a method of encryption.

CS15

Compound Interest

I'm spending the year dead for tax reasons.
—Douglas Adams

The Problem Description

The idea of compound interest arises when interest is added to the principal, so that from that moment on, the interest that has been added also earns interest. The process of adding interest to the principal is called *compounding*. An investment of $1000, for example, with an interest rate of 0.85 percent per month would have a balance of $1008.50 after the first month, $1017.07 after the second month, and so on.

Program Requirements

The exact formula for compound interest is

$$A_t = A_0 \left(1 + \frac{r}{n} \right)^{nt} \tag{1}$$

where

A_t = amount at time t (compounding amount)
A_0 = amount at time 0 (principal amount)
t = time in years
r = interest rate
n = number of compounding periods per year

However, the interest can also be calculated for each period using the following formula:

$$I_t = A_t r \left(\frac{1.0}{n} \right) \tag{2}$$

$$A_{t+1} = A_t + I_t \tag{3}$$

where I_t is the interest calculated. The assumption is made that the interest is calculated per annum. This iterative formula allows us to see what happens at each step.

Program Specification

Input(s):   Principal amount   (>$0.0)
              Interest rate   (0.0–100.0)
              Number of years   (>0)
              Number of compounding periods per year   (>0)

Output(s):   Cumulative values for the compound interest at each period.

Algorithm Design

1. Obtain input for the principal amount.
2. Obtain input for the interest rate.
3. Obtain input for the number of years.
4. Obtain input for the number of periods per year.
5. Convert the interest rate to a value between 0.0 and 1.0.
6. Calculate the total number of periods.
7. Calculate the compound interest and compounded value of the principal for each period, and output to the user.

   Step 5 requires the input interest rate to be divided by 100.0, such that an input value of 5.0 would be converted to 0.05. Step 6 involves multiplying the number of years times the number of periods per year. Finally, Step 7 involves the use of a looping structure that iterates the total number of periods, performing the calculations in Eqs. 2 and 3 each time and outputting the calculated value.

The Program

```
#include <stdio.h>
#include <math.h>

int main(void)
{
    double prinAmt, cmpdAmt, intRate, interest;
    int Nyears, Pyears, i, Nc;

    printf("Enter the principal amount (>$0.0): ");
    scanf("%lf", &prinAmt);
    printf("Enter the interest rate (0.0-100.0): ");
```

```
scanf("%lf", &intRate);
printf("Enter the number of years (>0): ");
scanf("%d", &Nyears);
printf("Enter the number of periods per year (>0): ");
scanf("%d", &Pyears);

intRate = intRate / 100.0;

Nc = Nyears * Pyears;

cmpdAmt = prinAmt;

printf("Compound Interest calculated: \n");
for (i=1; i<=Nc; i=i+1)
{
    interest = (cmpdAmt * intRate * (1.0/Pyears));
    cmpdAmt = cmpdAmt + interest;
    printf("Period %3d = $%.2f\n", i, cmpdAmt);
}

return 0;
}
```

Code Walkthrough

This problem has three main parts to the algorithm:

1. Obtain the input.
2. Calculate the compound-based formula.
3. Output the result obtained.

The next part of deriving a solution is identifying the type of data involved. Is it whole numbers or floating-point numbers? We essentially have four pieces of data as input:

1. Principal amount
2. Interest rate
3. Time period in years
4. Number of compounding periods per year

Chances are that most of this data involves fractional numbers, so we will create the first two pieces of data as variables of type **double**, and the last two as integers. Now we have to think up some good names:

1. Principal amount: **prinAmt**
2. Interest rate: **intRate**
3. Time period in years: **Nyears**
4. Number of compounding periods per year: **Pyears**

In addition, we need variables to store the intermittent values of the interest and compounded value, as well as a variable for controlling the loop, and a value for the total number of periods.

1. Compounding amount: **cmpdAmt**
2. Interest calculated: **interest**
3. Loop control variable: **i**
4. Total number of periods: **Nc**

We can now declare these in the program skeleton:

```c
#include <stdio.h>
#include <math.h>

int main(void)
{
    double prinAmt, cmpdAmt, intRate, interest;
    int Nyears, Pyears, i, Nc;

    return 0;
}
```

The first part of the program is no different from any program we have written so far. We are basically going to deal with program input. This should be self-explanatory.

```c
printf("Enter the principal amount (>$0.0): ");
scanf("%lf", &prinAmt);
printf("Enter the interest rate (0.0-100.0): ");
scanf("%lf", &intRate);
printf("Enter the number of years (>0): ");
scanf("%d", &Nyears);
printf("Enter the number of periods per year (>0): ");
scanf("%d", &Pyears);
```

Notice that we have specified ranges of values for each input to make it clearer to the user. Now we can perform some calculations prior to performing the compounding calculations. First, because we have specified the interest rate as a value in the range 0.0–100.0, we have to convert this to a value in the range 0.0–1.0. The range 0.0–100.0 is chosen because of the use of terms such as 4.37 percent in banking, rather than 0.0437.

```c
intRate = intRate / 100.0;
```

Next, we have to calculate the total number of periods, which is simply a product of the number of years and the number of periods per year:

```
Nc = Nyears * Pyears;
```

Finally, we initialize the value of the compounding amount to the principal:

```
cmpdAmt = prinAmt;
```

Now we can set up a loop that iterates **Nc** times, once for each period. The loop variable is initialized to 1 and iterates through every value up to and including **Nc**:

```
for (i=1; i<=Nc; i=i+1)
{

}
```

The body of the loop essentially performs the compounding interest calculations. Eq. 2 becomes

```
interest = (cmpdAmt * intRate * (1.0/Pyears));
```

whereas Eq. 3 becomes

```
cmpdAmt = cmpdAmt + interest;
```

Incorporated into the loop, and with the addition of a **printf** statement to output the compounded amount for every period, the loop looks like this:

```
printf("Compound Interest calculated: \n");
for (i=1; i<=Nc; i=i+1)
{
    interest = (cmpdAmt * intRate * (1.0/Pyears));
    cmpdAmt = cmpdAmt + interest;
    printf("Period %3d = $%.2f\n", i, cmpdAmt);
}
```

Testing the Program

Calculate the compound interest for $1000.00 over a 12-month period, with an interest rate of 5 percent. The program will run as follows:

```
Enter the principal amount (>$0.0): 1000.0
Enter the interest rate (0.0-100.0): 5.0
Enter the number of years (>0): 1
Enter the number of periods per year (>0): 12
Compound Interest calculated:
Period   1 = $1004.17
Period   2 = $1008.35
Period   3 = $1012.55
Period   4 = $1016.77
Period   5 = $1021.01
Period   6 = $1025.26
```

```
Period    7 = $1029.53
Period    8 = $1033.82
Period    9 = $1038.13
Period   10 = $1042.46
Period   11 = $1046.80
Period   12 = $1051.16
```

Defensive Programming

If we were to add defensive programming, it would be based on the correctness of the principal amount (>$0), interest rate (0–100 percent), number of years (>1), and number of periods per year (>1). For checking the principal amount, we could use a **do-while** loop to loop until such time as the value input is greater than 0.0:

```
do {
            printf("Enter the principal amount (>$0.0): ");
            scanf("%lf", &prinAmt);
} while (prinAmt <= 0.0);
```

We could make it more user-friendly by providing more feedback:

```
int valid=0;
do {
    printf("Enter the principal amount (>$0.0): ");
    scanf("%lf", &prinAmt);
    if (prinAmt <= 0.0)
        printf("Values should be greater than $0.0\n");
    else
        valid = 1;
} while (valid == 0);
```

This uses a variable **valid** to maintain a value of 1 (true) or 0 (false). If the principal amount is less than $0.0, then the message is printed, and the user asked to re-input the amount. If not valid, the value of the variable **valid** does not change. If the amount is greater than zero, the value of **valid** is changed to 1; when the loop checks this value, the expression **valid == 0** will become false, and the loop will exit.

Improving Efficiency

This is one of those situations in which improvements can be made to the program's efficiency, albeit small ones. The major improvement involves streamlining the loop, that is, removing the expression **(1.0/Pyears)** from the loop. Why? Mainly because its value doesn't change throughout the loop iterations; so instead of the calculation being performed Nc times in the loop, it can be removed and calculated only once. We'll need another variable for this:

```
double perA

perA = 1.0 / Pyears;

for (i=1; i<=Nc; i=i+1)
{
    interest = (cmpdAmt * intRate * perA);
    cmpdAmt = cmpdAmt + interest;
    printf("Period %3d = $%.2f\n", i, cmpdAmt);
```

In fact, both equations could probably be folded into one, reducing the need for the variable **interest**, which is somewhat redundant:

```
double perA

perA = 1.0 / Pyears;

for (i=1; i<=Nc; i=i+1)
{
    cmpdAmt = cmpdAmt + (cmpdAmt * intRate * perA);
    printf("Period %3d = $%.2f\n", i, cmpdAmt);
}
```

Identifying the Age of a Tree

The possible solutions to a given problem emerge as the leaves of a tree, each node representing a point of deliberation and decision.

—Niklaus Wirth

The Problem Description

Dendrochronology, or tree-ring dating, is the method of *historical dating* based on the analysis of tree-ring growth patterns. Many trees in temperate zones grow one growth ring each year, with the newest ring under the bark. For the entire period of a tree's life, a year-by-year record or ring pattern forms that reflects the climatic conditions in which the tree grew. Adequate moisture and a long growing season result in a wide ring. A drought year may result in a very narrow one.

Program Requirements

How do we estimate the age of a tree, without cutting it down to count its rings? If we know the circumference of a tree (in inches), we can calculate its diameter:

$$diameter = \frac{circumference}{\pi} \tag{1}$$

We can now calculate the age of a particular tree using the formula

$$age = diameter \times growth\ factor \tag{2}$$

and information on growth factors from the following table:

Tree Species	Growth Factor	Tree Species	Growth Factor
Red Maple	4.5	White Oak	5.0
Silver Maple	3.0	Red Oak	4.0
Sugar Maple	5.0	Basswood	3.0
White Birch	5.0	Ironwood	7.0
Black Walnut	4.5	Cottonwood	2.0
Black Cherry	5.0	Dogwood	7.0

Program Specification and Algorithm Design

Input(s):   The circumference of the tree and the tree species

Output(s):   A value representing the age of the tree in years

Algorithm:

1. Prompt the user for the species of tree.
2. Prompt the user for the circumference of the tree (in inches).
3. Calculate the diameter of the tree using Eq. 1.
4. Calculate the approximation of age using Eq. 2.
5. Output the tree age.

The Program

```c
#include <stdio.h>
#include <string.h>
#include <stdlib.h>

#define PI 3.14159

int main(void)
{
    char tree[12][13] = {"Red Maple", "Silver Maple",
                "Sugar Maple", "White Birch",
                "Black Walnut", "Black Cherry",
                "White Oak", "Red Oak",
                "Basswood", "Ironwood",
                "Cottonwood", "Dogwood"};
```

```
double growthF[] = {4.5, 3.0, 5.0, 5.0, 4.5, 5.0, 5.0,
                    4.0, 3.0, 7.0, 2.0, 7.0};

char species[20];
double circ, diameter, treeAge;
int i, T, found=0;

printf("Enter the tree species: ");
fgets(species,20,stdin);
species[strlen(species)-1]='\0';

// Identify the growth factor for the tree
i = 0;
while (found == 0 && i<12)
{
    if (strcmp(species,tree[i]) == 0){
        T = i;
        found = 1;
    }
    i = i + 1;
}

if (!found){
    printf("Sorry the species does not exist.\n");
    exit(0);
}

printf("Enter the tree circumference (inches): ");
scanf("%lf", &circ);

// Calculate the tree diameter
diameter = circ / PI;

// Calculate the age of the tree
treeAge = diameter * growthF[T];

printf("The age of the %s tree is %.2f years\n", tree[T],
        treeAge);

return 0;
}
```

Dissecting the Program

The first thing we will deal with in this program is storing the table in some sort of structure. The structure that makes the most sense is an array. The table contains two types of data: a string representing the name of the tree species and a number representing the growth factor. This requires the declaration of two separate arrays: a character array and a floating point array. The first of these is the character array:

```
char tree[12][13] = {"Red Maple", "Silver Maple",
                     "Sugar Maple", "White Birch",
                     "Black Walnut", "Black Cherry",
                     "White Oak", "Red Oak",
                     "Basswood", "Ironwood",
                     "Cottonwood", "Dogwood"};
```

Note here that we have declared a two-dimensional string, essentially a string containing 12 strings, each 13 characters in length. The next array is a 1D array of type **double**:

```
double growthF[] = {4.5, 3.0, 5.0, 5.0, 4.5, 5.0, 5.0, 4.0,
                    3.0, 7.0, 2.0, 7.0};
```

The indices should match, so that **tree[0]** is "Red Maple," and **growthF[0]** is its corresponding growth factor, 4.5. Next we need a string to hold the species entered by the user:

```
char species[20];
```

We also have another user input in the form of the tree circumference and two calculated values representing the tree diameter and age:

```
double circ, diameter, treeAge;
```

We need a few ancillary variables, but we will declare them later. Just leave a space. Now we will deal with the input of the tree species:

```
printf("Enter the tree species: ");
fgets(species,13,stdin);
```

Note that we have used the **fgets** function here instead of the normal **scanf ("%s", species)**. This is because **scanf** will only read up until a space is encountered, and many of the tree species actually have two parts to their names. The **fgets** will read everything up until enter is input. Now we have to strip the return key from the string.

```
species[strlen(species)-1]='\0';
```

This statement replaces the return key character with the end-of-string character. Next we have to search the 2D string **tree** to make sure the species exists:

```
i = 0;
while (found == 0 && i<12)
{
    if (strcmp(species,tree[i]) == 0){
        T = i;
        found = 1;
    }
    i = i + 1;
}
```

This is the basis for a simple search algorithm, assuming that the list is by no means in any sort of order. Basically we use a loop to cycle through each of the "row" strings within **tree**. For each string, pass it to the function **strcmp** as well as the string input by the user. **strcmp** will compare the two and return a value of 0 if they match. If a match is found, the variable **T** is set to the value of the index of the matching string, and **found** is set to 1. If no match occurs, the index **i** is incremented. The entire cycle is controlled by a **while** loop that continues while both **found** is 0 AND i has a value less than 12. If we leave out the latter part of this expression (i<12), then the loop will become infinite if the user types a species that is not included in the program. Next we actually deal with the fact that a user may enter a species that does not exist in the database:

```
if (!found){
    printf("Sorry the species does not exist.\n");
    exit(0);
}
```

This basically says if **found** is false, output a message to the user and exit the program. We could have made it more user friendly and actually included a key with the list of trees available, or a menu, but we will leave this as an exercise for the reader. In the last **while** we have used two functions that need to have their respective libraries included: **strcmp** and **exit**.

```
#include <string.h>
#include <stdlib.h>
```

If the species match, we can allow the user to enter the circumference of the tree.

```
printf("Enter the tree circumference (inches): ");
scanf("%lf", &circ);
```

We can now deal with the actual calculations:

```
diameter = circ / PI;

treeAge = diameter * growthF[T];
```

From these statements we know that we need a value for **PI**, defined as:

```
#define PI 3.14159
```

Note that in the calculation for **treeAge**, we now use the index **T** to identify the appropriate growth factor to use. The last thing to do is actually output the result:

```
printf("The age of the %s tree is %.2f years\n", tree[T],
        treeAge);
```

As usual, the actual calculation of the values took up very little time from a coding point of view.

Testing the Program

Here's a test run of the program:

```
Enter the tree species: Black Cherry
Enter the tree circumference (inches): 2.4
The age of the Black Cherry tree is 3.82 years
```

Coding Improvements

We could allow the input of the tree species to become cyclic, so that if the user gets it wrong, the program allows the tree species to be reentered.

```
do {
    printf("Enter the tree species: ");
    gets(species);

    i = 0;
    while (found == 0 && i<12)
    {
        if (strcmp(species,tree[i]) == 0){
            T = i;
            found = 1;
        }
        i = i + 1;

    }

    if (!found)
        printf("Sorry the species does not exist.\n");

} while (found == 0);
```

Here we have just encapsulated the code that reads the tree species and searches the database within a **do-while** loop. We could also have used an infinite **while** loop or some other construct. Now the loop continues to iterate until **found** becomes true (1). We might also like to deal with the problem of when a user enters "**black cherry**" instead of "**Black Cherry.**" The difference is subtle, but not enough to throw them out of the program or make them reenter it. The easiest way of doing this is first to change the elements of the string **tree** to lowercase:

```
char tree[12][13] = {"red maple", "silver maple",
                "sugar maple", "white birch",
                "black walnut", "black cherry",
                "white oak", "red oak",
                "basswood", "ironwood",
                "cottonwood", "dogwood"};
```

Next convert the user input to lowercase before checking to see if it is valid. We can achieve this using a function called **to_lowercase**:

```
void to_lowercase(char species[20])
{
    int i, L;
    L = strlen(species);
    for (i=0; i<L; i=i+1)
        if (isupper(species[i]))
            species[i] = tolower(species[i]);
}
```

This function basically calculates the length of the string using the function **strlen**, then cycles through each of the elements in the array **species**. At each element it checks to see if the character is an uppercase character using the function **isupper**. If it is, then it converts it to lowercase using the function **tolower**. The result is a lowercase string. The function is called just after the user enters the string:

```
to_lowercase(species);
```

Remember to include the **ctype.h** library, or **isupper** and **tolower** won't work.

Epilog

Did you know there are an estimated 100 billion board feet of lumber underwater? These submerged trees exist due to forests that were flooded years ago to make way for hydro-electric dams.

A Global Positioning System

Logic is the beginning of wisdom; not the end.

—Spock

The Problem Description

The global positioning system (GPS) is a constellation of satellites that orbit the Earth, transmitting precise time and position information. With a GPS receiver, users can determine their location anywhere on Earth. Global positioning systems often use latitude-longitude to represent a position on the surface of the Earth. The system is based on similar ground-based radio navigation systems, such as LORAN ((Long-range Radio Aid to Navigation), developed in the early 1940s and used during World War II. After several experimental satellite navigation systems, the first GPS satellite was launched in February 1978. By 1994 a complete constellation of 24 satellites was in orbit. The Galileo Positioning System is a satellite navigation system being developed by the European Union as an alternative to GPS. The GPS has many uses, including providing timing information (each satellite carries multiple atomic clocks) and tracking and forecasting the movement of freight, air traffic management, agriculture, transportation, and recreation. For example, companies use GPS to time-stamp business transactions, providing a consistent and accurate way to maintain records and ensure their traceability.

Program Requirements

On the earth, lines of *latitude* are circles of different size. The longest is the equator, whose latitude is zero, while at the poles—at latitudes 90° north and 90° south—the circles shrink to a point. On the globe, lines of constant *longitude* ("meridians") extend from pole to pole. For historical reasons, the meridian passing the old Royal Astronomical Observatory in Greenwich, England, is the one chosen as zero longitude. There are 360 degrees of longitude; 180 degrees are labeled west and the remaining 180 degrees are labeled east. Latitude and longitude are represented in the following **DMS** format:

AAA **Degrees,** BB **Minutes,** CC **Seconds, DIRECTION**

For example:

```
The position of Montalcino, Italy, is 43 degrees 03 minutes
North and 11 degrees 29 minutes East
```

The first step is to convert the measurements of latitude and longitude into a more usable form: Since there are 60 seconds in a minute and 60 minutes in a degree, the number of decimal degrees (DD) is given by:

$$
\begin{aligned}
D &= AAA \\
M.s &= BB + (CC/60) \\
d &= M.s/60 \\
DD &= D + d
\end{aligned}
\tag{1}
$$

The latitude and longitude coordinates can be expressed in spherical coordinates:

$$(r, f, q)$$

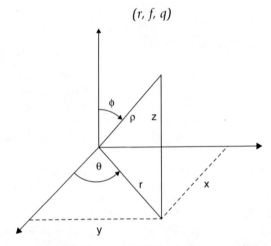

The first of these coordinates, rho, denotes the distance from the origin, in this case the average radius[1] of the earth $\rho = 6{,}367$ (km). The second coordinate, phi, is very similar to the latitude; it measures the angle ϕ from the north pole.

$$\phi \tag{2}$$

The third coordinate, theta, measures the angle θ starting at the prime meridian (longitude 0) and moving east.

$$\theta \tag{3}$$

---

[1]average radius = (Equatorial_radius + Polar_radius)/2

Both ϕ and θ, as described previously, are normally measured in degrees. It is better to express the angles in radians. The conversion formula is:

$$\angle radians = \frac{\angle degrees \times 2\pi}{360} \tag{4}$$

To express the location of a point in Cartesian coordinates with the origin at the center of the Earth, the conversion formulas are:

$$x = \rho \cos\theta \sin\phi$$
$$y = \rho \sin\theta \sin\phi \tag{5}$$
$$z = \rho \cos\phi$$

For example:

A = 35 degrees 17.299 minutes North and 120 degrees 39.174 minutes West
B = 46 degrees 36.003 minutes North and 112 degrees 02.330 minutes West

	A	B
x=	−2650	−1641
y=	−4471	−4055
z=	3678	4626

The distance between these two points (the straight line distance through the Earth) is 1,446 km and can be calculated using the formula:

$$d = \sqrt{(x_B - x_A)^2 + (y_B - y_A)^2 + (z_B - z_A)^2} \tag{6}$$

The distance along the surface of the Earth (great circle distance) can be calculated from the straight line distance:

$$surface\_distance = 2\rho \sin^{-1}\left(\frac{straight\_line\_distance}{2\rho}\right) \tag{7}$$

Program Specification

The program should calculate the surface distance between two points given two GPS coordinates in *degree-minute-second-direction* format. The program should prompt for the position of two coordinates and calculate the distance along the surface of the Earth.

Input(s): Two GPS coordinates in Degree-Minute-Second, Direction format

Output(s): A number representing the surface distance between the two coordinates

Modularity:

`read_pos`	a function to read in the latitude and longitude values for each location
`convert_DD`	a function to convert Degree_Minute_Seconds to decimal degrees
`deg2rad`	a function to convert degrees to radians
`calc_SphereCoord`	a function to convert latitude/longitude to spherical coordinates
`calc_3DCoord`	a function to calculate the 3D Cartesian coordinates from the spherical coordinates
`straight_D`	a function to calculate the straight line distance between two points
`surface_D`	a function to calculate the surface distance between two points

Algorithm Design

1. Obtain the two GPS coordinates.
   a. Input degrees, minutes, seconds.
   b. Input direction.
2. Convert the coordinates to decimal degrees (Eq. 1).
3. Convert the decimal degrees to spherical coordinates Eqs. 2 and 3.
4. Convert the spherical coordinates to 3D Cartesian coordinates (Eq. 5).
   a. Convert the degrees to radians using Eq. 4.
5. Calculate the straight line distance (Eq. 6).
6. Calculate the surface distance (Eq. 7).

Building the Program

This program seems colossal compared to what we have done so far. A lot of data must be shuffled to and fro. It encompasses seven different functions in addition to **main.** But the information is paramount here, so we will first deal with that. There are two positions, each which has a latitude and longitude, with each of those containing four pieces of information. In total 16 pieces of information must be input. We will use the prefixes **deg, min,** and **sec** to denote degrees, minutes, and seconds, respectively; the terms **Lat** and **Lng** for latitude; and longitude; and the suffixes **P1** and **P2** to distinguish the positions. The variable to hold the degrees for the latitude in the first position would be:

```
degLat_P1
```

These are all whole numbers, with degrees having a range 0 to 90 for latitude, 0 to 180 for longitude, minutes 0 to 60, and seconds 0 to 60. The declarations for all the input variables in the main program look like:

```
int degLat_P1, minLat_P1, secLat_P1;
int degLng_P1, minLng_P1, secLng_P1;
int degLat_P2, minLat_P2, secLat_P2;
int degLng_P2, minLng_P2, secLng_P2;
```

We also need some variables to store the directions for each position and latitude/longitude. We use the prefix **dir** to denote direction:

```
char dirLat_P1, dirLng_P1, dirLat_P2, dirLng_P2;
```

Now that we have these values, we can create the function **read_pos**, whose job is to read the values into each of these variables. These take the values N (north)/S (south) for latitude and E (east)/W (west) for longitude. Here's what the function looks like:

```
void read_pos(int *deg, int *min, int *sec, char *dir)
{
    printf("Degrees: ");
    scanf("%d", deg);
    printf("Minutes: ");
    scanf("%d", min);
    printf("Seconds: ");
    scanf("%d", sec);
    scanf("%c", dir);
    printf("Direction: ");
    scanf("%c", dir);
}
```

Note that the parameters in the function are all pass-by reference, because the values have to be passed back from the function. Note also that within the **scanf** function we don't use an & in this case because the asterisk already denotes an address. If we used an ampersand, we would probably imbed a subtle bug into our code. There are also two **scanf** statements that read characters. The first actually reads the enter key pressed after you enter the value for **sec**. Without it, it would store an enter character in the variable **dir**. Now when we call this function, we can store the first series of values for the latitude component of the first position:

```
read_pos(&degLat_P1, &minLat_P1, &secLat_P1, &dirLat_P1);
```

We can do the same for the remaining three sets of input, remembering to put some prompts in between.

```
read_pos(&degLng_P1, &minLng_P1, &secLng_P1, &dirLng_P1);
read_pos(&degLat_P2, &minLat_P2, &secLat_P2, &dirLat_P2);
read_pos(&degLng_P2, &minLng_P2, &secLng_P2, &dirLng_P2);
```

Now let's move onto the next function which converts from the Degrees-Minutes-Seconds format to decimal degrees using Eq. 1:

```
double convert_DD(int deg, int min, int sec)
{
    double ms, d;
    ms = min + (sec/60.0);
    d = ms/60.0;
    return deg + d;
}
```

Here there are three inputs and one output, the latter representing the decimal degrees. We use two temporary variables, **ms** and **d**, to break the equation up, although we could have just as easily written:

```
return deg + (min + (sec/60.0))/60.0;
```

Remember to use **60.0** instead of **60**; otherwise, integer division will be performed. We can call this function directly after the **read_pos** series in **main**:

```
decLat_P1 = convert_DD(degLat_P1, minLat_P1, secLat_P1);
decLng_P1 = convert_DD(degLng_P1, minLng_P1, secLng_P1);
decLat_P2 = convert_DD(degLat_P2, minLat_P2, secLat_P2);
decLng_P2 = convert_DD(degLng_P2, minLng_P2, secLng_P2);
```

We call it once for each of the latitude/longitude in each position. Now we have to create some more variables to hold the results, using the prefix **dec** to denote direction:

```
double decLat_P1, decLng_P1, decLat_P2, decLng_P2;
```

Now we can move onto the function **calc_sphereCoord**, which calculates the spherical coordinates for each position using Eqs. 2 and 3:

```
void calc_sphereCoord(double decLat, double decLng,
                      char dirLat, char dirLng,
                      double *phi, double *theta)
{
    if (dirLat == 'n' || dirLat == 'N')
        *phi = 90.0 - decLat;
    else if (dirLat == 's' || dirLat == 'S')
        *phi = 90.0 + decLat;
    if (dirLng == 'e' || dirLng == 'E')
        *theta = decLng;
    else if (dirLng == 'w' || dirLng == 'W')
        *theta = -decLng;
}
```

This function looks first at the latitude and decides whether the direction is north or south, using Eq. 2. Allowances are made in the expressions for either lowercase or upper-case letters. It then processes longitude in a similar fashion using Eq. 3. The way the equations are set out makes it easy to convert them to **if** statements. This function returns two of the spherical coordinates using pass-by-reference: *phi* and *theta*. The third, *rho*, represents the average radius of the earth, and is defined in the following manner at the top of the program:

```
#define rho 6367.0
```

The next function calculates 3D Cartesian coordinates from the spherical coordinates using Eq. 5. It uses **phi** and **theta** calculated in the previous function.

```
void calc_3DCoord(double phi, double theta, double *x,
                  double *y, double *z)
{
    double phiRad, thetaRad;

    phiRad = deg2rad(phi);
    thetaRad = deg2rad(theta);

    *x = rho * cos(thetaRad) * sin(phiRad);
    *y = rho * sin(thetaRad) * sin(phiRad);
    *z = rho * cos(phiRad);
}
```

Lines 5 and 6 of the function:

```
phiRad = deg2rad(phi);
thetaRad = deg2rad(theta);
```

convert **phi** and **theta** to radians before they are used. This is because trigonometric functions used here require radians, not degrees, so we have to write a small function to convert our values of phi and theta to radians:

```
double deg2rad(double deg)
{
    return (deg * 2 * PI)/360.0;
}
```

For this we will also need to define PI:

```
#define PI 3.14159
```

The last three statements of **calc_3DCoord** deal with Eq. 5, returning all three components using pass-by-reference parameters.

Now we are onto the final two functions. The first of these calculates the straight line distance between two points using Eq. 6. It uses as input the two sets of 3D coordinates calculated by **calc_3DCoord** for each of the two positions.

```
double calc_straightD(double x1, double y1, double z1,
                      double x2, double y2, double z2)
{
```

```
    double dx, dy, dz;

    dx = (x2 − x1) * (x2 − x1);
    dy = (y2 − y1) * (y2 − y1);
    dz = (z2 − z1) * (z2 − z1);

    return sqrt(dx + dy + dz);
}
```

Finally we can calculate the surface distance using Eq. 7. Its sole input is the straight line distance calculated in **calc_straightD**:

```
double calc_surfaceD(double SLD)
{
    return (2.0*rho) * asin(SLD/(2.0*rho));
}
```

Now we are left with the **main** part of the program. Here it is in its entirety, with associated comments:

```
int main(void)
{
    int degLat_P1, minLat_P1, secLat_P1;
    int degLng_P1, minLng_P1, secLng_P1;
    int degLat_P2, minLat_P2, secLat_P2;
    int degLng_P2, minLng_P2, secLng_P2;
    char dirLat_P1, dirLng_P1, dirLat_P2, dirLng_P2;
    double decLat_P1, decLng_P1, decLat_P2, decLng_P2;
    double theta_P1, phi_P1, theta_P2, phi_P2;
    double x1, y1, z1, x2, y2, z2;
    double straight_D, surface_D;

    // Enter positional information
    printf("Enter position information for point 1\n");
    printf("Enter the latitude: \n");
    read_pos(&degLat_P1, &minLat_P1, &secLat_P1, &dirLat_P1);
    printf("Enter the longitude: \n");
    read_pos(&degLng_P1, &minLng_P1, &secLng_P1, &dirLng_P1);

    printf("Enter position information for point 2\n");
    printf("Enter the latitude: \n");
    read_pos(&degLat_P2, &minLat_P2, &secLat_P2, &dirLat_P2);
    printf("Enter the longitude: \n");
    read_pos(&degLng_P2, &minLng_P2, &secLng_P2, &dirLng_P2);

    // Convert from d-m-s to digital degrees
    decLat_P1 = convert_DD(degLat_P1, minLat_P1, secLat_P1);
    decLng_P1 = convert_DD(degLng_P1, minLng_P1, secLng_P1);
    decLat_P2 = convert_DD(degLat_P2, minLat_P2, secLat_P2);
    decLng_P2 = convert_DD(degLng_P2, minLng_P2, secLng_P2);
```

```
// Convert to spherical coordinates
calc_sphereCoord(decLat_P1, decLng_P1, dirLat_P1,
                 dirLng_P1, &phi_P1, &theta_P1);
calc_sphereCoord(decLat_P2, decLng_P2, dirLat_P2,
                 dirLng_P2, &phi_P2, &theta_P2);

// Convert to 3D Cartesian coordinates
calc_3DCoord(phi_P1, theta_P1, &x1, &y1, &z1);
calc_3DCoord(phi_P2, theta_P2, &x2, &y2, &z2);

// Calculate the straight line distance
straight_D = calc_straightD(x1, y1, z1, x2, y2, z2);

// Calculate the surface distance
surface_D = calc_surfaceD(straight_D);

printf("The distance is %.2f km\n", surface_D);
}
```

The entire main program is really just about calling the different functions we have created.

Testing the Program

Test your program on some different Canadian locations (available from here http://geonames.nrcan.gc.ca/english/cgndb.html) and overseas locations (you can find GPS coordinates in Wikipedia). Here are two examples:

Toronto	43° 39′ 00″ North; 79° 23′ 00″ West
Montalcino	43° 03′ 00″ North; 11° 29′ 00″ East
Loch Ness	57° 18′ 00″ North; 4° 27′ 00″ West

The surface distance between Toronto and Montalcino is ≈ 6,935 km
The surface distance between Toronto and Loch Ness is ≈ 5,219 km

Being Defensive

As the program stands, it works fine, *if* the input is entered correctly. Otherwise it bombs. Imagine if we accidentally enter *q* instead of *w*. The program won't process this error until it executes **calc_sphereCoord**, by which time it's already too late to go back. There are some constraints we can work with here:

Degrees	0–90 (latitude)
	0–180 (longitude)
Minutes	0–60
Seconds	0–60
Direction	N/n, S/s, E/e, W/w

There are likely some other constraints, as in finding sequences of numbers that just don't work, but these will do for now. We can deal with all of these in the function **read_pos**. Since the degrees are different for latitude and longitude, we can create two functions: **readpos_Lat** and **readpos_Long**. Let's looks at the first. The latter can be created by "reusing" information from the **readpos_Lat.**

```c
void readpos_Lat(int *deg, int *min, int *sec, char *dir)
{
    while(1) {
        printf("Degrees (0—90): ");
        scanf("%d", deg);
        printf("Minutes (0—60): ");
        scanf("%d", min);
        printf("Seconds (0—60): ");
        scanf("%d", sec);
        scanf("%c", dir);
        printf("Direction (N/n, S/s): ");
        scanf("%c", dir);
        if ((*deg >= 0 && *deg <= 90) &&
            (*min >= 0 && *min <= 60) &&
            (*sec >= 0 && *sec <= 60) &&
            (*dir == 'n' || *dir == 'N' ||
             *dir == 's' || *dir == 'S'))
            break;
        else
            printf("Error in input bounds, please re-enter\n");
    }
}
```

In essence we have just surrounded the body of the function with an infinite **while**, allowing input to iterate until it is correct. The only other difference is the presence of an **if** statement to control the loop. Here we use a uber-expression to determine whether all the inputs match the constraints:

```c
if ((*deg >= 0 && *deg <= 90) &&
    (*min >= 0 && *min <= 60) &&
    (*sec >= 0 && *sec <= 60) &&
    (*dir == 'n' || *dir == 'N' ||
     *dir == 's' || *dir == 'S'))
```

We could also have written this as:

```c
if (*deg >= 0 && *deg <= 90)
    if (*min >= 0 && *min <= 60)
        if (*sec >= 0 && *sec <= 60)
            if (*dir == 'n' || *dir == 'N' ||
                *dir == 's' || *dir == 'S'))
```

which in reality just tends to get messy. If they all match, a **break** is executed and the function ends, returning the information. If some piece of information is out of bounds, the user is asked to reenter the information. We could have also made it so only the incorrect input is reentered instead of *all* the information, but that does lead to more complexity. Then we could check to make sure the correct datatype is entered. We could go on forever. The function **readpos_Long** is the same; only the constraints change.

Epilog

The basic crux of these functions is the *parameter passing*. The equations are relatively straightforward and shouldn't be hard to decipher. What will catch most people is passing the information to and from the functions. There are many other ways to pass information to and from the functions. We could declare all our variables as global variables, but it is harder to keep track of them all throughout so many functions and even harder to trace errors. A further way might be to use an aggregate structure such as **struct,** to create "object"-type structures. I suggest writing programs like this in one of two ways:

1. Code the entire program in **main,** and then modularize it piece by piece when you know it works.

2. Code the program function by function. Don't be tempted to code ALL the functions at once and then compile.

For example, design and code the function **read_pos** and then test it to see if it actually reads the right data and prints it out. For example, execute the first coordinate:

```
read_pos(&degLat_P1, &minLat_P1, &secLat_P1, &dirLat_P1);
```

Then print them out to see if the function actually does its job:

```
printf("%d %d %d %c\n", degLat_P1, minLat_P1,
        secLat_P1, dirLat_P1);
```

Parking Cars

Anyone who considers arithmetical methods of producing
random digits is, of course, in a state of sin.
—John Von Neumann

The Problem Description

In the future, cars will park themselves. In fact some cars already have a system that assists
in parallel parking, such as the British Toyota Prius. Self-parking cars currently on the
market are not completely autonomous, but they do make parallel parking much easier.
Now imagine a car that drops you off at the front of a store and proceeds to park itself.

Program Requirements

Cars that are one unit long try to parallel park randomly along a street of length $N=10$
units. A car can park if there is at least one half unit of space on either side of its center. In
other words, no extra maneuvering space is needed. As an example consider the following
figure. The first random number generated is 4.0. After parking the car, you have 3.5 units
on the left side and 5.5 units on the right.

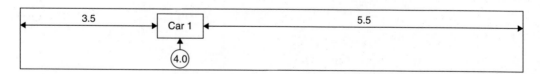

The next part of the algorithm requires you to generate a random number between 5.0 → 9.5 and 0.5→3.0, to be able to park a car on either side of the first car. Now we try and park a car in the right side by generating a random number between 5.0 and 9.5. The next car is parked at position 8.25. Now there are 3.25 units between the first car and the second and 1.25 units after the second car.

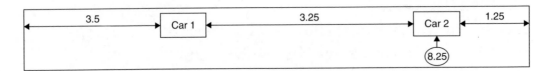

Next we generate a random number between 5.0 and 7.25. The next car is parked at position 5.5. This continues with all the spaces large enough until there is no space left to park cars.

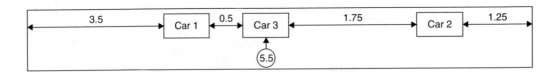

What we are trying to achieve here is a way of randomly parking cars until the car park is full. Once we have done this, we can run a simulation to try to find the average number of cars parked after, say, 1,000 runs of the simulation.

The Algorithm

The algorithm here is probably the most difficult part. How do we park cars so that every space is used up. To do it efficiently and get 10 cars parked every time, we would merely assign parking spaces, which is also easier because each spot could be delineated by a sensor. But let's add an element of randomness. There are two ways to design an algorithm to solve this problem: iterative and recursive.

Iterative Algorithm

The iterative algorithm requires us to start by finding a random number between 0.5 and 9.5, say p. Once the first car is parked, we then look to the left and right of the car and find the parking constraints for each, in this case 0.5 to $p-1.0$ and $p + 1.0$ to 9.5. Why do we subtract and add one respectively? Remember that cars are one unit in length and the random number generated represents the center of the car. To the left, we have to generate a new random number between 0.5 and one car length less than p. That's half a car for the car already parked and another half for the car being parked. If the parking area were 0.5 to $p-0.5$, we might end up parking one car atop the other!

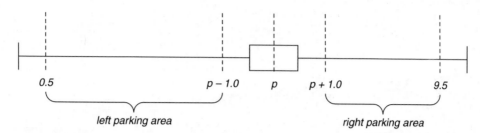

Parking the first car iteratively is easy. Parking the rest isn't so easy. To do this we have to use a data structure called a *stack*. This is a container with two basic operations *pop* and *push*. Push adds an element to the stack, pop removes one. A stack is a LIFO structure: *last-in, first-out*.

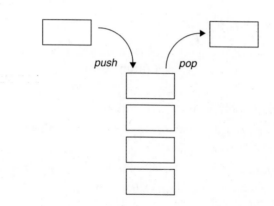

Basically, our algorithm works by storing the empty parking spaces. In the previous case, if p were 6.3, we would then push the pair (0.5, 5.3) and (7.3, 9.5) onto the stack. Then we would take one off and process it. In this case, we would pop (7.3, 9.5) off the stack, randomly park a car in the range 7.3 to 9.5, and any spaces either side would again be added to the stack. When the right side is entirely processed, and there are no spaces left, (0.5, 5.3) can be popped off the stack and processed in a similar fashion. But as functional as this is, we will focus instead on a recursive solution.

Recursive Algorithm

A recursive algorithm works well here because it is a very intuitive solution to the problem. It is intuitive because after we have parked the first car, we have space on *either* side to park another. So we run the algorithm again on both parts. Each of those parking spaces in turn will generate a parked car with space on either side, etc. This is essentially a *binary recursion* algorithm. Here's what a run of the algorithm could look like diagrammatically (*ns* represents no space):

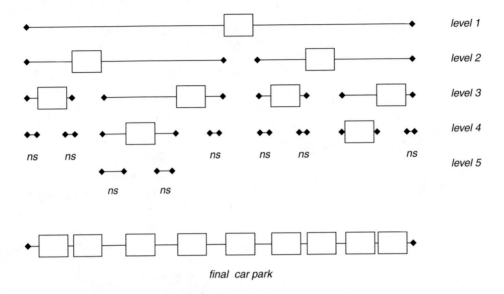

final car park

At each level in the diagram, the task is split into two, and cars are parked until no more spaces large enough are left. The algorithm for this goes something along the following lines:

1. Call the function **park**, parking the first car in the bounds (a=0.5,b=9.5).
2. The car is parked by randomly generating a number between **a** and **b** → **p**.
3. Increment the number of cars parked.
4. Determine the amount of space to the left of **p**. Is the space large enough to park a car?
   a. Yes, call **park** with the bounds (a,p−1.0). Go to 2.
   b. No (do nothing).
5. Determine the amount of space to the right of **p**. Is the space large enough to park a car?
   a. Yes, call **park** with the bounds (p+1.0,b). Go to 2.
   b. No (do nothing).

Calculating the amount of space is the crucial part of the algorithm. For the left side, we have to subtract 0.5 from **p** to account for the left half of the car and then subtract from this the value of the lower bound minus 0.5 (to account for half a car that *could* be parked). The equation for this is:

```
(p−0.5)−(a−0.5)
```

For example if **p**=6.3 (bounds 0.5,9.5), then the space to the left is (6.3−0.5) − (0.5−0.5) = 5.8. Note that you can't write this as:

```
(p−0.5−a−0.5)
```

This will result in an incorrect answer. For the previous example, the answer would be 4.8, which is one unit smaller than it should be. The equation for the right side is analogous:

```
(b+0.5)−(p+0.5)
```

Again for the example, this would result in a value of **(9.5+0.5) – (6.3+0.5)** = 3.2. Now let's implement this.

Deriving the Program

The first thing we have to think about is an algorithm to generate floating point random numbers in a certain range. Some implementations of C provide a floating point random number generator called **drand48**. The function **drand48** generates a double random number in the range 0.0 to 1.0. It uses the **srand48** function to seed the random number generator, so that the function **drand48** is initialized. If we do not have such a function, we must create our own. Here's what the function looks like:

```
double drand_RANGE(double low, double high)
{
    int randomNum;
    double drand, span;

    randomNum = (double)rand();
    drand = randomNum / (double) RAND_MAX;
    span = high — low;
    return low + span * drand;
}
```

The function **drand_RANGE** has two parameters representing the lower and higher bounds of the range. It returns a double number within this range. The first line in the function (outside the declarations) generates a random number (an integer):

```
randomNum = (double)rand();
```

The next line normalizes this number to a value between 0.0 and 1.0.

```
drand = randomNum / (double) RAND_MAX;
```

Next we calculate the distance between the high and low numbers

```
span = high — low;
```

Finally, we offset the range to begin at low and end at high, and return this value:

```
return low + span * drand;
```

Now let's turn to the recursive function, **park.** There isn't actually a lot to this function.

```
void park(double lower, double upper)
{
    double p;

    p = drand_RANGE(lower,upper);
    num = num + 1;
    printf("Car parked at position %.1f\n", p);
```

```
        if ((p—0.5)—(lower—0.5) >= 1.0)
            park(lower,p—1.0);

        if ((upper+0.5)—(p+0.5) >= 1.0)
            park(p+1.0,upper);
}
```

The function has two parameters representing the **lower** and **upper** bounds in which to park a car. First we generate a random number between **lower** and **upper**:

```
    p = drand_RANGE(lower,upper);
```

Then we increment the number of cars parked. This works because we only call **park** if there is enough space to park a car.

```
    num = num + 1;
```

We then print out where the car is parked (this isn't essential).

```
    printf("Car parked at position %.1f\n", p);
```

Next we get to the core part of the algorithm, where the recursion occurs. First we deal with the space to the left of the car:

```
    if ((p—0.5)—(lower—0.5) >= 1.0)
        park(lower,p—1.0);
```

Then we deal with the space to the right:

```
    if ((upper+0.5)—(p+0.5) >= 1.0)
        park(p+1.0,upper);
```

That's it! The recursive function is done. Note that **num** isn't declared in the function. That's because its value is incremented each time we park a car, so that means every time we call **park**. In this case we think it's better to use a global variable of the form:

```
    int num = 0;
```

Now here's the main program incorporating a run of 1,000 calls to park.

```
    int main(void)
    {
        int i, seed;
        double sum=0.0;

        seed = time(0);
        srand(seed);
        for (i=1; i<=1000; i=i+1)
        {
            num = 0;
            park(0.5,9.5);
            sum = sum + num;
        }
        printf("Average parked cars = %.2f\n",sum/1000);
```

```
        return 0;
    }
```

We initialize the random number generator in **main**:

```
    seed = time(0);
    srand(seed);
```

and then basically cycle through 1,000 iterations, using a **for** loop. The number of cars parked is added to **sum** after each call to **park**. At the end we divide the **sum** by **1000** to give us an average number of cars parked.

The Whole Program

```
    #include <stdio.h>
    #include <stdlib.h>
    #include <time.h>

    int num = 0;

    double drand_RANGE(double low, double high)
    {
        int randomNum;
        double drand, span;

        randomNum = (double)rand();
        drand = randomNum / (double) RAND_MAX;
        span = high — low;
        return low + span * drand;
    }

    void park(double lower, double upper)
    {
        double p;

        p = drand_RANGE(lower,upper);
        num = num + 1;
        printf("Car parked at position %.1f\n", p);

        if ((p—0.5)—(lower—0.5) >= 1.0)
            park(lower,p—1.0);
        if ((upper+0.5)—(p+0.5) >= 1.0)
            park(p+1.0,upper);
    }

    int main(void)
    {
        int i, seed;
        double sum=0.0;
```

```
    seed = time(0);
    srand(seed);
    for (i=1; i<=1000; i=i+1)
    {
        num = 0;
        park(0.5,9.5);
        sum = sum + num;
    }
    printf("Average parked cars = %.2f\n",sum/1000);

    return 0;
}
```

Testing the Program

Here's a run of a single call to park.

```
Car parked at position 3.4
Car parked at position 2.0
Car parked at position 0.9
Car parked at position 4.6
Car parked at position 8.8
Car parked at position 6.9
Car parked at position 5.7
```

If we sort and evaluate these, we get the following car parks:

```
0.9 → (0.4 to 1.4)
2.0 → (1.5 to 2.5)
3.4 → (2.9 to 3.9)
4.6 → (4.1 to 5.1)
5.7 → (5.2 to 6.2)
6.9 → (6.4 to 7.4)
8.8 → (8.3 to 9.3)
```

The following spaces are left: 0.4, 0.1, 0.4, 0.2, 0.1, 0.2, 0.9, and 0.7, none of which is large enough to park a car!

Epilog

After running our program five times over 1,000 iterations each, we get the following averages: 7.19, 7.24, 7.22, 7.20, and 7.21.

Image Processing

Light makes photography. Embrace light. Admire it. Love it. But above all, know light. Know it for all you are worth, and you will know the key to photography.

—George Eastman

The Problem Description

The word *image*, from the Latin *imago*, is an artifact that reproduces the likeness of some subject. One of the more interesting applications of two-dimensional arrays is the processing of digital images. A digital image may be created directly, for example by a digital camera, or obtained from an image in an analog medium, such as a photograph or slide using a scanner. Images are used in a diversity of applications, including health care (e.g., x-rays), law enforcement (e.g., forensics), space exploration (e.g., Mars Rovers), biometrics (e.g., fingerprint analysis), and personal photography. Images can be either color or gray scale. When you create a digital image, you are essentially creating a large mosaic of millions of separate picture elements called *pixels*. Each one of these pixels has a color, and when combined, they form an image. Sometimes it is necessary to process these images in some manner. For example, we might take a series of photographs that we wish to "stitch" together to form a panoramic view. An image might be somewhat blurred or contain some "noise," so we might wish to sharpen it or suppress the noise. An image of a text document might need to be processed to extract the individual characters so they can be passed to a character recognition algorithm. The act of manipulating the image is commonly known as *image processing*.

Program Requirements

An image is essentially a 2D array. Each array element (or pixel) holds the value of an 8-bit gray scale or a range of 256 possible values or intensities. This just means that the values range from 0 to 2^8-1 with 0 denoting black and 255 denoting white. You could think of this in the following way. A pixel with the value 0 contains no white; it is pure black. A pixel with intensity 1 has 1 part white and 254 parts black, a pixel with the value 254 has 254 parts white and 1 part black, etc. So the range of values we have to represent is 0–255, which means we could store this array using an **int**. For example, consider the image of a piece of text shown in the following figure. The image was extracted from a scanned version of *The Catacombs of Rome* (1854). Here the object of interest, the text, approaches black, whereas the background is near white (or off-white in this case).

To store this image as a 2D array, we could use an array declaration of the form:

```
int image[175][500];
```

This just says that we have a 2D array with 175 rows and 500 columns. Each location in the array has a specific pixel. That's equivalent to 87,500 pixels, or 0.0875 megapixels, which is not a very high resolution image. Now, let's progress to actually manipulating the image.

Image Histogram

Sometimes we want to look at the distribution of intensities (tones) in an image. We can do this by viewing the *histogram* of the image. A histogram is a plot of the frequency distribution of each of the values in the image. A histogram of a gray scale image has 256 *bins*, one for each of the representative grays, 0 to 255. Essentially we are creating an array of frequencies:

```
int histogram[256];
```

To create a histogram we start at 0 and count all the zero-valued pixels in the image, then assign the tally to the zeroth element of the array **histogram**. Here's the general equation:

$$h(k) = \sum_{i=0}^{X} \sum_{j=0}^{Y} 1 \quad if(I_{ij} = k)$$

Basically, *h(k)* is the number of pixels in the image *I* (of size *X*×*Y*) with intensity value *k* (*k* has values 0 to 255).

Image Thresholding

Thresholding is the simplest form of image segmentation, whereby we partition an image into components. In the case of the fingerprint image, we want to partition the image into background and the ridges of the fingerprint. Individual pixels in an image are labeled as either 0 or 1, depending on some *threshold* value. If we have an 8-bit image with 256 gray levels, then to select a threshold T = 100 will result in all pixels in the image less than 100 being reassigned the value 0, and all pixels greater than or equal to 100 being assigned the value 1. To look at it in equation form:

$$I_{Bt}(I) = \begin{cases} 0 & if \ I_{ij} < t \\ 1 & if \ I_{ij} \geq t \end{cases}$$

In this form, where only two *bins* are selected, so it is called *binary thresholding*. This is fine because there are essentially only two objects in a scanned image of text: the text and the background.

Program Specification and Algorithm Design

This program is composed of a series of four actions: reading an image, writing an image, image thresholding, and deriving an image histogram.

Reading an Image. This a function to read an image from a file. The image is stored in a text file as a series of integers, equivalent to the number of rows times number of columns in the image. The user is required to specify the number of rows and columns.

```
Input -> The number of rows and columns in the image
         The name of the file storing the image
Output -> Array containing the image

OPEN file for reading
FOR x = 1 to image_rows
    FOR y = 1 to image_columns
        READ value representing pixel from file
        ASSIGN pixel to 2D array element (x,y)
    ENDFOR
ENDFOR
CLOSE file
```

Writing an Image. The image is stored in a text file as a series of integers, equivalent to the number of rows times number of columns in the image. The user is required to specify the number of rows and columns.

```
Input -> Array containing the image
         The name of the file to store the image
Output -> Image stored in a file
```

```
OPEN file for writing
FOR x = 1 to image_rows
    FOR y = 1 to image_columns
        WRITE 2D array element (x,y) to file
    ENDFOR
ENDFOR
CLOSE file
```

Image Thresholding.   This function performs image thresholding.

```
Input -> Image to be binarized, a threshold value
Output -> New image containing the binary image

FOR x = 1 to image_rows
    FOR y = 1 to image_columns
        IF image[x,y] < threshold
            set binary image value to 0
        ELSE
            set binary image value to 255
        ENDIF
    ENDFOR
ENDFOR
```

Deriving an Image Histogram.   This function creates an image histogram.

```
Input -> Original image
Output -> An array containing the histogram.

SET all values in the histogram to zero.
FOR x = 1 to image_rows
    FOR y = 1 to image_columns
        INCREMENT the appropriate bin in the histogram
        relating to each pixel in the image
```

Deriving the Program

Since this is a large program, we will consider each function in turn. All programs that process images invariably use a nested-loop to access each of the elements of the image, from the top-left (the position of {0,0}), to the bottom right. This is basically the same for all functions, where **nrow** and **ncol** represent the number of rows and columns in the image respectively.

```
for (i=0; i<nrow; i=i+1)
    for (j=0; j<ncol; j=j+1)
        . . .
```

Reading an Image

The function that reads the image from a file into a two-dimensional array takes two arguments, the name of the file **fname**, stored as a string, and the two-dimensional integer array, **image**. This is what the function looks like:

```
void read_image(char *fname, int image[nrow][ncol])
{
    int i, j;
    int pixel;
    FILE *ifp;

    ifp = fopen(fname, "r");

    for (i=0; i<nrow; i=i+1)
        for (j=0; j<ncol; j=j+1){
            fscanf(ifp, "%d", &pixel);
            image[i][j] = (int)pixel;
        }

    fclose(ifp);
}
```

The body of the function basically involves opening the file for reading:

```
ifp = fopen(fname, "r");
```

This associates a *file pointer* called **ifp** with the actual file. Next we use a nested **for** loop to read the integer values from a file and store them in their appropriate position in the array.

```
for (i=0; i<nrow; i=i+1)
    for (j=0; j<ncol; j=j+1){
        fscanf(ifp, "%d", &pixel);
        image[i][j] = (int)pixel;
    }
```

The function **fscanf** is used to read directly from the file pointed to by the file pointer **ifp**. We know how many pixels are in the image (or elements in the array), since **nrow** and **ncol** were defined as global variables and given values before **read_image** was called. At the end of all this, we close the file:

```
fclose(ifp);
```

Writing an Image

The function **write_image** is really a carbon copy of **read_image**. The only thing that really changes is that the **fscanf** is replaced by a **fprintf** to print directly to a file opened for writing.

```
void write_image(char *fname, int image[nrow][ncol])
{
    int i, j;
    FILE *ofp;

    ofp = fopen(fname, "w");

    for (i=0; i<nrow; i=i+1){
        for (j=0; j<ncol; j=j+1)
            fprintf(ofp, "%d", image[i][j]);
        fprintf(ofp, "\n");
    }

    fclose(ofp);
}
```

So **fopen** uses the flag for writing **w** instead of **r**:

```
ofp = fopen(fname, "w");
```

Image Thresholding

This function has three parameters. The first represents the input image, and the second represents the binary image to be created and returned from the function. The third represents the threshold value passed to the function.

```
void threshold(int image[nrow][ncol],
               int binaryI[nrow][ncol], int threshold)
{
    int i, j;

    for (i=0; i<nrow; i=i+1)
        for (j=0; j<ncol; j=j+1)
            if (image[i][j] < threshold)
                binaryI[i][j] = 0;
            else
                binaryI[i][j] = 255;
}
```

All this function really does is cycle through each element of the image and ask the question:

```
Is the value of the pixel less than the threshold value?
```

If the answer is yes, then the corresponding pixel in the array **binaryI** is set to 0. Otherwise if it is greater than or equal to the threshold value, then the corresponding pixel is set to 255. At the end **binaryI** will be full of a combination of 0s and 255s. This is a binary image. All we need to do this is an **if-else** statement of the form:

```
if (image[i][j] < threshold)
    binaryI[i][j] = 0;
else
    binaryI[i][j] = 255;
```

Deriving an Image Histogram

The final function (well apart from **main**) derives a histogram of intensity values for the image in question. This function, aptly called **histogram**, has two parameters: the image to calculate the frequencies from and a 1D array to hold the frequencies.

```
void histogram(int image[nrow][ncol], int hist[256])
{
    int i, j;

    for (i=0; i<256; i=i+1)
        hist[i] = 0;

    for (i=0; i<nrow; i=i+1)
        for (j=0; j<ncol; j=j+1)
            hist[image[i][j]] = hist[image[i][j]] + 1;
}
```

The function first uses a single **for** loop to set all the values in the array **hist** to zero.

```
for (i=0; i<256; i=i+1)
    hist[i] = 0;
```

Then, we again use a nested loop to process each element of the image:

```
for (i=0; i<nrow; i=i+1)
    for (j=0; j<ncol; j=j+1)
        hist[image[i][j]] = hist[image[i][j]] + 1;
```

This basically uses the value stored in each element of the array image as an index to the array **hist**. So, if the pixel **image[i][j]** has the value 237, then:

```
hist[image[i][j]] = hist[image[i][j]] + 1;
```

is equivalent to:

```
hist[237] = hist[237] + 1;
```

It increments bin 237 of the histogram by one. Bin 237 holds the tally for all pixels in **image** with the intensity value 237.

The main Program

The role of the main program is to obtain the name of the image file to be processed, read in the number of rows and columns, obtain a threshold value, create the binary image, and write the binary image to file. Here is the whole **main** program:

```
int main(void)
{
    char fname[50];
    int hist[256];
    int T;

    printf("Enter a image filename: ");
    scanf("%s",fname);

    printf("Enter the number of rows: ");
    scanf("%d", &nrow);
    printf("Enter the number of columns: ");
    scanf("%d", &ncol);

    int image[nrow][ncol], binaryI[nrow][ncol];
    read_image(fname, image);

    printf("Enter a threshold value (0-255): ");
    scanf("%d", &T);
    threshold(image, binaryI, T);

    write_image("binaryM.txt", binaryI);

    return 0;
}
```

The first part of **main** has to do with input for the program:

```
printf("Enter a image filename: ");
scanf("%s",fname);

printf("Enter the number of rows: ");
scanf("%d", &nrow);

printf("Enter the number of columns: ");
scanf("%d", &ncol);
```

Once we have the filename and the number of rows and columns in the image, we can actually read in the data. However, first we have to create an array in which to store the image. Since we can use *variable length arrays* in C99, we will make use of this feature, declaring the array as the program runs. We create both an array to store the original image and an array to store the binary image.

```
int image[nrow][ncol], binaryI[nrow][ncol];
```

Now we can read the image in:

```
read_image(fname, image);
```

Then we can read in a threshold value:

```
printf("Enter a threshold value (0-255): ");
scanf("%d", &T);
```

After that we can perform the thresholding operation:

```
threshold(image, binaryI, T);
```

Now write the image to a file called **binaryM.txt**:

```
write_image("binaryM.txt", binaryI);
```

If we want to use the histogram function, we can use the following code:

```
histogram(image,hist);
for (i=0; i<256; i=i+1)
    printf("%d\n",hist[i]);
```

Testing the Program

To test the program we have to run it and view the various images. We can use a utility called **ImageJ** to import the images as **"Text Image."** If we choose a threshold with a value of 180, this is the image we will find in **binary.txt**:

ABOUT two miles from the gates of Rome, on that same Appian Way, over whose pavements once the legions of victorious Rome marched on their way to the Capitol, and whose stones were bedewed with the tears of captive princes as they were dragged along to swell the glory of the triumph, stands the church of St. Sebastian. The tide of population

Extending the Program

We could extent the program to calculate the threshold automatically. One way of doing this is to calculate the mean intensity value in the image. The mean can be calculated as follows:

$$\mu = \frac{\sum_{i=0}^{X}\sum_{j=0}^{Y} I_{ij}}{\sum_{i=0}^{X}\sum_{j=0}^{Y} 1}$$

when, we run this function on the test image, we get a threshold value of 99, resulting in the following image:

ABOUT two miles from the gates of Rome, on that same Appian Way, over whose pavements once the legions of victorious Rome marched on their way to the Capitol, and whose stones were bedewed with the tears of captive princes as they were dragged along to swell the glory of the triumph, stand the church of St. Sebastian. The tide of population

The result is similar except that the words in the lower right corner are now obscured. This relates to the fact that there is an artifact in the background of the original image. We could also use the *median,* or even the *mode,* instead of the mean. The function to calculate the mean looks like:

```
int calculate_mean(int image[nrow][ncol])
{
    int i, j, meanP;
    double sum=0;

    for (i=0; i<nrow; i=i+1)
        for (j=0; j<ncol; j=j+1)
            sum = sum + image[i][j];

    meanP = sum / (nrow*ncol);

    return meanP;
}
```

Moreover, it is called in the following manner:

```
meanT = calculate_mean(image);
printf("The mean intensity is %d\n", meanT);
threshold(image, binaryI, meanT);
```

Note we can use the same function **threshold** to create the binary image. It will take any value, calculated in any manner, as long as the value is between 0 and 255.

Epilog

The example we have used here is a small image. The original scanned image had a size of 2,469×4,293, which relates to approximately 10MB and is too large to process. It turns out we don't actually need all the information in these sort of images. We downsized the image by a scale of one to four, so that the dimensions became 617×1,073 and a more manageable 0.6MB. Of course the more resolution you maintain, the more accurate the results. There are many dozens of different thresholding algorithms. Each gives a slightly different result. Sometimes algorithms are used to improve the quality of the image before it is thresholded.

Counting Words

Not everything that counts can be counted, and not everything that can be counted counts.
—Albert Einstein

The Problem Description

Remember in Chapter 2 we talked about counting words? Well, it turns out that a simple algorithm isn't that hard to design. The program in this case study has been adapted from Kernighan and Ritchie's classic book on the C programming language. It counts the characters, words, and lines in a text file.

Program Requirements

A *word count* is the number of words a document contains. Knowing the number of words in a document is vital, since authors may have to write their work within certain minimum or maximum constraints. Word counting can be used in a primitive form of *statistical text analysis* (STA). STA is a technique that originated in attempts to determine if novels or plays of doubtful authorship were, in fact, the works of famous writers. For example, it could be used in the *Shakespeare authorship*, the scholarly debates over whether the works attributed to William Shakespeare, of Stratford-upon-Avon, were actually written by another writer or a group of writers, using the pen name "William Shakespeare." STA could help establish whether Shakespeare's works are similar to Sir Francis Bacon or Christopher Marlowe. The concept is based on the theory that different authors favor different words. For example, if we have two authors, say Shakespeare and Marlowe, we can sample the frequency of a word such as *bestrides*. In Shakespeare's work it may occur about once in every 4,000 words, while Marlowe rarely uses it, say once every 23,000 words. In a work where *bestrides* isn't used at all, it seems unlikely that it would have been written by Marlowe. However, we're going to concentrate on a simple implementation of word counting.

Program Specification and Algorithm Design

Input(s):   A text file containing text

Output(s):   A count of the number of characters, words, and lines contained in the input file

The basic algorithm is fairly simple:

1. Initialize a series of counters to count the number of words, lines, and characters.
2. Read each character from a text file.
3. Increment the character counter.
4. If a new line character is encountered, increment the line counter.
5. If a space, new line, or tab is encountered, increment the word counter.

The Program

```c
#include <stdio.h>

int main(void)
{
    int nlines, nwords, nchars, state;
    char c;

    state = 0;
    nlines = nwords = nchars = 0;

    while ((c = getchar()) != EOF) {
        nchars = nchars + 1;

        if (c == '\n')
            nlines = nlines + 1;
        if (c == ' ' || c == '\n' || c == '\t')
            state = 0;
        else if (state == 0) {
            state = 1;
            nwords = nwords + 1;
        }
    }
    printf("Text counting:\n");
    printf("Number of lines: %d\n",nlines);
    printf("Number of words: %d\n",nwords);
    printf("Number of characters: %d\n",nchars);

    return 0;
}
```

Examining the Program

The first part of the program deals with creating some variables in which to store our statistics. In this case we need a variable for the number of lines, the number of words, and the number of characters. We also need a variable to hold a toggle to determine the start and end of a word.

```
int nlines, nwords, nchars, state;
```

Now we need to create a variable to store a character as we process the text:

```
char c;
```

First we set the variable **state** to zero and initialize all the counters. The variable **state** is used to toggle the end of the word.

```
state = 0;
nlines = nwords = nchars = 0;
```

Now the program uses a **while** loop to process the file, reading each character one at a time until there are no more to read:

```
while ((c = getchar()) != EOF) {
}
```

We use **getchar** to read a character and assign it to the variable **c**, while at the same time checking to see if the end of file, or **EOF**, has been reached. Within the **while** loop, we process the character that has just been read. First we increment the character counter:

```
nchars = nchars + 1;
```

Then we process the character to determine what sort of character it is. First we determine whether or not the character is a return character. If it is, we know that a line has finished, so we can update the variable that counts lines:

```
if (c == '\n')
nlines = nlines + 1;
```

Then we determine the existence of if any space characters, which consist of single spaces, new lines, and tabs. If there are, we reset the variable **state** to 0, indicating the end of a word. If on the other hand, no space characters exist, then we check to see if **state** is zero. If it is, then a new word can begin, so **state** is set to 1, and the word counter incremented.

```
if (c == ' ' || c == '\n' || c == '\t')
    state = 0;
else if (state == 0) {
    state = 1;
    nwords = nwords + 1;
}
```

For example in the sequence:

```
coding monkey
```

When the program first starts, **state=0**. When it reads the first character, **c**, which is not a space character, it branches to the **else** portion of the statement. As **state** is initially zero, it sets **state** to 1 and increments the word counter to 1. Now it reads the next character, **o**, and does not process either part of the **if** statement. This continues until it reads the space after **coding**. Now the first part of the **if** statement becomes true, and **state** is reset to 0. When the next character, **m** is encountered, **state** is again set to 1 and the word counter is incremented to 2. And so on . . .

Finally we can print out the values of the counters:

```
printf("Text counting:\n");
printf("Number of lines: %d\n", nlines);
printf("Number of words: %d\n", nwords);
printf("Number of characters: %d\n", nchars);
```

Testing the Program

Once the program compiles, we run it. But what makes this program a little different is the fact that this program runs on the command line. That means you have to run the executable in the following fashion:

```
C:\>word_count < vader.txt
```

This basically uses the contents of the text file **vader.txt** as the input for the program. Now consider the contents of this file:

```
I've been waiting for you Obi-Wan. We meet again, at last.
The circle is now complete; when I left you, I was but the
learner, now I am the master. Only a master of evil, Darth.
```

Here are the results from the program:

```
Text counting:
Number of lines: 3
Number of words: 36
Number of characters: 178
```

In its simplest form, this program seems to do quite a good job. It delineates a word as a sequence of characters between two white spaces, which implies a space, tab, or new line (return) character. If we actually count the number of characters in the file, though, we get 175, which implies that it is counting new lines as well. This is fine, but they are invisible, so we should change the segment of the program that counts characters to:

```
if (c != '\n')
    nchars = nchars + 1;
```

thereby eliminating new lines. Let's try something a bit more challenging:

```
I amar prestar aen. Han mathon ne nen. Han mathon ne chae. A
han noston ned 'wilith. The world is changed. I feel it in
the water. I feel it in the earth. I smell it in the air.

Much that once was is lost, for none now live who remember
it. It began with the forging of the Great Rings. Three were
given to the Elves, immortal, wisest, and fairest of all
beings. Seven to the Dwarf lords, great miners and craftsman
of the mountain halls. And nine . . . nine rings were gifted
to the race of Men, who above all else desire power. For
within these rings was bound the strength and will to govern
each race. But they were all of them deceived, for another
ring was made. In the land of Mordor, in the fires of Mount
Doom, the Dark Lord Sauron forged in secret a master ring to
control all others. And into this ring he poured his cruelty,
his malice, and his will to dominate all life. One ring to
rule them all. One by one, the free lands of Middle-earth
fell to the power of the Ring. But there were some who
resisted. A last alliance of Men and Elves marched against
the armies of Mordor, and on the slopes of Mount Doom, they
fought for the freedom of Middle-earth.
```

Here are the results from the program:

```
Text counting:
Number of lines: 18
Number of words: 226
Number of characters: 1148
```

Again, the program works very well. Note, however, that it perceives "Middle-earth" as one word. However does it cope with the following input?

```
The Lord of the Rings is an epic fantasy saga by the British
author J.R.R. Tolkien, his most popular work and a sequel to
his popular fantasy novel, The Hobbit. The Lord of the Rings
was written during World War II and originally published in
three volumes in 1954 and 1955.
```

The output tells us there are 53 words, which is true—*if* we count numbers (e.g., 1954), Roman numerals (e.g., II), and single characters (e.g., J.) as words. If we take those out, we get 47 words. But are we just playing with trivialities? Probably. Don't forget in our interpretation of what a word is, we have some leeway. The program itself has to follow its set of rules, but *we* decide what those rules are. What about words joined by punctuation, or misspelled words? Well, we aren't designing a spelling fixer, so it probably doesn't matter. The program we have is *simple*. If we want to modify it, we could store each "series of characters" and check to see if it upholds all the rules.

Extending the Program

First let's modify the program so it will ignore numbers. This basically involves storing each set of characters that represents a word as a string and checking if the first element is a digit. If it is, we subtract the word from the counter. Here are the results from the program:

```
Text counting:
Number of lines: 5
Number of words: 51
Number of characters: 276
```

which is fine because it has excluded 1954 and 1955. Basically we use a counter **(index)** to track the start of each word. If the value of **index** is 0, then we store the character that has just been read into a variable, **checknum**.

```
if (index == 0)
    checknum = (char)c;
index = index + 1;
```

In the portion of code that checks the value of state to denote the end of a word, we then check to see if the first character of the word was a digit. If it is not a digit, we increment the word counter:

```
if (!isdigit(checknum))
    nwords = nwords + 1;
```

Therefore, the code within the main program becomes

```
        int nlines, nwords, nchars, state, index = 0;
        char c;
        char checknum;

        state = 0;
        nlines = nwords = nchars = 0;

        while ((c = getchar()) != EOF) {
            if (c != '\n')
                nchars = nchars + 1;

            if (index == 0)
                checknum = c;
            index = index + 1;

            if (c == '\n')
                nlines = nlines + 1;

            if (c == ' ' || c == '\n' || c == '\t'){
                state = 0;
                index = 0;
```

```
        }
        else if (state == 0) {
            state = 1;
            if (!isdigit(checknum))
                nwords = nwords + 1;
        }
    }
```

Now let's add a counter that just counts alphabetic characters, so we can obtain an estimate of the average length of each word. The extended program follows. We will not dissect this program, but the code has been heavily commented. The full program can be found in Appendix F.

The output is:

```
Text counting:
Number of lines: 5
Number of words: 51
Number of characters: 276

The number of alphabetic characters is 209
The average length of a word is 4.10 characters
```

Now let's try it on a really large file, say Charles Darwin's *Origin of Species*. Here's the output:

```
Text counting:
Number of lines: 20552
Number of words: 213835
Number of characters: 1233743

The number of alphabetic characters is 1009653
The average length of a word is 4.72 characters
```

Reading from a File

Finally, we could modify our program so that it prompts us for the file we want to count. This requires us to change the I/O behavior. Essentially we have to wrap the entire algorithm around the file-handling processes. First create a string to hold the filename and a pointer to a file:

```
char filename[40];
FILE *ifp;
```

Next provide a means of asking the user for the file:

```
printf("Enter the text file to process: ");
scanf("%s",filename);
```

Open the file for reading:

```
ifp = fopen(filename, "r");
```

Then check to see if the file actually exists. If it doesn't—if the string is empty—then exit the program:

```
// If the file does not exist, exit the program.
if (ifp == NULL){
    printf("Sorry that file does not exist.\n");
    exit(0);
}
```

Now perform the guts of the algorithm, and before printing out the results, close the file:

```
fclose(ifp);
```

The full program can be found in Appendix F.

Epilog

Counting words is something we take for granted when we use programs such as word processors. The algorithms are usually much more akin to our first program in this section. Very rarely are they as elaborate as our word counter, which ignores numbers and gives a summary of average word length. We could pursue this and create quite an elaborate program. Here is a list of other features we could add:

- Count the number of articles (a, an) or adposition (of, to, in, for, on, with, as, by, at, from).
- Count the number of numbers.
- Count the number of paragraphs.
- Calculate word frequencies.

CS21

Great Circle Distance

It is not the mountain we conquer, but ourselves.

—Sir Edmund Hillary

The Problem Description

The *great circle distance* is the shortest distance between two points on the surface of a sphere, measured along a path on the surface of the sphere.[1]

Program Requirements

Since the Earth is approximately spherical, the equations for great circle distance are important for finding the shortest distance between points on the surface of the Earth and so have important applications in navigation. For instance, they can be used to calculate frequent flyer miles, or the fastest distance between two ports. An example follows, with the first decimal degree relating to the latitude and the second the longitude:

Montreal, Canada: 45.5091° N, –73.55° W
Bern, Switzerland: 46.95° N, 7.4333° E

We will now proceed to design a program that reads in four parameters L1, G1, L2, and G2 (the latitude and longitude of two points on the Earth) and prints out the great circle distance in miles between them. We will calculate the distance using the *spherical law of cosines:*

$$d = R \cdot \text{arccoss}(\sin(L_1)\sin(L_2) + \cos(L_1)\cos(L_2)\cos(G_1 - G_2)) \tag{1}$$

All angles are in degrees. The value of R used here is the radius of the Earth, which is 6,372.695 km.

---

[1]http://en.wikipedia.org/wiki/Great_circle_distance

Program Specification

Input(s):   The latitude and longitude for each of the two positions

Output(s):   The great circle distance (GCD)

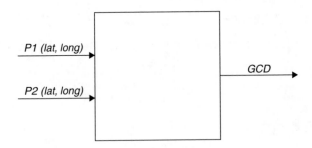

   The trigonometric functions in C take and return parameters in radians. We will use the C equation we created in Case Study 17 to convert from degrees to radians. Note that the shape of Earth is more like a flattened spheroid than a sphere, so formula is only an approximation (up to around 0.5% error).

Algorigthm Design

The basic algorithm is fairly simple:

1. Read in the latitude and longitude for both points as decimal degrees.
2. Convert the coordinates for each point from decimal degrees to radians.
   a. $radians = \left(\dfrac{\pi}{180}\right) degrees$
3. Calculate the great circle distance using Eq. 1.
4. Output the great circle distance.

The Program

```
#include <stdio.h>
#include <math.h>
#define PI 3.14159
#define R 6372.695
// Program to calculate the "great circle distance" using the
// "Spherical Law of Cosines"

int main(void)
{
```

```
double p1_latD, p2_latD, p1_longD, p2_longD;
double p1_latR, p2_latR, p1_longR, p2_longR;
double sin_lat, cos_lat, longD, dist;

// Input the latitudes and longitudes for each point
printf("Enter the latitude for point1: ");
scanf("%lf", &p1_latD);
printf("Enter the longitude for point1: ");
scanf("%lf", &p1_longD);

printf("Enter the latitude for point2: ");
scanf("%lf", &p2_latD);
printf("Enter the longitude for point2: ");
scanf("%lf", &p2_longD);

// Convert from decimal degrees to radians
p1_latR = (PI / 180.0) * p1_latD;
p1_longR = (PI / 180.0) * p1_longD;
p2_latR = (PI / 180.0) * p2_latD;
p2_longR = (PI / 180.0) * p2_longD;

// Perform the distance calculation using the
// "Spherical Law of Cosines"

longD = p1_longR - p2_longR;
sin_lat = sin(p1_latR) * sin(p2_latR);
cos_lat = cos(p1_latR) * cos(p2_latR);
dist = R * acos(sin_lat + cos_lat * cos(longD));

// Output the resulting great circle distance
printf("The great circle distance is %.2f km\n", dist);

return 0;
}
```

Dissecting the Code

The first thing we will do is create some storage for the information, in this case the latitude and longitude for each of the two points. We have decided to use the prefixes **p1** and **p2** to denote the two points, and two phrases to denote latitude (**lat**) and longitude (**long**) respectively in degrees (**D**):

```
double p1_latD, p2_latD, p1_longD, p2_longD;
```

We also need corresponding variables to store the radian versions (**R**):

```
double p1_latR, p2_latR, p1_longR, p2_longR;
```

Now we will prompt for input:

```
printf("Enter the latitude for point1: ");
scanf("%lf", &p1_latD);
printf("Enter the longitude for point1: ");
scanf("%lf", &p1_longD);
printf("Enter the latitude for point2: ");
scanf("%lf", &p2_latD);
printf("Enter the longitude for point2: ");
scanf("%lf", &p2_longD);
```

We now have to convert each of the decimal degrees to radians. This involves a series of equations of the form:

```
p1_latR = (PI / 180.0) * p1_latD;
p1_longR = (PI / 180.0) * p1_longD;
p2_latR = (PI / 180.0) * p2_latD;
p2_longR = (PI / 180.0) * p2_longD;
```

Now we can perform the actual calculations. We achieve this by actually splitting up the equation, which represents the spherical law of cosines:

```
longD = p1_longR - p2_longR;
sin_lat = sin(p1_latR) * sin(p2_latR);
cos_lat = cos(p1_latR) * cos(p2_latR);
dist = R * acos(sin_lat + cos_lat * cos(longD));
```

Now remember to declare the temporary variables:

```
double sin_lat, cos_lat, longD, dist;
```

and define the values of **PI** and **R**:

```
#define PI 3.14159
#define R 6372.695
```

Now that we have the distance, we can output it:

```
printf("The great circle distance is %.1f km\n", dist);
```

Testing the Program

We can test the program using the example of Montreal-Bern given in the problem explanation. The output we get is:

```
Enter the latitude for point1: 45.5091
Enter the longitude for point1: -73.55
Enter the latitude for point2: 46.95
Enter the longitude for point2: 7.4333
The great circle distance is 5939.04 km
```

Epilog

While this offers a solution, it goes to illustrate one of the caveats of choosing the first solution you find. Although this formula is mathematically exact, it is unreliable for small distances because the inverse cosine is ill-conditioned. Sinnott[2] offers the following table to illustrate the point:

```
cos (5 degrees=5.0) = 0.996194698
cos (1 degree=1.0) = 0.9999847695
cos (1 minute=0.01667) = 0.9999999577
cos (1 second=0.00028) = 0.9999999999882
cos (0.05 sec=0.00001) = 0.999999999999971
```

A computer carrying seven significant figures cannot distinguish the cosines of any distances smaller than about 1 minute of arc. Instead, we can use a simpler equation known as the *Haversine formula:*

$$d = R \cdot 2 \text{ arcsin}$$

We just have to change the formula portion of the program:

```
longD = p1_longR − p2_longR;
latD = p2_latR − p1_latR;
sin2_lat = pow(sin(latD/2.0),2.0);
sin2_long = pow(sin(longD/2.0),2.0);
cos_lat = cos(p1_latR) * cos(p2_latR);
dist = R * 2 * asin(sqrt(sin2_lat + cos_lat * sin2_long));
```

[2]Sinnott, R. W., "Virtues of the Haversine," *Sky and Telescope,* 1984, Vol. 68, No. 2, 159.

Bubble Sort

. . . bubble sort seems to have nothing to recommend it.
—Donald Knuth

The Problem Description

Sorting is the process of rearranging a given set of objects in a specific order. Sorting is a fundamental problem in many algorithms. When we look up a word on Wiktionary (http://en.wikipedia.org/wiki/wiktionary), it uses an algorithm that searches through a list of words to find one that best matches our request. We presume the list is kept in some sorted manner, similar to a paper dictionary. Searching is very efficient if a list is first sorted. There are many different algorithms for sorting; some are fast, some are slow. Some examples of sorting algorithms include: selection sort, insertion sort, shell sort, mergesort, heapsort, and quicksort.

We will investigate one of the oldest and probably most controversial sorting algorithms: the *bubble sort.*

Program Requirements

The bubble sort probably had its origins in a paper published in 1956 by Friend entitled "Sorting on Electronic Computer Systems," which uses the term "sorting by exchange."[1] The term *bubble sort* does not really appear until 1962 in Iverson's book *A Programming Language.*[2] The effect of the algorithm is to "bubble" the largest elements in a list to the end of the list and the smallest elements to the start of the list. The effect of the first pass

---

[1]Friend, E. H., "Sorting on electronic computer systems," *Journal of the ACM,* 1956, Vol. 3, No. 4, 134–168.
[2]Iverson, K. E., *A Programming Language,* John Wiley & Sons, 1962.

is to "bubble" the smallest value in the array into the element a[0]. In the second pass a[0] is not examined, so the smallest value is placed in a[1]. It takes n-1 passes to put all the elements in order. For example:

```
Original   44   57   12   42   4
           44   12   57   42   4
           44   12   42   57   4
           44   12   42   4    57
           12   44   42   4    57
           12   42   44   4    57
           12   42   4    44   57
           12   4    42   44   57
           4    12   42   44   57
```

The underlined pair signifies the two numbers that are compared and swapped. In this manner the largest number always bubbles to the end.

Program Specification and Algorithm Design

Input(s):   A list of integers

Output(s):   The sorted list of integers

Modularity: A function called bubblesort to perform the sort.

The basic algorithm is fairly simple:

1. Initialize an array, A, to store a series of n numbers.
2. Input numbers into the array.
3. Pass the array to the function bubblesort, which will return a list of sorted numbers.
4. Output the sorted numbers.

The algorithm for the function **bubblesort**:

1. Select an element in the array, i, starting from the last element in the array, and traversing the list backwards: $i = n : 1$
   a. Traverse through all the elements in the array from 1 to i: $j = 1 : i$
   b. If the element $A[i]$ is less than the element $A[j]$
      i. Swap the elements.

The Program

```c
#include <stdio.h>

// Program to sort a list of integers using bubble
// sort algorithm

void swap(int*, int*);
void bubblesort(int [], int);

int main(void)
{
    int sorted[100], i, N;

    printf("How many numbers to sort? ");
    scanf("%d", &N);
    printf("Enter a list of %d numbers: ", N);
    for (i=0; i<N; i=i+1)
        scanf("%d", &sorted[i]);

    bubblesort(sorted, N);

    printf("The sorted list of numbers is : ");
    for (i=0; i<N; i=i+1)
        printf("%d", sorted[i]);
    return 0;
}

// Function to swap two integer values
void swap(int *x, int *y)
{
    int temp;
    temp = *x;
    *x = *y;
    *y = temp;
}

// Function to perform the bubblesort
void bubblesort(int sorted[100], int N)
{
    int i, j;

    for (i=N-1; i>0; i=i-1)
        for (j=0; j<i; j=j+1)
            if (sorted[j] > sorted[j+1])
                swap(&sorted[j],&sorted[j+1]);
}
```

Dissecting the Code

We have been through many **main** programs now, so we won't dissect this. Its basic role is identifying the number of numbers to be sorted (stored in **N**), inputting the numbers and storing them in an array **(sorted)**. **main** then calls the function **bubblesort** in the following manner:

```
bubblesort(sorted, N);
```

After the **main** resumes control from the function, it prints out the sorted list, also stored in **sorted**. Note that the original array has been overwritten by the function **bubblesort.** If we want to keep this array, we should have made a copy before passing it to the function, as any function will treat an array passed to it as *pass-by-reference*. The function **swap** has also been explained earlier. We are starting to build new programs using components of older programs. This is a good example of code reuse. We shall concentrate on dissecting the function **bubblesort.** First we deal with the function skeleton, which takes as input the array to be sorted and an integer representing the number of elements stored in the array:

```
void bubblesort(int sorted[100], int N)
{

}
```

Next we look at the actual algorithm, which consists of a nested **for** loop:

```
for (i=N-1; i>0; i=i-1)
    for (j=0; j<i; j=j+1)
        if (sorted[j] > sorted[j+1])
            swap(&sorted[j],&sorted[j+1]);
```

In the outer **for** loop, we set the scope of the search, from N–1 to 0, which denotes the elements of the array, from the last to the first.

```
for (i=N-1; i>0; i=i-1)
```

The inner **for** loop deals with traversing the array from the first element up until the element whose index is **i**:

```
for (j=0; j<i; j=j+1)
```

Now within this loop we compare the value of two neighboring elements in the array and swap the elements if the one closest to the beginning of the array is greater than the other:

```
if (sorted[j] > sorted[j+1])
    swap(sorted[j],&sorted[j+1]);
```

Note the use of the ampersands as we are passing the address of individual elements of the array to the function **swap**. For an array with five **(N)** elements, the values of **i** are 0 to 4 and the values of **j** for each value of **i** are:

```
outer loop 1 (i=4) : j = 0:3
outer loop 2 (i=3) : j = 0:2
outer loop 3 (i=2) : j = 0:1
outer loop 4 (i=1) : j = 0
```

Testing the Program

We can test the program using the numbers of our earlier example:

```
How many numbers to sort? 5
Enter a list of 5 numbers: 44 57 12 42 4
The sorted list of numbers is : 4 12 42 44 57
```

Here is a breakdown of what happens:

The first iteration of the outer loop will check:

```
sorted[0] > sorted[1]?    44 > 57 = false, ignore
sorted[1] > sorted[2]?    57 > 12 = true, swap
Array =   44   12   57   42   4
sorted[2] > sorted[3]?    57 > 42 = true, swap
Array =   44   12   42   57   4
sorted[3] > sorted[4]?    57 > 4  = true, swap
Array =   44   12   42   4    57
```

Now 57 is locked in place, and we don't have to check it. The second iteration of the outer loop gives:

```
sorted[0] > sorted[1]?    44 > 12 = true, swap
Array =   12   44   42   4    57
sorted[1] > sorted[2]?    44 > 42 = true, swap
Array =   12   42   44   4    57
sorted[2] > sorted[3]?    44 > 4  = true, swap
Array =   12   42   4    44   57
```

Now 44 is locked in place, and we don't have to check it. The third iteration of the outer loop gives:

```
sorted[0] > sorted[1]?    12 > 42 = false, ignore
sorted[1] > sorted[2]?    42 > 4 = true, swap
Array =   12   4    42   44   57
```

Now 42 is locked in place, and we don't have to check it. The final iteration of the outer loop gives:

```
sorted[0] > sorted[1]?    12 > 4  = false, ignore
Array =    4   12    42   44   57
```

Now the entire array is sorted!

Epilog

In reality other sorting procedures, such as selection sort, are way faster and probably more intuitive. Its basic algorithm is:

1. Find the minimum value in the array.
2. Swap it with the value in the first position.
3. Repeat the previous steps for remainder of the list (starting at the second position).

The Calendar Problem

The early bird may catch the worm, but the second mouse
gets the cheese.
—Sanskrit Proverb

The Problem Description

We consider a problem that involves determining the number of days between two dates in the same year.

Program Requirements

We begin by discussing an informal strategy for the problem.[1] This basically sets out the rules:

1. If the given dates are in the same month, the number of days is the difference between them.
2. If the two given dates are in different months then:
   a. Determine the number of days from the earlier date to the end of its month.
   b. For each month starting from the first month after the earliest date and ending with the last month before the later date, count the number of days in each month.
   c. Add the day of the month of the latter date.
   d. Return the final sum as the number of days between the two dates.

Consider some test data to illustrate the algorithm: April 19 and November 6.

---

[1]Abbott, R. J., "Program design by informal English descriptions," *Communications of the ACM*, 1983, Vol. 26, 882–894.

The two dates are in different months so procedure 2 must be used:

    a. There are 11 days left in April.

    b. The months between April and November are May, June, July, August, September, and October. Sum up 31 for each of May, July, August, and October and 30 for each of June and September = 184.

    c. Add 6 for the first part of November.

    d. Sum = 11 + 184 + 6 = 201

Program Specification and Algorithm Design

Input(s):   Two dates, representing day of the month and month of the year

Output(s):   An integer representing the number of days between the two dates input

Additional information needed: Number of days in each month of the year.
    The basic algorithm is fairly simple:

1. Input a number representing the day and month for each date.
2. Identify if the months are the same?

    a. Yes—subtract the day from the second month from the day of the first. This represents the number of days between the dates.

    b. No—Calculate the number of days remaining in the first month from the first date.

        i. Cycle through the months from the month after the first month to the month before the last month. Add the number of days in each month to a running total.

       ii. Add the number of days in the month of the second date up until the day specified in that month.

3. Output the number of days between the two dates.

This results in the following sample pseudocode:

```
INTEGER: day1, day2, mon1, mon2, count
INTEGER CONTAINER: months[12]
months = [31,28,31,30,31,30,31,31,30,31,30,31]

READ: day1, month1
READ: day2, month2

IF month1 equals month2
    count = day2 - day1
ELSE
    count = months[mon1-1] - day1;
    FOR i : mon1+1 to mon2-1
        count = count + months[i]
    count = count + day2
ENDIF
```

The Program

```c
#include <stdio.h>

int main(void)
{
    int day1, day2, mon1, mon2, daycount, i;
    int months[12] = {31,28,31,30,31,30,31,31,30,31,30,31};

    printf("Please enter a start date (d/m): ");
    scanf("%d/%d", &day1, &mon1);
    printf("Please enter an end date (d/m): ");
    scanf("%d/%d", &day2, &mon2);

    if (mon1 == mon2)
        daycount = day2 - day1;
    else
    {
        daycount = months[mon1-1] - day1;
        for (i=mon1; i<=mon2-2; i=i+1)
            daycount = daycount + months[i];
        daycount = daycount + day2;
    }

    printf("The number of days is %d\n", daycount);

    return 0;
}
```

Dissecting the Code

The core skeleton of a C program we know all about, so we won't look at that. Let's skip straight into the actual body of the main program. First we have to create some variables:

```c
int day1, day2, mon1, mon2, daycount, i;
```

These are pretty self-explanatory. The first four variables are used to store dates, while **daycount** is used to store the incremented days, and **i** is an index variable for the loop. Next we use an array to store the number of days in each month.

```c
int months[12] = {31,28,31,30,31,30,31,31,30,31,30,31};
```

Now we move onto prompting the user for input:

```c
printf("Please enter a start date (d/m): ");
scanf("%d/%d", &day1, &mon1);
printf("Please enter an end date (d/m): ");
scanf("%d/%d", &day2, &mon2);
```

Note that the **scanf** formatting statement specifies **%d/%d**, which means that it expects an integer, followed by a /, followed by another integer. So the input will be of the form:

```
23/7
```

representing the 23rd day of the 7th month. Now we can process the data. The core part of the algorithm deals with an **if-else** situation. First the program checks to see if the two months are the same:

```
if (mon1 == mon2)
```

If they are, then both days occur in the same month, so it just calculates the difference between the two.

```
daycount = day2 - day1;
```

Otherwise the months are different, so the **else** clause is invoked.

```
else
{
    daycount = months[mon1-1] - day1;
    for (i=mon1; i<=mon2-2; i=i+1)
        daycount = daycount + months[i];
    daycount = daycount + day2;
}
```

Here we first calculate the days remaining in the first month.

```
daycount = months[mon1-1] - day1;
```

Then we use a **for** loop to iterate through the months in between **mon1** and **mon2**. So if the two dates are 23/7 and 11/10, it will iterate through months 8 and 9.

```
for (i=mon1; i<=mon2-2; i=i+1)
    daycount = daycount + months[i];
```

The loop starts at **mon1**, because array indices are one less. For example, the date mentioned previously is 23/7, so the month is seven. The months processed by the loop are 8 and 9, corresponding to elements **[7]** and **[8]** in the array **months**. In a similar fashion, ending the loop requires us to process months up to **mon2-2** (**mon2** equals 10, 10-2=8, and **months[8]** is the ninth month. Confused yet? Here's another way of looking at it:

```
month 8 = months[7] = months[mon1]
month 9 = months[8] = months[mon2-2]
```

For each of these intermediate months, we add the number of days to **daycount**. Now when the loop is finished, we can add the days in the second month, **day2**, to **daycount**. Now we just have to print out the result:

```
printf("The number of days is %d\n", daycount);
```

If we didn't know about arrays, we might have to use a **switch** statement.

```
for (i = mon1+1; i < mon2; i=i+1)
    switch (i)
    {
        case 2:  daycount = daycount + 28;
                 break;
        case 4:  ;
        case 6:  ;
        case 9:  ;
        case 11: daycount = daycount + 30;
                 break;
        \default: daycount = daycount + 31;
    }
```

Testing the Program

Run the program!

```
Please enter a start date (d/m): 23/7
Please enter an end date (d/m): 11/10
The number of days is 80
```

Now count the number of days on a calendar.

This should always work, right? Well, not really. Every four years we have a leap year, so February has 29 days. How do we incorporate this into our program? We have to change the algorithm, a process called *algorithm refinement*.

Algorithm Refinement

There is one caveat with the program as it currently stands. What happens when a leap year is encountered? We have to refine our algorithm to take this into account.

If the year is a leap year, and the earlier month is February, add a day.

```
if (isLeapYear(year) && (mon1 <= 2) )
    daycount = daycount + 1;
```

So now the program will look like:

```
#include <stdio.h>

int main(void)
{
    int day1, day2, mon1, mon2, daycount, year,i;
    int months[12] = {31,28,31,30,31,30,31,31,30,31,30,31};
```

```
    printf("Please enter a year (yyyy): ");
    scanf("%d", &year)
    printf("Please enter a start date (d/m): ");
    scanf("%d/%d", &day1, &mon1)
    printf("Please enter an end date (d/m): ");
    scanf("%d/%d", &day2, &mon2)

    if (mon1 == mon2)
        daycount = day2 - day1;
    else
    {
        daycount = months[mon1-1] - day1;
        for (i = mon1; i <= mon2-2; i=i+1)
            daycount = daycount + months[i]
        daycount = daycount + day2
    }

    if (isLeapYear(year) && (mon1 <= 2) )
        daycount = daycount + 1;

    printf("The number of days is %d\n", daycount);
    return 0;
}
```

Don't worry too much about the function **isLeapYear**. That's covered in Case Study 9.

Talking to Mars

Mars is there, waiting to be reached.

—Buzz Aldrin

The Problem Description

In 2004, NASA sent two rovers, Spirit and Opportunity, on seven-month, 515 million km journey to land on Mars. Mars is the fourth planet from the Sun in our solar system and is named after Mars, the Roman god of war. Mars is also known as the "Red Planet" due to its reddish appearance when seen from Earth. The rovers receive their commands from Earth via three onboard antennas: a movable high-gain antenna, a fixed low-gain antenna and a fixed, ultra-high frequency (UHF) antenna. Some data is sent directly to Earth and some is transmitted via the Mars orbiters Mars Odyssey and Mars Global Surveyor, which are constantly orbiting the red planet. This enables them to be updated with new software. In the latest software update (January 4, 2007), Spirit and Opportunity inherited four new skills. The first of these enables spacecraft to examine images and recognize certain types of features. The rovers can now recognize dust devils or clouds and select only the relevant parts of those images to transmit back to Earth. Another new feature, called *visual target tracking,* enables a rover to keep recognizing a designated landscape feature as the rover moves.

Program Requirements

Communication is achieved using radio waves, which are another form of light waves. They travel through space at the speed of 300,000 km per second. However due to the way that planets orbit, the distance of Mars from Earth can be anywhere from a minimum of 56,000,000 km to a maximum of 399,000,000 km. So, there is a time lag between sending a message on Earth and the message being received by a rover. Calculating the delay is as simple as dividing the distance by the speed of light.

Program Specification and Algorithm Design

Input(s): A number representing the distance in kilometers between Earth and Mars

Output(s): The time lag in both minutes and seconds

The basic algorithm:

1. Read in the value for the distance between the Earth and Mars.
2. Calculate the delay as the distance divided by the speed of light.
3. Calculate the delay in minutes by dividing the delay by 60.
4. Output the delay in both seconds and minutes.

The pseudocode might look like:

```
READ distance
INITIALIZE the value for the speed of light
CALCULATE delay as distance divided by speed of light
CALCULATE delay in minutes
OUTPUT delay in both minutes and seconds
```

Building the Program

We start the program with the normal C skeleton:

```
#include <stdio.h>

int main(void)
{
    return 0;
}
```

Now we will add some variables to store information. From the description of the program, we need storage for the following entities:

```
speed of light, delay in seconds, delay in minutes, distance
```

From these descriptions, we could select from the following identifiers:

speed of light:	speed_of_light, lightspeed
delay in seconds:	delay_sec, delay, delayS
delay in minutes:	delay_min, delayM, delay_in_minutes
distance:	distance, distanceEM,
	distance_between_earth_and_mars

Which ones should we choose? Probably not an identifier like **distance_between_earth_and_mars** because it's just too long. Very descriptive, but way too long. Let's try the following group of identifiers:

```
distance, lightspeed, delay, delay_min
```

Since we are probably dealing with real numbers, we should create them all as type **double**.

```
double distance, lightspeed, delay, delay_min;
```

Now we can define the default value for the speed of light in km per second:

```
lightspeed = 299792.458; //km per second
```

Prompt the user to input the distance between Mars and Earth:

```
printf("Enter the distance from Mars to Earth (km): ");
scanf("%lf", &distance);
```

Remember, because distance is a **double,** we have to use **%lf** when using **scanf.** Next we perform the delay calculation:

```
delay = distance / lightspeed;
```

Along with the conversion from seconds to minutes:

```
delay_min = delay / 60.0;
```

Finally we can print out the results:

```
printf("The time delay when communicating with\n");
printf("Mars is %.2f seconds OR %.2f minutes\n", delay,
        delay_min);
```

The conversion character used here is **%.2f,** which prints out the floating point number to two decimal places.

The Program

```
#include <stdio.h>
int main(void)
{
    double distance, lightspeed, delay, delay_min;
    lightspeed = 299792.458; //km per second
    printf("Enter the distance from Mars to Earth (km): ");
    scanf("%lf", &distance);
    delay = distance / lightspeed;
    delay_min = delay / 60.0;
    printf("The time delay when communicating with\n");
    printf("Mars is %.2f seconds OR %.2f minutes\n", delay,
            delay_min);
    return 0;
}
```

Testing the Program

This is a fairly easy program to test. Run it and input 56,000,000. Here's the output:

```
Enter the distance from Mars to Earth (km): 56000000
The time delay when communicating with
Mars is 186.80 seconds OR 3.11 minutes
```

Being Defensive

The outline mentioned some constraints on the input, which we didn't include in our program, so let's look at them now. The distance from Mars to Earth can be a minimum of 56,000,000 km, or a maximum of 399,000,000 km, so we should vet our input. We can use a simple **if** statement and a **while** loop to validate the input, and if incorrect, prompt for the data again. This loop will only exit when the input distance matches the constraints. It probably would be nice to add some sort of error message if the input is outside the range specified.

```
while (1)
{
    printf("Enter the distance from Mars to Earth (km): ");
    scanf("%lf", &distance);
    if (distance >= 56000000.0 && distance <= 399000000.0)
        break;
    else {
        printf("Sorry, the distance must be within\n");
        printf("the range 56000000km to 399000000km\n");
    }
}
```

Epilog

The closest Mars has approached earth in 60,000 years occurred on August 27, 2003, when it was actually 55,758,006 km distant. This means that the bounds of our defensive check may not have been accurate. This is the reality of writing programs for applications which have parameters which may change. Always remember to allow for such contingencies when designing software.

Matching DNA

DNA was the first three-dimensional Xerox machine.

—Kenneth Boulding

The Problem Description

DNA, or deoxyribonucleic acid, is a long molecule, like a chain, where the links of the chain are pieces called nucleotides (sometimes also called *bases*). It encodes the genes present in animals, microbes, and plants. Each DNA molecule is made up of sequences of four simpler molecules: A (adenine), G (guanine), C (cytosine) and T (thymine). Genetic fingerprinting and DNA profiling are techniques used to distinguish between individuals of the same species using only samples of their DNA. It was invented by Sir Alec Jeffreys at the University of Leicester in 1985.

Program Requirements

DNA matching is often used in forensic science to match suspects to samples of blood, hair, or saliva. It is also used in such applications as identifying human remains, paternity testing, matching organ donors, studying populations of wild animals, and establishing the province or composition of foods. There are a number of different DNA fingerprinting techniques, but the one we are going to look at here is more akin to deciding whether two DNA strings match.

Program Specifications and Algorithm Design

The program to compare two strings of DNA uses the following functions:

read_DNA

- Read two DNA sequences from standard input.
- If the user enters any lowercase characters *(a, t, g, or c)*, the function should translate them into uppercase characters *(A, T, G, or C)*.

validate_DNA

- Validate that the DNA string contains only the appropriate molecules by checking each character to guarantee that it is A, C, G, or T.
- Returns 1 for a valid DNA sequence and 0 for an unacceptable sequence.

match_DNA

- Check if two DNA sequences match.
- Return the value 1 if they match.

Input(s):   Two strings representing DNA sequences
Output(s):   A message that reports whether or not the DNA sequences match

Here's the outline of the algorithm for the function **read_DNA**:

1. Read a string of characters representing a DNA string.
2. Make sure all characters in the string are uppercase.
   a.   Function **checkCase** checks each element of the string and, if a lowercase character is encountered, converts it to uppercase.
3. Return the string and a value of true if the string is not empty.

Here's the outline of the algorithm for the function **validate_DNA**:

1. Check to make sure all the characters in the strings are members of the set {A, C, G, T}.
2. Return 1 if the string is valid, 0 if it is not.

   Here's the outline of the algorithm for the function **match_DNA**:

1. Check to see if the strings match.
2. Return 1 if the strings match, 0 if they do not.

Now let's look at how each of these items can be implemented as a function.

Deriving the Program

We will build the program in stages, analogous to the different functions.

Reading the DNA Strings

The first function we create will deal with reading a DNA string from the standard input. The function **read_DNA** has one parameter, namely the DNA string, and one value that is returned upon completion to determine whether or not the function was successful.

```
int read_DNA(char dna[N])
{
    int L;
    scanf("%s", dna);
    L = strlen(dna);
    checkCase(dna);
    if (L != 0)
        return 1;
    else
        return 0;

}
```

The string is read into the character array **dna**. We then check the entire string to make sure all elements are in uppercase. Then we check to see whether the string is empty or not. Checking the case is performed by the function **checkCase**:

```
void checkCase(char dna[N])
{
    int i, L;
    L = strlen(dna);
    for (i=0; i<L; i=i+1)
        if (islower(dna[i]))
            dna[i] = toupper(dna[i]);

}
```

It basically cycles through the string from element **0** to **L-1** (where **L** is the length of the string), checking if each character is a lowercase character using the function **islower**. If it is lowercase, it is automatically converted to uppercase using **toupper**.

Validating the DNA Strings

The next function validates a string. The function **validate_DNA** returns a value of 1 if a string is valid, 0 if it contains invalid characters. This is what the function looks like:

```
int validate_DNA(char dna[N])
{
    int i, L, valid=1;
    L = strlen(dna);
    for (i=0; i<L; i=i+1)
        if (dna[i] != 'A' && dna[i] != 'C' &&
            dna[i] != 'G' && dna[i] != 'T')
            valid = 0;
    return valid;

}
```

Like **checkCase**, it cycles through every element in the string. If the element does not equal A, C, G, and T, then it is an invalid character, and the flag variable **valid** is set to 0. If all elements are valid, then **valid** retains its initial value of 1 (true). A simple **for** loop and **if** statement accomplish this.

Match DNA Strings

The final function actually deals with the matching. The function **match_DNA** returns a value of 1 if two strings match, 0 if they don't. The function is not at all complicated and takes two strings as input:

```
int match_DNA(char dna1[N], char dna2[N])
{
    if (strcmp(dna1,dna2) == 0)
        return 1;
    else
        return 0;

}
```

It then uses the string comparison function **strcmp**, from the **string.h** library to do the matching. If **strcmp** returns a value of 0, then the strings match. Any other value returned (i.e., greater than or less than zero), indicates a difference of some sort.

The main Program

Here is the core of the main program:

```
int main(void)
{
    char dna1[N], dna2[N];
    while (1)
    {
        printf("Enter the first DNA sequence: ");
        if (read_DNA(dna1))
            break;
    }
```

```
    while (1)
    {
        printf("Enter the second DNA sequence: ");
        if (read_DNA(dna2))
            break;
    }
    if (validate_DNA(dna1) && validate_DNA(dna2)){
        if (match_DNA(dna1,dna2))
            printf("The two DNA sequences match\n");
        else {
            printf("Sorry, the two DNA sequences ");
            printf("do not match\n");
        }
    }
    else
        printf("Sorry, one of the DNA sequences is invalid\n");
    return 0;
}
```

The first two parts of the program deal with reading in two DNA sequences, each of the form:

```
while (1)
{
    printf("Enter the first DNA sequence: ");
    if (read_DNA(dna1))
        break;
}
```

If the string **dna1** is empty (i.e., if the user hits enter without actually typing anything else), then it asks for the sequence again. The rest of the program is a nested **if** statement. The first **if-else** deals with the validity of the two DNA sequences:

```
if (validate_DNA(dna1) && validate_DNA(dna2)){
}
else
    printf("Sorry, one of the DNA sequences is invalid\n");
```

If they are both valid, they are matched; otherwise, an error message is returned. The inner **if-else** deals with matching the two sequences if they are valid:

```
if (match_DNA(dna1,dna2))
    printf("The two DNA sequences match\n");
else {
    printf("Sorry, the two DNA sequences ");
    printf("do not match\n");
}
```

Testing the Program

Test the program by running it with a number of different cases. First try the case where the sequences do not match:

```
Enter the first DNA sequence: acgtcgtcg
Enter the second DNA sequence: acgtcgggg
Sorry, the two DNA sequences do not match
```

Then the case where one of the sequences is not valid:

```
Enter the first DNA sequence: acgtgctgx
Enter the second DNA sequence: aggctgcgg
Sorry, one of the DNA sequences is invalid
```

Then the case where they actually match:

```
Enter the first DNA sequence: accgtcgtcg
Enter the second DNA sequence: accgtcgtcg
The two dna sequences match
```

Calculating π

Noli turbare circulos meos

—Archimedes

The Problem Description

Pi or π is one of those numbers that is often used in everyday life. It represents a mathematical constant whose value is the ratio of a circle's circumference to its diameter, and it is approximately equal to 3.14159. Given any circle of radius r and area A, the ratio A/r^2 is a number independent of the size of the circle chosen and is usually called π, whose value is 3.14.... The value of π is known to great accuracy today; however, this was not always the case. The first recorded mention of π is in the Bible (1 Kings 7:32 and 2 Chron. 4:2), which gave the value as 3. The symbol π was first proposed by Welsh mathematician William Jones in 1706, although the earliest evidence of approximations to π date from around 1900 BC and can be attributed to the Babylonians (25/8) and the Egyptians (256/81), both values are within 1 percent of the true value. The author of the Rhind Papyrus in 1650 BC described the following rule:

> "Cut off 1/9 of a diameter and construct a square upon the remainder; this has the same area as the circle."

For a circle of diameter 9, $8^2 = 64$, whereas $\pi 4.5^2 = 63.617$, so this is not strictly correct. The first accurate attempt to compute π is often attributed to Archimedes of Syracuse (c. 287–212 BC), who used a sequence of regular polygons inscribed in and circumscribed about a circle. The perimeters may be used to give lower and upper bounds for the value of π, and as the number of sides increases, these bounds give better and better estimates. Beginning with regular hexagons and doubling the number of sides successively, Archimedes computed the perimeters of inscribed and circumscribed polygons with 6, 12, 24, 48, and 96 sides. For a 96-sided polygon he found that

$$3\ 10/71 < \pi < 3\ 10/70$$

which is equivalent to a value for π of 3.14. The astronomer Ptolemy of Alexandria (A.D. 150) used

$$3.1408 < \pi < 3.1428$$

Program Requirements

Many different series are used to calculate π; however, one of the oldest to pose a solution of more than 10 digits was that of Madhava of Sangamagrama around 1400 using the following formulation:

$$\frac{\pi}{4} = 1 - \frac{1}{3} + \frac{1}{5} - \frac{1}{7} + \frac{1}{9} - \dots \tag{1}$$

Madhava was able to calculate π correct to 11 decimal places. It is now known as the *Madhava–Leibniz* series or *Gregory-Leibniz* series since it was rediscovered by James Gregory and Gottfried Leibniz in the 17th century. It is an infinite "alternating" series, a series in which consecutive terms have opposite signs.

Program Specification

Input(s):   A value n representing the number of terms in the series to calculate.

Output(s):   The value of π.

Modularity: The series is calculated within a function named **Leibniz_pi**.

Algorithm Design

To derive an algorithm to calculate this series, we have to decide what the series represents. First of all, the "..." implies that there could be infinite terms in the series, and the very nature of the terms, -ve/+ve, -ve/+ve, and so on, describes some form of repetitive structure. The denominator in each of the terms also contains a pattern, with each value being a consecutive odd number. So here is a preliminary algorithm:

> CREATE a variable pi to store the series as it is calculated.
> PROMPT for the number of terms in the series.
> SET pi to 1.0 to represent the first value in the series.
> LOOP index i from 1 to some number determined to be the scope of the series, n.
> > IF the value of the i is odd
> > > MULTIPLY i by 2, and add 1 to obtain the denominator
> > > DIVIDE 1.0 by the denominator to calculate the term
> > > SUBTRACT the term from the value of pi
> > ELSE IF the value of the i is even
> > > MULTIPLY i by 2, and add 1 to obtain the denominator
> > > DIVIDE 1.0 by the denominator to calculate the term

ADD the term to the value of pi
END IF
END LOOP
MULTIPLY the final value of pi by 4.0

Basically, for the terms whose denominators are 3, 7, 11, 15, . . . , we subtract them from 1.0, and if the denominators are 5, 9, 13, 17, . . . , we add them to 1.0.

The Program

We will represent this algorithm in the form of a function:

```
double Leibniz_pi(unsigned long n)
{
    double pi;
    unsigned long i;

    pi = 1.0;

    for (i=1; i<n; i=i+1)
    {
        if (i%2 == 1)
            pi = pi - (1.0 / ((2.0*i)+1));
        else
            pi = pi + (1.0 / ((2.0*i)+1));
    }

    return pi * 4.0;
}
```

Here is the code snippet from **main** used to call the function **Leibniz_pi**:

```
int main(void)
{
    unsigned long n;
    double pi;

    printf("How many terms to calculate pi to? ");
    scanf("%lu", &n);

    Leibniz_pi(n,&pi);

    printf("The value of pi is: %.20f\n", pi);

    return 0;
}
```

Code Walkthrough

The function has one input (the number of terms in the alternating sequence), and one output (the value of π). The code assumes the variable **pi** is of type double, and **n**, **i** are of type unsigned long, allowing for a large number of terms to be selected. If we were to use an **int** instead, the program would not function correctly for a number of terms greater than the maximum value for **ints**, effectively causing an integer overflow to occur. Here is the skeleton of the function:

```
double Leibniz_pi(unsigned long n)
{
    double pi;
     unsigned long i;
}
```

The first line of code after the variable declarations sets pi to 1.0, essentially the first term in the series.

```
pi = 1.0;
```

The third line of code sets up the **for** loop, to run with **n–1** terms (the nth term is the first one). The **if** statement asks if the value of the loop index, **i**, has a leftover of 1, making it odd. If it is odd, the appropriate term is calculated and subtracted from the variable **pi**. Conversely, if i is even, the term is added to **pi**:

```
for (i=1; i<n; i=i+1)
{
    if (i%2 == 1)
        pi = pi - (1.0 / ((2.0*i)+1));
    else
        pi = pi + (1.0 / ((2.0*i)+1));
}
```

The last line in the function body multiplies the final value of **pi** by 4.0 to get the appropriate value:

```
return pi * 4.0;
```

Testing the Program

Let's try the program with 4000 terms:

```
How many terms to calculate pi to? 4000
The value of pi is: 3.14134265359370434822
```

Comparing this to the actual value of π, we notice that it is correct to 3 decimal places:

```
3.14159265358979323846264338327950288
```

For 1,000,000 terms, we get π accurate to 5 decimal places:

```
The value of pi is: 3.14159165358977432447
```

For 4,000,000,000 terms, we get π accurate to 9 decimal places:

```
The value of pi is: 3.14159265333793946695
```

Calculating π using this last run took 2.24 minutes, which is an extremely long time for 9 digits of significance.

An Alternate Algorithm

Calculating π can be achieved using a different set of calculations inside the **for** loop. For an input value of 4,000,000,000, the algorithm takes 1.42 minutes. This algorithm may run faster because of the removal of the **if**-statement. In the body of the **for** loop, the first expression calculates the fraction representing the term in the alternating sequence. Initially, this has the value -1.0/3.0. The second line updates the value of pi using the fraction calculated. Then both the numerator and denominator are updated for the next pass through the loop. The numerator has its sign changed, and the denominator is increased by 2 to give the next odd number.

```
double Leibniz_pi(unsigned long n)
{
    unsigned long i;
    double pi, numer=-1.0, denom=3.0, frac;

    pi = 1.0;

    for (i=1; i<n; i=i+1)
    {
        frac = numer / denom;
        pi = pi + frac;
        numer = -numer;
        denom = denom + 2.0;
    }

    return pi * 4.0;
}
```

Epilog

In practical terms, using this formula to calculate π is extremely inefficient because the rate of convergence is too slow to calculate many digits in practice; about 4000 terms must be summed to improve upon Archimedes' estimate. To calculate π to 10 accurate decimal places requires more than 10,000,000,000 operations.

Random Password Generator

Treat your password like your toothbrush. Don't let anybody
else use it, and get a new one every six months.
—Clifford Stoll

The Problem Description

A *random password generator* (RPG) is a program that takes input from a pseudo-random
number generator and automatically generates a password. We commonly encounter
these type of passwords on systems where we create accounts on the Internet.

Program Requirements

Random password generators normally output a string of symbols of specified length.
These can be individual characters from some character set (e.g., ASCII), syllables
designed to form pronounceable passwords, or words from some word list. An RPG can
be customized to ensure the resulting password complies with the local password *policy*,
say by always producing a mix of letters, numbers, and special characters.

Program Specifications and Algorithm Design

Functionality:	A password containing lowercase and uppercase characters, which is eight characters in length.
Input(s):	None
Output(s):	A string representing a randomly generated password

The algorithm takes the following form:

1. Store the series of *N* characters to be used to generate the password in a string.
2. For each element of the output password (8 elements):
   a. Choose a random number *between* 0 and *N-1*.
   b. Output the appropriate character from character table.

The Program

```c
#include <stdlib.h>
#include <stdio.h>
#include <time.h>

int main(void)
{
    int length = 8;
    int i,r;
    char AlphaChar[] = {"abcdefghijklmnopqrstuvwxyz"\
                        "ABCDEFGHIJKLMNOPQRSTUVWXYZ"};

    srand((unsigned int)time(0));

    for(i=0; i<length; i++)
    {
        r = 0 + rand() / (RAND_MAX / ((51 - 0) + 1));
        printf("%c", AlphaChar[r]);
    }
    printf("\n");

    return 0;

}
```

Dissecting the Program

We aren't going to bother with the program skeleton. The first line in the body of the program sets the length of the password:

```c
int length = 8;
```

Next we declare an integer to store the random number:

```c
int r, i;
```

Now store the character table that will be used to select characters from which to form the password. Here we chose a string of the form:

```c
char AlphaChar[] = {"abcdefghijklmnopqrstuvwxyz"\
                    "ABCDEFGHIJKLMNOPQRSTUVWXYZ"};
```

Note the use of the continuation character at the end of the first line. We have to use two series of characters enclosed in double quotes joined by the \ character. This is merely for aesthetic purposes, so our string doesn't wrap around in the program. If we did the following:

```
char AlphaChar[] = {"abcdefghijklmnopqrstuvwxyz\
                     ABCDEFGHIJKLMNOPQRSTUVWXYZ"};
```

The program wouldn't work properly, although it will probably compile. The next statement in the program randomly generates an integer using the **time** function to provide a seed value.

```
srand((unsigned int)time(0));
```

The core working of the program revolves around a **for** loop of the form:

```
for(int i=0; i<length; i++)
{
    r = 0 + rand() / (RAND_MAX / ((51 − 0)+ 1));
    printf("%c", AlphaChar[r]);
}
```

The loop cycles around **length** times (8 in this case), generating a random number in the range 0 and 51, which corresponds to the bounds of the string **AlphaChar,** and storing the value in the variable **r**. The **printf** function is now used to print the character associated with the element **r** of **AlphaChar**. Note that we have used an inline declaration of **i** in the loop (C99), implying that **i** only exists for the lifetime of the loop. After eight iterations, we terminate the string with a new line:

```
printf("\n");
```

Testing the Program

Run the program once, and we will get something like:

```
sLZldIME
```

Run the program ten times and we get:

```
bfStrtwS
pEFCDXmm
PpnUPKhK
ecqzEKLK
qoQZlYSK
SxvMPlAv
yDmVsuxZ
eVqQvDUJ
WrhmdQFB
waUpSLTd
```

Extending the Program

If we wanted to change the rules and add numeric characters to make the password harder to crack, we could change two things in the program. First, change the definition of **AlphaChar** to:

```
char AlphaChar[] = {"abcdefghijklmnopqrstuvwxyz"\
                    "ABCDEFGHIJKLMNOPQRSTUVWXYZ"\
                    "0123456789"};
```

Now change the range calculator:

```
r = 0 + rand() / (RAND_MAX / ((61 - 0) + 1));
```

This might give a password like:

```
kPx9EVZE
```

You could also change the program to include punctuation characters, change the length of the password, or expand the number of numbers in the password.

Epilog

In reality this is a pretty simplistic password generator, but adding numbers, increasing the size of the password, or defining more rules would definitely make it more crack-proof.

Round-off Errors

The only way for errors to occur in a program is by being put there by the author. No other mechanisms are known. Programs can't acquire bugs by sitting around with other buggy programs.

—Harlan Mills

The Problem Description

Here's a simple problem to illustrate the problem with round-off errors.

Program Requirements

The example we use is to compute the square root of a number, r, by iterating Newton's method. The algorithm for Newton's method is roughly:

1. Start with some positive value, x_0, which is close to the root.
2. Calculate x_{n+1} as the average of x_n and r/x_n.
3. Repeat steps 2 and 3, until the desired accuracy is reached.

Mathematically, the sequence of iterates converges to $\sqrt{r}$, so that $t^2 - c > 0$. However, a floating point number only has finitely many bits of accuracy, so eventually, an error is likely to occur.

The Program

```c
#include <stdio.h>

int main(void)
{
    double r, x, EPSILON = 0.0;
    printf("Enter a value: ");
    scanf("%lf", &r);

    x = r;

    while (x*x - r > EPSILON)
        x = (x + r/x) / 2.0;

    printf("The square root of %.2f is %.15f\n", r, x);

    return 0;
}
```

Dissecting the Program

The program is centered on two core statements. The first assigns an approximation of the root to x_0. We chose to use the original number entered.

```c
x = r;
```

Next we use a simple **while** loop to continuously calculate the average of x_n and r/x_n until some accuracy is achieved. Accuracy here is denoted by the difference between the calculated value squared and the original value **r**. When the difference is less than the value of **EPSILON** (which in this case is 0.0), the loop ends.

```c
while (x*x - r > EPSILON)
    x = (x + r/x) / 2.0;
```

Testing the Program

Here is where the fun begins. Try the following numbers: 2.0, 4.0, 10.0

```
Enter a value: 2
The square root of 2.00 is 1.414213562373095

Enter a value: 4
The square root of 4.00 is 2.000000000000000

Enter a value: 10
The square root of 10.00 is 3.162277660168379
```

If we stopped after the first three tests, we could assume our program worked okay, right? Okay, so now let's try 20.0. Did we get an answer? No, just what seems like an infinite loop. So let's look at the value of the difference calculated with input 10.0.

```
Enter a value: 10
90.000000000000000
20.250000000000000
3.388946280991736
0.214448483368569
0.001125566203939
0.000000031668918
-0.000000000000002
The square root of 10.00 is 3.162277660168379
```

Eventually the difference becomes negative and the loop ends. Somewhere *round-off error* kicks in and the value of **x*x** becomes less than **r**, resulting in a negative number when the difference is calculated. We could provide a temporary fix by making **EPSILON** some very small positive value:

```
double r, x, EPSILON = 1.e-8;
```

Now when we enter 20.0, we get:

```
Enter a value: 20
The square root of 20.00 is 4.472135955001610
```

The actual value of **x*x** turns out to be:

```
20.000000000018161
```

which when we subtract 20.0, we get 0.000000000018161, which is less than 0.00000001. Every time we perform an arithmetic operation, we are adding errors.

A More Reliable Program

A reliable way to do the computation is to choose some error tolerance, say **1.e-15**, and try to find a value x so that $|x^2 - r| < r*EPSILON$. The program now becomes:

```
while (fabs(x*x -r) > r*EPSILON)
    x = (x + r/x) / 2.0;
```

The result is:

```
The square root of 20.00 is 4.472135954999580
```

ISBN Validation

The laws of nature are but the mathematical thoughts of God.
—Euclid

The Problem Description

The International Standard Book Number (ISBN) is a code that uniquely specifies a book. It is based on the nine-digit Standard Book Number (SBN) created by Gordon Foster for the bookseller W.H. Smith in 1966.[1] The number is either 13 or 10 (before January 1, 2007) digits long and consists of four or five parts:

1. if a 13-digit ISBN, a GS1 prefix, either 978 or 979
2. the country of origin or language area code
3. the publisher
4. the item number
5. a checksum character or check digit

The 10-digit ISBN was developed by the International Organization for Standardization and released in 1970. Since January 2007, ISBNs have contained 13 digits to enable conformance with the European Article Numbering EAN global numbering system (a barcode standard), and to allow for an increase in the available number of ISBNs. When looking at an ISBN as printed on the back of a book, the sections are separated by hyphens, for example:

1-558-70840-5

---

[1]F. G. Foster, "Standard Numbering in the Book Trade," 1966; available at www.informaticsdevelopmentinstitute.net/isbn.html

Program Requirements

In both the 10- and 13-digit ISBNs, the last digit is known as the *check digit*. Its value is calculated from the other digits in the ISBN, and its purpose is to check the validity of the ISBN. If a mistake is made in copying the ISBN, the resulting number will be invalid, which indicates an error. For the 10-digit ISBN, the rightmost digit is a checksum digit, which can be uniquely determined from the other nine digits from the condition using the equation:

$$x = 10d_1 + 9d_2 + 8d_3 + 7d_4 + 6d_5 + 5d_6 + 4d_7 + 3d_8 + 2d_9$$

where d_i denotes the ith digit of the ISBN from the left. The checksum digit d_{10} can have any value from 0 to 10: the ISBN convention is to use the value X to denote 10. The resulting value is used to calculate x modulo 11, which is the remainder on division of x by 11. The resulting modulus is subtracted from 11, giving the check digit. If the check digit is 10, it is replaced with "X." For example, the calculation for the 10-digit ISBN whose first nine digits are 0-201-31452 is

```
= 10x0 + 9x2 + 8x0 + 7x1 + 6x3 + 5x1 + 4x4 + 3x5 + 2x2
= 0 + 18 + 0 + 7 + 18 + 5 + 16 + 15 + 4
= 83
```

The value of **83 mod 11** is 6, and so **11 − 6 = 5**. Therefore, the check digit is 5, and the complete sequence is 0-201-31452-5. This can also be calculated using the equation

$$d_{10} = 11 - (10d_1 + 9d_2 + 8d_3 + 7d_4 + 6d_5 + 5d_6 + 4d_7 + 3d_8 + 2d_6) mod 11$$

Note: If the value of the final checksum is 11, then the value changes to zero.

Program Specification

Input(s):   A 10-digit ISBN number.

Output(s):   A statement relating to the ISBN's validity.

Modularity: The program will incorporate four functions: **read_ISBN, isValid_ISBN, checkSum, main.**

                read_ISBN
                Task: read the ISBN and store it in a character array.
                Output: ISBN string.

                isValid_ISBN
                Task: check the length of the ISBN, and whether or not it contains characters it shouldn't.
                Input: ISBN string.
                Output: 1 if the ISBN is valid, 0 otherwise.

checkSum
Task: extract the individual digits, convert them to integers, and calculate the checksum digit.
Input: ISBN string.
Output: numeric checksum value.

main
Task: call **read_ISBN**, **isValid_ISBN**, and **checkSum**, check the checksum against the check digit and perform appropriate actions.

Algorithm Design

Designing an algorithm to validate ISBNs is not that challenging; in fact, it really involves only four steps:

1.1. Call the function **read_ISBN** to prompt for, read in the ISBN, and return it in a character array (i.e., string).
1.2. Check whether the ISBN input is correct using the function **isValid_ISBN** (i.e., is it made up only of digits, and maybe an X in the check-digit position)
 1.2.1. Determine if the ISBN string is long enough.
 1.2.2. Identify non-digit in elements 1–9, or noncompliant characters in element 10.
 1.2.3. Return 1 if the ISBN is valid, 0 otherwise.
1.3. Calculate the checksum for the ISBN using the function **checkSum**.
 1.3.1. Convert the digit characters in elements 1–9 of the string to integers.
 1.3.2. Apply the equation to calculate the checksum value.
 1.3.3. Return the checksum value.
1.4. Compare the calculated checksum to the check digit in the ISBN.
1.5. Output a result of "valid" or "invalid" to the user.

Usability and Input

The actual calculation of the ISBN checksum isn't that difficult; more challenging is the actual *input* of the data. The way the user inputs the ISBN will directly affect the design of the algorithm. The focus of the ISBN checksum program is to enter the ISBN data. This choice in many ways dictates how the rest of the algorithm will evolve. A 10-digit ISBN looks like this:

0-914894-65-X

The first nine elements have the values 0 through 9, the tenth element has the values 0 through 9 OR the character X, representing 10. From a usability context, there are a number of ways of inputting a 10-digit ISBN. A table of usability (input) versus portability (moving data from function to function) and data structure (how to store the data) is given here with a scale of 1–5 for each criterion (5 represents the best option).

	Usability	Portability	Data structure	Algorithm complexity
integer variables for digits 1–9 + character	1	1	1	2
integer array + character	1	3	3	2
9–digit integer + character	3	3	3	4
string	5	5	5	4.5

Simple

The simplest way of storing the information in the ISBN is storing each individual element in a variable. The first nine could be stored as integers, the tenth as a character. For example:

```
int isbn1, isbn2, isbn3, isbn4, isbn5;
int isbn6, isbn7, isbn8, isbn9;
char isbnX;
```

There are, of course, variations on this: (i) prompting the user to enter "10" when X occurs in the 10th element, meaning that **isbnX** could be declared as an **int**, or declaring all the variables as type **char**. This works quite well, although it requires being very specific with the input. For example, if we read in the first nine elements as follows:

```
scanf("%d%d%d%d%d%d%d%d%d", &isbn1, &isbn2, &isbn3, &isbn4,
                 &isbn5, &isbn6, &isbn7, &isbn8, &isbn9);
```

we have to make sure that the **printf** statement that precedes the **scanf** makes it clear that the digits of the ISBN should be separated by a space:

```
0 9 1 4 8 9 4 6 5
```

Otherwise, if the user enters **091489465**, this number will be stored in **isbn1**. Not exactly what is called for. The 10th element is acquired in a similar fashion:

```
scanf("%c", &isbnX);
```

The second caveat is that passing this information to a function requires more parameters. For instance, the function prototype would be

```
int isValid(int isbn1, int isbn2, int isbn3, … char isbnX);
```

This approach is simple from a data point of view, and easy to incorporate into the equation, but challenging from a portability standpoint between functions. Usability is inherently low because it forces users to enter each digit separately, which is counterintuitive, as users will be inclined to enter 1856266532 or 1-85626-653-2.

Simple and Compact

Another spinoff of the first approach is to store the data for the first nine digits using an integer array, and reading each element directly into the array. For example:

```
int isbn[9], i;

for (i=0; i<9; i=i+1)
    scanf("%d", &isbn[i]);
```

This also makes passing to a function more efficient. For example:

```
int isValid_ISBN(int isbn[9], char isbnX);
```

This still has a low usability, but improved portability and enhanced logistics with respect to algorithm design.

More Compact

A more compact approach is to separate the data into two pieces, one that deals with the first nine elements, and another that deals with the 10th. This is best achieved by storing the first nine digits as a complete number, and the 10th digit as a character.

```
long isbn;
char isbnX;
```

This makes it easier to input the information:

```
scanf("%ld%*c%c", &isbn, &isbnX);
```

And correspondingly, easier to pass the information to a function:

```
int isValid_ISBN(int isbn, char isbnX);
```

However, here the caveat lies in being able to "peel" off the information from the large number. This can be done by extracting the information and using it directly, or storing it in an accompanying integer array. Applying the latter gives

```
int i, isbnNUM[9];
for (i=8; i>=0; i=i+1){
    isbnNUM[i] = isbn % 10;
    isbn = isbn / 10;
}
```

The first line calculates the remainder of ISBN when divided by 10, effectively peeling off the number 5 from the example. After this, the number is reduced by using integer division. This approach is simple from a data standpoint, and reasonable from a portability standpoint, until the separate digits had to be peeled off the nine-digit integer. This increases the complexity of the algorithm. This is easier from a usability stance, as the user has to enter only two pieces of data, but there is still a disconnect. Choosing to store the first nine elements as a long has its virtues, but what happens when the input is 0864500572? The input will be truncated to 864500572 due to the leading zero being ignored.

Compact and Efficient

The problem with each of the attempts so far is that although the code is somewhat compact, the 10th element is still entered separately, which is probably annoying for some users. The most efficient way of tackling this problem is to use a string. So we could declare the string in the following manner:

```
char isbn[11];
```

Input is likewise less challenging:

```
scanf("%10s", isbn);
```

This also makes passing to a function more efficient. This approach is the simplest from a data standpoint, as the entire ISBN is stored as a string, which can be simply translated into a integer array with X stored as 10. Only one piece of data needs to be transferred between functions, and usability is high because the user can enter data as it appears on the book. It is even possible to format the data exactly as it appears on the book, 0-914-8946-5, and ignore the "-" characters when it comes to converting the ISBN from a string to an array of integers.

Deriving the Program

Due to the nature of the input, we have decided to use the compact and efficient approach to inputting the ISBN based on the use of strings. We will first deal with the skeleton of the main program:

```
#include <stdio.h>

int main(void)
{

    return 0;
}
```

Now we can deal with the first function, **read_ISBN**. The purpose of this function is to prompt the user for the ISBN and to return the value entered to the main program, from which it can be passed to the next function. As we have decided to use a string to accomplish this, the parameter for the function will be a single character array containing enough room for 10 characters in addition to the end-of-string character:

```c
void read_ISBN(char isbn[11])
{
    printf("Enter the ISBN (e.g.0864500572): ");
    scanf("%10s",isbn);
}
```

This is a reasonably simple function with one input that also acts as the conduit for the output from the function. The function **scanf** is used to read the string and store the string in the character array **isbn**. We use the specifier **%10s** to limit user input to 10 characters. An example is given in the prompt of the format of the ISBN required. We can now change the main program to reflect the implementation of the first function:

```c
#include <stdio.h>

int main(void)
{
    char isbn[11];

    read_ISBN(isbn);

    return 0;
}
```

When the function **read_ISBN** is called, the ISBN is stored in the character array **isbn**, because it is intrinsically passed by reference. Moving on to the next function, **isValid_ISBN**, we can validate the ISBN; **fgets** takes care of strings longer than 10 characters, but the ISBN has to be checked to make sure it is not shorter. Also each individual element should be checked to make sure it is a digit, with the exception of the last character, which could be a digit or an x/X. This function takes one input and returns one output: a true/false value to indicate whether or not it is valid. This function acts as a safeguard and actually does our defensive programming:

```c
int isValid_ISBN(char isbn[11])
{
    int i, L, valid=1;

    L = strlen(isbn);
    if (L < 10){
        printf("ISBN is too short\n");
        valid = 0;
    }
    else {
        for (i=0; i<L-1; i=i+1)
            if (!isdigit(isbn[i]))
                valid = 0;
```

```
        if (!isdigit(isbn[L-1]) && isbn[L-1] != 'x'
                              && isbn[L-1] != 'X')
            valid = 0;

        if (valid == 0)
            printf("ISBN contains incorrect characters\n");

        return valid;
}
```

The first line of code uses the **strlen** function to calculate the length of the string **isbn**. An **if** statement is then used to determine if the length of the ISBN is less than 10. If it is less than 10, an error message is displayed and the variable **valid** is set to zero. Then the first nine characters are checked to make sure they are digits. If a non-digit is encountered, **valid** is set to zero. Finally, the last character is checked to make sure it is a digit or x/X. If not, **valid** is set to zero. If value is zero, then an error message is displayed and the value of **valid** is returned: 1 to indicate valid (assuming none of the tests changed the value), and 0 to indicate that there is a problem. This function can now be integrated into **main**:

```
#include <stdio.h>
#include <string.h>
#include <ctype.h>

int main(void)
{
    char isbn[11];
    int cSum;

    read_ISBN(isbn);

    if (isValid_ISBN(isbn))
    {
        cSum = checkSum(isbn);
    }

    return 0;
}
```

Notice that we have used the function **isValid_ISBN** in the context of an **if** statement. The function **checkSum** will be called only if the ISBN is valid. Now, let's create **checkSum**:

```
int checkSum(char isbn[11])
{
    int isbnNUM[9], i, checkD=0;
```

```
    for (i=0; i<9; i=i+1)
        isbnNUM[i] = isbn[i] - 48;

    for (i=10; i>=2; i=i-1)
        checkD = checkD + isbnNUM[10-i]*i;

    checkD = 11 - (checkD % 11);

    if (checkD == 11)
        checkD = 0;

    return checkD;
}
```

The first **for** loop in this function iterates through the first nine characters of the string **isbn**. For each character, the value 48 is subtracted from the ASCII value associated with the digit. For example, if the ASCII value of "0" is 48, then the numeric value will be 0; if the ASCII value of "9" is 57, then when 48 is subtracted, it gives 9. These converted values are stored in an integer array. The checksum value is then calculated using a reverse loop with the loop index starting at 10 and counting down to 2. The index is then multiplied by the associated element from the integer array. The remainder of dividing the checksum by 11 is then subtracted from 11, with the result being the calculated check digit. There is a special case when the value of the check digit is 11: then it is reset to 0. Now the main program can be modified to make use of the check digit calculated:

```
#include <stdio.h>
#include <string.h>
#include <ctype.h>

int main(void)
{
    char isbn[11];
    int cSum, cDigit;

    read_ISBN(isbn);

    if (isValid_ISBN(isbn))
    {
        cSum = checkSum(isbn);
        if (isbn[9] == 'x' || isbn[9] == 'X')
            cDigit = 10;
        else
            cDigit = isbn[9] - 48;
```

```
            if (cSum == cDigit)
                printf("ISBN has a valid checksum\n");
            else
                printf("ISBN has an invalid checksum\n");
        }

    return 0;
}
```

The first **if** statement determines if the check digit is "x" or "X," and if so converts it to 10; otherwise, it converts the character digit to an integer by subtracting 48 (ASCII). The second **if** statement checks the calculated checksum against the check digit and outputs an appropriate response. We can also modify the program to allow the user to reenter the ISBN if it is not valid:

```
#include <stdio.h>
#include <string.h>
#include <ctype.h>

int main(void)
{
    char isbn[11];
    int cSum, cDigit, again=0;

    do {
        read_ISBN(isbn);

        if (isValid_ISBN(isbn))
        {
            cSum = checkSum(isbn);
            if (isbn[9] == 'x' || isbn[9] == 'X')
                cDigit = 10;
            else
                cDigit = isbn[9] - 48;

            if (cSum == cDigit)
                printf("ISBN has a valid checksum\n");
            else
                printf("ISBN has an invalid checksum\n");
        }
        else
                again = 1;
    } while (again == 1);

    return 0;
}
```

Testing the Program

To test the program, we can create a series of test cases, some to test the function **isValid_ISBN**, others to test the function **checkSum**:

1856266532	correct and valid
0864500572	correct and valid with leading zero
0201314525	correct and valid with leading zero
159486781X	correct and valid with trailing uppercase X
159486781x	correct and valid with trailing lowercase X
0743287290	correct and valid with leading and training zero
081185213X	correct and valid with leading zero, trailing X
185626653	incorrect, too short
1B56266532	incorrect, contains a non-digit
159486781Z	incorrect, contains a non-digit/X in check digit
1856266537	correct, but not valid (invalid check digit)

For example:

```
Enter the ISBN (e.g.1234567890): 0864500572
ISBN has a valid checksum

Enter the ISBN (e.g.1234567890): 185626653
ISBN too short
Enter the ISBN (e.g.1234567890): 1856266532
ISBN has a valid checksum

Enter the ISBN (e.g.1234567890): 1B56266532
ISBN contains incorrect characters
Enter the ISBN (e.g.1234567890): 1856266532
ISBN has a valid checksum
```

Timber Reforestation

People love chopping wood. In this activity one immediately
sees results.

—Albert Einstein

The Problem Description

A problem in timber management is to determine how much of an area to leave uncut so
that the harvested area is reforested in a certain period of time. It is assumed that reforestation takes place at a known rate per year, depending on climate and soil conditions. A
reforestation equation expresses this growth as a function of the amount of timber standing and the reforestation rate. For example, if 100 acres are left standing after harvesting
and the reforestation rate is 0.05, then 100 + 0.05 * 100 (or 105 acres) are forested at the
end of the first year. At the end of the second year, the number of acres forested is 105 +
0.5 * 105, or 110.25 acres.

Program Specifications

Input(s):	Number of uncut acres	(>0)
	Forest regrowth rate	(0.0–1.0)
	Input option of acres or years	(A/a,Y/y)
	Acres or years	(>0)

Output(s):   Years (to regrow) or acres (regrown)

Formula(s):   Reforested acres = uncut acres * regrowth rate

Calculating the number of reforested acres is an iterative process, with the
formula given able to calculate regrowth per annum.

Algorithm Design

1. Prompt user for data.
2. Input the number of uncut acres and reforestation rate.
3. Prompt user for forest regrowth data: years or acres.
4. If the option chosen is years, the program will calculate the number of years to regrow n acres.
   4.1. Prompt the user for the number of acres, *n*, to regrow.
   4.2. While the number of acres of regrowth calculated is not greater than *n*, increment a counter for years.
   4.3. Output the number of years.
5. If the option chosen is *acres*, the program will calculate the number of acres regrown after *n* years.
   5.1. Prompt the user for the number of years, *n*, allocated for regrowth.
   5.2. For each of the 1 . . . *n* years, calculate the compounded acres regrown.
   5.3. Output the number of acres regrown.

The Program

We will represent this algorithm in the form of a function:

```
#include <stdio.h>

int main(void)
{
    double uncutAcres, regRate, regAcres, acres=0.0;
    char opt;
    int i, years=0;

    printf("COMPUTATION OF TIMBER REGROWTH\n\n");
    printf("Enter number of uncut acres: ");
    scanf("%lf", &uncutAcres);
    printf("Enter reforestation rate (0.0-1.0): ");
    scanf("%lf%*c", &regRate);
    printf("Enter criteria to calculate: "
            "A (acres) or Y (years): ");
    scanf("%c", &opt);

    // Calculate the number of reforested areas based on acres
    // or number of years it will take to reforest n acres.
    if (opt == 'A' || opt == 'a')
```

```
        {
            printf("Enter years: ");
            scanf("%d", &years);

            regAcres = uncutAcres;
            for (i=1; i<=years; i=i+1)
                regAcres = regAcres + (regAcres * regRate);
            printf("After %d years there will be %.2f "
                    "acres.\n", years, regAcres);
        }
        else if (opt == 'Y' || opt == 'y')
        {
            printf("Enter acres: ");
            scanf("%lf", &acres);

            regAcres = uncutAcres;

            while (regAcres < acres)
            {
                regAcres = regAcres + (regAcres * regRate);
                years = years + 1;
            }
            printf("It will take %d years to reforest"
                    " %.2f acres.\n", years, regAcres);
        }
        else
            printf("Sorry, that option is not available\n");

        return 0;
    }
```

Code Walkthrough

The first portion of the code deals with the creating variables:

```
double uncutAcres, regRate, regAcres, acres=0.0;
char opt;
int i, years=0;
```

The next portion of code deals with data input. Note that the format string in the second **scanf**, "%lf%*c", uses the * modifier to discard the space character entered after the regrowth rate.

```
printf("COMPUTATION OF TIMBER REGROWTH\n\n");
printf("Enter number of uncut acres: ");
scanf("%lf", &uncutAcres);
printf("Enter reforestation rate (0.0-1.0): ");
```

```
scanf("%lf%*c", &regRate);
printf("Enter criteria to calculate: "
       "A (acres) or Y (years): ");
scanf("%c", &opt);
```

The first **if** statement encountered checks to see if the user selected the "acres" option. If true, the block of code associated with the **if** is activated. The user is prompted for the number of years over which to calculate the forest regrowth, and then uses a **for** loop to calculate the forest acreage as each year progresses.

```
if (opt == 'A' || opt == 'a')
{
    printf("Enter years: ");
    scanf("%d", &years);

    regAcres = uncutAcres;
    for (i=1; i<=years; i=i+1)
        regAcres = regAcres + (regAcres * regRate);
    printf("After %d years there will be %.2f "
           "acres.\n", years, regAcres);
}
```

If the first **if** expression evaluates to false, then the second **if** statement is evaluated to determine if the user selected the "years" option. If true, the block of code associated with the second **if** is activated. The user is prompted for the number of acres of regrowth to calculate and then uses a **while** loop to calculate the number of years it takes to regrow n acres. A **while** loop is chosen because it is not evident from the outset how many iterations of the loop will be required.

```
else if (opt == 'Y' || opt == 'y')
{
    printf("Enter acres: ");
    scanf("%lf", &acres);

    regAcres = uncutAcres;

    while (regAcres < acres)
    {
        regAcres = regAcres + (regAcres * regRate);
        years = years + 1;
    }
    printf("It will take %d years to reforest"
           " %.2f acres.\n", years, regAcres);
}
```

If neither of the options is chosen, then the user is directed to an error message using a default **else** statement:

```
else
    printf("Sorry, that option is not available\n");
```

Testing the Program

There are basically four inputs to this program, three of which are static, with the fourth chosen based on the value of the third option, which allows for "acres" or "years" to be calculated:

1. Number of uncut acres
2. Reforestation rate
3. Criteria to be calculated: acres or years
4. If acres, enter years; if years, enter acres

Each one of these requires that the data is within certain constraints:

- Uncut acres must be > 0.
- Reforestation rate must be > 0 but < 1.0, as it is expressed as a ratio.
- Type of criteria must be a y/Y or a/A.
- Years must be > 0.
- Forested acres must be > 0.

Knowing these constraints,ß we can set up a series of black-box test cases, as shown in the accompanying table.

Test case	Input				Expected outcome	Actual outcome
	uncut acres	*rate*	*opt*	*acres/years*		
1	1000	0.05	"a"	10	1628.89	1628.89
2	1000	0.07	"y"	5000	24	24
3	0	0.07	"a"	10	error: uncut acres = 0	0
4	1000	1.1	"a"	10	error: rate > 1.0	1667988.10
5	1000	0.05	"b"	10	error: "b" is not an option	program exited
6	1000	0.05	"a"	0	1000.0	1000.0
7	1000	0.05	"y"	0	0	0
8	1000	-0.02	"a"	-2	error: negative years 1000.0	1000.0

Here are the results of running the first test case:

```
COMPUTATION OF TIMBER REGROWTH

Enter number of uncut acres: 1000
Enter reforestation rate (0.0-1.0): 0.05
Enter criteria to calculate: A (acres) or Y (years): A
Enter years: 10
After 10 years there will be 1628.89 acres.
```

In some cases, such as when the number of **uncut_acres** is zero, the actual results produced are correct, even though no defensive code has been added. When the option is to calculate reforestation in acres and the number of years entered is negative, the program also responds well, retaining the original number of acres.

Appendix A

Common Error Messages

There's always one more bug.

—Lubarsky's Law of Cybernetic Entomology

Syntax Errors

Missing Semicolon

```
5    int a, b;
6    printf("Enter a number: ")
7    scanf("%d", &a);
```

The gcc C compiler would generate the following error message:

```
error.c: In function 'main':
error.c:7: parse error before "scanf"
```

The Pelles C compiler would generate the following error message:

```
error.c(7): error: Syntax error; found 'scanf' expecting ';'.
```

The Digital MARS C compiler would generate the following error message:

```
(7) : Error: ';' expected following declaration of struct member
```

To fix this error, simply add a semicolon at the end of line 6.

```
6    printf("Enter a number: ");
```

Undeclared Variables

```
5    int a;
6    int b
7    double sum;
8    sum = a + b;
```

The gcc C compiler would generate the following error message:

```
error.c: In function 'main':
error.c:7: syntax error before "double"
error.c:8: 'sum' undeclared (first use in this function)
error.c:8: 'b' undeclared (first use in this function)
```

The Pelles C compiler would generate the following error message:

```
error.c(7): error: Syntax error; found 'double' expecting ';'.
```

This is a case where there is actually no syntax error on the line flagged, and the real error occurs on line 6. If the error on line 6 is corrected (missing semicolon), the error reported on line 8 will disappear. What about this?

```
5    int a;
6    int b;
7    double sum;
8    Sum = a + b;
```

The gcc C compiler would generate the following error message:

```
error.c: In function 'main':
error.c:8: 'Sum' undeclared (first use in this function)
```

The Pelles C compiler would generate the following error message:

```
error.c(8): error: Undeclared identifier 'Sum'.
error.c(7): warning: Local 'sum' is not referenced.
```

This is a different problem; in this case the error actually exists on line 8. The uppercase **S** in **Sum** must be changed to a lowercase **s,** or else the variable does not match its declaration. Remember, C is case sensitive, so the variable **PI** is not the same as **pi** or **Pi.** The Pelles compiler actually notes that the variable **sum** is not referenced.

The Digital MARS C compiler would generate the following error message:

```
Sum = a + b;
      ^
(8) : Error: undefined identifier 'Sum'
```

Unmatched Parentheses

```
5    int a=2, b=4;
6    double sum;
7    sum = (a + b / 12.0;
```

The gcc C compiler would generate the following error message:

```
error.c: In function 'main':
error.c:7: parse error before ';' token
```

The Pelles C compiler would generate the following error message:

```
error.c(7): error: Syntax error; found ';' expecting ')'.
```

The Digital MARS C compiler would generate the following error message:

```
sum = (a + b / 12.0;
        ^
(7) : Error: ')' expected
```

To fix this error, simply add a matching parentheses.

```
7    sum = (a + b) / 12.0;
```

Similar errors occur for unmatched braces {, and }, or < and >. For example:

```
1    #define <stdio.h
```

The gcc C compiler would generate the following error message:

```
error.c: In function 'main':
error.c:1: missing terminating > character
```

The Pelles C compiler would generate the following error message:

```
error.c(1): fatal error: Could not find include file
<stdio.h.
```

Unterminated Strings

```
5    int a=2, b=4;
6    double sum;
7    sum = (a + b) / 12.0;
8    printf("%f\n, sum);
9    }
```

The gcc C compiler would generate the following error messages:

```
error.c:8:12 missing terminating " character
error.c:8:12 possible start of unterminated string literal
error.c: In function 'main':
error.c:8 parse error at end of input
```

The Pelles C compiler would generate the following error message:

```
error.c(8): error: Unterminated string or char const.
error.c(9): error: Illegal expression.
error.c(9): error: Syntax error; found 'end of input' expecting ')'.
error.c(9): error: Syntax error; found 'end of input' expecting ';'.
error.c(9): error: Syntax error; found 'end of input' expecting '}'.
```

The Digital MARS C compiler would generate the following error message:

```
}
^
```

```
(9)  : Lexical error: unterminated string
(10) : Lexical error: unterminated string
Fatal error: premature end of source file
```

To fix this error, simply add a matching ".

```
7    printf("%f\n",sum);
```

Left Side of an Assignment Statement Does Not Contain an L-Value

Consider the following C code where the aim of the assignment statement on line 7 is to add **a** and **b** and store the result in **sum**:

```
5    int a=2, b=4;
6    double sum;
7    a + b = sum;
8    printf("%f\n",sum);
```

The gcc C compiler would generate the following error messages:

```
error.c: In function 'main':
error.c:7 invalid lvalue in assignment
```

The Pelles C compiler would generate the following error message:

```
error.c(7): error: Lvalue required.
```

What does this mean? An l-value is really just a place where the result of an assignment statement can be stored. The left side of an assignment statement must always contain the name of a variable. Therefore, to fix this error:

```
7    sum = a + b;
```

Parse Errors

Parsing is the process of determining the structure of a program by checking that it is syntactically correct (e.g., correct number of matching parentheses, semicolons).

```
5    double a=4.0, b=3.4, m;
6
7    if (a => b)
8        m = a/b;
```

The gcc C compiler would generate the following error messages:

```
error.c: In function 'main':
error.c:8 parse error before '>' token
error.c:6 warning: unused variable 'b'
error.c:6 warning: unused variable 'm'
```

The Pelles C compiler would generate the following error message:

```
error.c(7): error: Illegal expression.
error.c(7): error: Syntax error; found 'b' expecting ')'.
```

```
error.c(7): error: Syntax error; found ')' expecting ';'.
error.c(7): error: Illegal statement termination.
```

The equal sign in a greater than or equal (or less than or equal) comparison operator always follows the greater than or less than sign. To fix this error, simply change the relational operator to >=.

```
7    if (a >= b)
```

Using the Wrong Operands

```
4    {
5        double a=4.0, b=3.4, rem;
6        rem = a % b;
7        printf("Remainder = %f\n",rem);
8    }
```

The gcc C compiler would generate the following error messages:

```
error.c: In function 'main':
error.c:7 invalid operands to binary %
```

The Pelles C compiler would generate the following error message:

```
error.c(6): error: Operands of % have illegal types 'double' and 'double'.
```

The Digital MARS C compiler would generate the following error message:

```
rem = a % b;
          ^
(6) : Error: illegal operand types
Had: double
```

The operands used with the modulus operator % were not integers. To calculate the remainder for floating point numbers, the following code should help:

```
4    {
5        double a=4.0, b=3.4, m, rem;
6        m = (int)(a / b);
7        rem = a - (b*m);
8        printf("Remainder = %f\n",rem);
9    }
```

Too Few Arguments When Calling a Function

```
1    #include <stdio.h>
2
3    double div(double a, double b)
4    {
5        if (b != 0)
6            return a/b;
7    }
```

```
8
9    int main(void)
10   {
11       double a=3.4, b=2.0;
12       printf("%f\n", div(a));
13       return 0;
14   }
```

The gcc C compiler would generate the following error messages:

```
error.c: In function 'main':
error.c:12 too few arguments to function 'div'
error,c:11 warning: unused variable 'b'
```

The Pelles C compiler would generate the following error message:

```
error.c(7): warning: Missing return value.
error.c(12): error: Insufficient number of arguments to 'div'.
```

The function **div** was declared with two input parameters, yet when the function was called only one was used. It can be corrected in the following manner:

```
12  printf("%f\n", div(a,b));
```

The second problem, a warning tagged by Pelles C, indicates that the function is missing a return value. This is because the function will only return a value when **b** does not equal zero. A better way to write the function would be to add:

```
3    double div(double a, double b)
4    {
5        if (b != 0)
6             return a/b;
7        else
8             return 0;
9    }
```

Syntax Warnings

Using '=' When '==' Is Intended

```
5    int a=2, b=4;
6    if (a = b)
7         printf("equal");
8    else
9         printf("not equal");
```

The gcc C compiler would generate the following error message:

```
error.c: In function 'main':
error.c:6: warning: suggest parentheses around assignment
      used as truth value
```

What is the problem with this code? Notice that the equal sign used in the if statement is actually the assignment operator, not the relational operator, which tests for equality. In this code **a** is set to 4 because of the assignment, and the expression **a** = **b** is *always* true, because the value of the expression is 4. To fix this error, simply replace the = (assignment) with the == comparison operator:

```
6    if (a == b)
```

The Digital MARS C compiler would generate the following error message:

```
if (a = b)
      ^

(6) : Warning 2: possible unintended assignment
```

Value Returning Function Has No Return Statement

```
3    int add(int a, int b)
4    {
5        int temp;
6        temp = a + b;
7    }
```

The C compiler would generate the following error message:

```
error.c:7: warning: control reaches end of a non-void function
```

The Pelles C compiler would generate the following error message:

```
error.c(7): warning: Missing return value.
```

The function calculates a correct result for the local variable temp, but it never returns the result. The error can be corrected by adding a return statement:

```
3    int add(int a, int b)
4    {
5        int temp;
6        temp = a + b;
7        return temp;
8    }
```

Runtime Errors

Array Index Bounds Error

The array index bounds error describes an attempt to access an element of an array that does not exist. Consider the following code to set all the elements in an array **snowfall** to zero.

```
int snowfall[7];
for (i=1; i<=7; i++)
    snowfall[i] = 0;
```

The problem here is that the array's correct indices range from 0 through 6, while the array indices used in the for loop range from 1 to 7. The array element **snowfall[0]** is never used. The attempt to access the array element **snowfall[7]** is erroneous, because **snowfall[7]** does not exist. Such an error can lead to a "Bus error" or "Segmentation fault."

Divide by Zero

Divide by zero occurs when the denominator is zero. It usually doesn't manifest itself until the variable assigned the result is printed out.

```
double a=13.7, b=0.0, sum;
sum = a/b;
printf("%f\n", sum);
```

The program will generate the following error message:

```
inf
```

This is short for *infinite* and implies a divide-by-zero error. Changing the code to integers yields:

```
int a=13, b=0, sum;
sum = a/b;
printf("%d\n", sum);
```

The Pelles C compiler would generate the following runtime error message:

```
Exception: Integer divide by zero
```

Logic Errors

Infinite Loop

An infinite (or "endless") loop is a loop that repeats indefinitely. A program executing an infinite loop is said to *spin* or *buzz* forever and goes catatonic (which describes a condition of suspended animation in which something is so wedged or hung that it makes no response). A *tight loop* is a loop of code that executes without releasing any resources. An infinite loop often occurs when a test condition continuously evaluates as true. For example:

```
int i=1;
while (i < 1000)
{
    sum = sum + i;
}
```

The expression **(i<1000)** is always true because although the value of **i** is initially 1, its value is never incremented. Because of this property the loop is infinite.

Dangling Else

The dangling else is a common and subtle error in the flow of control of a nested **if** statement. Since a compiler ignores indentation, it matches an **else** clause with the most recent unmatched then clause.

```
if (a > 0.0)
    if (a > maximum)
        maximum = a;
else
    minimum = a;
```

The following small change in the **if** statement solves the problem (use braces to enforce an association:

```
if (a > 0.0){
    if (a > maximum)
        maximum = a;
}
else
    minimum = a;
```

Off-by-One Error

The off-by-one error generally describes a loop that repeats one fewer or one more time than is correct. Consider the following loop, which is supposed to sum the first 100 integers:

```
int i, sum=0;
for (i=1; i<100; i++)
    sum = sum + i;
```

When this code is executed, the loop repeats 99 times, and only the first 99 integers are summed. The following small change in the **for** loop solves the problem:

```
int i, sum=0;
for (i=1; i<=100; i++)
    sum = sum + i;
```

Incorrect Shortcut Operators

Misuse of the shortcut increment and decrement operators:

```
int i=4, j;
j = ++i; //(j=5, i=5)
```

versus

```
j = i++; //(j=4, i=5)
```

Forgetting the Ampersand in `scanf()`

`scanf()` must have the address of the variable in which to store input. This means that often the ampersand address operator is required to compute the addresses. Consider the following code:

```
double radius;
scanf("%lf", radius);
```

This would generate an erroneous result if you tried to print out the value of radius. For example if you entered 37, the value printed out may be 2.165711. This can be fixed by including an ampersand operator.

```
double radius;
scanf("%lf", &radius);
```

Forgetting to Put a Break in a Switch Statement

Forgetting to place an appropriate break statement may lead to code "falling through." For example

```
int x=2, y;
switch(x) {
    case 2: y = x * x;
    case 3: y = x * x * x;
}
printf("%d", y);
```

will result in **y=8,** regardless of whether **x=2** or **x=3.** The correct version of this code would include a break statement:

```
int x=2, y;
switch(x) {
    case 2: y = x * x;
            break;
    case 3: y = x * x * x;
}
printf("%d", y);
```

Using the Wrong Format in `printf` and `scanf`

C compilers do not check that the correct format is used for arguments of a **scanf()** or **printf()** call. The most common errors are using the %f format for doubles (which must use the %lf format) and mixing up %c and %s for characters and strings.

Improper Numeric Conversions

If both operands are of type integer, integer division is used; otherwise real division is used. For example:

```
double radians;
radians = 15/360;
```

This code sets radians to 0.00, not 0.0416! Why? Because 15 and 360 are integer constants. To fix this, change at least one of them to a real constant.

```
double radians;
radians = 15.0/360;
```

If both operands are integer variables and real division is desired, cast one of the variables to double (or float).

```
int x=5, y=2;
double d = ((double)x)/y;
```

Incorrect "Blocks" of Code

For example the code:

```
if (x == 0)
    printf("error, x is zero\n");
    exit(1);
```

This code segment will

- check if x is zero
- print "error . . ." if this is true
- then exit
- exit anyway if x != 0, but without printing "error . . ."

It should read:

```
if (x == 0)
{
    printf("error, x is zero\n");
    exit(1);
}
```

Empty Statements

For example the code:

```
if (x == 0);
{
    printf("error, x is zero\n");
    exit(1);
}
```

is the same as typing

```
if (x == 0)
{

    ;

}
{
    printf("error, x is zero\n");
    exit(1);

}
```

So, if **x** = **0** nothing is executed and the error statement and the exit command are executed all the time. This error also manifests itself as "loop has no body":

```
for (i=1; i<1000; i++);
```

Appendix B

Code Profiling

That's the thing about people who think they hate computers.
What they really hate is lousy programmers.

—Larry Niven and Jerry Pournelle

Introduction

Sometimes it is difficult to determine *why* a program is slow when you run it. The problem is you don't really get a feel for what is causing the lack of speed. You just know it's slow. Understanding what parts of a program contribute to this slowdown is the job of the *profiler*. A profiler helps diagnose where the bottlenecks are in your program. Let's take a lead into this problem from Jon Bentley who wrote a column for *Communications of the ACM* entitled "Programming Pearls."[*] The example he gives prints all primes less than *n*, not unlike the program we wrote illustrating functions.

```
        #include <stdio.h>
        #include <math.h>

        int prime(int n)
        {
            int i;
999         for (i=2; i<n; i=i+1)
78022           if (n % i == 0)
831                 return 0;
168         return 1;
        }

        int main(void)
        {
            int i, n;
1           n = 1000;
1           for (i=2; i<=n; i=i+1)
```

---

[*]*Programming Pearls*, Jon Bentley, ACM Press, 1986.

```
999            if (prime(i))
168                printf("%d ", i);
1        return 0;
     }
```

The numbers to the left of the program signify how many times each of the lines is executed. It tells us that when **main** was called, it tested 999 integers and found 168 primes. The function **prime** was called 999 times, returning one 168 times and zero 831 times. This program works quite well.

The program is obviously correct but somewhat slow. The profile shows that the greatest amount of time is spent testing factors. There must be a way of cutting back on this time, right? There is. Let's consider testing as factors only those integers up to **sqrt(n)**. We can do that using a call to **sqrt**.

```
        #include <stdio.h>
        #include <math.h>

        int root(int n)
        {
5456      return sqrt(n);
        }

        int prime(int n)
        {
            int i;
999         for (i=2; i<=root(n); i=i+1)
5288            if (n % i == 0)
831                 return 0;
168         return 1;
        }

        int main(void)
        {
            int i, n;
1           n = 1000;
1           for (i=2; i<=n; i=i+1)
999             if (prime(i))
168                 printf("%d ", i);
1           return 0;
        }
```

It appears that the changes were quite effective. Only 5,288 factors had to be tested.

Where is the bottleneck? Well, you might be surprised to learn it is in the function **sqrt** that is hogging the CPU. We could fix this by taking the call to **root** out of the loop:

```
        int prime(int n)
        {
            int i, bound;
999         bound = root(n);
```

```
999        for (i=2; i<=bound; i=i+1)
5288           if (n % i == 0)
831               return 0;
168        return 1;
       }
```

The next version of the program incorporates two more speed-ups. Every even number except for 2 is not a prime, so removing them cuts down on the amount of numbers we have to check by about 50 percent!

```
           int prime(int n)
           {
               int i, bound;
999            if (n % 2 == 0)
500               return 0;
499            bound = root(n);
499            for (i=3; i<=bound; i=i+1)
5288              if (n % i == 0)
831                  return 0;
167            return 1;
           }
```

Okay, so this works very fast! Just one little problem. Can you spot it? There are only 167 primes! Where is the missing prime? When we checked the number 2 to see if it was divisible by 2, the function reported that it wasn't a prime. We essentially added a *logic error*, but it is one that can be easily fixed:

```
if (n % 2 == 0 && n != 2)
    return 0;
```

OR

```
if (n % 2 == 0)
    return (n == 2);
```

Tricky! If **n** is divisible by 2, it returns 1 if **n** is 2 and 0 otherwise. You could do the same with **n=3** and **n=5**.

The next variant of this program replaces the computationally expensive square root function with a multiplication:

```
499        for (i=3; i*i<=n; i=i+1)
5288           if (n % i == 0)
831               return 0;
167        return 1;
```

The final program just uses integers that have previously been defined as primes.

```
#include <stdio.h>
#include <math.h>

int x[1000],xc;
```

```c
int prime(int n)
{
    int i;
    for (i=0; x[i]*x[i]<=n; i=i+1)
        if (n % x[i] == 0)
            return 0;
    x[xc] = n;
    xc = xc + 1;
    return 1;
}

int main(void)
{
    int i, n;
    n = 1000;
    x[0] = 2;
    xc = 1;
    for (i=3; i<=n; i=i+1)
        if (prime(i))
            printf("%d ", i);
    return 0;
}
```

To compare the run times of each of these algorithms we use four values for **n**: 1,000, 10,000, 100,000, and 1,000,000. The results follow.

Algorithm	Run Time (sec) for n=			
	1,000	10,000	100,000	1,000,000
P1 original	0.015	0.25	8.75	617.171
P2 restrict to root(n)	0.015	0.171	1.812	22.828
P3 bound = root(n)	0.031	0.14	1.468	13.656
P4 ignore evens	0.015	0.156	1.484	15.046
P5 use i*i<=n	0.015	0.156	1.484	15.656
P6 using previous primes	0.031	0.218	2.125	21.234

As we can see, the changes have little effect when the values of **n** are small. However, as the value of **n** grows, there are definite changes in the amount of time taken to execute the algorithm. The original algorithm takes more than 10 minutes to identify the primes for **n**=1000000, while only using approximately 15 seconds for P3, P4, and P5. This clearly shows that modifications in an algorithm are sometimes reflected at run time. All the algorithms from P2 to P6 use only 2 percent to 4 percent of the time that the original algorithm takes. Food for thought!

Appendix C

Common Problems

More than 50 percent of human programming will vanish as computers take over.
—R. W. Kristinat, Hughes Aircraft Co.

This appendix covers some of the more common problems encountered.

Problem	Symptom
Missing semicolon.	Syntax error at start of next statement.

Missing & before a variable in **scanf**.
 	
```int n;```
```scanf("%d", n);```
	The value read is stored somewhere, but because an address was not provided, when accessed, the variable will contain a garbage value.
	
	Value stored in n = -1073743196

Using **%d** to read in a **double**, or **%lf** to read in an **int**.
 	
```int n;```
```scanf("%lf", &n);```
	An unexpected value is stored in the variable concerned.
	
	Value stored in n = -1073743196

Mismatched parentheses in an expression.	Syntax errors at the end of the expression.
Wrongly placed or missing parentheses in an expression.	Wrong values are calculated.

Inadvertent use of integer arithmetic.
 	
```double Tc, Tf;```
```Tf = (9/5) * Tc + 32;```
	The 9/5 will always evaluate to 1, because integer division is used, resulting in Tf = 232 for Tc = 200, instead of the real value of Tf = 392. The problem can be fixed using (9.0/5.0) in the equation.

Problem	Symptom

Divide by zero.
 	
`double r;`
`r = 42.0/0.0;`
	A runtime floating-point error. On some systems, this may result in the phrase "**inf**" being output.

Using = instead of == in a condition expression. `if (a = 100)`	Program behavior is unexpected. The compiler may provide a warning, but the program will compile. The value of the expression will always be true. The value stored in **a** is set to 100, evaluating to true, regardless of what the value of **a** was prior to the if statement.
Wrongly placed semicolon in an if statement.	The behavior of the if statement is unexpected.
Comparing floating-point values in an if statement with **(x==y)** instead of with **(fabs(x-y) < 0.0001)**.	The behavior of the if statement is unexpected. The condition will rarely evaluate to true.
Missing braces around a compound statement.	Program behavior is unexpected. Only the first statement is activated.
Missing break in a case branch.	Program behavior is unexpected. More than one case statement may be evaluated.
Wrongly placed semicolon after a loop. `  for (i=1; i<=100; i=i+1);`	Loop will simply iterate and do nothing.
< instead of <= in loop condition.	Loop will make one too few iterations.
<= instead of < in loop condition.	Loop will make one too many iterations.
Infinite loop.	Loop will execute forever.
Failure to add a semicolon after a **do-while** loop.	Parse or syntax error during compilation.
Variable declared in the wrong place: globally versus locally.	Program behavior may be unexpected.
Failure to use a reference parameter when appropriate.	Values will be pass-by-value, meaning a copy is passed to the function.
Missing & before a reference parameter in a function call.	Program behavior will be unpredictable, and inappropriate values will be returned from the function.

Array subscripts go out of range.
 	
`int a[10];`
`a[12] = 1;`
	Program will attempt to access memory that it shouldn't, corrupting other variables. Many compilers will allow this, even though they shouldn't.

Problem	Symptom

Forgetting that array elements start with an index of 0, and whose last subscript is one less than the array size.
 	
``
int i,a[10];
for (i=1; i<=10; i=i+1)
    a[i] = 0;
``
	Array will go out of bounds.
	
	The range of indices is 1..10, when is should be 0..9. Most compilers won't check for this, leading to potential problems at runtime.

Reading or copying strings into arrays that aren't large enough.	Array will go out of bounds. Program may exhibit a runtime crash.
Using **%s** to read a string that contains spaces.	Only the first part of the string up to the first space will be read.
Confusion between rows and columns in 2D arrays.	Program will access the wrong element.

Failure to initialize a variable.
 	
``
int n;
n = n + 1;
``
	A random garbage value is assigned to **n**, leading to an unexpected value.

Variable hasn't been declared, but it seems as though it has.
 	
``
double soil;
soil = 49.7;
``
	The compiler complains about a variable not being declared; however, there could be some confusion—in this case, using a "one" instead of the letter "l."
	
	``
	soil, soil
	SOIL, S0IL, SOlL, 5OIL
	``

Mixed-mode computations.
 	
``
int m;
double r, s=5.7;
r = s + 3.69;
``
	Wrong values are calculated. Expecting 9.39? The floating-point calculation has been cast to an integer.

Order of calculations is wrong due to missing parentheses.
 	
``
double r, s=5.0;
r = s + 1.0 / 3.0;
``
	Wrong values are calculated. The division is performed first, with **r** assigned the value 5.3333, as opposed to 2.0.

Failure to store a number correctly.
 	
``
int m;
m = 57439183713;
``
	The variable **m** has the maximum value it can contain. Integer overflow will occur.

Problem	Symptom
Improper logical expressions. `if (a<0 && a>100)`	Expression will not evaluate properly. The value of **a** cannot be less than zero AND g reater than 100. && should be replaced with || (OR).

Loop does not terminate: infinite loop.
 	
`int i=0;`
`while (i < 100){`
 	
`   .…`
 	
`}`
	Loop will execute forever. The value of **i** was never incremented, so its value will always be less than 100.

Comparing strings with ==.
 	
`char s1[] = "vad";`
`char s2[] = "vad";`
 	
`if (s1 == s2)`
`    printf("strings match");`
	The expression **s1 == s2** will never evaluate to true. Use **strcmp**:
	
	`if (strcmp(s1,s2) == 0)`
	`        printf("strings match");`

Strings too short. For example, storing a six-character postal code:
 	
`char pc[6];`
`scanf("%6s",pc);`
	The string has room for only five characters (not six), since one element must be saved for the string terminator "\0". In reality, this may actually work on most systems.

Characters left in the input buffer.
 	
`char ch;`
`int num;`
`scanf("%d", &num);`
`scanf("%c", &ch);`
	Using **scanf** to read a number (**int**), followed by **char** causes the **char** to be skipped. The Enter key pressed after **int** is left in the buffer and read into the variable **ch**. Instead discard the Enter key:
	
	`scanf("%*c%c", &ch);`

Appendix D

To Binary and Back

There are 10 kinds of people in this world . . . Those who understand binary and those who don't.

—Anonymous

Decimal to Binary

Conversion of integers to binary can be achieved by dividing by 2 until you get to 1. Take the example of converting 24 to binary:

```
24/2 = 12 remainder 0
12/2 = 6 remainder 0
6/2 = 3 remainder 0
3/2 = 1 remainder 1
1/2 = 0 remainder 1
```

So the binary equivalent of 24 is 11000.

Binary to Decimal

Conversion of binary numbers to decimal is achieved by adding the appropriate powers of 2. Take the example of converting 11 to decimal:

$$0\times2^0 + 0\times2^1 + 0\times2^2 + 1\times2^3 + 1\times2^4 = 8 + 16 = 24$$

Appendix E

Using C Compilers
As a programmer, I write programs.
—Ken Thompson

Compiling a Program

In this section we will briefly look at the process of compiling using gcc and Pelles C. When you compile a program, the compiler passes the source code through the preprocessor, the compiler, the assembler, and finally the loader. This is usually done pretty transparently. That is, we don't have to run different programs for each of these tasks.

Compiling with gcc

A command-line driven compiler, **gcc** is the GNU compiler collection and contains front ends for C, C++, Objective C, Chill, Fortran, and Java, as well as libraries for these languages. GNU is a recursive acronym for "GNU's Not Unix" and is pronounced "guh-NEW." Note that there is no graphical user interface. Consider a source code file named **test.c**, containing the C program. To compile the program using **gcc**:

```
gcc test.c
```

This will preprocess the code and compile, assemble, and link the code into a program that can be executed, creating a file called **a.out**. The first step performed by gcc is to send the source code through the C *preprocessor*. The C preprocessor is responsible for three things: text substitution, comment stripping, and file inclusion. Text substitution and file inclusion are requested in the source file through the preprocessor directives #define and #include, respectively. You can see what happens in preprocessing using the "-E" flag in gcc. Preprocessing produces a fairly large file because it incorporates information from **stdio.h** and any other libraries included. All the comments are removed during preprocessing, and the code is now ready for *compilation* into assembly language. The results of the compilation process can be viewed using the "-S" flag in gcc:

```
gcc -S test.c
```

This creates a file called **test.s,** which contains the assembler code. The next step *assembles* the assembler code into an object file, which essentially turns the human-readable assembler into machine-readable language. The object file can also be created using the gcc "-c" option:

```
gcc -c test.c
```

This essentially says, "compile but do not link," creating an object file called **test.o.** The final stage involves *linking,* which produces an executable program. To link the .o file:

```
gcc test.o
```

which creates the executable **a.out.** The entire process is depicted in the accompanying diagram. When using **gcc,** all these processes are performed internally unless an explicit compiler option is used.

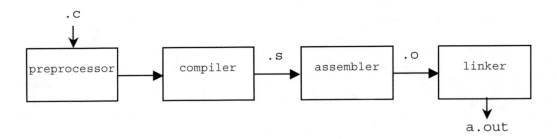

It is possible to create a file other than a.out using the "-o" option:

```
gcc test.c -o test
```

which creates an executable named **test.** There are a number of options that can be used with **gcc.** The first is the -**Wall** option:

```
gcc -Wall test.c
```

This lists all warnings generated during compilation. When the program compiles without any messages using this option, it will likely be syntactically correct. To have the compiler enforce the ISO C89 standard, use the -**ansi** option:

```
gcc -ansi test.c
```

This is equivalent to -**std=c90** (dialect) option. To use features compatible with the ISO C99 standard requires the -**std=c99** option:

```
gcc -std=c99 test.c
```

More about Stacks and Memory

The a.out file that gcc creates contains the following information:

a.out magic number
other a.out contents
size needed for BSS ("better save space") segment
data segment (initialized global and static variables)
text segment (executable instructions)

Local variables don't go into a.out; they are created at runtime and stored in the stack. When an executable, such as a.out, is run, the parts of the program are put into memory. Memory space for items such as local variables, parameter passing in function calls, and so on is created in a stack segment, often called the *runtime stack*, and heap space is allocated for dynamically allocated memory. As discussed in Chapter 20, the stack provides a storage area for local variables. The stack stores the "housekeeping" information associated with function calls, known as a *stack frame*. The stack also works as a scratch-pad area for temporary storage.

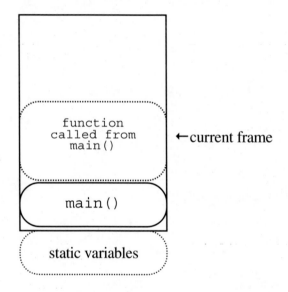

```
        function
     called from
        main()
```
← current frame

```
        main()
```

static variables

On many systems, the stack grows automatically as more space is needed. When all the space in the stack has been used up, *stack overflow* occurs. Consider the follow examples of variables declared in a function:

```
char str[]="Do or do not, there is no try!";
char *s="I am the master!";
int x;
```

In the stack region of memory, the following data is stored:

Name	Type	Value
str	array of char, size=[31]	Do or do not, there is no try!\0
s	pointer (to char)	00E9
x	int	

In the heap region of memory, the following data is stored:

Type	Address	Value
string literal, size=[31]	00E9	I am the master!\0

The implicit size of **str** is set at 31 (for the 30 characters enclosed in double quotes, and the \0 terminating character). It has memory reserved for it in the stack. The pointer variable **s** is declared to hold the address (00E9) of the first character of the string. The string is stored in the heap region of memory, not the stack.

Consider the following program:

```c
#include <stdio.h>

double pi = 3.14159;

double circleArea(double r)
{
    return pi * r * r;
}

int main(void)
{
    double area, radius;
    scanf("%lf", &radius);

    area = circleArea(radius);
    printf("Area = %.2f\n", area);

    return 0;
}
```

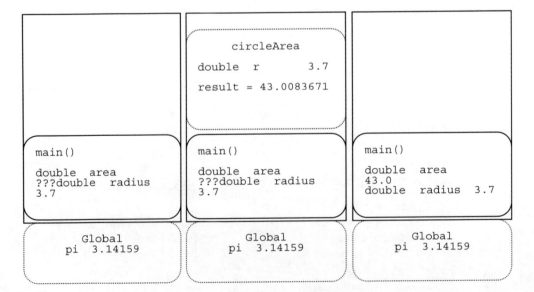

The left part of the accompanying diagram represents the stack up to the point in the program when the user has entered a value for the radius and it has been stored in the variable **radius**. The value stored in the global variable **pi** is stored in the static region. The middle part of the diagram represents the call to the function **circleArea**, which has created a new frame in the stack showing various internal variables. The right part of the diagram shows the stack after the call to **circleArea** has been completed. The function stack frame has been deleted and note that the variable **area** contains the value of the area calculated, which was returned from the function.

Appendix F

Program Code

Nathan's First Law: Software is a gas; it expands to fill its container.

—Nathan Myhrvold

Satellite Orbit Velocity

```c
#include <stdio.h>
#include <math.h>
#define Earth_rad 6378.0
#define uGravConst 6.67e-11
#define Earth_mass 5.98e24

/* Program to calculate the orbital velocity of a satellite */

int main (void)
{
    double orbit_Ht, sat_OVms, sat_OVkms, centre_Ht;
    int i, reloop=1;

    do
    {
        // Input for the height of the orbit in kilometres
        printf("Enter the height of the satellite orbit (km): ");
        scanf("%lf", &orbit_Ht);

        // Only perform the calculation if the orbit is greater
           than 320km
        if (orbit_Ht > 320.0)
        {
```

```
                    reloop = 0;
                    // Calculate the distance from the satellite to the
                    // centre of the earth
                    centre_Ht = (orbit_Ht + Earth_rad) * 1000.0;
                    // Calculate the orbital velocity in metres per
                       second
                    sat_OVms = sqrt((uGravConst * Earth_mass) /
                    centre_Ht);
                    // Convert the orbital velocity to kilometres per
                       second
                    sat_OVkms = sat_OVms / 1000.0;

                    // Output the result
                    printf("The orbital velocity of the satellite"
                            " is %.2lf km/s\n", sat_OVkms);
              }
              else
                    printf("The height of the satellite is too low.\n");
        } while (reloop);

        return 0;
}
```

Word Counting with Statistics

```
#include <stdio.h>
#include <string.h>
#include <ctype.h>
#include <limits.h>

// Function to calculate the number of punctuation characters in
   a word
int contains_punc(char word[50], int L)
{
    int i, pc=0;
    for (i=0; i<L; i=i+1)
        if (ispunct(word[i]))
            pc = pc + 1;
    return pc;
}


int main(void)
{
    int nlines, nwords, nchars, index = 0;
```

```c
int L, cL=0, punc;
char c, word[50];

nlines = nwords = nchars = 0;

while ((c = getchar()) != EOF) {
    // Increment the number of characters if it isn't a
       newline
    if (c != '\n')
        nchars = nchars + 1;

    // If a newline is encountered, increment the line
       counter
    else if (c == '\n')
        nlines = nlines + 1;

    // Store each word in a string
    if (!isspace(c)){
        word[index] = c;
        index = index + 1;
    }

    // If a space, newline or tab is encountered,
    // set the end of the word.
    if (c == ' ' || c == '\n' || c == '\t'){
        // Add an end-of-string character
        word[index] = '\0';
        index = 0;
        // Determine if the first element in the word is a
           digit.
        if (!isdigit(word[0])){
            // Increment the word counter
            nwords = nwords + 1;
            // Calculate the word length
            L = strlen(word);
            // Calculate how many punctuation characters are
               in the word
            punc = contains_punc(word,L);
            // Calculate the number of alphabetic characters
            cL = cL + L - punc;
        }
    }
}

// Output the statistics
printf("Text counting:\n");
```

```
    printf("Number of lines: %d\n",nlines);
    printf("Number of words: %d\n",nwords);
    printf("Number of characters: %d\n",nchars);
    printf("The number of alphabetic characters is %d\n", cL);
    printf("The average length of a word is %.2f "
            "characters\n", (double)cL/nwords);

    return 0;
}
```

Word Counting with File I/O

```c
#include <stdio.h>
#include <string.h>
#include <ctype.h>
#include <limits.h>
#include <stdlib.h>

// Function to calculate the number of punctuation characters in
    a word
int contains_punc(char word[50], int L)
{
    int i, pc=0;
    for (i=0; i<L; i=i+1)
        if (ispunct(word[i]))
            pc = pc + 1;
    return pc;
}

int main(void)
{
    int nlines, nwords, nchars, index = 0;
    int L, cL=0, punc;
    char c, word[50], filename[40];
    FILE *ifp;

    // Prompt the user for the input text filename
    printf("Enter the text file to process: ");
    scanf("%s", filename);

    // Open the file for reading
    ifp = fopen(filename,"r");

    // If the file does not exist, exit the program
    if (ifp == NULL){
```

```c
        printf("Sorry the file %s does not exist.\n", filename);
        exit(0);
    }

    nlines = nwords = nchars = 0;

    while ((c = fgetc(ifp)) != EOF) {
        // Increment the number of characters if it isn't a
           newline
        if (c != '\n')
            nchars = nchars + 1;

        // If a newline is encountered, increment the line
           counter
        else if (c == '\n')
            nlines = nlines + 1;

        // Store each word in a string
        if (!isspace(c)){
            word[index] = c;
            index = index + 1;
        }

        // If a space, newline or tab is encountered,
        // set the end of the word.
        if (c == ' ' || c == '\n' || c == '\t'){
            // Add an end-of-string character
            word[index] = '\0';
            index = 0;
            // Determine if the first element in the word is a
               digit.
            if (!isdigit(word[0])){
                // Increment the word counter
                nwords = nwords + 1;
                // Calculate the word length
                L = strlen(word);
                // Calculate how many punctuation characters are
                   in the word
                punc = contains_punc(word,L);
                // Calculate the number of alphabetic characters
                cL = cL + L - punc;
            }
        }
    }
```

```c
    // Close the input file
    fclose(ifp);

    // Output the statistics
    printf("Text counting:\n");
    printf("Number of lines: %d\n",nlines);
    printf("Number of words: %d\n",nwords);
    printf("Number of characters: %d\n",nchars);
    printf("The number of alphabetic characters is %d\n", cL);
    printf("The average length of a word is %.2f "
            "characters\n", (double)cL/nwords);

    return 0;
}
```

Caesar Cipher with Spaces Stripped

```c
#include <stdio.h>
#include <ctype.h>
#include <string.h>

// Function to strip a string of spaces
void strip_string(char *s, char *r)
{
    int i, j, L;
    j = 0;

    L = strlen(s);
    for (i=0; i<L; i=i+1)
        if (isalpha(s[i]))
        {
            r[j] = s[i];
            j = j + 1;
        }
    r[j] = '\0';
}

// Function to convert a character from ASCII to integer
int char2int(char c)
{
    return (c - 97);
}

// Function to convert a character from integer to ASCII
char int2char(int d)
{
```

```
        return (d + 97);
}


// Function to encode a plaintext string using an offset
void encode(char *plainT, char *cipherT, int offset)
{
    int i, L, shift, n;

    // Calculate the length of the string
    L = strlen(plainT);
    // Iterate through the string
    for (i=0; i<L; i=i+1)
        if (!isspace(plainT[i]))
        {
            // Determine the integer value of the character
            n = char2int(plainT[i]);
            // Calculate the encoding shift using the offset
            shift = (n + offset) % 26;
            // Determine the character value of the integer
            // and assign it to the ciphertext string
            cipherT[i] = int2char(shift);
        }
        else
            cipherT[i] = plainT[i];
    // Terminate the ciphertext string
    cipherT[L] = '\0';
}

// Function to decode a ciphertext string using an offset
void decode(char *cipherT, char *plainT, int offset)
{
    int i, L, shift, n;

    // Calculate the length of the string
    L = strlen(cipherT);
    // Iterate through the string
    for (i=0; i<L; i=i+1)
        if (!isspace(cipherT[i]))
        {
            // Determine the integer value of the character
            n = char2int(cipherT[i]);
            // Calculate the decoding shift using the offset
            shift = (n - offset + 26) % 26;
            // Determine the character value of the integer
            // and assign it to the plaintext string
            plainT[i] = int2char(shift);
        }
```

```
        else
            plainT[i] = cipherT[i];
    // Terminate the plaintext string
    plainT[L] = '\0';
}

// Function to convert a string to lowercase
void string2lower(char *s)
{
    int i, L;

    L = strlen(s);

    for (i=0; i<L; i=i+1)
        if (isupper(s[i]))
            s[i] = tolower(s[i]);
}

int main(void)
{
    char plainT[40], plainT_stripped[40], cipherT[40];
    int offset, code;

    // Prompt the user for the type of operation
    printf("Caesar Cipher\n\n");
    printf("(1) encode or (2) decode? ");
    scanf("%d%*c", &code);

    // Prompt the user for the string, convert to
    // lowercase and strip spaces
    if (code == 1)
    {
        printf("Enter a plaintext string: ");
        fgets(plainT,40,stdin);
        string2lower(plainT);
        strip_string(plainT, plainT_stripped);
    }
    else if (code == 2)
    {
        printf("Enter a ciphertext string: ");
        fgets(cipherT,40,stdin);
        string2lower(cipherT);
    }
```

```
    // Prompt for the offset value
    printf("Enter an offset: ");
    scanf("%d", &offset);

    // Perform the encoding/decoding of the string
    if (code == 1)
    {
        encode(plainT_stripped, cipherT, offset);
        printf("The ciphertext is: %s\n", cipherT);
    }
    else if (code == 2)
    {
        decode(cipherT, plainT, offset);
        printf("The plaintext is: %s\n", plainT);
    }

    return 0;
}
```

Climate Data: File I/O

```
#include <stdio.h>
#define N 8

int main(void)
{
    int i, j;
    FILE *ifp, *ofp;
    double sum;

    double yr1659_2005[N][12];
    double yr_Means[N];

    // Open the file for reading
    ifp = fopen("HadCET_act.txt","r");
    // Open a file for writing
    ofp = fopen("yearly_means.txt","w");

    if (ifp == NULL)
    {
        puts("Sorry the file does not exist\n");
        return 1;
    }
```

```c
    // Read the temperature from the file into the 2D array
    for (i=0; i<N; i=i+1)
        for (j=0; j<12; j=j+1)
            fscanf(ifp, "%lf", &yr1659_2005[i][j]);

    // Calculate means for each year
    for (i=0; i<N; i=i+1)
    {
        sum = 0.0;
        for (j=0; j<12; j=j+1)
            sum = sum + yr1659_2005[i][j];
        yr_Means[i] = sum / 12.0;
    }

    // Output the means for each year to file
    for (i=0; i<N; i=i+1)
        fprintf(ofp, "%.2lf\n", yr_Means[i]);

    // Close the files
    fclose(ifp);
    fclose(ofp);

    return 0;
}
```

Index